PERGAMON INTERNATIONAL LIBRARY
of Science, Technology, Engineering and Social Studies
*The 1000-volume original paperback library in aid of education,
industrial training and the enjoyment of leisure*
Publisher: Robert Maxwell, M.C.

CHINA'S
CHANGED ROAD TO DEVELOPMENT

THE PERGAMON TEXTBOOK
INSPECTION COPY SERVICE

An inspection copy of any book published in the Pergamon International Library will
gladly be sent to academic staff without obligation for their consideration for course
adoption or recommendation. Copies may be retained for a period of 60 days from
receipt and returned if not suitable. When a particular title is adopted or recommended
for adoption for class use and the recommendation results in a sale of 12 or more copies
the inspection copy may be retained with our compliments. The Publishers will be pleased
to receive suggestions for revised editions and new titles to be published in this important
international Library.

Other titles of interest

BROWN, L. B.
Psychology in Contemporary China

CHEN, T. H.
Chinese Education since 1949

DJERASSI, N.
Glimpses of China from a Galloping Horse

LOZOYA, J.
Asia and the New International Economic Order

MAXWELL, N.
China's Road to Development, second edition

POSTLETHWAITE, T. N. and THOMAS, R. M.
Primary and Secondary Education in the ASEAN Countries

RODZINSKI, W.
A History of China, Vols. 1 and 2

SIGURDSON, J.
Technology and Science in the People's Republic of China

Related Journal

WORLD DEVELOPMENT*
The multidisciplinary journal devoted to the study and promotion of world development.

Chairman of the Editorial Board:

Dr Paul Streeten, Center for Asian Development Studies, Boston University, 264 Bay
State Rd., Boston MA 02215, USA

*Free specimen copy available on request

CHINA'S
CHANGED ROAD TO DEVELOPMENT

Edited by

NEVILLE MAXWELL

Contemporary China Centre, Queen Elizabeth House, Oxford, UK

and

BRUCE McFARLANE

University of Adelaide, Australia

PERGAMON PRESS

OXFORD · NEW YORK · TORONTO · SYDNEY · PARIS · FRANKFURT

U.K.	Pergamon Press Ltd., Headington Hill Hall, Oxford OX3 0BW, England
U.S.A.	Pergamon Press Inc., Maxwell House, Fairview Park, Elmsford, New York 10523, U.S.A.
CANADA	Pergamon Press Canada Ltd., Suite 104, 150 Consumers Road, Willowdale, Ontario M2J 1P9, Canada
AUSTRALIA	Pergamon Press (Aust.) Pty. Ltd., P.O. Box 544, Potts Point, N.S.W. 2011, Australia
FRANCE	Pergamon Press SARL, 24 rue des Ecoles, 75240 Paris, Cedex 05, France
FEDERAL REPUBLIC OF GERMANY	Pergamon Press GmbH, Hammerweg 6, 6242 Kronberg-Taunus, Federal Republic of Germany

First edition 1984

Library of Congress Cataloging in Publication Data
Main entry under title:
China's changed road to development.
(Pergamon international library of science, technology, engineering, and social studies)
Bibliography: p.
1. China — Economic conditions — 1976—
— Addresses, essays, lectures.   2. China — Social conditions — 1976—   — Addresses, essays, lectures.
3. China — Economic policy — 1976—   — Addresses, essays, lectures.   4. China — Social policy —
1976—   — Addresses, essays, lectures.
I. Maxwell, Neville George Anthony.
II. McFarlane, Bruce J.   III. Series.
EC427.92.C46465 1984   338.951
83—23679

British Library Cataloguing in Publication Data
China's changed road to development.
1. China — Economic conditions — 1976—
I. Maxwell, Neville   II. McFarlane, Bruce
330.951'057   HC427.92

ISBN 0—08—030849—X (Hardcover)
ISBN 0—08—030850—3 (Flexicover)

Printed in Great Britain by A. Wheaton & Co. Ltd., Exeter

Preface

NEVILLE MAXWELL

Contemporary China Centre, Queen Elizabeth House, Oxford, UK

and

BRUCE MCFARLANE

University of Adelaide, Australia

There is sharp disagreement among Western observers about the new course China has taken since 1976, and how to evaluate it. That China has quit what used to be called 'the Maoist road to development' is evident, but the disagreement begins with efforts to describe China's 'new road' and to discern its destination. Consideration of the nature of what the post-Mao Chinese leadership describes as 'pragmatic reforms' turns to their social implications and thence to the political ideology they express. Here the system's self-definitions cease to serve, so a broader question may be posed. For whom? For whose benefit is China's development now being planned? And then, perhaps, by whom? In the periods of Mao's predominance development planning by specialists was repudiated; the answers would, it was maintained, be thrown up by the experience, the practice, of China's working multitudes, organized in the countryside in their new cooperative communities, in the industrial sector in factories under varying degrees of worker control. Now that the specialists and the managers have come triumphantly back into their own, are the interests of the great majority of the Chinese as well served as they were? Or, as those who speak for China's new order claim, better?

Four years ago, in the Preface to a previous collection of papers on 'China's Road to Development',* Maxwell wrote:

> China's road to development has followed a zigzag course. The alternate stretches can be signposted 'right' or 'left' in terms of the priority given to economic over political goals. On rightward stretches, under the direction of the group in the Chinese Communist Party whom Western observers call 'moderates', priority is given to economic growth, and the implementation of socialist values is made a long-range objective. On the leftward stretches, when 'radicals' are in control, economic development and progress towards socialism are seen as inseparable and mutually reinforcing. The differences between the two schools are more than tactical, since the radicals hold that policies which fail to consolidate and advance socialism for that reason undermine it — that policies which encourage the reassertion of individualism and its offspring, privilege and hierarchy, in effect work towards restoration and the emergence in China of a class society on Soviet lines. A fundamental ideological divide thus underlies differences over development strategy. This means that the changes of course, the angles in the zigzag, are abrupt and politically convulsive; while the current ideological expression will always repudiate that of the previous phase, and denigrate its economic achievements.

It was already apparent in 1979 that another change of course in China was in the making, only the sharpness of the turn was still in question. Would that come to be seen as a 'right turn', corrective of Maoist emphases now judged 'ultra left'? Or would it go much further, as some evidence already suggested, and become a U-turn — not just a correction of course, but a reversal? Those questions are still at issue, so sharply indeed that, after a rare period of consensus in the field of China studies that began in the early 1970s, approaches and positions are now again becoming conflictual. So the Conference convened in September 1982 by the Contemporary China Centre at Oxford had as its purpose the clarification of such conflicting views, and, if possible, their harmonization. The Conference was therefore given the title, 'China in Transition', and in the opening session, the question was put, 'Transition — from what? to what?'

> From an ultra-left phase of Maoist excesses that had left the Chinese people wounded and their economy stagnant; to a corrective period of pragmatic reforms, in which yesterday's maxims can

---

*Second edition (Pergamon Press, 1979).

be dismissed as shibboleths, and the revolutionary leadership concentrates on policies aimed at improving the economic condition of the masses? Or . . .

From a period in which the Maoist leadership sought and struggled for a social and economic strategy that would consolidate the revolution by carrying it onward to a further stage, in the direction of greater equality and fuller participation by the people in China in controlling and managing their own lives; to a phase of reversal that reflects the restoration to power of the emergent elite challenged in the Cultural Revolution, which has reformed economic strategy to serve its own class interest?

Such was the formulation that informed discussion around the papers submitted for the Conference, the majority of which are included in this collection.

The papers published in this book cover the issues one needs to make an informed judgment about the very different attitudes to social and economic development that have emerged in China since 1978. The authors tell us the details about the new policies in the economy, agriculture, industry, as well as new measures in relation to population, education, income distribution and political power. They also indicate how much of the Marxism of Mao, and, indeed of Marxism itself, has been jettisoned to fit in with new precepts and an alternative 'vision' as to how Chinese society should operate.

A common theme in most of the papers that follow is that the process of transition from capitalism to socialism has, from the beginning, been complicated by the fact that the overwhelming majority of the population has consisted of peasant households, and those employed in industry; science and technology only a small (if compact) minority. The four modernizations aim to bring a quick, even abrupt change in this situation by 2000 AD. This would mean that ideologies and policies based on priority to socialization within agriculture ('narrowing the three great differentials', rural egalitarianism within communes) would become less relevant. It would mean that a serious challenge would be mounted to the contention that under socialism markets and market-relations would disappear — important political ideas dominant 1968—76.

It is shown in the essays of Watson, Blecher, Keating and Croll that economic and social policies related to agriculture have been overturned in the years since Mao's death. Not only has the Chinese Communist Party and State tolerated a massive flight from communes to a system of peasant households contracting with the State and 'enriching' themselves, but birth control policies have been disrupted (Croll), education policy for rural people seriously undermined (Keating) and control over movement of peasants to towns weakened (Blecher).

In the management of more modern sectors of the economy profound changes in attitudes in *political economy* may be detected. Selden argues these were necessary to end excesses of various speed-up campaigns and 'Left turns'; McFarlane shows the impact of political as well as economic cycles on the broad course of social development; Ishikawa lays out the conditions under which centralized and decentralized models can succeed in avoiding structural disequilibrium of the economy and establishing a reasonable long-term growth rate.

What were the reasons that prompted major changes in the organization of the economy, of its major sectors and China's basic social policies? The authors of this book show they derived from the actual experience of centralization of economic and political power in the Mao period — experiences which promoted a thirst for decentralization, even if the practical consequences of this change were not fully thought out.

Arising from the studies here by Pairault, White and Lockett-Littler is the obvious link which has eluded the planners of China in the past — that between price policy and decentralized economic mechanisms. If output decisions are decentralized, knowledge of the global situation can only be transmitted by price indicators (whether these be actual transactions-prices or accounting prices). What comes through in the surveys of the Chinese debates published here is that 'economic reformers' in that country, in their opposition to continuance of the centralized planning system, often do not distinguish the many different kinds of prices (with different functions) in a socialist economy. They adopt a *simpliste* attitude to this question and often make uncritical use of analogy with a free market economy. Yet our authors also show that the debate in China is vigorous, that a kind of revival of the NEP of Soviet Russia of the 1920s is under way and that broader questions of workers' rights and self-management in economic units are beginning to be seriously discussed.

The political implications of changes in the degree of decentralization in the economy are important. Kraus shows that new privileged social strata are the strongest proponents of the reforms. Saich indicates how the Chinese

Communist Party is having to learn how to share power with state institutions, managers and even peasant associations, and to change its style of work. Accompanying these, as Brugger and Mackerras indicate, there has been an ideological re-vamping of Chinese Marxist precepts, including re-evaluation of key elements in the thinking of Mao and a re-writing of the history of the Party and of China's post-revolution experience.

The international shock-waves of this new course have been felt on many overseas left movements and countries, and, as Kim concludes, has brought into question the policy of self-reliant development in Third World countries and China's alliance with Western and Eastern radicals opposing 'dependency' by the Third World on European and Japanese centres of economic power.

Contents

x

CONTENTS

The Logic – and Limits – of Chinese Socialist Development

MARK SELDEN*

Department of Sociology, State University of New York, Binghamton

Summary. – In many ways 1949–55 was a golden age of Chinese socialism because progress in cooperation was achieved with minimum violence. When the pace was forced after that, peasant mistrust grew. Successes in the Great Leap and the Cultural Revolution were short-lived, illusory, or at best in the earlier period there were fewer zig-zags in ideology and in economic policy of the sort which came with the Great Leap. However, wild swings of this kind are apt to divert us from the continuities which come out of the power structure, the class structure and the decision to promote a rapid rate of economic growth. These include the institutional transformation of the economy; economic planning; expanded state welfare functions; the effort to avoid foreign dominance; elimination of exploitation and of certain kinds of social inequalities. The limits to *socialist* development appear to be set by the size of agricultural surplus that can be extracted without exacerbating tensions and the high rate of investment that industrialization requires. On the political front, the limits are set by peasant attitudes to government policy, the power of structural hierarchies (and their associated vested interests) and excessive Party interference in areas of social life best left to more democratic decision-making processes.

How are we to comprehend the sharp swings of the policy pendulum which stand as the most distinctive feature of China's socialist development since the 1950s? The present essay seeks to identify sources of this pattern of dramatic and often quite unexpected changes with respect to the rural areas where the Chinese Communist Party had developed its most distinctive approaches to revolutionary change, where many believe it to have achieved its most impressive feats but where, as recent events make plain, the problems have been and remain formidable. Before turning to the tensions and conflicts which have produced the zig-zags alluded to above, we note certain structural and policy continuities, some so axiomatic as to be beyond debate or challenge by major groups within the Party-state, throughout these tumultuous decades.

The following explicit core goals of China's socialist development have been shared by all significant elements of the Chinese leadership throughout the People's Republic.

A. *Institutional formation and transformation,* including:
1. Ownership and management of the economy centred in state and co-operative (or collective) institutions;
2. Planned economy;
3. Expanded political, economic, educational and welfare functions of the Party-state, penetrating and transforming economy and society.

B. *Rapid economic development and the improvement of the livelihood of the people.* Industry, particularly state-owned heavy industry, would lead the way, but agricultural development was vital to the achievement of national goals.

C. *Breaking the fetters of foreign domination and the achievement of worldwide recognition of the Chinese nation.* China would emphasize self-reliance while seeking appropriate allies.

D. *Elimination of exploitation and of certain inequalities,* notably:
1. Those exploitative relationships associated with the landlord, capitalist and merchant classes;
2. Relations of inequality between women and men, minority and Han, and

*I am grateful for the critical comments of Victor Nee on the draft of this paper. The usual disclaimer is particularly apt in this case.

(eventually) those between rural and urban people.

These goals, lent urgency by the formidable economic and political tasks following decades of national humiliation, foreign invasion and social disintegration, provided a basis for a national leadership consensus around core propositions of socialist development. Beneath the surface, however, lay profoundly different assessments of the relative priority of these sometimes conflicting goals, different approaches to their realization, and the clash of interests of groups and sectors within the Chinese polity.

In retrospect, what seems most extraordinary is the broad unity within the Chinese leadership and its ability to forge a popular consensus as it initiated the re-fashioning of the Chinese state and society. Beginning with land reform, initiated in 1947 in the midst of civil war, continuing through the formation of new Party and state institutions and the promulgation of the fundamental laws of the People's Republic by 1950, it included the initial stages of institutional transformation, involving the restructuring of the class relations in agriculture, industry and commerce. These changes were not affected without conflict. The early land reform in particular involved intense struggle and resulted in hundreds of thousands of deaths. Nevertheless, beginning in the late 1940s the passage to state ownership of vital sectors of national industry and commerce, the beginnings of mutual aid and cooperation in agriculture and handicrafts, and the creation of a rudimentary planning network, proceeded without serious disruption. The bases for a national consensus rested on the Communist Party's demonstrated achievements during the anti-Japanese resistance and civil war, the widespread recognition of the bankruptcy of the earlier social order, and the perception that state policies were working to the advantage of the great majority including the rural and urban producers and intellectuals. Particularly important is the fact that the major changes — including some involving direct conflicts of interest — produced improvement in the livelihood of the majority of people in the initial stages of institutional transformation, planned accumulation, and industrial growth. Remarkably, all this was accomplished while China fought a draining civil war followed almost immediately by the Korean War and in the face of blockade and economic boycott by the United States and other leading powers.

To sum up, the achievements in the transitional years from the civil war to the early People's Republic rested on two foundations. First, thorough-going institutional transformation coincided with, even contributed to, rapid economic recovery and growth, the expansion of state sector administrative and industrial jobs, the reduction of property-based forms of inequality, *and* improved living standards for most rural and urban people. Second, the changes rested on high levels of consensus within the Party-state leadership with respect both to long-term goals and concrete policy measures for their step by step achievement.

Chinese rural policy in the early years of the People's Republic marked a striking departure from the Stalinist strategy which sacrificed the countryside in the course of imposed collectivization to developmental goals centred on heavy industry and the cities. The distinctive features of Chinese practice, building on important lessons derived from the symbiotic relationship of Party and rural producers established during the years of anti-Japanese resistance and civil war, included the following: first, social change could proceed no faster than popular consciousness of and desire for change. This was the basis for mobilization of the rural majority in land reform and in state supported efforts to promote small-scale mutual aid teams and cooperatives. Second, popular support rested on implementation of policies which boosted the incomes of most rural producers. This was realized both during the drive in the early 1950s to encourage households to enrich themselves and in the explicit promise of early cooperatives that they would ensure mutual prosperity (*gongtong fuyu*). Third, local innovation and adaptation was encouraged so that new cooperative forms would be suitable to local conditions and local preferences. Fourth, the leadership achieved fair success in implementing gradual, voluntary institutional development by stages. The long-term vision of collectivized agriculture on the Soviet model would be achieved, according to the leadership consensus of the early 1950s, in conjunction with mechanization, a process requiring a minimum of several five-year plans to complete. In this view, technological advance would demonstrate to rural producers the material benefits of large-scale collective agriculture, and the collectivization process, building on decades of small-scale cooperation, would then permit a voluntary transition.[1]

If these points constitute a leadership consensus on principles of rural development in the early 1950s, in practice sharp conflicts developed centred on competing conceptions of sectoral investment priorities (agriculture, light industry and heavy industry), rates of accumulation, the appropriate speed of viable institutional transformation, and the role of market and plan in the national economy.

Three important sets of policy decisions implemented in 1954, in the autumn of 1955 to the spring of 1956, and in 1958–60, initiated a course which undermined both in practice and in theory the above-stated core principles, set the state on a collision course with the rural population, destroyed the leadership consensus and eventually sowed the seeds for the collapse of collective agriculture which is in progress in the early 1980s.[2]

As China embarked on her first five-year plan in 1953, the state imposed high rates of accumulation on the countryside for investment in the urban industrial sector. Heavy industry was the focus of national investment, and rural handicrafts and private markets were deliberately constricted as both competed with the state for resources. The heart of the problem was the conflict between a state bent on centralizing resources for modern processing and export, and rural handicrafts and private marketing which could contribute to expanding incomes and a pattern of decentralized rural accumulation. The state won. In 1953–54, the combination of state controls on marketing and handicrafts and excessive tax and grain sales quotas (forcing Mao Zedong, Zhou Enlai and other leaders to apologize and re-allocate grain to the countryside) cut into rural incomes in ways that set back the contemporary drive to build cooperation on foundations of mutual prosperity. Meanwhile differences grew over the pace of cooperative formation with some leaders urging acceleration but the majority in the Central Committee and Politburo contending that cooperation had proceeded too fast so that some units existed in name only or could be sustained only by means of coercion. By the spring of 1955, backlash against excessive state procurement and pressures toward cooperative formation had produced a leadership consensus to ease the financial and organizational pressures on the countryside. It appeared to represent a return to first principles.

From Marx and Engels through Lenin, Stalin and leaders of several socialist states, we note a recognition of the sensitivity of the 'agrarian problem', that is of integrating rural producers into a socialist developing society. But it was a sensitivity which would more often than not be honoured in the breach as it conflicted with more pressing goals. Lenin once put the point at issue well in a prescient statement which also sheds light on the most glaring failures of subsequent Soviet collectivization policy:

In relation to the landlords and the capitalists our aim is to complete expropriation. But we shall not tolerate any violence towards the middle peasantry . . . *coercion would ruin the whole cause.* What is required here is prolonged educational work. We have to give the peasant, who not only in our country but all over the world is a practical man and a realist, concrete examples to prove that cooperation is the best possible thing . . . cooperatives must be so organized as to *gain the confidence of the peasants.* And until then we are pupils of the peasants and not their teachers. . . . *Nothing is more stupid than the very idea of applying coercion in economic relations with the middle peasants.*[3]

There is abundant evidence from the internal and public policy debates on cooperative transformation that the Chinese leadership recognized the necessity to adhere to policies which protected the interests not only of the poorest strata but also of the middle peasants as well to ensure the creation of cooperatives which could ensure both equitable growth and rising rural incomes.

In the summer of 1955, two events set China on a new course. First, the five-year plan, with its ambitious targets and focus on heavy industry to the detriment of light industry and agriculture, was finalized and published. And second, with Mao Zedong throwing his authority behind a new drive, plans for gradual voluntary cooperation were discarded. In a matter of months, large collectives were being organized everywhere. Collectivization was virtually completed throughout the Chinese countryside in just six months, that is at a speed far greater than that achieved in the Soviet Union. Several features of China's instant, imposed collectivization bear note. Mao Zedong put forward three important reasons for abandoning previous cooperative principles. These were, first, the necessity for decisive action to assure that the ambitious production targets of the five-year plan would be reached; second, the perception that growing class polarization in the rural areas jeopardized the entire process of socialist transformation; and finally, that the poor peasants were urging, even demanding, collectivization as the only way forward. In addition to these factors, a fourth which was undoubtedly important in securing the support of grassroots cadres, was the fact that these cadres faced great difficulties in coping with the complexities of a mixed private–cooperative economy.

Close reading of the contemporary documentation reveals that already by the summer of 1955 it had become clear that in the absence of a dramatic change, China would indeed fall far short of unrealistically high plan targets.

Collectivization did, moreover, increase state access to the agricultural surplus, but only at a very heavy cost to the countryside, to rural producers, and to future production. Second, although we can find examples of some peasants losing their land and others prospering through the market, the weight of evidence convincingly presented by Vivienne Shue and others suggests that policies of gradual transition were curbing rural inequalities.[4] Third, there is abundant evidence of peasant willingness to participate in well-run small cooperatives which boosted household incomes, but I have been able to find no credible evidence of the demand by poor or any other rural producers for collectivization which involved the transfer of land and other resources from the household to village-wide or even multi-village units and required large-scale organization of agriculture for which there was little precedent. As we will note, resistance to the change — by no means confined to the prosperous — strongly suggests otherwise. Fourth, imposed collectivization simplified rural organization in the sense of establishing a single administrative and ownership pattern across the countryside, but it also presented immense organizational hurdles involved in non-mechanized farming on a scale dozens or hundreds of times larger than that of the household which had previously been its locus, and in a virtual absence of technical and administrative preparation for the changes. Although the model regulations for rural co-operatives issued on 17 March 1956 stipulated that 'the only way to ensure that the peasants take the road of cooperation voluntarily is by adherence to the principle of mutual benefit',[5] in 1955–56 the reality was an instantaneous process of state-imposed collectivization throughout the countryside.

One of the most deeply entrenched myths about the transformation of the countryside is that China carried to its logical conclusion gradual, voluntary cooperation culminating in 1955–56 in the 'high tide' and the rapid advance to full-scale collectivization.[6] The reality was quite different. Nationwide collectivization eliminated the largest remaining property-based income differentials between prosperous and poor households within each community, essentially completing the egalitarian redistributive logic set in motion in the land reform. It eliminated the fragmented land tenure system based on private ownership which land reform had actually strengthened. It opened new possibilities for coordinated agricultural planning and modernization in such areas as water conservancy and capital construction in the fields. But those achievements were won at a very high price, including betrayal of promises to rural producers of gradual, voluntary cooperation. The large new collectives lacked the experience and technological foundation for outproducing the smaller-scale producers, and above all they lacked an effective system of incentives which would encourage collective members to surpass the economic performance of private farmers and smaller cooperatives. The Party-state and China's hundreds of millions of rural producers were moving toward an antagonistic relationship.

But if China's imposed collectivization produced major problems, the fact is that the process was not only completed with extraordinary speed but (it appears) in the absence of major violence. To be sure, millions of pigs and cows were slaughtered and eaten, but damage to livestock and other property was on a scale far smaller than that in the Soviet Union, and agricultural production did not collapse. The differences lay above all in the credibility of the Chinese leadership after several decades of successful rural work, and the high degree of state penetration to the village level well before the collectivization drive. Yet, if our analysis is correct, a collectivization process which turned its back on promises of voluntary participation, which ignored the wide range of experiences of diverse communities and imposed a single administrative model, which placed particularly heavy burdens on a large middle peasant stratum, which sought to organize rural production on a large scale in the virtual absence of modern inputs, and which provided a vehicle for siphoning the rural surplus out of the countryside, created formidable problems.

Recent research, and the release of important Chinese documentation, have clarified important elements of the Great Leap Forward, particularly the price it imposed on the countryside. Here we wish to emphasize the ways in which the leap built on and extended tendencies and approaches which took shape during the collectivization drive. In the leap the Chinese leadership carried to new heights the logic of large-scale collectivization and elimination of the market and the private sector; it encouraged ultra-accumulation and virtually limitless demand for labour while in practice flagrantly disregarding the livelihood of rural producers. The promises of the leap that all would realize the fruits of abundance in a few short years as China zoomed past the most advanced industrial powers quickly gave way to the reality of mass hunger, starvation and economic collapse with the countryside bearing the brunt of the policy disasters of the period. We wish to focus here on the consequences of policies which divorce state goals of accumulation, collectivization and industrialization from the demands of rural producers for improved livelihood. This formula for disaster, not the ravages of nature and the withdrawal of Soviet technicians, bears primary responsibility for the economic collapse which began in 1959 and continued into the early 1960s until major policies associated with the leap could be overturned with the restoration of the private sector and the market, the scaling down of production units, and the implementation of more effective incentive systems.

The price was extremely heavy from multiple perspectives. As the economist Sun Yefang reported, the death rate soared from 10.8 per thousand in 1957 to 25.4 per thousand in 1960. This meant additional deaths of close to 10 million in 1960 alone, and a total in the range of 15–20 million deaths for the leap years. By the time the leap reached its nadir in 1960, grain production had fallen to 143.5 million metric tons, down 52 million from 1957.[7] The grain stocks required to feed China's cities, which expanded rapidly during the leap, had dropped from a high of 21 million tons in 1956 to less than a month's stock by the summer of 1961. The drawing down of grain stocks, and the beginnings of foreign grain purchase in the early 1960s provided a buffer against starvation for the urban population, leaving the countryside to bear the real brunt of the starvation brought about by the leap. It would be two decades before the Chinese leadership would acknowledge that per capita grain production in 1977 was no greater than it had been in 1955, prior to collectivization and the great leap,[8] and per capita *consumption* in the countryside may well have been lower than twenty years earlier.

The record of the Chinese revolution through the early 1950s, perhaps more than that of any other twentieth-century revolution, attests to the efficacy of the transformation of social relations linked to the welfare of rural producers as a lever for economic development and social progress. This outcome was closely related to the confluence during these years of revolutionary goals and values with the interests and participation of the majority of rural producers. Within the framework of policies assuring subsistence and security, making possible the re-creation of shattered families, and moving toward a modicum of prosperity, China's rural producers prepared to participate in and to shape a variety of new cooperative institutions.

The imposed collectivization of 1955–56, followed almost immediately by the impossibilism and disruptive state pressures of the Great Leap Forward, brought to an end that era in which state-led social change rested on strong leadership consensus and broad popular unity. It also initiated a period in which:

1. All attempts at implementing more advanced socialist forms (larger collective units, more egalitarian patterns of remuneration) encountered fierce resistance and in virtually every instance were soon reversed.
2. Leadership unity at the top gave way to bitter recrimination, sharp intra-leadership conflict, and an increasingly manipulative and conspiratorial political milieu.

The crisis of the Chinese state since the 1950s centres on the fact that proposals for social change and mobilization, while proclaiming goals of productivity and income breakthroughs, have frequently produced contrary results. Inevitably, many Chinese have come to view with suspicion both the state and the models it has proclaimed, particularly those viewing the future from positions of poverty and insecurity convinced that the message of collectivism and self-reliance could not solve their problems. This helps to explain the rush in the early 1980s to leave collective agriculture.

The overdetermined swing of the pendulum from the politics of collective mobilization to the economics of modernization, the market and high growth since the late 1970s raised impossible expectations of gains in productivity, income and consumer goods in a manner which bears comparison with the Great Leap Forward, though the politics of the two movements were profoundly different. Once again it has been necessary to cut back sharply on grandiose economic projects for which the technical–material–financial foundations were lacking.

Nevertheless, the preoccupation with the developmental project, the recognition of the heavy price which China must now pay for decades of stagnant per capita incomes amidst rising population, and the recognition that 'bigger and more public' may not necessarily produce salutary development results in the absence of technical–material foundations and human support for change . . . all these tendencies suggest signs of leadership recognition of some of the important lessons for socialist development which were discarded at such a heavy price in the mid-1950s. The realization that imposed collectivization and the great leap cut away at the genuine foundations of cooperation and hence of socialism in the countryside; the awareness that social change to succeed in the long run must be linked to higher productivity *and* higher incomes for the majority; the perception that more goods and services for people, even at the expense of heavy industrial growth, are preconditions for restoring unity and for overall advance . . . these are among the positive lessons to be drawn from the present cycle.

Again, as in the 1950s, the most profound changes are taking place in the countryside, this time with the vast expansion of the private sector, proliferating free markets, and the dismantling of most collective structures in agriculture. Numerous observers have pointed out that this may lead China to the virtual abandonment of cooperative and collective forms in favour of a household-based agriculture; and it may produce mounting class inequality in the countryside and lead to the demise of socialist institutions generally as China opens her doors wider to international capital. Yet the present course opens other possible options. At its best, in the early 1950s, Chinese socialism made available to the rural population options of effective cooperation sweetened with state material and organizational support. We should not rule out the possibility of the emergence over the next decade of strategies which make available new and more flexible options for defining the relationship among state, cooperative and household in the urban and rural economy; which produce an expanded state financial role in supporting and assisting poorer communities; which encourage both accelerated accumulation and consumption; and which place on a firmer foundation the cooperative and collective institutions which constitute the soil on which socialist development can thrive.

China's state socialism has important achievements to its credit, as well as profound failures. Its further advance is likely to require approaches which restore the confidence and basic unity shattered in the late 1950s and damaged in subsequent campaigns which drove a further wedge between the developmental and egalitarian goals of Chinese socialism and undermined the credibility of the state. This is likely to require a diminished role by the Party-state, sharing greater power in the production and marketing spheres with cooperatives, collectives and households. It is likely to require 'retreat' on many fronts from the forward positions taken over the decades with scant attention to the creation of material and popular foundations for institutional change. Such a course, fraught with difficulties and pitfalls, nevertheless holds out the brightest prospects for the future of a Chinese socialism.

NOTES

1. The classical statement is in Mao Zedong (1977), pp. 184–207.

2. I have explored the issues raised in this essay in Selden (1978, 1982 and 1983).

3. Lenin (1959), pp. 276, 282–283.

4. Vivienne Shue (1980).

5. See 'Model regulations for an agricultural producers' cooperative', in Tung Ta-lin (1959), p. 96.

6. For representative expressions of this view see Nolan's (1976) eloquent and richly informed analysis, Gray (1973) and Shue (1980).

7. Sun Yefang (1981), and the discussion by Nicholas Lardy and Kenneth Lieberthal (1982), pp. xviii–xxix.

8. Hu Qiao-mu, *People's Daily* (6 October 1978), cited in Lardy and Lieberthal (1982), p. xxxvi.

REFERENCES

Gray, J., Chapter in S. Schram (ed.), *Authority, Participation and Cultural Change in China* (Cambridge University Press, 1973).

Lardy, N. and K. Lieberthal (eds.), *Chen Yun's Strategy for China's Development. A Non-Maoist Alternative* (Armonk: M.E. Sharpe, 1982).

Lenin, V. I., *Alliance of the Working Class With the Peasantry* (Moscow: Foreign Languages Publishing House, 1959).

Mao Zedong, 'On the cooperative transformation of agriculture', in *Selected Works of Mao Tsetung*, Vol. 5 (Beijing: Foreign Languages Press, 1977).

Nolan, P., 'Collectivization in China: some comparisons with the USSR', *Journal of Peasant Studies* (January 1976).

Selden, M. (ed.), *The People's Republic of China: A Documentary History of Revolutionary Change* (New York: Monthly Review Press, 1978).

Selden, M., 'Co-operation and conflict: co-operative and collective formation in China's countryside', in M. Selden and V. Lippit (eds.), *The Transition to Socialism in China* (New York: M.E. Sharpe, 1982).

Selden, M., 'Socialist development and the peasantry: crisis of collectivization', in Albert Bergesen (ed.), *Crises in the World System* (Los Angeles: Sage, 1983).

Shue, V., *Peasant China in Transition. The Dynamics of Development Toward Socialism* (Berkeley: University of California Press, 1980).

Sun Yefang, 'Strengthen statistical work, reform the statistical system', *Jingji guanli* (Economic Management), Nos. 2, 3–5 (1981).

Tung Ta-lin, *Agricultural Cooperation in China* (Beijing: Foreign Languages Press, 1959).

China's Economic System Reform: Underlying Factors and Prospects

SHIGERU ISHIKAWA*

Aoyama Gakuin University, Tokyo

Summary. – Three important determinants of economic growth in the Chinese context are: the motivation of economic units, the absorption of foreign technology and its diffusion and agricultural productivity. The Stalin model of the 1950s served China well, especially when sustained by 'Chinese sub-models' such as ties of trust with rural brigades, workers' innovation etc. After that investment effectiveness declined, and today the structural changes necessary point to the need to alter existing institutions which have become obsolete. In agriculture, the use of cash inputs is more common now and a sense of economic efficiency is increasingly required. Care should be taken in comparing China with East European countries given that China's per capita gross domestic product is much lower as is the percentage of agricultural output reaching the market. The comprehensiveness of the economic reform likely in China means that it will only be possible to judge it over a time horizon longer than five years. For such economic reforms to be wholly successful, they need to continue to incorporate Chinese 'sub-models' mentioned in the paper and must develop a network of supplying industries and inter-dependent factories.

1. INTRODUCTION

This paper aims to investigate various factors and their interaction which affected the nature and viability of China's economic system[1] in the period of Mao Zedong's regime and on the basis of that to explore the prospects of the economic system reform which China's new regime has been attempting since the end of 1978.[2] As is known, this 'system reform' constitutes only one component of the overall economic reform contemplated, another closely related component being a readjusting of an economic structure biased by a policy favouring high accumulation rates and high priority given to building heavy industry towards one based on a more normal pattern, putting emphasis on realizing a steady increase in personal consumption. Here the discussion is concentrated on the former: the reform of the economic system.

The investigation is facilitated by a comparison of the Chinese changes with the experience of the economic system reform which was attempted in the East European countries much earlier than in China, toward the end of the 1950s. As is well known, China, like the East European countries, adopted the centralized physical planning model developed by Stalin in the pre-war plan era (hereafter abbreviated as the Stalin model) as the basic design of the economic system for economic reconstruction after the establishment of the socialist regime. It was also those aspects of the economic system which were shaped by the Stalin model that were made the object of the systemic reform common to both China and the East European countries. The essential components of the reform as far as the original design aiming at decentralized price planning was concerned, had a large degree of similarity. As for the *retreat* from the reform which later took place in East European countries (with the exception of Hungary) in the direction of recentralization, we are not yet at a stage to be able to make any final comparison.

Although my own knowledge on the East European economies is very limited and depends upon English-language literature,[3] a comparative analysis, starting from confirmation of the similarities on the level of the system model, seems useful in making explicit both similar and dissimilar aspects of the actual economic systems as between China and the East European

* I would like to express my sincere appreciation to Professors W. Brus, Dong Fureng, Nicholas Lardy, Victor Lippit and Thomas Rawski for their comments and criticisms on the original version of this paper. For any remaining errors I am solely responsible. I would also like to thank Professor Bruce McFarlane for his editing of my manuscript.

countries. In fact, we find as a result of such a comparative analysis that:

(1) the Stalin model adopted in China brought a number of sheer inefficiencies[4] into the economy, which necessitated a serious attempt at economic system reform to achieve their removal — a sequence similar to the one which had taken place in the East European countries;

(2) the Stalin model, however, made a significant contribution to the economic transformation of China in the relatively early phase of the People's Republic;[5]

(3) in China, the Stalin model was in many respects introduced in combination with peculiarly Chinese policies and practices which can be called 'Chinese sub-models'; the results of this combination were mostly favourable in making the system viable;

(4) any evaluation of the economic system reform in China should be made on the basis of more comprehensive criteria than those for the economic reforms in the East European countries.

Such a comparative analysis is also useful in obtaining from the East European experience certain important insights into factors to be taken into consideration when the *implementation* of the system reform is at issue.

To state the main conclusion from comparative analysis more concretely: the kind of factors which affect the nature and viability of the economic system or the reform are never simply the system-characteristics which relate to the particular model adopted or which the particular reform intends to introduce to replace the existing one. The Chinese experience indicates that there are, in addition, cultural and social traditions to be taken into account, in particular the village community tradition and urban employment practices. The political and social environment relating to the mutual trust (or distrust) between government and people is crucial. Other relevant factors include the level of output and market development, factor endowments, and the possibility of dualistic development. The experience of Eastern Europe suggests further factors that are likely to affect the implementation of the reform, such as the strength of vested interest groups in the existing system and, in particular, the amount of tautness in the current economic plan.

2. THE STALIN MODEL

In the light of the East European experience,

three points may be noted with regard to the content and characteristics of that Stalinist model which provided them with the basic design of the post-war economic system:

(1) The content of the Stalin model has been ably stylized by many expert economists, and may be summarized most simply by three items: (i) the entire economy was controlled through the system of 'centralized, physical planning'; (ii) the modern, industrial sectors consisted of state enterprises with the characteristics that (a) they were engaged in production and marketing, mostly according to the detailed plan targets that were determined by the upper organs and transmitted to the enterprises as government orders, (b) they had neither power nor responsibility to ensure that their products were finally sold to consumers, and (c) they were not expected universally to achieve financial self-reliance; (iii) the agricultural sector consisted of state and collective farms, the latter having developed through the land reform and collectivization movements. The activities of the collective farms, in turn, were subjected to the procurement plan for main farm products and sometimes to a detailed product-by-product plan directed from above. It should be noted that the above summary excludes the experience of Yugoslavia which, since the 1940s has developed a unique course of 'market socialism', or that of Poland which gave up collectivization in 1956 and pursued an agricultural system based on private family farms.

(2) The Stalin model was developed on the basis of earlier Russian experience of rapid industrialization and was geared to the state of excess demand in all the production sectors of the economy which accompanied a high rate of capital accumulation and high output growth.

(3) The model was seen to have caused disruption of the main balances of the economy and the disappearance of *microeconomic* efficiency, resulting in avoidable losses of national output and consumption. For this reason, the Stalin model of Eastern Europe was made the object of reform during the trend of de-Stalinization after Stalin's death.

The basic design of the economic system constructed during the First Five-Year Plan period (1953—1957) was the Stalin model with the three components listed in (1) above. However, the Stalin model brought to China not only demerits of the kind similar to those described in (3) but also benefits that were probably unique to China.

3. MERITS AND DRAWBACKS OF THE STALINIST MODEL IN CHINA

Drawbacks of the Stalin model ranged over both microeconomic and macroeconomic aspects of the economy. The demerits in the microeconomic aspects were most clear in the inefficiencies that flowed from the fact that the state enterprises were deprived of almost all decision-making powers relating to production and management. Just two examples, which can be well documented[6] may be cited: toward the end of the 1970s there was increasing evidence that the state industrial enterprises were producing a considerable amount of products which were actually unsaleable to the consumers and simply piled up in the warehouses of the Materials Bureaux or the State Trading Companies. The reason for this was either that the quality of the products was inferior, or the kinds of products supplied were not those actually required by consumers. More fundamentally, these malpractices occurred because the responsibility for marketing products of whatever quality or kind was not taken by the state industrial enterprises themselves but by the Materials Bureaux or the State Trading Companies. The former were simply interested in the increase in the amount of output valued at the officially fixed price, since this was the main 'success-indicator' for these enterprises. Moreover, during the same period, it became clear that the rate of utilization of fixed assets in state enterprise was very low, and that ordinary levels of maintenance and repair of these assets was neglected. The main reason was the practice by which construction of fixed assets was decided by the upper levels of government and executed by construction firms under contract, in a system where the completed fixed assets were transferred to the state industrial enterprises for their free use. Hence, the enterprise had no incentive to use the transferred assets economically.

Inefficiency of investment allocation in the macroeconomic sense arose for technical reasons. When the industrial structure became more complicated, it was not easy to proceed with centralized, physical planning without significant errors. Centralized planning under this new structure also brought about a tendency of ministerial autarchy, preventing horizontal cooperation. In connection with this aspect of bureaucratism, the tendency of provincial autarchy can also be noted. This is perhaps a specially important issue for China due to its vastness: whenever decentralization of some of the central government power to the provincial government was attempted, with the aim of arousing local initiatives to assist in local industrialization, it brought about as a by-product the duplication of investments (especially when the decentralization extended to the financial aspects after 1977).[7]

In agriculture, the strict procurement and production plans for food grain were imposed on the production teams without any adjustment of the procurement prices. The necessity for this became obvious in the 1970s in the light of the changed price—cost relationships which created conditions under which the larger the increase in the production of food grain, the poorer the production team and family members became. The incentive to increase food grain production for market was apparently declining in the low productivity regions where the opportunities for side-line production and local industry were very limited.[8] The net marketed surplus of food grains in the whole of China significantly declined in the 1970s as compared to the 1950s and reached a level as low as 10% of total output.

The merits of the Stalin model on the other hand, can be indicated by the fact that China, which before the start of the First Five-Year Plan lacked most branches of heavy industry, has now been transformed into a country with large-scale heavy industries consisting of comprehensive and well-balanced branches. This transformation was inconceivable without the support of the system of centralized, physical planning. Focusing on the machinery industries, the Chinese have not yet reached the stage of technological development in which new generation manufacturing technologies centring on automatic control of production processes are capable of being mastered, but a state that is fairly close to it, while imported technologies on the level of pre-automatic process control have been steadily mastered and then diffused widely. The proportion of machinery industry output to total industrial output has already reached the level of 30%, close to the Japanese level of 36%.

In agriculture too (as recently stressed by some Chinese economists) without 'artificial' emphasis on food grain production for marketing with the aid of planning, the amount of marketed food grain would have been smaller, and the speed of industrialization lower in the past 30 years than otherwise.[9]

Why did the Stalin model in some cases

exhibit merits, while producing demerits in others? My hypothesis is that apart from the cases where the merits arose with the aid of the Chinese sub-models, the question can be answered mainly by the compatibility (or otherwise) of an economic system with the economic structure to which the system was applied. (The 'economic structure' here denotes the industrial, size and locational structure of productive forces as well as the form and intensity of interdependence of economic units in the economy.) Essentially, I consider that the Stalin model achieved success in transforming China from an agricultural country into an industrial country because it was compatible to the economic structure in the earlier phase of the People's Republic period. Remember the state of heavy industries at that time, in which there was no need or possibility of increasing the effectiveness of investment in the heavy industries by marginal adjustments to the industrial branches or factories: macroeconomic adjustment by the Stalin model sufficed.

On the other hand, the Stalin model turned out to be inefficient as the economic structure evolved further, and became incompatible to the changed economic structure. It is not easy to know precisely when this change took place, as the disturbance to steady economic change caused by the post-Great Leap disaster and the Cultural Revolution was so large.[10] The inefficiency became manifest, however, in the 1970s. To cite a few examples: large adjustment of investment and production within the machinery industries was unsuited to the state of the same industries in 1978, for the weight of their output in total industry had come closer to the developed country level and the number of enterprises in industries was now more than 100,000 units. A turn to a policy of marginal adjustment must then have been on the agenda. Interdependence among these enterprises was limited even though most of them started as comprehensive and vertically integrated firms. In 1978, only 20% of the enterprises under the jurisdiction of the First Machinery Industry Ministry were buying from outside the parts and components or production processes required for making complete products. The structural change in agriculture occurred largely because the production of food grains and other main agricultural products came to depend significantly upon the purchased agricultural inputs and machinery with an industrial origin.

4. SUPPORT FROM THE CHINESE SUB-MODELS

There were four conceivable Chinese submodels that worked well in combination with the Stalin model; they are described in the following four theses:

(1) Production teams, the basic units of the people's Commune, were organized in the same geographical areas where traditionally natural villages or their neighbours had been located, and taking the families residing in these areas as the team members. Such production teams were capable of utilizing mutual trust among the traditional villagers, and their community-type solidarity was an essential organizational element of the production teams.

The favourable effect of this 'Chinese subsystem' upon the rural economy is exemplified by similar Japanese experience. The community solidarity of the natural villages in Japan was exhibited most clearly in the activities of the so-called 'minor cooperatives' which were organized all over the country in the early 1920s, with individual natural villages (called *buraku*, distinct districts below the administrative towns or villages) taken as units. Their activities ranged over (1) joint purchase and joint utilization of newly introduced farm machinery and equipment, such as electric or oil pump sets, motorized threshers and even power tillers, (2) joint farm operation and protection, especially in connection with innovative production methods, and (3) joint purchase of current inputs and joint marketing of farm products.[11] Without such community solidarity, organization of these types of joint undertakings of individual farmers (or even before that, the organization of the *minor cooperatives* themselves) would have been difficult. For individual farmers were likely to feel unsure as to whether the fruits of the joint operation of joint investment would be distributed among them according to the savings they had contributed to the joint undertaking. Comprehensive organization of the minor cooperatives itself was not seriously considered. In the system of production teams in China, labour remuneration was determined according to the mixed principle of payment for work and payment for needs. When there was no community solidarity among the team members, there arose a possibility that even for ordinary farming operations by members on the collectively run farmland, all the members chose to work lazily. Joint investment was also disliked and not pursued. (This represents, in pure economic theory, the case of 'prisoner's dilemma' first postulated by Amartya Sen.[12])

In China, however, as far as production for self-provisioning of the production team members was concerned, community-type solidarity among the members worked well for bringing about joint undertakings, thus preventing the occurrence of 'prisoner's dilemma' circumstances.

In this connection, a question may be raised as to whether in rural China the community solidarity of the traditional natural villages remained in operation in the production teams, as it evidently did in the *buraku* of Japan until at least a few years ago. As far as one can check with the evidence, it certainly remained in rural Guangdong,[13] but did not exist in rural Heilongjiang.[14] One may surmise that more generally it remained in the wider area of Southern China but not in the Northern regions where the village communities had been destroyed by the invading non-Han races from the northern inland as early as the 10th century. However, it is not necessarily valid to conclude that where there was no traditionally based community solidarity there was no community-type solidarity of any sort. Even if a farming group is organized, say, by government regulation in a small local area where information about each person was almost complete, and if all the members came to realize that the egotistic behaviour of individual members eschewing community-type solidarity would result in the disaster described by the case of prisoner's dilemma, it is likely that they would come to agree to act in such a way as to avoid such disaster. This would be true where it was not possible to act in the same way as if traditional community solidarity existed.[15]

(2) If and when the responsible party or government officials (*cadres*) of the people's Communes, districts and/or *hsien* behaved unselfishly and indiscriminatingly and trusted the cooperation of the common people (*masses*) in the locality, it was possible for mutual trust between the *cadres* and *masses* to emerge, and on that basis it became possible to initiate local undertakings and projects utilizing surplus labour and surplus materials.

The relationship between the *cadres* and *masses* relevant here can be regarded as one between the *cadres* who were anxious to have agricultural production of production teams for marketing substantially increased and the *masses* who feared the loss that would be inflicted by following the *cadres*' guidance or directives. What would happen if mutual distrust between the two prevailed? Two examples from actual cases might be suggested:

First,[16] the *cadres* in many localities (who had to secure a certain minimum quantity of the marketed food grains) felt insecure when only the compulsory procurement plans of food grains were transmitted to the production teams. They therefore issued detailed product-by-product sowing plans and, moreover, centralized many of the decision-making powers for routine farming operation, causing 'absentee control'. If the production team members were free to make any decisions regarding the management of the team with the only constraint being set by the compulsory procurement plan, it would have been possible for them to achieve the plan target efficiently and to devote the rest of the time to various non-food grain production activities, thereby obtaining a significant amount of net revenue. However, if action of the *cadres* had been as indicated above, it might have become more profitable for the production team members to limit their effort on the collective production of food grains, and then to go out of the teams to seek temporary off-farm employment. Here there was a strong likelihood that the case of 'prisoner's dilemma' would arise.

Second,[17] when the additional increase in the marketable output required prior execution of irrigation and drainage projects with the scope of the commands wider than the area of individual production teams or brigades, the *cadres* might have felt compelled to appeal to the local masses for participation using the surplus labour and surplus material under their command. However, where these *cadres* were not trusted by the *masses*, it is likely that the production teams would not have responded favourably to the *cadres*' appeal, or even if they did, that the quality of the completed project would be inferior. This is another theoretical case of prisoner's dilemma.

The incessant exhortation by the Chinese leadership to ensure the local *cadres*' selfless attitude, and the practice of the 'mass line' was not simply an appeal based on idealism. It was also motivated by the necessity to avoid the occurrence of cases of 'prisoner's dilemma' and to convert ôtherwise unused surplus labour and surplus material into productive wealth.

(3) Under conditions in which the production capacities of those state industrial enterprises under centralized investment allocation were not sufficient to satisfy the entire demand, in particular local demand, a policy of liberalizing rights to establish local industries which used local resources with low opportunity costs (and which catered to local needs) played a useful role in achieving overall efficiency of resource use.

While the policy of encouraging local industries was first initiated during the Great Leap period (1958–60), it was discontinued thereafter and revived only after 1966. In the early 1970s it contributed to creating a fairly comprehensive and balanced system of local industries in each individual province with the ultimate aim of provincial self-sufficiency in agricultural producers' goods. The scope of operation comprised the *hsien*-run, district-run and sometimes provincial-run state enterprises as well as some enterprises run by the People's Communes and brigades. Three points may be noted. First, the construction of local industries was very labour-intensive. Equipment was universally of small size and inexpensive. Often recycled equipment could be used. The most decisive advantage from the national economic point of view, however, lay in the fact that surplus local resources could be brought into active use in the construction and later the production process of local industries by means of the pump-priming effect of a small amount of centralized funds and resources which nevertheless involved high opportunity costs. We can say that the *investment inducement* effect of this centralized investment was very large. Second, the establishment of local industries, especially of *hsien*-level enterprises, was not conceivable without the strong leadership displayed by the local party and government officials. As the establishment of local enterprises was largely an affair determined singly by the local leaders, there was not here any game-theoretic situation.[18] Third, in most of the local factories and local industries, production costs were necessarily higher than the officially set ex-factory prices. However, this in itself did not mean that these factories were inefficient, as often claimed. The ex-factory prices were set by choosing the average cost of the most marginal enterprise in the central state-enterprise sector. As the establishment of local industries was encouraged to offset some of the excess demand for the products of the central state enterprises, it was natural that the price which equilibrated demand and supply was higher than the marginal cost of the central state-enterprises.[19]

(4) All over the modern sector a policy of 'full employment with low wages' was enforced, and the Labour Office in each locality became an agency enforcing this policy,[20] which provided urban workers with an inducement to endure persistently low wages for longer periods than in cases where such a policy did not exist.

The policy of assuring full employment to the urban workers in this manner does not seem to have been adopted in Eastern Europe. This might have been due to the employment situation in these countries where the urban labour force was fully employed and no serious problem of unemployment remained. On the other hand, there was in China already a considerable degree of urban unemployment in the First Five-Year Plan period. The policy of 'full employment with low wages' was institutionalized with the aim of coping with this situation. Even after that period, the urban unemployment problem potentially existed in the sense that if the very tight control over the rural–urban population movement was ever to be relaxed, the problem would worsen.[21] The above policy might be considered simply as one to cope with such potential unemployment; it had, however, a different implication which came from the fact that the same policy contained elements of traditional Chinese employment practice of a paternalistic, non-contract type. The employed persons under this policy would have felt more secure than under ordinary measures for preventing unemployment.

Two comments on the above Chinese sub-models are in order. First, with regard to the traditional Chinese institutions and practices which provided the foundation of some of the above sub-models, it should be emphasized that they contain not only those favourable elements which could be transmitted to the new system to be utilized positively as in the above sub-models. They contain at the same time those unfavourable elements which had been criticized before as 'feudalistic elements' and which could play potentially and actually a harmful role for planned development. When we separate from the traditional Chinese institutions and practices each of these favourable elements and relate them to the Chinese sub-models, we are in fact assuming that the unfavourable elements were effectively controlled, largely by the 'mass' education and the disciplinary training of the party members along the lines of Maoism.[22]

Even with regard to these four sub-models, as in the case of the Stalin model, there were problems of whether or not they were themselves congruent with the underlying economic structure. Most were congenial to the economic structure of a low development level in the relatively early phase of the People's Republic and thereby contributed as much to accelerating economic growth as the Stalin model alone could have achieved. More specifically, sub-models (1) and (2) were obviously congenial to a Chinese agriculture with a predominantly subsistence structure. Sub-model (3) did fit well with the industrial structure where the weight of the large-sized, high-technology sector was still small. Sub-model (4) was congenial at a stage where the steady rise in per capita disposable personal income was still the task for a distant future. With the inevitable changes of such an economic structure, the role of these sub-models became problematic — necessarily so.

5. REFORM PLANS OF THE NEW REGIME

Turning to the problems of the economic system reform of the Deng regime, I first point to past experience of reform in the East European countries. Three points may be made.

First, leaving aside the so-called model of 'market socialism' of Yugoslavia (in which individual state enterprises enjoy autonomy in management decision-making), the major alternative model to Stalin's which was available just after Stalin's death was, to use W. Brus' phrase, a 'centrally planned economy with regulated market mechanism' (or in short, a 'decentralized model').[22] In contrast to the Stalin model, the characteristics of such a decentralized model may be summarized as follows: (1) The central plan is confined to the macroeconomic determination of the national saving and investment ratios, the allocation of national investment among the major sectors, the outputs of major commodities and some other major economic and financial variables. (2) The main performance indicator of the state enterprises is limited to profit results. Other indicators of a directive nature are abolished. Decisions on current production and management are now made by the enterprise. Purchase of raw materials and selling of products are made through the market and by contracts. (3) Government exerts mainly indirect influence upon decisions made by the enterprises and individuals, using the instruments of price policy, taxation policy and interest rate policy.

Second, except for Hungary, the decentralized model has now been turned back to a partially-revised Stalin model. On the one hand, constraints upon enterprises through indicators with a directive nature have now been relaxed, and the role of profit and sales as 'success indicators' has been strengthened. Price reforms have been carried out on the basis of a broadly uniform profit: asset ratio for 'prices of production' set by the centre. In agriculture, the compulsory delivery system has been now replaced by a system of marketing by contracts. However,

this 'reform' is not really comprehensive and consistent enough to be able to reactivate the enterprises and collective farms on the basis of a strengthened market mechanism. Many aspects of centralized, physical planning continue to be in operation. Only in Hungary has the decentralized model survived, though with various revisions.

Third, a variety of observations may be presented as to why the decentralized model has been turned back to a partially revised Stalin model. Three points may be referred to here: (1) Leaving aside the external opposition to the reform, the decentralized model was also opposed from internal sources, notably party and government officials who feared that the reform would deprive them of the existing power they had been able to hold within the administrative set-up of centralized, physical planning. Some workers in state enterprises also feared that the reform would threaten the 'vested interest' they had already acquired in the form of welfare and secured employment. (2) When there was severe tautness in the Plan, and the economy was in a state of seller's market, it was difficult to expect real efficiency from the use of the market mechanism; the centralized, physical planning was always likely to revive. (3) The decentralized model required a high level of sophistication in planning techniques in achieving proper combination of macroeconomic planning and market regulation, and such sophistication had not been shown in practice.

That the original design of China's economic system reform was along the lines of the decentralized model is evident in two authoritative documents. One is the article written by the President of Chinese Social Science Academy, Hu Qiaomu, in *Renmin Ribao* for October 1978[23] and the other is the book of the Director of the Economics Institute of the State Planning Commission, Xue Muqiao, *Studies on the Problems of Chinese Socialist Economy* (1974).[24] The latter is more specific in indicating the basic design of a desirable Chinese system. The scope of the national economic plan of a directive nature would be limited to determining the major economic variables which more directly affect the direction of national economic development. The determination of the rest of the variables would be dealt with in the plan only as targets of a projection nature, formulated by assuming the working out of the market mechanism and the law of value. If and when the economy deviated from the lines indicated in economic plans, then it would be controlled by the more indirect instruments of taxation policy, price policy, material supply policy, government investment policy, and credit policy. It was proposed that the state enterprises be provided with real decision-making power on production, marketing and enterprise financing, so that their initiatives would be unleashed. In the People's Commune sector, it was proposed that private plots and sideline production of the individual member families be allowed and restored, autonomy of the production teams be re-established, and with improvements in the present excess demand situation, the planned purchase and planned supply system of food grains and other main agricultural products might be abolished.

Finally, some comment on the actual process of implementation of the reform plan up to the present seems in order. It has not been steady and uniform over various sectors. In the state enterprise sector, the reform plan was implemented in a small number of the well-established enterprises on an experimental basis and is of limited scope: experimental enterprises were merely allowed to retain a certain proportion of the realized profit for internal use under their own discretion, instead of surrendering almost all of it to the state.[25] However, in late 1980, under the impact of an inflationary situation which followed the increase in the budget deficit, further increases in the number of the experiment enterprises were stopped by a central government directive. While since then there have been some renewed attempts at furthering the state enterprise reform, real progress to that end seems to have been negligible.

On the other hand, the systemic reform in the agricultural sector has been going strong on two fronts: (1) separating the administrative functions of the area under the People's Commune from the economic functions of the People's Commune; (2) introducing a production responsibility system into the *modus operandi* of production teams. While the former is still in the experimental stage, the latter is already widespread and has exerted a profound impact upon the rural organizational set-up. Although precise information is still lacking, it is certain that the size of operation and in some cases that of management has become smaller. *De facto* collapsing of the production teams into family farms also appears to have been going on over wide areas of the country.

As for the method of national economic planning, no change has yet been made with respect to the practice of centralized, physical planning.[26] In the process of enforcing measures for structural readjustment, a large number of state enterprises in the heavy industrial sector (especially in the machinery industries) were forced to find consumers for their products by themselves, and accordingly the concept of 'market adjustment' has been introduced by contrast with the concept of 'plan adjustment'. For 1982 the importance of narrowing down the scope of the economy under the market adjustment tended to be stressed by the central planners.[27]

6. VARIOUS FACTORS AFFECTING FUTURE PROSPECTS

Although one may wonder if the development of the economic system reform implies that China has been following the course of recentralization seen in the majority of the East European countries, our investigation here of the underlying factors affecting the viability of the economic system suggests that it is still premature to judge the final outcome of the reform. It is more relevant to view recent events as one phase of the trial-and-error process needed to assess the effects of each of the underlying factors,[28] irrespective of whether those factors are perceived by the planners in the way described above.

In what follows, five statements are made, linking underlying factors to proposed reforms:

(1) Insofar as these economic spheres are those where the Stalin model had already lost its effectiveness in promoting further evolution of the economic structure, and had clearly become the sources of inefficiency, certain elements of the decentralized model must be introduced as part of an effective alternative. But their effectiveness seems to be conditioned by the degree of development in the economic structure and, in particular, the degree to which interdependence among the sectors and units of the economy has really increased.

This statement seems to be applicable to those aspects of the economic reform which relate to the state enterprises and production teams having autonomy in management decisions as well as an enlargement of the domain under *indirect* planning in macroeconomic control. The autonomy in management decision becomes effective, however, only when the markets of products and factors have been firmly established. This is also the case with regard to the expansion of indirect planning using instruments of price, taxation and interest policies. The problem is to what extent the evolution of China's economic structure achieved over the past thirty years has been sufficiently deep and widespread in achieving a modern system, so that the introducing of market mechanism into a wider sphere of the economy becomes really effective. It is not easy, however, definitively to answer this question: the interdependence among the machinery industry enterprises themselves increased considerably during the past thirty years, but the proportion of these enterprises under the jurisdiction of the First Machinery Industry Ministry (which buys the parts and processes) is currently only 20%. In agriculture, while the proportion of the value of cash inputs to the value of final output in grain production increased during the 1970s, the absolute level is still very low, the marketable ratio of food grains produced has decreased over time, while the 1978 level was as low as 12% (excluding the food grains that were rationed back to the agricultural sector). More generally, we have to remember that whereas per capita GDP in 1978 in East European countries ranged from US$1750 in Rumania to US$5710 in East Germany, that of China for the same years was only US$260. The proportion of agriculturally employed persons to total employed persons in the same year ranged from 10.6% in East Germany to 32.8% in Rumania, but it was as high as 73.8% in China.[29] Although the precise degree and the detailed process are yet to be investigated, it is beyond doubt that the state of the economic structure thus exemplified will offer significant resistance to the attempt to introduce the market mechanism, at least to the extent observed in the East European countries, and probably more, due to the differences between China and Eastern Europe just cited.

(2) Insofar as the product and factor markets in the economy are still more or less partitioned and in some local markets certain commodities are in short supply, the enterprises engaged in production of these commodities in short supply are not necessarily inefficient even if they are inferior to other enterprises in terms of relative production costs or profit rates, or other technical economic standards uniformly applied to them disregarding the dualistic market conditions. Selection of a certain portion of 'five small' industries would have to be made, in the final analysis, in terms of comparative marginal effectiveness of investment using the centralized funds with positive opportunity costs.

This statement refers to specific aspects of the issue taken up in (1). It questions the appropriateness of the major criterion according to which selection was done for a considerable portion of the 'five small industries' campaign when it was discussed and enforced. I would point to the relative magnitude and duration of the financial deficit that the individual enterprises incurred. The main area of large loss occurred in the 'five small' industries (altogether 2.2 billion yuan in 1980, of which 'small iron and steel' occupied 0.9 billion yuan and 'small chemical fertilizer' 0.8 billion yuan) and is a great burden on the economy.[30] Regarding great variance of the production costs as between 'small cement' factories, two factors are cited: the difference in effort for achieving efficiency and differences in objective conditions (e.g. availability of limestone, transport facilities, distribution channels).[31] The financial loss incurred from the first cause may be made a legitimate criterion for selecting such small industries for development, but the loss due to the latter should not, insofar as excess demand still exists and causes losses or windfalls unrelated to effort.

With the progress of local industrialization, the demand and supply situation of products and the availability of local resources with a low opportunity cost is liable to change. The tendency toward provincial autarchy which was touched upon previously has been instigated by the recent decentralization of financial power to the provincial government, and has accelerated this change. Conditions seem to vary significantly among the different 'small industries'. It is desirable, as a first step, to investigate in each industry whether the supply from the state enterprises producing centrally-allocated commodities has come to satisfy the national demand, and, if the supply is found to be still short of the demand, whether the local enterprises have been competing with the state enterprises in the above category for scarce resources, including the centrally-allocated commodities.

(3) If it is proved that the role to be played by market adjustment is not very large due to the still underdeveloped market conditions, it is still necessary to look for systemic measures to supplement it. It seems important, for example, to examine the possibilities for the community-type solidarity in the production teams to continue to play a supplementary role, in this case, within the context of the decentralized model.

It should be noted that community-type solidarity does not necessarily conflict with the market mechanism, and can sometimes play the role of strengthening the latter. The experience of Japan is illustrative of the point. Community-solidarity of the *buraku* was exhibited in the buying and selling activities of the minor cooperatives through markets. This strengthened the community-solidarity further, which, in turn, facilitated market development in the rural areas.[32] If this Japanese experience has general applicability, then any policy measure which is likely to weaken the existing community-type solidarity might be carefully reconsidered.

> (4) Where it is not possible to expect market adjustment to play a significant role, it is useful to attempt to recover and strengthen the relationship of mutual trust between the government, enterprises, People's Communes, workers and peasants, and thereby to create the conditions where central government appeals for moral support will get a favourable response from local governments, enterprises and the masses.

The implication of this statement is particularly important in the context of current political situation in rural China, where the introduction of various forms of the Production Responsibility System have been at issue. There seem to be a number of factors which were responsible for the advent of this system, in particular for the form of contracting production with individual households (*baochan-daohu*) or all-round contract with the household (*baogan-daohu*). First, there was the necessity to overcome the anarchic situation of the production teams relating to task assignment to individual members which have prevailed in the 1970s; second, the need to recover losses and improve an incentive system for work; third, the organization of the production teams as the basic ownership units in some regions may still be too large in size and scope to be suitable at the present stage of productivity development — the need is to revise it toward a smaller size.[33] More important here is another factor: the coercive attitude and corruption of rural cadres, fairly widespread in the 1970s, has caused the rural mass to distrust the cadres, which in turn has stimulated the production team members' choice of the *baochan-daohu* and, in particular, *baogan-daohu* system within the general movement towards a Production Responsibility System.[34]

> (5) As the decentralized model is not effective

when the economy is experiencing excess demand conditions and if China still wants to have a high growth economy, some *ad hoc* measures may have to be devised. As one of them, some *interim* period may be usefully set in which a high growth rate is restrained while various component measures in the decentralized model are implemented, so that the conditions that are required for achieving high growth are created without bringing about a state of excess demand. Some special resources are necessary for operating a reform during such interim periods. A cadres—masses relationship in which the government's moral appeals were favourably received would be helpful for proceeding with such measures.

To refer to an example of such a possible *interim* measure: while China imported grains from about 1961 at a maximum level of 6 million tons, the level rose steadily after 1978 and reached about 15 million tons in 1981. This change in the trend of grain import corresponds to the period when the government publicized a policy enabling the farm population to 'take rest and restore vitality' (*xiuyang shengxi*); and for the enforcement of this policy large grain imports were deliberately made on a continual basis so that the output structure of agriculture (which has been too much geared to food grains) could be adjusted to a normal one with an appropriate emphasis on non-food production.[35] For the same purpose, increases in the amount of tax in kind on agriculture and compulsory procurement of main agricultural products were withheld. In addition, the 1979 procurement prices of these products were substantially raised. The recovery of the production teams' autonomy in management decisions, as well as the introduction of the Production Responsibility System, was made easier by these interim measures. On the other hand, the measures taken incurred a considerable cost in the forms of foreign currency expenditure and internal inflation. It seems urgent, therefore, to establish a viable rural system within a period in which the economy can afford to maintain such an interim period of 'relaxation'.

NOTES

1. In this paper, 'economic system' is used as a generic term denoting all the institutions and organizations of the economy. It determines ownership relations regarding various assets of the economy. It also determines what organs, units or individuals are making decisions on production and management, carrying on the routine affairs on the basis of these decisions, and how these economic subjects are sharing powers for decision-making and implementation. It further

determines how in this connection cooperation and/or competition is developed among these economic subjects.

2. To be precise, the reform plan was adopted at the Third Plenary Session of the Eleventh Central Committee of the CCP held in December 1978.

3. In connection with the comparative analysis in

this paper, the following literature was most useful. Morris Bornstein, 'Economic reform in Eastern Europe', in JEC, U.S. Congress, *East European Economies Post-Helsinki* (1977); W. Brus, *Problems of the Incipient Reform of the Economic System in the People's Republic of China,* Background Paper for the World Bank (September 1980); J. F. Karcz, 'An organizational model of command farming', in M. Bornstein (ed.), *Comparative Economic Systems: Models and Cases* (Third Edition) (Irwin, 1974); K. E. Wädekin, *Agrarian Policies in Communist Europe* (London: Allanheld, Osmun, 1982).

4. In this paper the term 'economic inefficiency' is used mostly in the sense of H. Leibenstein's 'X-inefficiency' concept.

5. A statistical assessment for the whole period from 1949 to date which looks at macroeconomic growth and fluctuations is found in my 'China's economic growth in the PRC period — an assessment', *The China Quarterly* (forthcoming issue).

6. My chapter in S. Ishikawa (ed.), *1980-nendai no Chugoku keizai (The Chinese Economy in the 1980s)* (Tokyo: Japan International Affairs Institute, 1980) contains the essential documentation for these two examples.

7. For the history of administrative decentralization, see Liu Suinien, 'Problems of correctly handling the relationship between the centre and provinces in the economic system', in Liu Guoguan (ed.), *Guomin Jingji Guanli Tizhi Gaiquo di Ruogan Lilun Wenti (Some Theoretical Problems concerning the Reform of the National Economy Control System)*, *Zhongguo Shehui Kexuo Chubanshe* (Peking: 1979).

8. See also S. Ishikawa, 'China's food and agriculture: performance and prospects', in Erwin M. Reisch (ed.), *Agriculture Sinica* (Giessener Abhandlungen Europaischen Ostens Band 114), (Berlin: Duncker and Humblot, 1982).

9. Wong Yangxi *et al.*, 'Views on strategic problems in China's agricultural development', *Jingji Yanjiu*, No. 11 (1981); and Ding Shengjun, 'On the position of grain in the development strategy of China's agriculture', *Jingji Yanjiu*, No. 3 (March 1982).

10. The analysis of economic fluctuation and its various implications is given in S. Ishikawa, 'China's economic growth in the PRC period — an assessment', *op. cit.*

11. S. Ishikawa, *Essays on Technology, Employment and Institutions in Economic Development: Comparative Asian Experience,* (Tokyo: Kiuokuniya, 1981).

12. Amartya Sen, *On Economic Inequality* (Oxford University Press, 1973), pp. 94–99. The problem was discussed in the Chinese context in greater detail in S. Ishikawa, 'Personal income differentials in China and their underlying factors', *Ajia Keizai,* Vol. 17, No. 6 (June 1976).

13. W. L. Parish and M. K. Whyte, *Village and Family in Contemporary China* (University of Chicago Press, 1977), ch. 15.

14. Katsuji Nakagane, 'People's Commune and community', in T. Shimakura and K. Nakagane (eds.), *Jinmin-Kosha Seido no Kenkyū* (Studies on the System of People's Communes) (Tokyo: Institute of Developing Economies, 1980), ch. 1.

15. The solution is similar to the case of 'conventions' postulated by H. Leibenstein, in 'The prisoners' dilemma and the invisible hand: an analysis of intra-firm productivity', *American Economic Review*, Vol. 72, No. 2 (May 1982).

16. Zhao Ziyang, 'Study a new situation and thoroughly enforce the readjustment measures', *Hongqui*, No. 1 (1980).

17. *Ibid.*

18. Regarding these two points, see S. Ishikawa, 'A note on the choice of technology in China', *Journal of Development Studies*, Vol. 9, No. 1 (August 1972).

19. See also the discussion in Statement 2 of section 2 above.

20. Sun Ping, 'Why it is necessary to implement a rational low-wage system?', *Xuexi*, No. 23 (1957).

21. See S. Ishikawa, 'China's economic growth in the PRC period — an assessment', *op. cit.*

22. This paragraph was added to clarify my standpoint, in the light of the cordial criticisms made by Dong Fureng. He rightly pointed out that the Chinese tradition in some cases weakened the negative role of the Stalin model, but in other cases strengthened it; the Chinese tradition in some cases strengthened the positive role of the Stalin model, but in other cases weakened it. As an example of the unfavourable aspect of the Chinese tradition, he cited certain remaining elements of the feudal *clan* rules which were contained in the community solidarity, and which conditioned the interrelationship between the cadres and the mass of people in certain localities, thus making the negative role of the Stalin model even more serious. Thomas Rawski also raised a similar point in connection with a job-inheritance-like practice in the labour market.

23. Hu Qiaomu, 'Adhere to the economic law and speedily realize four modernizations', *Renmin Ribao* (6 October 1978).

24. Xue Muqiao, *Zhongguo Shehyi-Zhuyi Jingji Wenti Yanjiu* (Renmin Chubanshe, 1979).

25. In the second quarter of 1981, an attempt was made to improve this profit retention system by fixing the rate of taxation on the enterprises and making them responsible for the ultimate gains or loss. However, no fundamental measures were taken

to remove the differential conditions among the enterprises which was a basic cause of the differential financial performance among them. See Huang Zhenqi, 'Several questions related to enlarging the right of self-management: state enterprises', *Jingji Yanjiu*, No. 3 (March 1982); and also Xue Muqiao, 'Problems to be solved in reforming the economic management system', *Jingji Yanjiu*, No. 1 (Jan. 1981).

26. Xue Muqiao, *op. cit.*; and Xue Muqiao, 'Planned adjustment and market adjustment reconsidered', *Hongqi*, No. 1 (1981).

27. Xue Muqiao, 'Planned economy as the principal and market adjustment as supplement', *Hongqi,* No. 8 (1982).

28. In the terminology used in my paper, 'China's Economic Growth . . .', the 'trial-and-error' process mentioned here is of a marginal nature and not on a gigantic scale.

29. Figures for East European countries taken from World Bank, *World Development Report* (1980), p. 111; and from Wädekin, *op. cit.*, p. 145.

30. Ma Hong and Sun Shangqing (eds.), *Zhongguo Jingji Jiegou Wenti Yanjiu (A Study on the Problem of China's Economic Structure)*, (Renimin Chubanshe, 1982). See ch. 23 by Chen Shengcheng and Li Yue.

31. Sun Yangchu, 'Report on the survey of 'small cement' enterprises in Shangdong', *Renmin Ribao* (29 February 1980).

32. S. Ishikawa, *Essays on Technology, Employment and Institutions in Economic Development, op. cit.*, pp. 325–335.

33. *Ibid.*

34. Xue Muqiao, *Chongguo Shehui-Zhuyi Jingji Wenti Yanjiu*, pp. 42–44 and 66.

35. Zhao Ziyang, *op. cit.* See also Wang Songpei and Guo Ming, 'On "contracting production with the individual household" and "all-round contracts with the household" ', *Jingji Yanjiu*, No. 10 (October 1981).

Political Economy of Class Struggle and Economic Growth in China, 1950–1982

BRUCE McFARLANE*

University of Adelaide, Australia

Summary. – The Chinese economic cycle is both a cycle of accumulation and construction activity and a political cycle exercising its influence by trial-and-error methods and changes from voluntarist to pragmatic planning approaches. As a result of some excessive accumulation in the form of net investment in non-productive sectors, there was a lag in infrastructures like energy and transport and trade-off against consumption more severe than expected. Structural imbalances in the economy would have had to have been tackled after 1976, even if the voluntarists had been in office. The eclipse of central planning supporters was of 1979–1980 duration only. Thereafter the line on 'planning and the market' became less enthusiastic as the concept of 'market socialism' faded. 'Stabilization' of the relative growth rates of heavy industry and light industry was compatible with both the programme of the Chen Yun reformers *and* those reluctant to give ground from 'realistic plans' to tł e 'law of value'. In agriculture, the masses of small peasant proprietors rather than Part factions decided the shift to the new system of material incentives based on households. In this, weaknesses of Maoist practice in solving rural poverty played a role. Nevertheless, the left can defend collectivist ownership to some extent by adopting a more reasonable programme than in 1966–1976.

1. INTRODUCTION

Attempts to promote higher living standards in a large, poor country such as China or the USSR necessarily involve considerations of the agricultural/industry balance; the dependence of rates of economic growth on the allocation of new investment funds to the capital goods sector; sectoral trends; the possible dangers involved in excessive capital accumulation rates for personal consumption; the effectiveness of investment and new technology.[1]

Serious planners, economists, bureaucrats, government officials, cadres and Party-branches have since 1979 increasingly paid attention to these questions in China, since they are part of the agreed Party objective of raising mass living standards.

There are a number of ways these issues can be faced. One is to stress motivation not by material reward alone but by participation in decision-making, the need to pursue class struggle, and the drive for social aspects of socialism (such as egalitarianism). The other is a more *technocratic approach*. While favouring central plans, socialist orientation in distribution, social control over production, it seeks a steady growth of output as the primary

foundation on which social experiments can be developed.[2]

It is, of course, theoretically possible to work out a growth model or planning model that can guide a technocratically inclined socialist government in achieving a growth path that will not cause too many bottlenecks or a fierce 'trade-off' of economic growth against the living standards of the poorest in society. The purely technical side of this task was outlined in the work of Feldman and Gustav Groman in the USSR and Adolph Lowe who developed his ideas at Kiel in the early 1930s (later in the USA). Kalecki in Poland developed this tradition.[3] However, socialist economic planning in China, and indeed in the Soviet Union, has to encompass much else besides, while in *practice* the desired rate of growth of the economy or of living standards may be unattainable for unforeseen reasons.

To explain this, some arguments will be put forward about the nature of the long-term economic cycle in Communist China and then the political reactions to it by the 'voluntarist' and 'economistic' factions will be discussed.

* My thanks to Peter Nolan for systematically helpful comments on an earlier draft of this article, and to Professor Shigeru Ishikawa for making available Table 1 from a recent publication of his in Japanese.

2. THE ECONOMIC CYCLE

The primary concern of the planner or technocratic economist (and an important part of the story, if not all of it) is the movement of production and capital accumulation. These are shown in Tables 1—3.

Table 1[4] shows yearly growth paths and annual growth percentages for main indicators in various socio-economic phases defined (following Ishikawa's suggestion) as pre-Cultural Revolution (I), Cultural Revolution (II) and Economic Reform period (III). The most striking trough is 1960—1966, reflecting the bad agricultural seasons and some dislocations caused by the Great Leap Forward. A second trough covers the peak Cultural Revolution period of political debate accompanied by a reduced interest in investment effectiveness and maximizing outputs. The industrial output figures for this period are thought (by Ishikawa and other observers) to be exaggerated to the extent that they may include articles rejected for reasons of poor quality by consumers.

Leaving aside the troughs, Table 1 also shows that phases I and II featured a steady growth of agricultural and industrial output which fed 400 million persons and transformed the structure of production, thereby achieving a modern heavy-industry sector. It should also be noted that in this phase, 'infrastructure' was by no means neglected, since China's definition of industry used here included electricity, gas and water supply in addition to manufacturing. In phase III, the infrastructure lagged as a result of the neglect of electric power developments in particular.

The third phase, or the period of major economic reforms, achieved high growth rates in the first few years but, it may be argued, these results could have been of the 'once-and-for-all' type associated with the unleashing of initiatives after any economic reform.

Looking at agricultural trends, it should be remembered that land-saving and labour-using technical variants were widely adopted in pre-Cultural Revolution phase I. The type of capital investment backing these technologies was often of the kind the Chinese call 'accumulation' by which they mean *accumulation by labour*. The concept includes irrigation works, flood-control projects and accumulation of farmyard manures. These were usually carried out, in this earlier period, by voluntary labour of cooperatives and communes. In the later phases of the development path (II and III), investment in agriculture changed its character and came to mean modern and large-scale engineering works for pumps, tractors, mechanical threshers, chemical fertilizers and pesticides. Land cultivated may have decreased a little, but the capital investment of phases II and III resulted in significant yield improvements per hectare planted.

It is to Professor S. Ishikawa that we owe an explanation for the *shape* of the overall fluctuations in GNP, national income and investment implied in Table 1 and the graphs that can be drawn from it.[5]

Apart from fluctuations caused by a 'political trade cycle' (i.e. sudden changes in planners' and politicians' minds on priorities, or use of trial-and-error methods on a large scale), Ishikawa has identified equipment and construction cycles *within* the overall cycles. The first cycle, 1952—1962, he explains by the capital construction and equipment investment effort occasioned by the introduction and diffusion of Soviet aid to China in this period. Soviet technical aid embodied technology of vintages 1940 and 1960. The second cycle is a construction cycle for 1962—1978 using the same kind of technology, now copied by the Chinese. The second cycle may have also been stimulated by waves of technology imported during 1962—1965 and 1973—1976, although on these occasions they embodied foreign technology which was not as massively copied and diffused as in the case of the Soviet aid.

The political trade cycle, however, seems to have been even stronger than construction changes in its overall effect on the total economic cycle, presumably distorting the more technical cycles and compounding their effects. Such a political trade cycle also influenced the fluctuations in *investment* which we see in Tables 2 and 3, although these investment cycles do have technical aspects as well.

After the Cultural Revolution the question of the future of the Chinese economy was widely canvassed. It was broadly agreed then that two technical factors and one 'social relations' factor would be operative. The first two were the productivity achieved in agriculture and the ability to absorb foreign technology. The social relations aspect was whether deep changes in motivation of peasants, workers and managers set in train by Mao with his slogans of 'fight self' and 'grasp revolution to promote production' would take deep root and have favourable effects on production.

Analogously, a judgment about the future course of the Chinese economy over the years 1980—2000 will be some mix of technical factors and 'social relations' considerations. To explain it is necessary to consider further

Table 1. *National income, outputs of industry, agriculture and food grains, and population: absolute amounts and growth rates by phases, 1952–1980*

	Phase 1 (1952–1966)			Phase II (1966–1976)		Phase III (1976–1980)		Annual rate of growth: 1952–1980
	1952	1966	Annual rate of growth	1976	Annual rate of growth	1980	Annual rate of growth	
1. National Income (NDMP) – billion yuan in 1970 prices	65.4	151.0	6.2 (4.0)	245.6	5.0 (7.0)	338.9	8.4 (8.5)	6.1 (5.5)
2. Total value of industrial production – same	27.5	144.8	12.6 (10.6)	326.1	8.5 (11.3)	499.2	11.2 (11.2)	10.9 (9.8)
3. Of which, heavy-industry production – same	8.7	72.3	16.3 (14.4)	183.1	9.7 (13.6)	264.8	9.7 (13.6)	13.0 (11.3)
4. Of which, light-industry production – same	18.7	72.3	10.2 (7.4)	143.0	7.0 (8.5)	234.4	13.2 (12.6)	9.5 (8.4)
5. Total value of agricultural production – same	63.6	94.7	2.9 (1.4)	131.7	3.4 (3.8)	162.7	5.4 (6.1)	3.4 (3.4)
6. Amount of food grain production – unprocessed, million tons	163.9	213.9	1.9 (0.6)	286.30	3.0 (3.4)	318.22	2.7 (3.8)	2.4 (2.5)
7. Population – yearly average per million persons	568.2	735.6	1.9 (1.7)	926.19	2.3 (2.4)	976.74	1.3 (1.3)	2.0 (2.0)
8. Per capita national income – yuan in 1970 prices	115.0	205.3	4.2 (2.3)	265.2	2.6 (4.4)	347.0	7.0 (7.1)	4.0 (3.5)
9. Per capita food grain output – unprocessed (ton)	288	291	0.1 (–1.0)	309.0	0.6 (1.0)	326.0	1.4 (2.4)	0.4 (0.5)

Annual rate of growth is derived as a compound *annual rate* of growth between the years at both ends of the phase indicated. Figures in parentheses are derived as the annual growth rate estimated by the least-squares method.
Source: S. Ishikawa, 'Major factors in medium and long-term projections on the Chinese economy', Japan–China Association (Tokyo: 1982) (in Japanese).

Table 2

(1) Period	(2) Percentage of accumulation in national income	(3) Average rate of growth of industrial and agricultural production (%)	(4) Average rate of growth of national income (%)	(5) Rate of increase of financial revenue (%)	(6) Rate of increase of labour productivity in enterprises owned by the whole people (%)
1st 5-Year Plan (1953–1957)	24.2	10.9	8.9	11	8.7
2nd 5-Year Plan (1958–1962)	30.8	0.6	–3.1	0.2	–5.4
Period of Readjustment (1963–1965)	22.7	15.7	14.5	14.7	23.1
3rd 5-Year Plan (1966–1970)	26.3	9.6	8.4	7	2.5
4th 5-Year Plan (1971–1975)	33	7.8	5.6	4.2	–0.3
5th 5-Year Plan (1976)	31.1	1.7	–2.3	–4.8	–8.6
1977	32.3	10.7	8.3	12.6	8.1
1978	36.5	12.3	12.3	28.2	12.3
1979	33.6	8.5	6.9	–7.9	6.4

Source: *Peking Review* (23 March 1981).

Table 3. *Changes in the accumulation rate in different periods* (*in percentages*)*

	Average rate of accumulation (rate of investment)	Approximate range of fluctuation	
		Lowest	Highest
1st FYP Period (1953–1957)	24.2	23	26
IInd FYP Period (1958–1962)	30.8	10	44
The 1963–1965 Period	22.7	18	27
IIIrd FYP Period (1966–1970)	26.3	21	33
IVth FYP Period (1971–1975)	33.0	32	34
The 1976–1978 Period	33.4	31	37

*For figures, see *People's Daily* (15 May 1980), p. 5; *Social Sciences in China*, English ed., No. 2 (1980), pp. 193–198.

the 'social relations' which operated in phases II and III of the Chinese economic cycle.

3. 'CLASS STRUGGLE' IN CHINESE POLICY DEBATES

During the Leap Forward, Mao was concerned with speeding up the pace of economic growth. At his second Chengdu talk he characterized the overstrained pace of development of the Great Leap as follows: 'while one wave has not yet fallen, another rises in turn; this is the unity of the opposites'. The Great Leap was a 'wave-like form of progress', illustrated as follows:

'sowing is transformed into reaping; reaping is transformed into sowing. Spring, summer, autumn and winter are transformed into one another'.[6] But for Mao progress was the result, *even if there is chaos*: 'the appearance of disorder contained within it some favourable elements', as it will lead to 'order' on a higher level.[7] Another Maoist economist put it this way too, stressing 'spiral progress' to socialism.[8] As is well known, deep concern about 'chaos' and a determination to achieve 'great order' dominated official thinking in 1978 and thereafter, while notions of 'wave-like' movements or 'spiral progress' have been savagely criticized. The reassessment of the history of the Chinese

Communist Party (CCP) of June 1981[9] is full of this distaste, a reaction which led eventually to the assessment that there was a rupture in Mao's thinking on economic and social questions after 1958. This is hardly surprising. At the 10th Plenum of the 8th Central Committee meeting of September 1962 Mao had already come into conflict with that *liberal-technocratic* group around Liu and Deng that has controlled economic policy since 1978.

During the Cultural Revolution there was an official policy of 'grasping revolution *to promote* production'. Both ultra-Lefts and Mao's critics often forget this. The workers' innovation movement and mass campaigns based on ideological motivation were not designed merely as exercises in talking, but as motivating forces for accelerating the rate of economic growth in all sectors. It was Michal Kalecki's '*u*' factor (investment by workers' initiative) that was relevant here.[10]

Since 1976 the objective of changing/ improving social relations in the short-run between groups (peasants and workers) has had a low priority. Those parts of Maoism related to 'changing human nature' and 'developing a new socialist man' appreciated by such Western writers as J. G. Gurley, Jack Gray, and Neville Maxwell seem to have been consigned to a lesser role. The 'human factor', which was added to the usual growth and planning equations, has partly dropped out. Kalecki's '*u*' factor has been relegated, in the minds of some planners (though not of the President of the Chinese Academy of Social Science), to merely saving waste, better repair of machines and workers' suggestions, thereby losing its wider implications. Developments which western observers found new and appealing have been systematically wound down: barefoot doctors have been told to get shoes and higher skills; tertiary students have been told they may be exempt from labour (except where the school can use the proceeds of the sale of things produced by student labour to become self-sufficient); and a 'peasants first' policy has lost its egalitarian underpinnings. In their place have appeared a reassertion of Chinese traditional values about hard work and in favour of self-interest, frugality and self-sufficiency (in schools and welfare institutions as well). Such ideas are, of course, familiar in the West in the writings of Samuel Smiles, Mrs. Thatcher and Milton Friedman.

What needs to be pointed out here is that the apparent official disillusionment with an emphasis on social relations is not only a political issue of attacking a key tenet of the 'Gang of Four', or even just a renewed interest in a doctrine of 'productive forces first'. It clearly implies an abandonment of the drive to egalitarianism with which any such 'new man' approach must be linked. In this, disappointment with results of Maoist practice in relation to narrowing regional and income differentials and abolishing poverty have played a role.[11]

Some examples are:

(a) such a basic need as adequate access to drinking water had not been delivered to 40 million people as of 1980;[12]

(b) only 4.2% of children in the appropriate age bracket were enrolled in middle school in the 1970s;[13]

(c) during the Cultural Revolution, 100 million peasants still received less than 150 kg of grain ration, when it was known that the national 'mean' had been 163.5 kg in 1960 (it subsequently rose to 173.5 kg in 1972);[14]

(d) according to official estimates in 1980, about 100 million peasants were subsisting on state relief, while one in ten peasant households and 200 counties had a mean per capita income no higher than in 1949.[15]

These trends would seem to indicate that against the undoubted positive policies of Maoism in certain areas such as health services, industrialization of the country areas by downward transfer of technology, diffusion of appropriate technology, we have to put the continuance of undemocratically imposed planning norms, and the persistence of large-scale poverty at the bottom of the rural income pyramid up to the present time.

The gap between rhetoric about 'narrowing the three great differentials' between agriculture and industry (though not between areas within the rural sector),[16] pushed in periods of Leftist revolt against bureaucratization of the revolution, and what was actually achieved, allowed Deng's technocratic line to gain plausibility and legitimacy in wider circles than the top cadre. It meant that Deng could claim to have done more to raise the incomes of many peasants at the bottom income level in the poorest counties simply by moving the terms of trade in favour of agriculture, than Maoism had been able to achieve over 25 years. It meant that the ground was prepared for new household-based agricultural policies (*San Zi Yi Bao*) for poor areas that were not accumulating surpluses. It meant that the encouragement of private plots, even in urban areas, would take off once a new official tolerance of small peasant proprietorship became known to farmers.

After 1976 the four modernizations took pride of place in plan efforts, so 'reducing the three great differentials' was postponed. The key to poverty relief was now seen to be in a long-term growth of real product per man hour. Above all, modernization as a goal meant that the transformation of productive forces was seen by many political leaders to be a *pre-condition* for transforming social relations by first raising income levels, although the way in which higher consumption would transform social relations has been left vague in political ideology since 1978.

4. 'PRODUCTIVE FORCES' VS 'SOCIAL RELATIONS' IN CHINA: PRAGMATISM AND VOLUNTARISM IN PLANNING POLICY

At the time of the 1960s Sino-Soviet dispute about 'peaceful co-existence', it was not difficult to find quotations from both the USSR and China enthusiastically supporting peaceful co-existence between systems, though both sides accused the other of foreswearing it.[17] Cardboard cut-outs of both sides' positions did exist: similarly with the 'productive forces' vs 'social relations' debate in China after 1976. For example, in relation to the USSR, it had already been the case that both moral and material incentives were harnessed by government officials, party cadres and managers. There was never a *complete* reliance on one *rather than* the other form of incentives, although the use of piece-work rates in the USSR always meant the amalgam was tipped more in favour of material incentives. Despite what is often thought, Mao emphasized the need to develop the productive forces[18] while it was Liu Shao-qi who said that 'on the basis of increasing production, and taking into account the need, effort should be made to improve step by step, the workers' material and cultural life'.[19] However, it was Liu and not Mao who said: 'under socialist conditions, he who devoted his mind to working for personal benefits will never achieve them. He who devotes his mind to serving the people will achieve personal benefits also'.[20] This point is made because some interpreters see the new line on material incentives as reflecting a class takeover by capitalist roaders in collusion with small peasant proprietors unleashed by the new 'responsibility system' in agriculture. This 'transformation of the social relations', however, only exists in the minds of those who link the struggle over 'productive forces' and

social relations with each other, and not with class struggle.

The real content of China's debates and practice can be assessed in part by querying whether there ever was a *consistent* push of 'social relations' (class struggle) over 'productive forces'. In reality no sharp dichotomy existed in practice, or for long periods, between policies geared to continuing 'class struggle' and those based on planning and economic growth — the supremacy of the forces of production. Such a sharp dichotomy is largely a fiction promoted both by a relatively few ideological pronouncements of a small group of Leftists, and the considerable 'frame-up' of the 'Gang of Four' pursued after 1977, in which their views were caricatured by government and party polemicists. What there existed in practice (and this can be seen from the statistics quoted in this article) was a changing set of objective conditions which produced an inevitable subjective response. Thus, from 1959 to 1964 there was an increasing awareness that while 'moral incentives' would assist in making the rationing system work, the dwindling grain supply which made that rationing necessary would have to be solved by technical inputs, organizational rearrangements in agriculture and the restoration of rural fairs. After 1970, the high costs of a low international trade turnover were met by increased trade and overseas commercial contact. After 1977, serious structural imbalances in the economy, especially between wage-goods production and heavy-industry production, led first to a rise in the investment rate, later to a sharp cut in the rate of accumulation and then to 'economic reforms' aimed at raising the overall effectiveness with which resources were used, especially as investment inputs.

Conversely, failures or perceived failures of Mao's economic policies and actions on poverty relief plus mistakes in left leadership paved the way for the present reforms. This is why Chen Yun as well as China's leading economists of today can support[21] not only a reduction in the overall growth rate and the decrease in expansion of heavy industry, but also 'cutbacks and restrictions on capital construction, a readjustment of the internal structure of production, and acceleration of housing construction, a lowering of production costs and a reduction in enterprise losses'. All of these measures aim to stabilize the economy. They might raise consumption standards. Whether they will eliminate structural crisis in the balance of the economy and future economic cycles will depend on how the basic causes of the cycle are perceived and handled. If left to technocrats and planners alone, a better investment programme might be designed, but it is hard to see it being immune to Party interference and pressure from below, while the dangers of neglecting infrastructure investments, even from the standpoint of 'effectiveness of investment' are considerable and will require the most careful handling. What is not clear in this kind of advocacy is an account of how China will go from 'more consumption' (albeit a modest jump) to transformation of social relations in a socialist direction.

The decade of the 1970s had opened with serious disagreements about industrial policy and contracted output in some sectors (including a loss of 20 million tons of steel production in 1974–1976). Up to 1975 the Left, while including a range of technocratic planning problems in its strategies, was still arguing[22] for gradually increasing priority to be given to changes in 'social relations' even if the degree of direct participation above the level of the workshop in practice was limited. They did not undermine in a serious way the commodity system and monetary-based exchange, or status differences in enterprises. Rather, the decade of the 1970s ended with the status quo in all these matters largely consolidated. The factory general manager has authority over the use of enterprise assets, and is responsible for welfare, discipline and technical operations. He also represents the enterprise on outside bodies. While trade unions as representatives of workers have been revived as participants in factory decision-making, they have a minority of advisory directors. A 'representative' principle has replaced the 'participatory' principle of the Left.

The aim of this was (a) to eliminate worker opposition to higher norms needed to raise productivity, (b) to strengthen the quasi-market system of enterprise competition, which would be hampered if decisions about pricing, investment and profits had to await the approval (and discipline) of mass meetings of blue-collar workers.

By eliminating an approach based on technological determinism, Chinese socialists opened up the question of the political context of the process of a changing social division of labour: control of the labour process and the political objectives which motivate the accumulation process are part of a government's political outlook. Kalecki made the same point in relation to his 'government decision function' curve. Chinese leaders since 1976 have gradually dismantled the previous relatively democratic

mass-decision-making process in factories[23] and gone back to a hierarchical style of management of industrial enterprises, although minor reforms such as election of group chiefs and workshop leaders are now being introduced. Moreover, the demise of 'barefoot engineers' who used to diffuse minor innovations, means that attempts to increase Kalecki's 'u' factor by participation of workers will be less successful and result in a lower growth of potential production. In rural development programmes, the communes' role seems certain to be largely replaced by contracting enterprises hired to build social overhead capital and by the burgeoning 'household responsibility system', neither of which is designed to lead to participation of rural workers in rural development programmes. In China today, there is nothing like the popular science movement in Kerala or even some of the participatory rural schemes of Colombia and Thailand.[24]

This was, to a large extent, an overreaction against previous mass campaigns and 'social relations first' propaganda of the Left which had set in by 1979. The overreaction itself has been modified by events at the top levels of Party economic policy since early 1981, with the change to some recentralization and the calling of limited elections within factories. One should also mention the paying of more attention to peasant livelihood and communal distribution problems as well as curbing cadre corruption. The political economy emphasis was firmly shifted after March 1981, however, to (a) provincial planning within a new Stalinist framework; (b) continuing and increasing discipline over the work force; (c) more power to factory managers; and (d) streamlining of central plans rather than abolishing them. Market forces, while being encouraged, have not developed into market socialism but the reformers have some consolation in trends in industrial management and the amazing growth of spontaneous small peasant proprietorship in rural areas.

5. REFORM OF INDUSTRIAL MANAGEMENT IN THE CONTEXT OF CENTRAL PLANNING: SURPLUSES, PROFITS, PROFITABILITY

After 1978 there was certainly a drive for autonomy of enterprises to be extended. The view of the Chen Yun group was that 'if enterprises do not have a suitable amount of autonomy, then there is no point in talking about market regulation'. However, many central controls remained within a decentralized Stalinist system, and were only slowly being removed. Even this process was halted by the Central Committee meeting of June 1981.

Why are 'reforms' in relation to enterprise autonomy *important* as an indicator of trends in the 'political economy' of Chinese socialism (e.g. the degree to which there has been regression to capitalist mentality and methods)? One obvious reason is that the *specifica differentia* of a socio-economic system is the way that an economic surplus is formed and extracted: the social-existence form of labour power.[25] Industrial enterprises, which in China always transferred their profits to the State budget, have been a key source of the Chinese economic surplus which provides the collective investment fund for re-investment in new industries. Any tendency towards a real widening of market forces-based recruitment of labour power to service industrial enterprises, with the new trends in the new wage system, would certainly strengthen and not merely modify the role of the law of value in influencing the contribution to surplus and the control of the distribution of that surplus by non-producers. While it is true that all socialist economies have to make 'profit' in the sense of 'surplus' to aid the state budget,[26] there is still room for serious differences concerning how the decisions about that process are taken. Market decisions can be just as much outside direct worker participation in decisions as are vertical bureaucracies handing down plans from on high with little real consultation.

However, the scope for more and increasing market freedom in China today is perhaps still problematic — the shift is still of the nature of a limited decentralization, and the shift itself has been of a zig-zag type. For instance, it would be possible, in relation to 'industrial strategy', to describe 1979 as the year of the concept of the economic reform, with 1981—1982 as years of consolidation of a number of firms into trusts, with their ministerial counterparts included (the same kind of development occurred in the USSR in 1969—1972 and in Poland in 1958). While the changes in allocation of resources as between heavy and light industry during 1979—1982 have been clear and consistent, the issues of democratization of management, autonomy and degree of market forces allowed have been taken up in a ramshackle and pragmatic way. This perhaps reflects the zig-zags at the controls of the top planning agencies: the creation of a State Commission for Economics and Finance under Chen Yun in July 1979, a new State Commission for

Manufacturing under Bo Yibo in February 1980, the replacement of Hua Guofeng by Zhao Ziyang as Prime Minister in September 1980, the removal of Yu Qiuli (for Yao Yilin) as head of the Planning Commission, and the fall of Kang Shi'en and Gu Mu from the Planning Commission in February—March 1981.

It is still not possible, from a political economy standpoint, to be certain whether 1982 was a year of pause before the economic reform in industry was deepened and continued, or a period of halt and reversal towards planning and controls for commodities originally destined for allocation by quasi-market forces. It appears, for instance, that by mid-1982, only 10% of the gross value of output of the state-influenced and industrial sector had been seriously adjusted to the reform.

During the zig-zag period of 1979—1982, the earlier pro-market socialist advocacy of some economists (who nevertheless agreed that Stalinist economic planning had brought many benefits in the past) has been replaced by a political economy which insists on a combination of plan, regulation and market which would have a different mix according to which sector of industry is involved. (It will be recalled that S. Vukmanovic-Tempo's 1957 speech in Belgrade launching market socialism for Yugoslavia made similar reservations, while the Hungarian economic reform of the late 1960s had a three-tier system of prices under various degrees of control, according to the type of commodity involved.) In a number of the 1981—1982 China press articles (for example the *People's Daily* editorial of 24 February 1982) it was argued that planning and regulation will be needed for heavy industry and manufacturing exports, but can be relaxed for provincial-level industrial activity.

This raises the problem of two areas of industry that are being more strongly affected by the new reforms in industry. They are rural factories and manufacturing which is linked to foreign trade. Under the previous regime (to 1978), local industry had been expanding rapidly, especially in the 1970s. It was seen as a source of inputs for agriculture and a means of obtaining surpluses for savings and investment for collectivist units in rural areas. Their future (e.g. the five small industries campaign and Mao's horizontal economic zones of 1972—1973) is in some doubt, partly because Mao believed, in opposition to Deng, that local industry maximized participation in cooperative enterprises, providing a quick route to socialism and socialist man. The short-term profits of small industrial enterprises in local areas with almost a zero gesta- tion period could supply profits for longer-term investments with longer gestation periods, thereby putting short-term interests at the service of long-term interests. Or as Dobb put it with more academic precision in his 1960 book, *An Essay on Economic Growth and Planning*, the Chinese investment selection methods of the peak Mao period 1958–1959 'may have the offsetting advantage of a shorter period of production, contributing to the growth rate via the compounding effect by shortening the time-lag of the process and having increments of investment at earlier dates'.

Mao had envisaged that the high degree of popular participation involved in small industries would help in preventing bureaucracy, which was represented not as a political style but a fundamental bastion of class power. In 1965 Mao had said 'the officials of China are a class, and one whose interests are antagonistic to those of the workers and peasants'. The industriali- zation of rural areas would also in Maoist terms gradually reduce distinctions between industry and agriculture, mental and manual labour, and city and countryside.

The new industrial reforms and the new criteria for investment choice being suggested run counter to Mao's vision of the *central* role of small industries in economic development and social change, although they are likely to be one area where market forces rather than bureaucratic control will rule in the future. It would seem, however, that the new techno- cratic consciousness about 'effectiveness of investment' will have a negative effect on much of the small-scale rural industries, involving as it does not only consideration of the impact of macroeconomic investment rates but internal choice *within* sectors.

China's manufacturing industries linked to foreign trade remain comparatively small. Their future is likely to be governed by the Law on Foreign Investment of 1979, joint ventures and the practice of export-promotion zones. To a great extent they will be marginal to the 'commanding heights' of the economy for the foreseeable future, although the social relations involved (more employment of women wage labourers, as well as use of technology from abroad embodying capitalist production rhythms and wage relativities) are sure to pose problems for the Party in the political and ideological sphere, even if the economy will be benefiting.

The main advantage of free trade zones is in being able to build up a sector which has

not kept up with others, posing the threat of structural disproportion. This is sector Ib — that producing machines to make consumer goods, an example of which is textile looms. This sector is ideally suited for foreign coopera- tion or for importing, as it then releases internal resources for productive real-capital formation. It would be foolish to deny that what has already happened in foreign trade-linked investment is a retreat into non-socialist political economy. However, China is still a planned economy and can switch its investment policies in the future, given the political will to do so. Already there are signs of a desire to cut back on the original programme for a large number of joint ventures.

Since 1978 the reform of industrial enter- prise management has been taking place under conditions of accelerating inflation, which has forced a policy of financial rectitude (balanced budgets, reduction of money income pressures, more financial control through central budgets). Under these conditions, there is a tendency to assign to enterprise profits a key role (along with the issuing of savings bonds) in balancing state budgets. The pressure has been to seek higher profits (and reduced subsidies) in industry as contributions to budget income. This, in turn, has led to higher wholesale prices, to enable enterprises to retain profits for self- finance (as envisaged in the economic reforms giving quasi-autonomy) *and* take off some of the burden of delivering higher surpluses to the budget. To the extent that reduced sub- sidies from a higher level of retained enterprise profits make higher taxation less necessary, this helps the situation. But the inevitable results of relying on transfers of enterprise profits *and* granting more retained profits is the setting of higher and higher levels of whole- sale prices: inflation is the result, from the supply side. Not only that, but the turnover taxes have also been increasing (both as revenues for the budget and to balance supply and demand), adding to household burdens. As popular reaction against this amounts, it is possible to predict that any decentralization of fiscal control will be followed by a tightening of Communist Party control within economic units. Any losses in tax revenues from decen- tralization will accentuate the possibility of this sort of action being taken by the authorities.

6. AGRICULTURAL REFORM, EGALITARIANISM AND THE ECONOMIC SURPLUS

It is familiar to readers of Kalecki, Dobb

or Joan Robinson that a certain role is played by agricultural results in overall development strategies. When in the pre-socialist regime the peasant and the landlord had taken their share of the wheat (or rice), the remainder was used for wages. The real wage of workers in investment-goods industries had to be found from the surplus created by agricultural workers.

Where, as in China, the state intervenes to snare that surplus, it also diverts it to the work-force in investment-goods industries. What is the effect on the poor classes of farmers?

Deng's government has pointed[27] to the fact of continuing poverty and scarcity of basic necessities for 100 million peasants and claimed to have done more with a stroke of the pen (raising agricultural prices) than Mao's policies of agrarian egalitarianism over 20 years. This has had some persuasive power, even if published figures show a low 'commodity turnover' for total agricultural production. Perhaps the higher rewards attained by peasants in the last few years have sustained the per-suasiveness of the anti-Mao claims here. They have also justified the new management respon-sibility system in agriculture as a way of helping peasants previously locked into rural people's communes that have been unable to accumulate surpluses for various historical, geographical and economic reasons. It has been argued that 'narrowing the three great differentials' has not worked for these categories, that only wealthier communes have a continuing stake in the 1960—1980 commune system. The new system will give material rewards for those willing to work hard on family-based farms:[28] *San Zi Yi Bao* in agriculture has virtually been re-instated.

Why did the official Maoist policy of egali-tarianism break down in agriculture, paving the way for the apparent popularity of the present trends toward small peasant proprietor-ship within the new responsibility system? To answer this it is necessary to look at the kinship system, the pre-World War II social relations as they actually existed, and the fissures in the bonds of trust between rural cadres and masses that opened over the last 20 years.

In rural society, exchange of women, ex-change of gifts, bride prices etc., reflecting older tribal and kinship social relations, are deeply rooted and well organized. In China the custom of brides going to the husband's village, arranged marriages, and payment of bride price is still common, because exchange of women and gifts is an integral part of production and repro-duction of peasant proprietor systems — as Gregory's analysis clearly shows.[29]

This means that pre-war China was not a pure case of feudalism at all, hence collecti-vization did not produce a wholly new society. Rather, China before communism was a rural society in which hangovers of an Asiatic mode of production and feudal elements co-existed with a parallel system of owner-cultivation. It is the culture (and some economic aspects) of the latter that has provided the fertile ground for the resurgence of peasant interest in owner-cultivation, material reward and dismantling of the collectivized rural economy.

The CCP's analysis of social relations in agriculture has not been a shining star in its political economy: the continuing relevance and dynamism of peasant proprietorship was ignored; cardboard figures of large-scale oppres-sive landlords and suffering landless peasants were substituted for historical and political analysis. The differences between a flexible system of peasant owner-cultivation (subject to weather cycles) and the rigid hierarchical system of feudalism were passed over. A similar error was made in other Maoist com-munist parties — in Bangladesh and especially in the Philippines[30] in relation to alleged 'feudalism' there in the 20th century, while neglecting peasant proprietorship, dynamism, and kinship ties.

Even without complications arising from the factors just discussed, objective contradictions existed in the Chinese collective economy itself. The question of inter-commune differentials is an example as recognized by the Party and the government. Assume a number of com-munes in a given county, all wishing to enjoy the fruits of rural industrialization. The county will, by the downward transfer of technology, seek to build up the industrial potential of selected communes. (This can be done, for example, by sub-contracting for spare parts to be supplied to new county-owned enterprises. This will transform the repair shops of the selected communes and generally make the degree of rural industrialization a little more sophisticated.) Notice, however, that the suc-cessful commune will surge ahead of those who miss out. In other words, such growing dif-ferentials between communes are inherent in the process of economic development itself — in the absence of equalization, punitive taxation of successful communes etc.

The same principles apply to the difficulties of ironing out the net value of output per worker as between regions, and hence living standards. Established areas retain their pull on resources, making it difficult to achieve any evening-out of regional differences.

The suggestion, then, is that agricultural policies during 1965–1974 produced the worst of both worlds: they produced neither a better share for the lowest 20% of peasants in total agricultural income nor a rising flow of net agricultural marketable surpluses to the state. A change in such a situation was inevitable and in 1978 it came with a vengeance.

In what ways can the new Production Responsibility System, legalizing *San Zi Yi Bao* and reviving small peasant proprietorship, produce both higher surpluses for the state *and* a better deal for poorer peasants in poorer areas? According to its supporters[31] it will increase the *marketed* proportion of total agricultural production, which has been falling since the 1950s. This presumably will result from a new release of incentive occasioned by a reduction in bureaucratic control, a diminution of the power of local cadres to decide a peasant household's access to jobs, scarce consumer durables and education, and a greater degree of autonomy for peasants in managing their own affairs. Losses to the economy presumably include a drop in the kind of social overhead investment previously done by commune labour at little cost to the state, and the switch to profitable cash-croppings, necessitating imports of grain. Some collectivist elements may be preserved even if the *baochan* (household contracting) and *tongyi jingying lianchan davlao* (unified management combined with linkage to individual worker's reward) are emphasized. This would be done, for example, by specifying that the production team must adopt 'unified planning for cultivation and unified ploughing, sowing and irrigation'. But will this check hold? The experience of the 1960s suggests severe problems in this direction while the speed with which the chief 'unified plan indicator' (acreage to be sown) disappeared may be a lesson here.

The whole structure is precariously balanced: it depends on the *behaviour* and the *interaction* of the key economic agents involved here — the peasants and the middle- and lower-level bureaucrats. The former will be pushing to the limit of any loopholes in the announced principle of 'emphasizing the planned economy while giving market the supplementary regulatory role'. It cannot be ruled out altogether that the trend to small peasant proprietorship will seriously erode the collective structure in many areas. Farmers will be looking to the cadres to push out large numbers of unproductive workers. Cadres will want to concentrate short supplies of modern inputs in key areas with a proven comparative advantage in the production of particular products. (Comparative advantage in farm production may, of course, be altering as high yield areas find it hard to raise yields from their already high levels.) But whether encouragement of side-line crops, private plot production and price adjustment will prove highly compatible with a strategy of concentration and concern for ecological balance, remains to be seen. In an optimistic scenario for the future, individual peasant proprietors may come to develop a symbiotic relationship with a collective agricultural economy.

The recent reforms in Chinese agriculture have come about for three main reasons. The first was growing disenchantment on the part of 100 million economic agents with their lot in rural life. The second was to support the acceleration of needed agricultural surpluses in the wake of the sudden switch to the 'four modernizations' programmes. The third was the switch to a consumption goods priority in 1980, after the halt to further high construction levels to reverse previous record investment in such construction.

7. CONCLUDING REMARKS

First, it is necessary to raise the issue of using a political economy approach to Chinese economic policy change. A wide variety of writers from Trotskyists to modern Chinese technocrats have seen the backward level of productive forces as the source of Stalinism, or Maoism, and of the kind of economic contradictions discussed in this paper. The task of political economy is to give content to these generalizations in order to gauge their relevance for the events of the last decade. It is suggested that in doing this the following three economic features stand out:

(a) investment cycles with periods of severe 'trade-off' against consumption;

(b) structural disproportions in the economy in relation to the balance of machine building, machines to make consumer goods and social overhead capital (infrastructure);

(c) the fact that in agriculture the very process of rural industrialization, downward transfer of technology to communes and the absence of a 'Ricardian-rent' tax to even out living standards between communes made egalitarianism in the rural sector difficult. It may also have made 'narrowing the differential' between agriculture and industry (measured as net value of output per worker or as living standards) inoperative.

Second, it is important that political economy should incorporate an instrumental analysis, which makes explicit some of the things positivism and narrow empiricism hide. It should combine a study of economic cycles and models of planned growth with an analysis of the motivation and behaviour of economic agents. Positivist theory claims its propositions have empirical relevance, but the 'facts' in China do not display enough regularity for positivism to be solidly based. Rather it is necessary to transform the discussion of linear models of accumulation and production into political economy by the use of relevant theory. Theory must have a factual base though. Here we need to sum up the experiences in China with those key elements in pre-Deng political economy: 'spiral growth', 'narrowing the three great differentials', promoting at least some participation in planning above the workshop level, and egalitarianism. These can only be fully evaluated by studying how economic agents really behaved in each phase of the economic cycle, and is, unfortunately, beyond the scope of this article. Nevertheless it can be suggested that Mao had an analysis both of growth and motivation of economic agents, as is well-known to readers of his *60 Work Points* and *Ten Great Relations*. But while some of his summings-up of experience (e.g. worker-innovation movement) fit the bill, the later ones, indicating a severe pessimism about experience in China's socialist construction, were at the *system* level and not at the *action* level. (Many of his ten great relations are a case in point: heavy industry never seems to have taken its designated third place and how often was bureaucracy cut by two-thirds?) In neither capitalist nor socialist societies do economic agents pursue the *macroeconomic* goal of the reproduction of the system as a whole. The social dimension of economic agents acting and interacting has to be brought in. It is not enough to claim that if you have the correct theory of growth or an accurate planning model you can get the correct growth path. If this were true Kalecki would not have had to bring in his 'government decision curve'.[32]

Today, reform-minded Chinese economists[33] with their stress on the need for a certain amount of enterprise autonomy, the responsibility system in agriculture, and protection for people against accumulation policies which produce severe trade-offs against consumption are emphasizing a specific kind of behaviour of economic agents and moving towards their own version of instrumental analysis. They, together with some Party leaders, recognized the major structural crises which had arisen in the Chinese economy after 1969. If I could venture an opinion here it is that it would be a pity if all of the kind of instrumental analysis done by Mao himself should be wholly lost. His concepts of motivation of economic agents also produced some worthwhile things for China such as 'barefoot' engineers and doctors; the workers' innovation movement; 'walking on two legs' in technology policy; and some degree of 'equal sacrifice' in periods of accelerating accumulation. The effective short-run political opportunism of Deng in producing a 'new course' (frame-up of the Gang of Four, falsely claiming Mao as the author of the 70-point industrial charter, selective use of 'Mao thought') should not prevent us from seeing some longer-term benefits for the masses in China in remembering Mao's diagnosis.[34]

NOTES

1. 'Political economy' in PR China lately has become involved with questions of economic growth, capital accumulation, sectoral imbalances in the economy, reforms of economic management of planning in enterprises, farms and the economy as a whole. Here China has rejoined the 'economics of socialism' as seen in the works of Dobb, Kalecki, Brus, Popov, Feldman, Khachaturov. 'Class struggle' around issues of living standards in Chinese policy-thinking increasingly has begun to look like Kalecki's 'government decision function' which traces out a series of compromises between the demands of a socialist government for higher rates of investment and the needs/resistance of people at the lower end of the income scale who wish to increase their consumption standard.

2. Under different circumstances, a similar debate took place in Cuba on the merits of guerrilla and mass mobilization campaigns. At the beginning of 1963 Guevara launched a discussion on the role of the law of value under socialism and favoured a centralized system backed up by mass campaigns and ideological fervour. His opponent in this debate was the Cuban Foreign Trade Minister Alberto Mora, who argued that the law of value and market prices must be valid economic categories under socialism. Mora described the idea of the economy as a single enterprise as a day-dream, the pursuit of which leads to bureaucracy and unnecessary conflicts between the centre and enterprises. Mora's advocacy of market socialism can be found in his 'Concerning the question of the law of value in the Cuban economy', *Commercio Exterior* (June 1963). Guevara's articles in the 'Maoist' style are in J. Gerassi (ed.), *Venceremos.* As with the present

Chinese rulers, the Cubans later condemned the Guevarist line as counter-productive in practice, with Umberto Perez, as President of the Cuban Economists' conference and Chairman of the Cuban Planning Commission producing, in 1979, an unfavourable ex-post evaluation of Guevarist experience within Cuba.

3. M. Kalecki, *Introduction to the Theory of Growth in Socialist Economy* (Oxford: Blackwell, 1969); G. Groman in N. Spulber (ed.), *Foundations of a Strategy of Economic Growth in the USSR* (Indiana University Press, 1964); and in N. Jasny, *Soviet Economists of the Twenties* (Cambridge University Press, 1972), Ch. 6; Adolf Lowe, 'A structural model of production', *Social Research* (1952) and *Path to Economic Growth* (Cambridge University Press, 1976); G. A. Feldman in Spulber, *op. cit.*, and in E. Domar, *Essays in the Theory of Economic Growth* (1957), Ch. 9.

4. Table 1 has been translated from the article in Japanese by Professor S. Ishikawa: 'A study of the major factors in the medium and long-term projections on the Chinese Economy' (Tokyo: Japan–China Association, 1980).

5. Ishikawa, *ibid.*

6. Mao Tse-Tung, *Selected Works*, Vol. 1 (Peking), p. 108.

7. *Ibid.*, p. 112.

8. Lui Ku-Kang, 'Spiral waves of growth in socialism', *Ta-Kung Pao* (2 June 1961), reprinted in *Far Eastern Economic Review* (12 October 1961).

9. 'On questions of party history', *Beijing Review* (7 July 1981). See resolutions 20 and 35.

10. The '*u*' factor in Kalecki's equation covers extra growth from moral incentives working out, so that there is no demand on state funds.

11. See P. Nolan, *Growth Processes and Distributional Change in a South China Province: the Case of Guangdong* (London: C.C.I., 1982).

12. Quoted in Suzanne Paine, 'Spatial aspects of Chinese development', *The Journal of Development Studies* (1981).

13. *Ibid.*, p. 116.

14. *Ibid.*

15. Official Report of NCNA of 7 November 1980.

16. The lessons of the Great Leap Forward showed very clearly the social and technical limits of equalizing spatial income differences.

17. Gregory Clark, *In Fear of China* (Landsdown Press, 1969), pp. 107–108.

18. Jack Gray, 'The Chinese model: some characteristics of Maoist policies for social change and economic growth' in A Nove and M. Nuti (eds.), *Socialist Economics* (Penguin, 1973).

19. C. P. Fitzgerald, *Quotations from President Lui Shao-Chi*, p. 130.

20. *Ibid.*, p. 61.

21. Dong Fureng, 'Relationship between accumulation and consumption' in Xu Dixin *et al.*, *China's Search for Economic Growth* (Beijing: New World Press, 1982).

22. *Peking Review* (7 March 1975), pp. 5–10; 4 April 1975, pp. 5–11.

23. W. Brugger, *Democracy and Organization in the Chinese Industrial Enterprise* (Cambridge University Press, 1976), describes this for the 1950s.

24. See A. Pearse and M. Stiefel, *Inquiry into Participation* (Geneva: UNRISD, 79/C.14, 1980).

25. This refers to the status of labouring classes in relation to employers. See K. Takashashi, 'A contribution to the discussion', in Rodney Hilton (ed.), *The Transition From Feudalism to Capitalism* (London: New Left Books, 1976), p. 70.

26. Wu Jinglian, Zhou Shulian and Wang Haibu, *Jingji Yanjiu*, No. 9 (1978). See also G. G. Garvy, 'The monetary system and the payments flow' in Nove and Nuti (eds.), *op. cit.*, pp. 281–305. For an account of industrial strategy generally up to 1979 see Thierry Pairault's chapter in Gordon White and Jack Gray (eds.), *China's New Economic Strategy* (New York: Academic Press, 1982).

27. Official report issued on 7 November 1980 by NCNA on peasant incomes since 1949.

28. Wang Gengjin, Yang Zhangfu and Wang Songpei, 'To speed up the development of agricultural production requires adequate concern for peasants', *Economic Research* No. 3 (1979), pp. 23–24.

29. C. A. Gregory, 'A conceptual analysis of a non-capitalist gift economy', *Cambridge Journal of Economics*, Vol. 5 (1981), pp. 119–134.

30. J. Richardson and J. Fast, *Roots of Dependency* (Manila: Foundation for Nationalist Studies, 1979).

31. Su Xing, 'The Production Responsibility System in the Chinese Countryside', Paper at the Asian Studies Association Conference, Melbourne (10 May 1982). Su Xing does admit the possibility of some rich households stimulated by individual incentives carrying out 'new acts of exploitation' and says 'this in fact has already happened where people contracted for a lot of land, they basically rely on hired labour'. (p. 13).

32. M. Kalecki, *Selected Essays on the Economic Growth of the Socialist and Mixed Economy* (Cambridge University Press, 1972), p. 41.

33. Su Xing, 'China's Planned Economy and the Market', Paper to Australian Association for Study of Socialist Countries, Sydney (May 1982), p. 11.

34. At the same time there are many benefits in a 20-year stabilization programme. It seems, in retrospect, that the socio-economic vision of Mao (as expressed in such writings as *60 Work Points* and *Ten Great Relations*) has been difficult to fulfil in the context of accelerated industrialization. Ground made in education and health was not backed up by gains for 100 million peasants at the bottom of the income scale in relation to their wage goods. In industry, many years went past before substantial income gains were widely achieved. An appeal to the Chinese people to support a government policy of encouraging more consumerism was bound to meet a positive response *under these circumstances*. The socialist investment cycle had done its work in preparing the political ground for a longer-term stabilization policy and possibly for market socialist experiments. When we note the intensity of permanent political excitement generated by Maoism, and that the Left was exhausting itself by the early 1970s, it is possible to see the twin circumstances of a revived demand for wage goods and disaffection with mass mobilization campaigns producing the political climate for the present trends in the political economy of China.

Chinese Market Mechanism: A Controversial Debate

THIERRY PAIRAULT

Centre National de la Recherche Scientifique, France

Summary. – The points made in works of Engels and Stalin on the 'law of value' under socialism remind us of the problem of the law of value's relationship to commodity production under socialism, to market mechanisms, to planning. A useful bit of conceptual clarity was proposed by W. Brus who argued that the major economic decisions concerned with macroeconomics and economic growth need a degree of centralization; market forces can assist plan implementation in the circulation of agricultural and light industrial goods. Chen Yun stood for a wider role for market forces and decentralized decision-making. In the 1950s and again in 1979 he gained a good deal of support from the Deng faction. However the need for an adjustment policy of restricting the dominance of heavy industry and capital construction works led after December 1980, not to a deepening of economic reform but to the growing strength of centralizers like Li Xiannian supported by the military for their own ends.

Three years ago, Chen Yun, at a meeting of the Central Committee (March–April 1979) launched the basis of a vast movement of economic reform by stating: 'in the concurrent utilization of the regulatory mechanisms of planning and market, the role of the plan has pre-eminence but that of the market is to be fully developed'.[1] Chen Yun became President of the State Commission for Economy and Finance on a programme of introducing market mechanisms. After the disappearance of this Commission, Chen Yun was reduced to defending his economic opinions in semi-governmental meetings and cadre gatherings.[2] Some practical and theoretical aspects of the system reform experiment are presented here in order to evaluate the consequences for planning and to understand them more fully in the context of recent political changes.

1. THE REVIVAL OF THE MARKET MODE OF PRODUCTION AND ITS CONSEQUENCES

Summarizing the arguments being put forward by Chinese economists in criticizing Stalin on the law of value[3] is a useful starting-point in confronting the growth of market mechanisms within a socialist economy. The theoretical problems implied are important, as is the task of explaining the limits imposed by the planning system and centralized decision-making on the free play of market mechanisms. In his *Economic Problems of Socialism in the USSR*,

Stalin recognized that the collectivization of agriculture in the USSR had not allowed 'socialization of all the means of production' as had been forecast by Engels in *Anti-Duhring*:[4] hence the coexistence of two forms of socialist ownership — collective and state. Stalin was led to the conclusion that the law of value had a purely accounting role in the state sector, but that market relations remained to produce a regulatory role for the law of value in the collective or cooperative sector.

This vision led Stalin to attribute the character of commodities to goods in the non-state sector but not in the government sector. Goods exchanged between the state sector and the collective sector also took on the character of commodities. From the Stalinist theoretical point of view, if such a good is sold to the collective sector it *changes* its character. This ignores the fact that it originated in the state sector, and, being already owned by the whole people, it is also in fact the property of those working in the collective sector before changing hands.

According to Chinese analysts, the posited coexistence of the two sectors does not *explain* anything, and it is only possible to 'resolve' the contradiction by denying the character of a commodity to *all* goods, *or* by proclaiming them all to be commodities.

The existence of a market economy in a socialist regime resulted, according to the Chinese, in the following trends:

(i) Relative autonomy was given in the

social division of labour to the units of production (state, collective, individual) whence the appearance of divergent interests and of contributions of a different quality. To develop production it was necessary to stimulate units of production by payment according to work and to distribute turnover tax by some reference to costs of production. Since it was impossible to use the labour time incorporated in products as a measure, the necessity arose of an *indirect* comparison by means of the Marxian formula $C + V + S$, hence the survival of market relations and the regulatory role of the law of value in all sectors of the economy.

(*ii*) The imperfections of the planning system led to social *labour* diverging from social *needs*, so the manufacturing sector (following the plan) made certain products which were useless or unsaleable. Such a situation meant that waste of social labour was acute and the structure of production did not correspond to the structure of social needs. The fact that the plan tried *a-posteriori*, to alleviate the maladjustment by a reallocation of social labour merely indicated the persistence of the law of values operations in Marx's sense, i.e. the law of the reallocation of social labour in the market mode of production.[5]

This analysis posed problems of theory:

(*a*) The existence of the social division of labour and the necessity of autonomy for units of production required by the remnants of the market mechanism gave rise to the following conclusion: in order to realize the ownership of all the means of production by *society* (and not just the *state*), and to bring about the elimination of market relations, China, like other socialist countries before it, has to precisely, if paradoxically, encourage capitalism.[6]

(*b*) The development of productive forces was held back by imperfections in the planning system, especially a centralized system of management earlier successful in the first 5-year plan, when China was very poor and had only a small number of production units. The justification for the economic reforms was based on the need to decentralize the management of the economy and have recourse to indirect levers of control. The logic in such (Chinese) reasoning was strengthened when it was realized that the economy had become more complex and the need for decentralized decision-making had accelerated, leading to an enhanced role for the market mechanism. A theoretical impasse was soon reached, for according to the original Marxist schema, the evolution should have been in the reverse direction: planning and production by society ought to have progressively replaced the law of value as the organizing method of production, responding to social needs.[7]

(*c*) The autonomy of units of production and the decentralization of management was deepened and set in motion a new division of the net product. However, all the net product ('*S*'), or at least the greater part of it, returns to the state where the apparatus is dominated by the Party. The state's grab for net product transformed the latter into means of production legally owned by the working class. But, because the units of production now retain a growing part of the net product, they substitute themselves for the state and bring about a separation of the workers from their means of production (in the absence of genuine self-management). In other words, the actual reforms undertaken accentuate the double separation also characteristic of capitalist enterprises: separation of economic units from each other and separation of the workers from their means of production.

(*d*) Finally, the Chinese only bring out the above problems very indirectly in discussion; instead they tend to proclaim they will use *Zijue*[8] — harness the law of value in order to avoid a complete return to capitalism. Yet Engels said this procedure can only bring to an end the process of superseding capitalism.[9]

The *theoretical* point involved here is that in a socialist economy the law of value is limited by the degree of centralization over major economic decisions. To recall the formulation of Professor Wlodimierz Brus, there exist three types of economic decision-making:

(*a*) Macro-economic decisions defining long-term growth of output, the rates of investment and consumption. These inevitably remain in the hands of central authorities.

(*b*) Micro-economic decisions relating to individual consumption. Market forces here can play a free role, although there can never be full 'consumer sovereignty' since the macro-economic decisions will impinge to a certain degree on the structure of consumption.[10] It is from this standpoint that one can interpret the price rises for consumer goods, agricultural goods and goods still rationed in order to relieve inflationary demand pressure on light industrial goods;

(*c*) Micro-economic decisions relating to the structure of production. Here the nature of the profit of socialist enterprises fixes the limit to decentralization. In an economy of economic liberalism profit is the result of good enterprise management, while in a socialist economy it is the result of the degree of success in plan-fulfilment.

However, the greater the autonomy of socialist enterprises, the more their profits will also reflect successful management, although never wholly independent of the need to fulfil plans.

These considerations need to be taken into account in assessing the potential role of new market mechanisms in their practical effects. Experience with this in other socialist countries has been mixed in achieving the slogan 'the socialist market is a planned market'.[11] For China, in the sphere of allocation of consumer goods, two possibilities exist:

(*a*) The state does not intervene and prices are set by supply and demand. The difference with capitalism would then be that there is still central control over the structure of investment and production, hence, even if more indirectly, over the level of consumption.

(*b*) The state intervenes to fix a number of prices, and the market mechanism is used to ensure social needs are met as set out in the plan. Two cases where this occurs are, first, when there is an inelastic demand for consumer goods so that firms can fix prices high - above cost of production and make windfall profits. Here the state's intervention is to correct market imperfections; second, the state wishes to encourage certain production by subsidies. The market here is regulated to counter the law of value which normally ensures that products exchange at their full value.

When we come to the sphere of capital goods, the problems are more complex. Adaptation of supply to demand conditions depends finally on the structure of investments and the relation of the investment goods sector to the consumer goods sector. Any new structure of consumption brought about by the market need not be consistent with the preferences of socialist planners in this matter. Moreover, in the case of 'means of production' (capital goods) it is by no means obvious that supply and demand *should* set the relative prices on the basis of relative scarcity because these goods are inputs into the production of *all* goods and

have a decisive role in setting the whole production structure. The market will necessarily be controlled in this case because it will itself not permit the working out of the law of value.

If we look at the general issue of investment planning, experience shows that the market mechanism can influence the *choice of methods* of implementing investments, but not the determination of the investment rates and structures, which are geared to politically-determined rates of economic growth.

2. POLICY CHANGES IN PRACTICE

In the middle of 1979, reforms were introduced. They allowed fluctuations in demand and supply to influence prices of light-industry goods, but heavy industry remained under central planning.[12] This was seen as a method of rejecting 'voluntarist' planning which, under the slogan of giving *priority* to investment in fact produced too high a rate of capital accumulation and under the slogan of priority for heavy industry imposed excessive burdens on light industry and agriculture.

'Realistic' planning, by contrast, was to accept a real role for the law of value and to allow agriculture and light industry to grow at the same rate as heavy industry if this were so desired. In this way, the rate of growth of the Chinese economy would emerge mainly as a result of concrete economic calculations and no longer from abstract political voluntarism.

Perhaps we can simplify a bit by saying that 'voluntarist' planning corresponded to the slogan *zhong, qing, nong* (heavy industry first, light industry second, agriculture last), while the 'realistic' planning slogan was *nong, qing, zhong* (agriculture first, light industry next, heavy industry last). However, it should be pointed out that this should not be taken too literally; a preference for one of these forms of planning does not produce an order of priorities since, in the end, priorities rest on the idea of heavy industry as the key to the 'law' of socialist development, which gives priority to the capital goods sector — a 'law' reaffirmed in an editorial of the *People's Daily* of 20 October 1979.

The concept of 'realistic' planning had been put forward at the beginning of the 1950s by Chen Yun and some other economists. One of the objectives of Mao Zedong was to firmly oppose a version of such planning suggested by Sun Yefang. By contrast 'realistic' planning at the beginning of the 1960's was implemented under the policy 'take agriculture as the base and industry as the dominant factor'. The first part of this slogan foreshadowed the policies later elaborated as *nong, qing, zhong*. Here it is accepted that the rate of growth of industry itself depends on agriculture; that Department 1 (capital goods) depends ultimately on Department 2 (consumer goods), and Chinese economic thinking at the top by no means involves abandonment of the idea of priority development for Department 1.

In the course of 1979, some economists attacked the 'law' of priority for Department 1 as mathematically and historically unjustified, but the debate was suddenly cut off by the 20 October editorial of *People's Daily* which reaffirmed the validity of such a law of socialism, using the authority of Stalin.

It is necessary here to distinguish current and future trends. The present period is characterized by a higher growth rate of the consumer-goods sector (Department 2) than Department 1. However, Chinese commentators such as Xue Muqiao have stressed that this policy is provisional and a response to the need for a policy of readjustment. With the achievement of a better balance between investments in Departments 1 and 2, the possibility will arise again for priority growth of Department 1.

A wider issue is involved here. 'Voluntarist' planning results in a policy of absolute priority for investment, with consumption treated as a residual. Conversely, 'realistic planning' results in an attempt to stimulate the masses by better satisfying their material needs and better management of enterprises in order to shape investment. This second option was, above all, the line of Chen Yun.[13] It had been tested in nine provinces during the second half of 1956, but at the beginning of 1957 an end was put to the experiment, largely because of fears that the system would necessitate a major reform of the taxation system, without which the State Treasury would have suffered serious losses.

In the Chen Yun formula, the market is not considered as a method of planning, but merely a flexible way of management of the Chinese economy — the use of indirect economic levers rather than administrative methods in plan implementation.

The December 1978 Third Plenum of the Central Committee issued a call to 'combine the planned economy and the market economy'. This was ambiguous in its suggestion of two *separate* sectors, one planned and socialist, one market and, by implication, non-socialist. It was no surprise that shortly after (at the April 1979 Working Conference of the Central Com-

mittee), a new slogan appeared to clarify matters: 'combine regulation by the plan and regulation by the market; the regulation by the plan should take the lead, but full attention should be paid to regulation by the market'.

But ambiguity did not thereby disappear. No clear distinction had been made between market, market economy and market mechanism. Commodity exchange takes place constantly in a socialist economy but this does not constitute a 'market economy'. No clear distinction had been made between a commodity economy, planned economy and market economy. A socialist economy can be a planned economy and a commodity economy, as Stalin pointed out. The issue here was not brought out clearly — a plan should take account of commodities without itself being dominated by free movements in commodity production.

It was the actual state of the Chinese economy which decided many of these issues. For its economic disorganization and lack of efficient controls looked very similar to the situation in which plan and market were working without contact with each other. New political solutions had to be found and new policies formulated. Chen Yun's State Economic Commission set up in June 1979 was dissolved in February–March 1981, having been under a cloud from December 1980. Its functions were taken over by a 'working group' led by Wan Li, a Deng Xiaoping man.

The temporary optimism exhibited at the Third Planning Session of the Peoples' National Congress (with Zhao Ziyang as Prime Minister, Yao Yilin as new Chairman of the State Planning Commission and Wang Bingquian as Minister for Finance) meant economic reform was being strongly encouraged.[14] By December 1980, there was a brutal return to reality — the actual condition of the economy deteriorated sharply. The law of value was taking its revenge on the former period of voluntarist planning, with strong inflationary trends[15] forcing recognition of the need for a major adjustment,[16] which culminated in a reassembled working session of the Central Committee from 16 to 25 December 1980.

This meeting resulted in a proposal to end experiments with economic reforms and to return to more centralist methods. It meant the eclipse of Chen Yun, despite denunciation of the 'left' for having disorganized the economy in the ten years 1966–76 and then having refused to adjust the economy during 1976–78 and 1978–80.[17]

The seventeenth meeting of the Permanent Committee of the 5th Peoples' Congress

(February—March 1981) endorsed the decisions of the working party of December 1980, with Deng and Zhao Ziyang taking the middle course between the opposed tendencies of planning. A strong showing was made by voluntarists despite the relative eclipse of Li Xiannian.[18] An editorial statement in the *Peoples' Daily* of 13 March 1982 advocated a policy of adjustment to restore equilibrium in the economy and permit orderly growth. An intervention was made by the economic reformers[19] in the shape of Xue Muqiao, who put an article in the *Peoples' Daily* critical of the 'voluntarists' and reaffirming that the principal issue in the adjustment policy was to prepare the ground for economic reform.

The military, which played a big role in the struggle against the 'left', now found itself in opposition to a rightist tendency.[20] The military had doubts on two counts. First, there was the cuts in credits to the army earmarked for modernization and preparation to combat a powerful aggressor.[21] (Indirectly this criticism of other policies of Deng gave a clue to the army's concern that heavy industry would be made to bear the brunt of adjustment.) On this basis, the military realigned with the 'voluntarists'[22] who refused to consider basic construction actively as a residual. With regard to the agricultural reforms, the army was concerned about the availability of recruits under conditions favouring families requiring members to cultivate family-worked land.

All of these tendencies[23] led to new concern for heavy industry. Cutbacks in this sector, at first desired to bring about the first step towards sound growth, were now considered to be a threat to other sectors' development, as well as a limit on state revenues.[24] It was noted that the continuing dominance of agriculture and heavy industry in the total Chinese economy were a clear sign of the latter's continuing state of underdevelopment. To really do something about this required a stronger and more orderly development of heavy industry.[25] There followed the instruction from Zhao Ziyang at the end of the Fourth Session of the 5th Peoples' Congress: 'readjust the orientation of the production of heavy industry'.[26] It was to make an occasion of this new policy that Zhao Ziyang and Wan Li (the new Chief Economic Adviser of the Government) went in mid-January 1982 to the Peking Iron and Steel Company which, despite a diminution of production in 1981, had seen its profits grow by 8.2%.[27]

The changes in policy have depended partly on people at the heart of the Government, although real power remained entirely in the hands of the Political Bureau, in particular with seven members of the Standing Committee of the Bureau where there were two major tendencies: that of Deng Xiaoping, Zhao Ziyang and Hu Yaobang and that of Li Xiannian, Hua Gofeng and Ye Jianying, with one independent: Chen Yun. The latter had been under the shadow of Central Committee decisions that were changing; despite the republication of his speech of 1945 at the 7th Congress of the Party,[28] he began to show more discretion in economic matters.[29]

After a period of relative quiescence Li Xiannian increased his influence in 1982. A speech at the Chinese New Year[30] was remarkable on a number of counts. It was the first speech of his published since 1979; the speech itself, though brief, was a virtual working programme touching on economic policy, internal and external affairs, the Party, with quite specific points of a precision lacking in Zhao Ziyang's discourse of December 1981 at the fourth session of the 5th Peoples' Congress.[31] Li announced the first convocation of the year of the 12th Congress of the Party; the speech contained no reference to themes and slogans dear to Deng Xiaoping.

From the economic viewpoint we may note the emphasis given to the need for a centralization of economic life, for coordination: *quanguo yi pan qi*.[32] This slogan pointed to the role required of the market:

> Regulation by the market and planning of the economy are not featured by relationships of equality, but by those of subordination. Market regulation should not impinge on areas of authority of the planning cadres . . . regulation by the market, if it is to be utilized properly, must also be carefully controlled.[33]

Such a definitive position could not have suited the centrifugal tendencies favouring enterprise reform in agriculture and Li Xiannian recalled that agriculture, like industry, had to be planned on the basis of contracts between the units of production (probably the brigades) and the state trading corporations.[34] If these remarks did not rule out reforms in the methods of exploiting agriculture, they certainly limited their scope.

It is important, too, to point to the stress on the problem of capital accumulation on the part of Li Xiannian. This can be seen more precisely in an editorial of the *Peoples' Daily* of 22 February 1982, which underlined the fact that the rate of accumulation between 1978 and 1981 had fallen considerably, a drop from 36.5 to about 30% of national income, a satisfactory trend when compared with the 25% target announced in 1979 as the aim of policy, and the 20% favoured by Chen Yun and Bo Yibo. Li indicated that the purchasing power of the masses should not grow at the expense of Government objectives, and the official view at this time concerning the budget deficit was that excessive investment was not to blame, but the sudden improvement in the standard of living was through welfare and subsidy measures. As a result, the *Peoples' Daily* of 22 February said that Government decisions aimed to limit the production of bicycles, sewing machines, watches and clocks.

Centralization was also being seen as a way of countering regional protectionism, which was resulting in a cut in deliveries to other provinces and protection of regional markets. The result had been a multiplication of small less efficient industrial units, involving duplication of the more profitable factories which produced higher quality output. In other words, the view was now taken that it is necessary to centralize many decisions relating to capital accumulation if only to guarantee the greatest

level of profitability ('rentability') in investments.[35]

These preoccupations of the Government explain the administrative reforms suggested at the 22nd meeting of the Standing Committee of the 5th Peoples' Congress, reforms in the area of reorganizing Government structures, notably a concentration of decision-making power into the hands of a smaller number of commissions and ministries. We were witnessing a return to administrative methods of management of the economy to the detriment of indirect economic levers.

This policy evolution has forced a defensive reply from those favouring market forces, who have had to use such expressions as 'indirect levers of planning' (*jiangie de jihva tiaojie*) as opposed to 'direct levers of planning' (*zhijie de jihua tiaojie*) to describe the role of the market.[36]

While the role of the market as regulator no longer can lead to deconcentration of power in favour of administrative regions, the task remains of encouraging economic units, a task formerly tackled with Maoist slogans like 'fear no difficulties, not even death' or 'study Daqing'.

NOTES

1. 'Jihua tiaojie he shichang tiaojie xianghiehe yi jihua wei zhu, tongshi, chongfen zhong shi shichang tiaojie de zuoyong,' in *Lun shangpin liutong (On The Circulation of Commodities)* (Peking: 1950), p. 88.

2. *Renmin ribao* (hereafter *RMRB*), 26 January 1982, p. 1.

3. The best sources of the debate are in *Jingji yanjiu (Economic Studies)* hereafter *JJYJ*, No. 5 (1979), pp. 46−55; No. 7, pp. 37−46; No. 8, pp. 58−64; No. 5 (1980), pp. 19−25; No. 11, pp. 19−32; No. 2 (1982), pp. 65−8, as well as *Shangpin sheng chan jiazhi guilü yu qiye quanxian (The Law of Value in Commodity Production and Increased Enterprise Power)* (Peking: 1980), 339 pp.

4. F. Engels, *Anti-Duhring* (Paris: Edition Sociales, 1977), p. 319.

5. K. Marx, *Capital* (Paris: Editions Sociales, 1973−5), Vol. 6, p. 207.

6. Engels, *op. cit.*, pp. 319−321.

7. Marx, *op. cit.*, p. 203.

8. As distinct from *zifa* or spontaneity as in the capitalist system.

9. Engels, *op. cit.*, pp. 347−349.

10. Lack of interest in the consumers by the Chinese Government becomes more unsupportable when it is realized that the consumption plan has in no way been linked to a plan for wage increases. See *JJYJ*, No. 12 (1979), p. 25.

11. *JJYJ*, No. 5 (1980), pp. 14−25.

12. *RMRB* (15 May 1979), p. 3; *JJYJ*, No. 5 (1979), p. 44.

13. See the Chen Yun theory of 'three equilibriums' and that of '2, 3, 4' of Bo Yi Bo in *Caimo zhanshe (Commerce and Finance)*, 16 February 1967; *Caizheng (Finances)*, No. 7 (1980), pp. 17−21; *RMRB* (24 April 1981), p. 5.

14. *RMRB* (30 October 1980), p. 1.

15. On inflation see *RMRB* (7, 8, 9, 10 and 14 December 1980), and for basic construction activity *RMRB* (28 November 1980), p. 5; (2 December 1980); (30 December 1980), p. 5.

16. *RMRB* (2 December 1980), p. 1; (3 December 1980), p. 5.

17. On these aspects see *RMRB* (2 December 1980), p. 1, (1 January 1981), p. 1.

18. Amongst whose numbers should be counted Li

Xiannan, Hua Guofeng and military leaders like Ye Jianying.

19. That is to say, *in fact*, the tendency of Chen Yun.

20. Article in *Jiefangjun bao* (*Liberation Army Daily*) reprinted in *RMRB* (27 April 1981), p. 4.

21. Editorial of *Liberation Army Daily* reprinted in *RMRB* (28 September 1981), p. 1. At the 5th session of the 5th Peoples' Congress, Hua Guofeng had insisted on the necessity of strengthening the army.

22. *China News Analysis*, No. 1219, pp. 5–6. The sixth plenum of the Central Committee of June 1981 attempted to deal with economic dislocation and confused thinking about the market mechanism by issuing a new slogan: 'On the Basis of Public Ownership Bring the Planned Economy Fully into Play, While at the Same Time Develop the Complementary Regulation by the Market'.

23. Perhaps this is why the 1982 budget provided for a growth of 6.2% in military expenditure against an average growth of all expenses of 4.1%.

24. *RMRB* (16 October 1981), p. 5.

25. *RMRB* (2 October 1981), p. 5.

26. *Tiaozheng zhonggongye de fuwu fangxiang*; see *RMRB* (14 December 1981).

27. *RMRB* (18 January 1982), p. 1.

28. *RMRB* (31 December 1981), p. 1.

29. *RMRB* (26 January 1982), p. 1. These quotations show the need to exercise caution in interpreting these ideas as 'voluntarist' and to note Ye Jianzhang summarizing anew the options of Chen Yun in *JJYJ*, No. 6 (1981), pp. 9–15.

30. *RMRB* (25 January 1982), p. 1.

31. *RMRB* (14 December 1981), pp. 1ff.

32. This slogan appeared to oppose 'disorganization' and favoured the planning system's return to favour.

33. *RMRB* (24 February 1982). This editorial on the continuing need for administrative methods is a thrust against the dominant trend of 1979; it supports replacing administrative means by economic methods in guiding the economy.

34. On this theme see *RMRB* (8, 22, 23, 25 February 1982), p. 1.

35. *RMRB* (24 February 1982), p. 1.

36. *JJYJ*, No. 6 (1982), pp. 3–21.

Changing Relations Between State and Enterprise in Contemporary China: Expanding Enterprise Autonomy

GORDON WHITE

Institute of Development Studies, University of Sussex.

Summary. — The first section of the discussion follows the fortunes of the policy of 'expanding enterprise autonomy' from its inception in late 1978 to the end of 1980 when the reform was halted, with particular emphasis on the actual effects of policy both intended and unintended, on industrial enterprises; the second section examines the ambiguous period of retrenchment, consolidation and continued reform during 1981 and 1982; the last section draws brief conclusions about the nature of the Chinese policy process and the prospects for further reform in the 1980s.

1. INTRODUCTION

One of the central dimensions of the programme of economic reforms in China during the post-Mao era has been the attempt to change the relationship between the state apparatus and basic units of industrial production in the state sector through the policy of expanding enterprise autonomy (*kuoda qiye zizhuquan*). While policy changes have been justified in terms of economic efficiency, their practical implications are far broader. They embody a fundamental change in the dominant 'mode of production' of state socialist societies — the plan-guided, state-administered system of decision and control over the basic processes of industrial accumulation, production, distribution, circulation and exchange. They involve a shift in the relationship between state and economy, thus raising perhaps the central issue of 'development policy' confronting societies in both North and South, East and West. The political implications are potentially profound since any decisive redistribution of economic power — directly or indirectly, sooner or later — brings a redistribution of political power in its train. Indeed, if we adopt a functional view of 'politics', economic reform is itself one arena of political reform. Since both state and economy are matrices of institutionalized interests, both horizontal (class, stratum or group) and vertical (institutions, localities, client systems), change in the relationship between state and enterprises affects the balance of resources between social groups. The issue of economic reform is apocalyptic, revealing the societal forces by an interplay of which it is itself determined, (for example, see Sabel and Stark: 1982).

This paper sets out to analyse the experience of official attempts to 'expand enterprise autonomy' in state-run industry in China between 1978 and 1983, examining the following key areas: the *rationale* of the policy in the wider context of the programme for reforming economic management in the state sector; the main *elements* of the new policy thrust and their practical *impact* on state-enterprise relations; the degree of *success* of policy reforms in the light of initial objectives and the key *constraints* operating to blunt or divert the course of implementation. My approach to analysis has two objectives: first, to grapple with the often bewildering relationships between theory and practice, policy statement and result, in the Chinese context; second, to link political, social and economic analysis, penetrating to the structurally-based interests lurking behind policy pronouncements and hopefully transcending the economism and technicism which characterize so much of the Chinese public debates.

2. EXPANDING ENTERPRISE AUTONOMY: POLICIES AND PROGRESS

2.1. *The reform critique of state-enterprise relations*

The policy of expanding the decision-making power of industrial enterprises is a basic component of a general analysis of Chinese political economy which I shall call the 'market reform' or 'reform' position. It advocates a process of economic decentralization away from *all* levels of the state apparatus to basic-level production units and a different type of relationship between state agencies and industrial enterprises, 'economic' rather than 'administrative'. Under the old system, it is argued, enterprises lacked any power of economic initiative and this brought economic passivity and inefficiency. The main thrust of economic reform should thus be to expand the decision-making power of enterprises (for example, see Jiang Yiwei: 1980 and Liu Guoguang *et al.*, 1979).

The main target of criticism has been the *overconcentration* of management power inherited from the Soviet system adopted during the First Five-Year Plan. Although successive waves of administrative decentralization had weakened the branch principle and diffused power to the localities, from the point of view of the enterprises, the identity of their superiors might have changed but the basic fact of administrative subordination had not. Regardless of whether the superior unit was a central or a local bureau, the same hierarchical logic of directive planning operated. Put another way, vertical economic linkages predominated over horizontal (Liao Jili: 1980 discusses the issue in these terms) or, in a metaphor popular among reformers, enterprises were treated like beads on an abacus pushed hither and thither by bureaucratic fingers (for example, Ma Hong: 1981, p. 19). Mandatory quantitative and qualitative targets were transmitted downwards to determine the amount and type of output and key elements of the production process, usually the perennial 'eight targets' [These were total output value, production mix, quality, consumption of raw materials and energy, wage fund, costs of production, profits and working capital (for a case study from 1972, see Meisner: 1972).] Investment funds were allocated administratively and enterprises had to apply formally for increments; technical innovations and new products also needed approval from above; sources of supply and outlets were arranged by superior organs (*tonggou tongxiao*) which also fixed prices; profits were returned to state agencies (*tongshou tongzhi*) with the exception of a small factory director's fund (which apparently lapsed during the Cultural Revolution decade); most of the enterprise's depreciation funds also reverted to the state. While detailed controls of this kind would be difficult to maintain and monitor in a relatively simple and small economy, in the Chinese case they were often inaccurate, hampered by a weak statistical system. The situation worsened as the economy grew more complex.

Planning deficiencies led to supply bottlenecks and overstocking of products. In this supply-driven system, the target of total output value, according to He Jianzhang (1979) tended to outrank the others (like 'the father of the emperor') with the result that enterprises were motivated to seek increased output value without sufficient consideration of whether or not products were needed, 'production for plan not market'. Although output was theoretically linked to demand through planning calculations and other mechanisms (such as commodity fairs), responsibility for product exchange rested not with the enterprise but with state commercial organs which had to 'sell what is produced'. He estimated that, by the end of June 1978, the value of unsold stocks amounted to the total value of industrial output over the first half-year and the cost of disposal amounted to 100 million yuan (a substantial proportion being written off as wastage). Enterprises also had little incentives to develop new products.

On the supplies side, the enterprise suffered from defects in the system of 'unified allocation' (*tongyi fenpei*) by state agencies. Ji and Rong (1979) described the situation thus:

> With regard to the supply of materials, the production tasks of a number of state-operated enterprises are handed down vertically according to the state plan, while the raw materials on the other hand are distributed and supplied on a geographical basis. Many enterprises have gaps in their raw materials when their plans are drawn up. When they order goods, they have to arrange a discount. In this way, the completion of production plans is difficult to guarantee and having purchasing personnel all over the place cannot be avoided.

Enterprises faced similar problems in the disposition of labour, which was subject to strict administrative controls (White: 1982). Enterprises with idle supplies and equipment found it difficult, within the formal framework at least, to reallocate or take on extra labour.

Lack of financial power in the context of 'unified receipts and unified expenditures' meant that enterprises failed to gain financial benefits for good performance and had received state subsidies for the kind of losses which may have reflected bad management – the phenomenon of enterprises 'eating from the same pot'. Lack of incentives also affected the performance of individual workers within enterprises. Financial resources formally subject to control by enterprise managers were meagre. A current joke went as follows: 'Question: which enterprises in China have independent economic accounting? Answer: Only one, the Ministry of Finance'. He Jianzhang (1979, p. 36) cites the case of the Beijing No. 1 Machine Tools Plant which during 1977–8 remitted annual profits of 33 million yuan to the state but was only allowed to keep 50 yuan for emergency use. Any expenditures above that amount had to be approved by a municipal bureau. The results, he argued, were damagingly paradoxical: some things could be done better by enterprises on their own initiative but were not allowed, i.e. 'rational but not lawful'; other tasks cost more if done by the book but were required by the state, i.e. 'lawful but not rational'.

Similar complaints were raised about enterprises' lack of control over their depreciation funds. Funds for renewing fixed assets came under the plan for capital construction and expenditures had to be submitted to higher organs for approval, a cumbersome procedure which impeded technical change. Depreciation rates also tended to be set very low (for example, 2.92% at the massive Anshan Iron and Steel Company, a 34-year regeneration cycle) and depreciation funds were often diverted to other uses.

The central theme running through these criticisms was the severe economic cost of a system of industrial management which either made enterprises passive or sluggish in their responses or, where it did stir enterprises into action, drove them in inefficient directions. The policy prescriptions of the reformers stem from this critique, the common denominator being a call for greater decision-making power for enterprises *vis à vis* their bureaucratic superiors – enterprise autonomy was described as the 'key link' in overall management reform. They supported this point theoretically with some abstruse arguments about the necessity of enterprise independency by virtue of their role

in a commodity economy. (For example, see Lin Qingsheng: 1980; Li Dehua: 1980).

Expanding enterprise autonomy was part of a wider reform package with four main components: first, a leaner, less extended state planning system with overall macro-economic functions, notably determination of the size and distribution of the national income, the ratio between investment and consumption and allocation of investment resources. The state is to play the crucial role of maintaining overall balances in physical and financial, domestic and international terms. (Ma Hong: 1981). Second, planners were to make greater use of 'economic mechanisms' or 'levers' (such as price, credit and taxation) to achieve their objectives. Third, market mechanisms were to be expanded to 'verify' enterprise performance and spread horizontal linkages throughout the economy. Fourth, there was to be a diversification of economic institutions, notably the formation of 'companies' (or 'trusts') at national and regional levels. These proposals involved changes at all levels, but in the rest of this paper, I shall focus on enterprises and their reactions to the changing policy environment.

2.2 *The policy process, 1979–81*

Other writers have provided chronological surveys of the emergence of the policy of expanding enterprise decision-making power during 1978–9 so I shall only use the broad brush (Watson, 1982) for that period. Although the central arguments for this reform were already receiving wide publicity from economists (notably those based at the new Chinese Academy of Social Sciences in Peking) to be translated into policy they required political sponsorship from the CCP leadership. This was delayed by the struggle between the 'pragmatic' faction led by Deng Xiaoping and the 'whateverist' group represented by Mao's chosen successor (and then CCP Chairman) Hua Guofeng. July 1978 was a crucial time of transition; it saw the issue of the CCP Central Committee's 'Draft Decision Concerning Some Problems in Speeding up the Development of Industry' (known as the 'thirty-point decision on industry' or just, 'thirty points'), allegedly drafted under the supervision of Deng Xiaoping, yet reflecting an unresolved balance of contending political groups and developmental programmes and couched heavily in the imagery and terminology of the Maoist era. The Decision's approach to industrial administration was still heavily administrative with enterprise activity subject to 'five fixes' and 'eight targets' determined by central or local administrative departments. [The 'five fixes' are fixing the nature and scale of production, personnel and organization, consumption quotas and supply sources, capital assets and liquidity and links with other enterprises].

The first major challenge to the kind of thinking embodied in the Decision was posed in the same month by an unpublished speech at a State Council meeting by Hu Qiaomu, President of the Academy of Social Sciences. Hu raised a series of basic issues, prominent among which was the relationship between state and enterprise. He criticized previous attempts to tackle problems in the economic management system by adjusting relationships *within* the state machine. The key issue, he argued, was to regulate correctly the relationship between three forces — the state, enterprise, workers. Specifically, enterprises should be granted more economic responsibilities, so that their managers and workers could develop greater interest in their own performance. This involved the 'transfer of the greater portion of our economic work from government administration to the field of enterprise management'. In concrete terms, however, Hu's proposals for expanding enterprise autonomy were comparatively modest, focusing on the need to develop a contract system to regulate economic links *between* enterprises. This, together with Hu's other proposals — for strengthening the role of banking, developing specialized companies and enlarging the scope of economic legislation — paved the way for a surge of critical reformist literature in the latter part of 1978, with specific attention to expanding contractual relations (both among enterprises and between state and enterprises) and increasing enterprise funds from retained profits (Wu Jinglian *et al.*, 1978). Pilot programmes for expanding enterprise autonomy were begun, most notably in Sichuan province in October 1978.

The watershed Third Plenum of the CCP Central Committee in December 1978 gave the green light for more extensive publication of the reform message and expansion of the pilot projects already under way. The programme covered six areas: the right for enterprises to draw up their own production plans in accordance with the requirements of both plan and market, to be regulated by contracts with both the state and customers; the right to market a portion of their own products (after meeting plan targets); the right to greater

financial control over funds for renewal or expansion of fixed assets, welfare measures and worker bonuses; the right to hire and re-assign labour power and adjust wage levels and scales; the right to arrive at 'negotiated' prices for their products subject to state guidelines; the right to refuse unreasonable requisitioning of funds, materials or labour by superior organs.

Though these rights implied an expansion of market-type relationships, reformers were careful to emphasize that they should be established within the framework of central planning, viz. 'the power for enterprises to make decisions under centralized guidance'. But beneath this general consensus lay wide disagreements about the state-enterprise relationship and the precise nature and degree of central planning. Indeed, during 1978 to 1980, the reformers seem to have been a temporary coalition of different groups with varying view points. There was disagreement over *how much* to reform, some being willing to countenance only marginal changes, while others advocated a more radical approach (for a summary of some areas of disagreement see Zhang Xiang, 1980). There was disagreement about the precise *forms* that reform should take: for example, some emphasized the need for expanding the autonomy of existing enterprises while others laid more stress on the need to 'rationalize' the structure of industry by combining enterprises into 'companies' or 'trusts'. Reformers also disagreed about *how* reforms were to be introduced, some favouring a more piecemeal approach while others, mindful no doubt of the obstacles posed by bureaucratic opposition and foot-dragging, wanted to launch a vigorous movement to create a new situation from which retreat would be difficult. There were varying views about the desirable *end-state* of the reforms, which we can clarify by referring to Eastern European experience: first, a system like the Soviet Union after the reforms, with a high degree of centralization and administrative control and severely circumscribed enterprises; second, the Hungarian system with less state intervention and considerable enterprise autonomy; and third, the Yugoslav model with a relatively weak 'parametric' state and higher enterprise autonomy (for an indirect discussion of these positions, see Jiang Yiwei, 1980). Such differences were crucial in determining both the impetus behind the reform process during 1978—81, and the range of reactions to problems which emerged as reform policies were actually put into practice.

The first pilot programme, based on six enterprises, was begun in Sichuan province in October 1978. In July the following year, the State Council decided to expand the programme both within Sichuan and across the nation, issuing five documents providing guidelines for further experiments in a larger number of enterprises.[1] These guidelines were partly a programme for deepening the reform process; but they were also clearly an attempt to rationalize and rein-in unapproved local initiatives which had been mushrooming in previous months. The new stage embraced 2,600 state enterprises which were given greater power over finances (through their ability to retain a certain percentage of profits and most of their depreciation funds), materials (freedom to dispose of idle materials), hiring of personnel and marketing (of above-quota products). These regulations were complex, however, and brought confusion as well as order. In the financial sphere, for example, many finance officers in local governments and enterprises could not make head or tail of the new provisions, and the Ministry of Finance had to convene a press symposium in September 1979 to clarify the situation. By early 1980, however, over 3,000 enterprises were involved in the experiment, accounting for 7% of all state enterprises and over 30% of national industrial output. On February 19, the State Economic Comission reviewed progress, called for a better job in implementing new policies and signalled a further extension of enterprise autonomy in the new year.[2] In April, a National Work Conference on industry and communications, held in Nanjing, declared that the experimental enterprises (now 3,300) had achieved 'good results' in terms of increasing profits, enterprise funds and worker-staff incomes. 2,963 enterprises in 22 provinces and cities had reportedly increased their output value by 12.2% in 1979 and their profits by 20%, outperforming enterprises not participating in the experiment. Of the increased profits, the enterprises and their workforces retained 34.2%, while the state took the rest. In consequence, the conference concluded that the 'direction of the experiment to expand enterprise decision-making is in general correct' and called for a further increase in the number of participating enterprises.[3]

In August, the State Economic Commission called for further experiments with a more radical form of enterprise initiative whereby enterprises would be fully responsible for their own profits and losses (Watson, 1982, p. 116). Experiments with this system had already been in operation in Sichuan since the beginning of 1980. On September 2, the State Council approved the State Economic Commission's 'Report on the Experimental Expansion of Enterprise Self-Management and Opinions on Future Work' which stipulated that, beginning in early 1981, *all* state enterprises would join the experiment and enjoy 'greater decision-making powers in personnel, finances, materials, production, supply and marketing'.[4] By this point, participating enterprises had reached 6,600 enterprises and their success in increasing output, output value and remitted profits was again reported to be far greater than non-participating enterprises. The results appeared to be gratifyingly positive-sum: the state received more revenue, the enterprises retained more profits and their workers earned higher incomes.

In spite of these favourable evaluations and continued reform impetus, however, during 1980 there was mounting evidence of problems emerging in the implementation of the reforms and opposition to or disagreement about their continuation. In December, much to the disappointment of many reformers, the brakes were applied with a squeal. The CCP Central Committee convened a Central Work Conference late in the month which decided to halt the reform programme for the time being and sought to reassert controls over those areas of economic decision which had been delegated over the previous two years. By early 1981, it was clear that the programme for expanding enterprise autonomy, while not repudiated, had been dropped from the policy agenda for the time being.

How do we account for this decision? Part of the reasons can be traced to the way in which reform policies had been implemented during 1979–80. In spite of a plethora of policies, there appears to have been no overall programme which mapped out in advance the scope, pace and phasing of policy implementation. There was, however, a basic procedure, which is a familiar feature of the Chinese Communist policy process. viz. initial concentration on selected 'trial-points' and gradual expansion of new policies on the basis of results achieved. While this approach can claim the usual advantages of incrementalism, it has characteristic problems which cropped up in this specific case. First, while its logic called for gradual change, the highly-charged ideological atmosphere surrounding the new policy initiatives created a kind of 'reform-mania'. While the Maoist campaigns of the past had encouraged people and institutions to show their mettle (and reliability) through left-wing radicalism, the new environment evoked a comparable passion (and pressure) for reform-mongering. Second, since central policy directives, particularly in the early stages of the movement, were overly vague and general, lower-level units were given great licence to interpret policies in original ways. In some cases, this meant positive action to seize the initiative and push policies through; in others, it meant negative action to block, change and reinterpret policy for conservative purposes. In consequence, reform policies had a highly uneven and ambiguous impact. Third, official policies were subject to systematic distortion from a familiar mechanism: first, the initial batch of trial enterprises tend to be chosen for their superior performance, thus the initial results of reform may be unrepresentative and misleading; second, there is both implicit and explicit pressure to produce good results which vindicate the new policy (and its proponents), with the result that the pace and scope of reform are accelerated prematurely with many problems lying undetected.

While some critics blamed the *way* reform policies were being implemented, others blamed their *substance*. In the latter's eyes, the reforms in general and the expansion of enterprise autonomy in particular, had either created or exacerbated economic 'anarchy' and social discontent. Were the effects of the enterprise autonomy movement in fact so negative as to justify halting it in late 1980? To the extent that economic problems emerged during 1979—80, were these the result of greater enterprise autonomy or other factors? To answer these questions, we must now investigate the precise impact of the autonomy experiment, both positive and negative.

2.3 *The impact of policies to expand enterprise autonomy: 1979—81*

One can only 'blame the reform' for the socio-economic problems of 1979—80 and the policy shift of December 1980 if it can be shown that reform policies actually had a significant impact on enterprise behaviour. In fact, the impact of reform policies was very uneven, both across regions and across policy areas. In regional terms, there were pace-setters such as Sichuan province and Shanghai, but reformers were aware that regional conditions — both between and within provinces — affected attitudes to reforms. From the viewpoint of poorer areas, the reforms could

be seen as embodying a weakening of centralized redistribution and an implicit re-allocation of resources and opportunities towards richer and more technologically advanced areas. The expansions of markets meant that products from advanced areas, notably Shanghai, with cost and quality advantages reinforced by increasing use of advertising, could penetrate other regional markets and undermine local industries. Significant changes were mainly confined to financial policy, as the reformers ruefully admitted (e.g. Xue Muqiao, 1980, p. 15; Ren and Zheng, 1982). In other areas, such as production planning and marketing outside the plan, there was very limited movement and in others, notably the assumption of independent pricing power by enterprise managers and greater control over hiring and firing labour, progress was marginal or non-existent (White, 1982).

I shall focus now on the area of most movement, finance. Even here, progress fell short of the reformer's plans. Some limited progress was made in expanding the role of the banking system in providing funds to enterprises on a credit basis (with interest to pay) as opposed to 'free' allocations from the state budget. Enterprises were also granted control over a larger proportion of their depreciation funds and depreciation schedules were adjusted. But the most widespread changes involved a series of measures designed to increase the 'economic responsibility' of enterprises by allowing them control over variously defined and calculated 'funds', retained profits or net revenues on an annual basis. One can discern three major measures, each of which progressively increases the financial independence of the enterprise and in the reformers' eyes would increase the economic initiative and efficiency of enterprises and their personnel (Reynolds, 1982; Mun, 1981). The first system, of *enterprise funds*, which had been advocated by the Draft Decision of July 1978 (Section IX), merely set up a fund equal to a certain percentage (up to 11%) of the total wage-bill which the enterprise could use for investment, incentive bonuses or welfare projects. It was introduced on a trial basis in 1978 under the guidance of State Council regulations. But the discretion of enterprise managers was limited in various ways. Superior organs were often reluctant to relinquish control over finances earmarked for enterprise funds. For example, the 1978 profits of the Wuhan Iron and Steel Company were ¥ 60 million over target and the company should have retained 10% or ¥ 6 million for its enterprise funds. But the Hubei Provincial Metallurgy Bureau re-allocated a large percentage of this sum to offset losses in other enterprises and the WISC only received ¥ 1 million.[5] The 1978 State Council regulations specified that enterprises could not draw on the funds unless the eight annual plan targets had been achieved. This provision serves to reinforce the process of haggling, characteristic of the unreformed system of centralized planning, whereby enterprises under-estimate their productive potential and push for low targets which would allow easier access to their enterprise funds. The link between enterprise funds and increased efficiency is also problematic. If enterprise funds were based on the total wage-bill, for example, poorly managed enterprises with a larger workforce might fare better than well-managed enterprises with fewer employees. Enterprise funds thus either failed to reward levels of enterprise performance differentially, or in certain conditions, rewarded poor performance. As critics pointed out, enterprise funds only made sense if they were in some way calculated on the basis of differential economic performance, measured by indices such as increase or decrease in output, quality and variety of products, cost levels and efficiency in use of fixed capital. The litmus test for these various elements of performance was seen as the indicator 'enterprise's profit level', for the following reasons (Wu Jinglian, 1978, p. E7):

> The socialist profit target is a target used to check on the operations of an enterprise when carrying out socialist emulation drives and economic accounting . . . An enterprise's profits are in direct proportion to the results of its production but in inverse proportion to its consumption. Therefore, when production is carried out according to plan, products are sold at prices specified by the state and other relevant state rules are observed, the level of profits of an enterprise or the level of accomplishment of the profit target will comprehensively reflect the good or bad operation of an enterprise. The above premise shows that the more profits an enterprise obtains, the better it has been run and the more it will benefit the whole society.

This analysis led to greater concentration on methods for allowing enterprises to *retain profits*, which, like enterprise funds, could be used on managers' discretion for investment, personnel welfare or bonuses.

Ratios of retention were calculated on two broad bases:

(a) Annual increase in profits, usually based on an equation of current year's planned profit target with previous year's actual profit. This system was laid down on the Sichuan province reform regulations, known as the '14 articles' — we can refer to this as the 'incremental profit system' (IPS). While the IPS was designed to stimulate improvements in capacity utilization by 'ratcheting up' profit targets, in the short term at least it actually rewarded enterprises with previously poor performance and thus room for improvement while enterprises operating at high levels of efficiency found it hard to increase profit ratios. Similarly, a sharp increase in profit in year t might mean a small increase in year $t + 1$, with the result that enterprises would try to even out profit increases year by year to maximize opportunities for retention (Mun, 1981, p. 37).

(b) The second system, the 'current profit system' (CPS) was designed to eliminate this kind of problem by tying retained profits to the total amount of profits, both planned and unplanned, in the current year. There have been two basic ways of calculating this. First, different retention ratios are applied to planned and above-planned profits, with an incentive increment on the latter. This of course created another incentive, viz., for enterprises to strive for a low planned profit target to maximise above-plan results. The second method, whereby the retention rate is calculated on the basis of total profits, serves to reduce this kind of distortion and is particularly suited to enterprises of relatively stable profitability. The third means of expanding enterprise financial autonomy was that of 'own responsibility for profit and loss' (*zifu yingkui*) whereby enterprises were merely required to pay taxes on their profits and retain the rest — we can call this the profit and loss responsibility system (PLRS). Trial enterprises were liable to four sets of taxes or charges: income tax, revenue-adjustment tax, fixed assets charge and a working capital charge. The benefits arising from increased profits were potentially considerable, but the enterprise could not expect any subsidy from the state if it made a loss. This system was a more radical reorientation of state-enterprise relations but, due to the problems arising from and mounting opposition to its more moderate counterpart, the profit retention system and due to the lack of complementary reforms needed to create an environment favourable to its success (notably price and tax reform and far greater enterprise control over production and marketing), the PLRS made little headway in 1980. By early 1981, only about 270 enterprises throughout the country (with 10 pioneering enterprises in

Sichuan province) were using this system, but in a relatively restricted form which closely resembled the PRS. In practice, therefore, the basic similarity between the three financial systems far outweighed the differences.

These different efforts to expand the financial autonomy of enterprises have faced several characteristic problems in practice. First, in many cases, the formal right to certain funds has not been converted into real discretionary control by enterprise managements. As in the case of enterprise funds, superior state organs have been reluctant to slacken their grip on retained profits. For example, a report on a trial profit-retention scheme among commercial enterprises in Liaoning province complained that state organs still insisted that enterprises obtain approval for each item of spending, thus creating a disguised version of the previous system (Gao, 1980). Local government agencies preferred to calculate profit retention ratios on their own rather than at enterprise level, thus retaining the power to average out or otherwise redistribute 'retained' funds across enterprises. Managers' financial discretion was also hampered by the difficulties they faced in purchasing materials and equipment with retained funds — such items were accorded secondary priority by the state agencies which continued to determine their allocation administratively.

Second, most forms of profit retention actually in operation (since the second version of the CPS apparently made little headway, allegedly owing to opposition from the Ministry of Finance) tended to create pressures for enterprises to bargain over their annual planned profit targets and to minimize them where possible. As the above report on Liaoning province pointed out:

> To withdraw more managerial funds, a number of enterprises have intentionally exaggerated their unfavourable conditions and tried in every possible way to lower their targets when planning them and when reporting to higher management levels . . . or making reports to the financial departments at the same level.

More generally, campaigns by enterprises to increase their retained profits by hook or by crook put pressures on the revenue of superior organs, threatening, in the eyes of some administrators at least, to undermine the financial viability of the state and leading to complaints that 'greedy' enterprises were obstructing the overall accumulation process.

During 1980, the problem of state revenue generated increasing concern since the total amount of industrial profits remitted to the state decreased over 1979, even though total industrial output value increased. Though a review of ten provinces and cities revealed that enterprises involved in the new financial experiments increased their remittances by 7.9%, the profits of non-participating enterprises decreased by 17.4%, remittances dropping accordingly.[6] A study of Chongqing city pointed to similar problems at the local level, with industrial revenues to the state dropping 10.2% between January and September 1980 compared with the same period in 1979 (Tian Fang et al., 1981). Reformers tried to rebut alarmist critics with comforting statistics, but the statistical record was sufficiently uneven to fuel opposition.

Third, the ways in which many enterprise managers used the increased funds at their disposal were often inconsistent with the overall aims of improving levels of efficiency and the macro-economic objectives of the economic 'readjustment' programme. Managers were accused of erroneously equating an increase in financial autonomy with the right to 'spend more money' in often unconsidered ways. In the sphere of distribution, that portion of retained profits earmarked for bonuses was often distributed without regard for differential productivity in an 'egalitarian' fashion. In the sphere of investment, some enterprises used their development funds to expand productive capacity for goods already in full or excess supply, or to make their enterprises 'small but comprehensive', a phenomenon decried by the reformers as a characteristic feature of the old planning system; or they launched capital programmes without consideration for the availability of adequate power and material supplies, or redirected accumulation funds into showy but unproductive assets, such as cars and fancy office buildings.

Fourth, there was a tendency for the profit motive to eclipse other goals of enterprise activity. Managers were accused of making 'profit-seeking' their sole concern, a reflection of 'capitalist business thinking', which disregarded the interests of both state and consumers.

In consequence, the earlier stress on profitability as the key index of enterprise performance was increasingly downplayed, profit being relegated as one target among several, not the least of which was generation of revenue for the state. Many enterprise managers must have been exasperated by the perilously thin line between 'socialist entrepreneurship' and 'capitalist profit-seeking'.

Fifth, profit was at best an ambiguous criterion of performance. On the one hand it was rational in so far as it reflected effectiveness in factor utilization; on the other hand, it was an arbitrary standard in two senses: (i) differences in profitability between enterprises might reflect differences in objective conditions, such as plant, technology or location rather than organizational factors subject to managerial control. (ii) they also reflected varying price ratios (and taxation rates) within and between different sectors of industry which reflected planners' preferences rather than conditions of supply and demand. Zhao Ziyang referred to the problem of inter-sectoral differentials in a speech in Sichuan in April 1980, noting that profits were (arbitrarily) higher in the processing trades than in raw materials, fuel and agricultural machinery.[7] There were also variations *within* industries. Take the following examples of differential profit rates in the fuel sector

84 trial enterprises in Sichuan province: while the average profit rate was 21.4%, rates varied from 34.2% for the chemical industry, 23.8% for machinery, 11.7% for building materials and a loss for coal. On an inter-enterprise basis, profit rate ranged from 51% to 2.39% (Lin Ling, 1980). As Zhao pointed out, however, rectification of these arbitrary variations required basic changes in the price structure and a more thorough-going application of 'the law of value' but these changes were too fundamental to be on the agenda as yet.

However, even where variation in profitability *did* reflect 'subjective' factors under managerial control, resulting inequalities between enterprises were also a cause of concern since they affected 'neighbourly relations' between enterprises, i.e. increasing inequality of wage-rates between different factories within the same sector led to discontent in the 'poorer' factory. This created pressure for the state to

Table 1. *Profit Rates in the Fuel Industry*

	Electricity	Petroleum	Coal
I The rate of profit in an output of 100 yuan	40	46.1	2.3
II The rate of profit on every 100 yuan of capital	25	36	0.8
III Average profit per worker (yuan in one year)	16,286	12,214	73

(Lu Qikang: 1979). Within the textile industry, profits were relatively high for factories producing chemical fibre or blended fabrics. There were even variations within factories: for example, in the same knitwear plant, a nylon socks workshop might have higher profits than a cotton socks workshop. In Guangdong province, profit retention trials in 100 enterprises revealed immense, non-performance-related gaps in profitability between industries which were not related to performance. For example, a factory producing wrist-watches, which were priced at many times their cost, could reap high profits while a factory producing basic daily items, such as matches, whose prices were at cost, had far lower rates.[8] Both sets of factors — 'objective' differences and price differences — accounted for the phenomenon of 'hardship and happiness being uneven'. They were important in accounting for the wide variation in profitability among

intervene to prevent disparities from growing too large.

If we investigate the impact of the reforms in enterprise autonomy as a whole and relate them to overall economic trends in Chinese industry in 1979–80 the picture is ambiguous, not the least because statistics on 'success' or 'failure' were used by different groups to defend or discredit the reform process. Certainly there was no shortage of glowing accounts of the 'pleasing results' of expanding enterprise autonomy, notably in the financial sphere. In Sichuan province, for example, reform advocates such as Lin Zili claimed 'outstanding success', citing impressive increases in enterprise profits, revenue remittance to the state and worker incomes as a result of greater dynamism and efficiency on the part of enterprises (Lin Zili, 1980).

On the other hand, overall economic trends during 1979–80 provided considerable cause for alarm, particularly for those manning state industrial and financial departments. Growth in GNP (in value terms) declined from 12% in 1978 to 7% in 1979 and c.6% in 1980. 1979 and 1980 were also years of severe financial disequilibrium, with budget deficits of ￥17 billion (15.4% of total state revenue) and ￥12.1 billion in 1980 (10.5%) and an official (and therefore probably underestimated) inflation rate of 5.8% in 1979, 6% in 1980. Efforts to restrain the scale of capital construction had not proven effective, with state investment in 1979–80 exceeding budgeted targets at a time when state revenues were being squeezed. It is clear that these economic problems were posing severe political problems for the Dengist leadership. Inflation, particularly as it affected the prices of everyday items such as vegetables, was causing widespread social unrest among urban populations. Cadres in state organs at all levels pointed to evidence of a growing fiscal crisis of the state and accelerating economic 'anarchy'. Opponents of the reform at all levels could use these pressures to bolster their arguments and undermine Deng's credibility. Indeed, in the highest reaches of the CCP, Deng was finding it far more difficult than expected to demote the last representative of Maoist power, Hua Guofeng. The pressure for retrenchment was irresistible and the enterprise autonomy movement was a major casualty.

There was enough evidence to relate expansion of enterprise decision-making power to these overall economic problems to cause severe political problems for advocates of reform. As we have seen, higher enterprise profits did not necessarily mean higher state revenues or levels of efficiency; in fact, often quite the contrary. Enterprise accumulation funds increased significantly and were often, from the point of view of superior state organs at least, spent in 'blind investment' projects with exacerbated rather than eased problems of over-accumulation and inefficient capital use. To the extent that enterprises used their increased funds to increase the incomes of their workforce without corresponding increase in productivity and used their increased marketing power to increase prices through 'negotiation' with customers, they contributed to inflationary pressures. In the eyes of many, moreover, increasing the discretion of enterprise managers had encouraged a wave of 'improper practices', including 'speculation' 'profiteering', fraud and smuggling.

Just as clearly, however, there were differences about how these problems should be interpreted and what effect they should be allowed to exert on economic policy. Five broad positions can be identified.

(i) Those who had been sceptical of the reforms in the first place and who used mounting evidence of problems to discredit the experiment to expand enterprise decision-making and bring it to a halt. Most significant here, of course, would be representatives of Maoist thought at all levels, who regarded the reform as 'revisionist' and would rally behind Hua Guofeng in his struggle to avoid demotion.

(ii) Those who supported reform but were worried about its social, economic and political consequences and were willing to halt its expansion and settle for relatively marginal change in the short and middle term. In comparative terms they were settling for a situation analogous to that in the Soviet Union after the reforms of the mid-1960s.

(iii) Reformers who were sensitive to the economic and political problems of 1979–80, but diagnosed them partly as contextual viz. as the result of problems in the economy as a whole and partly as the inevitable result of a basic contradiction between the new and the old system, the reformed and the unreformed. In the latter category, the basically unchanged price system was the main obstacle. According to their analysis, partial and comprehensive reform were inextricable – the reform process could not stop half-way or it would be stifled by a combination of its opponents and its own consequences. For the short term, however, more thorough-going reform was out of the question – this would risk economic instability and political crisis. Rather the situation should be stabilized for the foreseeable future; limited gains should be consolidated and the preconditions for deeper reform established.

(iv) Reformers who, though sensitive to emerging problems, wished to press ahead incrementally, correcting and adjusting as circumstances required.

(v) Reformers who felt that reforms were faltering precisely because they have not gone far enough and were in favour of grasping the nettle and moving forward with a 'giant step', most notably through a comprehensive reform of the price system.

The official position adopted in late 1980 was essentially (iii). This was publicly espoused by Premier Zhao Ziyang and other key reformers in the top leadership and appears to have guided their policy strategy over the next two years. In the context of late 1890, it represented a balance between what was deemed economically necessary and politically feasible.

3. 1981–3. RECULER POUR MIEUX SAUTER?

After the cardinal Central Work Conference of December 1980, the programme of expanding enterprise decision-making power was shelved and the work of overall economic 'readjustment' emphasized. Did this shift in policy reflect a *de facto* abandonment of thorough-going economic reform behind a smokescreen of propaganda about the need for merely temporary consolidation? Did it reflect a loss of commitment to reform among the CCP leadership or demonstrate the naivety of expecting anything more than marginal change given the stifling constraints posed by the state-party apparatus? If the commitment to reform remained strong, how could the reform process best be restarted — with what policies and on the basis of what preconditions? These have been the major problems facing the Chinese leadership in the early 1980s and the answers to them will determine the shape of the Chinese politico-economic structure till the end of the century. We can improve our ability to answer by looking at policy debates and official behaviour on the crucial issue of enterprise autonomy during the two years after the Central Work Conference.

The key themes of policy analysis and practice during 1981–2 can be grouped under four main headings:

(i) Official analyses of economic strategy stipulated that, in the relationship between economic readjustment and reform, *readjustment should be primary*. More specifically, thorough-going reform could not be put on the agenda until basic disequilibria in the economy as a whole were rectified: between accumulation and consumption, prices and incomes, state revenues and expenditures, and different economic sectors.

We can interpret this formulation in both conservative and progressive terms. On the one hand, opponents of reform or marginal reformers could assert the primacy of readjustment as a way to rationalize the reimposition of central controls after a period of (to them) incautious relaxation and to oppose further reforms. At least one author, Cai Yanchu, defined the relationship between readjustment and reform as a struggle between state and enterprises over the extent of capital construction. Cai described the issue as follows: (1980, p. 14).

[We] have been baffled by the rising demand to expand the autonomy of enterprises which has almost drowned out the voices in support of readjusting the national economy. This unreasonable demand has forced people to study and search for the motive behind the proposal to expand enterprise autonomy. My surveys and observations reveal this fact; that the real aim behind their demand is to reinstate investment in capital construction through other channels — investment which has been cut off by the state.

Advocates of reform would clearly reject this kind of analysis, preferring to emphasize the role of readjustment as a temporary stage necessary to establish favourable overall conditions for further micro-economic reform. This argument was often couched in terms of the need for 'synchronisation between micro- and macro-economic reform.' (Ren and Zheng, 1982).

[Most] of the reform measures have been micro-economic and are concerned with a part of the economic system . . . The micro-economic and macro-economic reforms have not been coordinated . . . [But these] two aspects are interdependent and complementary. Macro-economic reform is the prerequisite for micro-economic reform . . . Our placing emphasis on strengthening macro-economic reform by no means signifies that we belittle the importance of micro-economic reform. On the contrary, it signifies that we want to create the external conditions for micro-economic reform.

This kind of analysis prompted greater interest among economists in questions of 'macro-economic management' and 'development strategy' — still fairly unfamiliar concepts — and in the theory and practice of planning, contrasting strongly with their earlier concentration on enterprise behaviour and markets.

(ii) Emphasis on the primacy of readjustment was accompanied by *greater analytical emphasis on the role of the state in the economy* and a *reimposition of specific administrative controls*. The previous system of economic management received a better press. Official commentaries admitted that even after the reforms, the basic system of administrative management of industry was still intact, and would remain 'for quite a long time to come' (Zhou and Wu, 1981). It should therefore be suitably strengthened and streamlined, but not subverted by excessive decentralization. Accordingly, the sphere of enterprise decision-making power was not to be extended for the foreseeable future. The State Council issued a circular to this effect in April 1981, emphasising consolidation and improvement of existing progress in experimental enterprises and summarization of reform experience at all levels.[9] In general, 1981 and 1982 saw a tightening of state controls over industrial enterprises to secure 'discipline' and ensure that enterprises fulfilled their responsibilities to the state. In late 1981, there was a move to introduce the principle of the 'economic responsibility system' (ERS) (*jingji zerenzhi*), which had been successful in agricultural reforms, into relations between state and enterprise, and between enterprise managers and workers. While some official statements attempted to present ERS as an expansion of enterprise decision-making, it seems rather to have embodied a reimposition of administrative requirements on enterprises, notably those old diehards, the 'eight [plan] targets' (for a fuller discussion, Fujimoto, 1982).

However, on another front, greater movement was allowed. Provision was made for a further reorganization of the industrial structure by amalgamating industrial enterprises according to principles of specialization and cooperation. By early 1981, 19,336 enterprises had been amalgamated in 1,983 companies or general firms, accounting for 5.13% of total enterprises (and 30% of enterprises in the three crucial cities of Peking, Tientsin and Shanghai). This type of industrial reform was seen as an attractive 'middle way', between the extremes of enterprise autonomy and central planning — indeed it was described as '*both* readjustment and reform' and therefore worthy of further development. Indeed, one can detect a distinct 'reform' position emerging in 1980—1 which sees the combination of state administrative and trusts as an alternative to markets and relatively autonomous enterprises which can solve the previous problems of administrative 'over-centralization' and bureaucratic rigidity yet without (and here the criticism of market reformers and enterprise autonomists is clear) 'over-decentralization and over-independence' which causes 'economic chaos'. Perhaps we could call advocates of this position 'trusties' (e.g. Li Zhisheng, 1981).

During 1981—2 there was a reaffirmation, in both theoretical and practical terms, of the over-riding primacy of state interests and overall political priorities *vis à vis* the interests and attitudes of individuals and economic or administrative units. A *People's Daily* editorial of February 1982 put it as follows:[10]

> The state is an organic entity. In carrying out economic construction, we must coordinate the forces of all quarters. It will not work if each moves in different directions and does things in its own way. . . . For some time, the leading cadres of a small number of departments, localities and enterprises have been putting the partial and

local interests of their units above everything else in approaching problems and handling work when they should have proceeded from the interests of the whole.

Premier Zhao Ziyang also took up this theme when he argued that 'efforts to expand decision-making powers [of enterprises and localities] are also apt to foster the trend towards departmentalism, decentralism and liberalism, to weaken and depart from the state's unified plan, [and] interfere with and break up the unified socialist market.'[11]

This kind of thinking brought an unambiguous reaffirmation of the *economic dominance of the plan*, under the general slogan of 'taking the planned economy as the key link, with regulation by the market mechanism playing the supplementary role'. In effect, this was putting the market in its place (and with it any ideas of rapid expansion of enterprise autonomy). It also marked a break from the main reform themes of 1979—80 in which lip-service was paid to the continued primacy of planning, but the role of the 'law of value' was stressed to the virtual exclusion of systematic thought about how to improve the planning system. This one-sidedness was admitted by no less a figure than Xue Muqiao in mid-1982 (Xue: 1982, p. 16).

The earlier period was now criticized — in the usual style of referring to the 'erroneous tendency' of 'some comrades' who identified defects in the previous economic mechanism with *planning itself* and thus ended up overstressing the role of market forces (e.g. Hao, 1982). The prime distinction, argued the new orthodoxy, was not between plan and market but between strong and weak planning — planning could be improved through better statistics, more diverse techniques, more careful investigation and research, or the use of more 'scientific' planning techniques (including computers). With regard to enterprise decision-making power, this position could imply that, as You Lin of the Research Office of the CCPCC Secretariat put it, 'generally speaking, state-owned enterprises must carry out production in accordance with state planning', their freedom of manoeuvre mainly limited to profit-sharing and with minimal scope for market-oriented decisions. You was in favour of confining the operation of market relations to small-scale, overwhelmingly collectively-owned industrial enterprises and was very sceptical about reformers' views on the relationships between 'macro' and 'micro' economies. (You, 1981).

Some comrades . . . advocate that the so-called macro-economy . . . should be subjected to planned regulation, while the economic activities of enterprises (the so-called micro-economy), including what and how much to produce, should be regulated by the market. It is undoubtedly very necessary to subject major matters concerning the whole economy to planning. But if the 'macro' is wholly different from the 'micro', the 'macro' will probably be made a mere figurehead, becoming just 'a gentleman on the rampart'. Just think! If all enterprises go their own way, how can a so-called 'macro policy decision' in state planning play its role? If all enterprises carry out their activities at the mercy of the market, how can state planning be realised?

For You and others like him, the aim of reform was 'to improve and strengthen the planned economy . . . and raise planning to the stage of being scientific.' The market, which had been lionized during 1978−80, was now subjected to a barrage of criticism: its ill effects during the period of reform were highlighted and the erstwhile virtues of competition between enterprises were ignored in the light of its 'unhealthy tendencies' (notably 'market blockade' created by local protectionism, technical secrecy, bribery and 'fixing', and destructive conflict among 'brother units').

While there appears to have been a superficial consensus between various opinion groups on the need for stronger planning, they have disagreed on the *forms* this planning should take. While a Party spokesman like You Lin appears to envisage a strengthening of traditional directive planning controls which severely restrict the economic initiative of enterprises, reformers such as Xue Muqiao define 'stronger planning' in terms of making greater use of parametric mechanisms, such as price, credit and tax, which is *compatible* with greatly increased enterprise power. In the words of Xue Muqiao, 'the greater the enterprise's autonomy, the more necessary it is for the state to guide and supervise economic activities by means of economic levers and legislation' (1982, p. K17). Conflicting positions apart, however, this debate about the nature of

planning was very illuminating since it provided a more precise definition of the different forms of planning and prepared the way for a more sophisticated understanding of the concrete relationships between planning and market, state and enterprise. The debate continued through 1981 and early 1982 and by September 1982 a compromise solution was reached, and ratified in general terms at least at the CCP's 12th Party Congress that month. This is essentially a notion of a three-tiered system of economic management with directive plans for key sectors and products (producer goods and crucial consumer items), non-obligatory guide-plans for a considerable range of industrial products, notably consumer goods and deregulation of non-staple foodstuffs and handicraft commodities. However, successful implementation of this new system depends on a thorough reform of the price system, a nettle which most socialist governments have been unwilling or unable to grasp.

(iii) Focusing on enterprises themselves, the main theme during 1981−2 was the proclaimed need for *rectification* (also called, more euphemistically, 'consolidation'). This reflected a feeling of disappointment among reformers about the performance of enterprise managements during the reforms and the realization that enlarging the decision-making powers of incompetent managers would subvert the purpose of the exercise. The level of enterprise management, declared *People's Daily*, was backward and chaotic.[12] More focused studies attempted to assess the range of managerial performance, (for example) in three areas which had been pacesetters in the experiment to expand enterprise autonomy: There was also a realization that the expansion of managers' discretion and greater use of the market did not in and of itself raise the level of management competence. Indeed, the experience of 1979−80 demonstrated, some argued, that the positive effect of 'economic mechanisms' generally were limited: (Su and Shi, 1981).

We should get rid of the erroneous idea that

Table 2. *Quality of Enterprise Performance in Peking, Tientsin and Sichuan*

Area	'Basic condition' of enterprises (%)			Number of enterprises in survey
	1st rate	2nd rate	3rd rate	
Peking	27	65	7	893
Tientsin	16.3	70.5	13.2	634
Sichuan	26.8	58.7	14.5	1,293

economic measures can be used to solve all problems in improving operations and management ... [Given] the limits of objective economic conditions, pricing and other important economic levers cannot for some time to come fully assert their role, nor can the market mechanism guarantee that an enterprise's operation activities will definitely conform to the demands of the state plan and the interests of the whole society. Under these circumstances, it is all the more necessary to adopt the method of combining economic and administrative means to consolidate enterprises.

The deficiencies to which such measures were to be applied were given a full public airing in 1981–2. First of all, many managerial cadres had proven unequal to the increased responsibilities offered by the reforms. They lacked the necessary training in business and technical know-how, were often too old and inured to the organizational logic of the old system and were unsympathetic to the reforms since they had been appointed on political grounds (for example as 'revolutionary cadres' demobilized from the People's Liberation Army). The reforms, it was felt with some justification, could not be entrusted to such people — a new managerial cadre had to be created — younger, better trained, professionals who could practice the kind of 'scientific management' which had proven so successful in capitalist enterprises in Japan and the West.[13] To this end over-aged cadres were retired, short-term management courses were mounted at various levels (for example, under the aegis of the Chinese Enterprise Management Association), management studies departments were opened in the universities, students were sent to Japan and the West to study, and foreign consultants were invited to lecture and establish management studies centres.

Specific management deficiencies have also received critical attention: wage and bonus distribution practices, investment decisions (notably the failure to use investment funds for 'intensive' rather than 'extensive' purposes) and the failure to establish concrete responsibility systems for production and distribution (there were attempts to establish more 'scientific' piece-rate norms, quality control circles, etc.) Most dramatically, a mounting campaign was conducted against management 'deviations' such as evasion of financial regulations and more serious 'economic crimes' such as smuggling, bribery, embezzlement, 'speculation' and 'swindling'. By early 1981, these 'crimes' were deemed so serious that Premier Zhao Ziyang said they were worse than the problems of the early 1950s which had prompted the

'Three Antis' and 'Five Antis' campaigns.[14]

Inevitably, the experiment to expand enterprise autonomy took some of the blame for these problems. Formerly pace-setting enterprises now came under fire. One such was the Sichuan No. 1 Cotton Textiles Printing and Dyeing plant which was one of the first trial enterprises in 1978 and one of the few chosen in 1980 to try out the third method of expanding the financial autonomy of enterprises, 'own responsibility for profit and loss'. As late as December 1980, this plant was receiving public attention as a successful example of the new financial system 'bringing great vitality to enterprises'.[15] The reported results of the experiment were indeed impressive, with an increase in profits of 96% between January and September 1980 compared with the same period in 1979. Advances were also claimed in product quality and variety, rate of turnover of funds, economical utilization of materials and power, and an ambitious programme of capital investment was in full swing. In February 1981, however, the factory was publicly criticized for financial irregularity, specifically for evading the payment of ¥ 2.4 m income tax.[16] The enterprise had falsified its accounts in three ways: first, it reduced its profit figures for May 1980 (and therefore its tax liability) through a fictitious ¥ 427,000 of 'increased production cost'; second, it substituted cheaper 25 mm for dearer 38 mm chemical fibres, increasing nominal production costs by ¥ 2,437,000; third, it allegedly creamed off ¥ 751,000 for a compensatory trade deal with a Hong Kong company. Although public accounts of the episode pointed out that such irregularities had no relation to the enterprise's participation in the trial 'zifu yingkuei' system, the scandal clearly rubbed off on the experiment itself and the Sichuan authorities who were sponsoring it. This case clearly reflected a general concern that enterprises were using their greater freedom to squeeze state revenues.

Another case with the same message was that of the Jiuan Petrochemical Works in Shandong province.[17] The plant was accused of withholding ¥ 4.5 m in state revenue, about 12.5% of the profits actually remitted to the State in 1980. This was done by fiddling the accounts by inflating 'production costs' and concealing sources of revenue. Plant managers were also castigated for squandering their discretionary funds on unnecessary luxuries (notably cars and calculators) and allowing the establishment of 24 slush funds (called 'small cash boxes') throughout the plant (including the trade union branch and the Young Communist

League committee) which were allegedly largely spent on unnecessary goods or entertainment.

The imposition of central administrative controls was orchestrated by a series of key policy documents during 1981 and early 1982. The State Council circular of April 1, 1981 was reinforced by documents issued in September on the rectification of enterprise managements and the establishment of economic responsibility systems in industry. In November, the State Economic Commission issued six criteria for consolidating enterprises, the fifth of which stipulated that 'the enterprise must fulfil state plans in an all-round manner'. The 'Provisional Regulations on the Institution of the Responsibility System in Industrial Production', issued in early December, also laid heavy emphasis on the need for enterprises to fulfil planned targets. Early in 1982, the CCP Central Committee and the State Council decided to expand the work of 'consolidating' enterprises to all state-run concerns over the next two to three years.[18]

Such measures were conservative to the extent that they sought to correct the instabilities which emerged in 1980 by reasserting central controls characteristic of the pre-reform system. But the impetus towards reform continued during 1981–2. Just as overall economic readjustment and the rectification of enterprise managements were seen as essential preconditions for *further* reforms two other preconditions were singled out and acted upon. First, it was agreed that the reform process could not continue without a systematic plan to guide implementation. Premier Zhao Ziyang had cited the need for an 'overall programme' in his report on the work of the government at a session on the National People's Congress in December 1981. To this end, the State Council decided in April 1982 to establish a high-level committee for economic reform 'which will be in charge of the overall research and planning for reform of the economic system and leading this work in a unified manner.'[19] Second, it was realized that reforming the relationship between state and enterprise could not be limited to changes in the enterprise; the state apparatus had to be reformed as well. A movement was launched in early 1982 to restructure and streamline government organs, which were seen as overstaffed, overlapping, top heavy, professionally incompetent and conservative. This movement was described as a 'profound revolution against overstaffed organizations, irrational systems and all sorts of bureaucratism' which 'lays the foundations for the reform of the over-centralized management system'.[20]

An attempt was also made to introduce the principle of economic responsibility into government work, a policy with potentially radical implications. Although this administrative reform met with bureaucratic obstacles and results fell short of objectives, considerable progress was made, enought to suggest that the CCP leadership's commitment to thoroughgoing reforms was far from spent (Lee, 1982). This and other trends suggests that 1981–2 was a complex transitional period with elements of retrogression, consolidation and preparation for forward movement, elements which reflected not merely a new stage in the policy process, but disagreements between contending positions. Wide-ranging policy debate continued up to the 12th Party Congress in September 1982 when some (probably temporary) compromise and partial consensus was reached.

CONCLUSIONS

What is the future likely to hold for the crucial relationship between state organs and industrial enterprises? 1981–2 was a period when advocates of reform were forced back on the defensive and forced to reconsider their position in the light of the preceding two years. As we have seen, overall progress in the enterprise autonomy experiments had been uneven: in certain areas, such as the labour system, precious little change had taken place; in other areas, such as movement towards greater market involvement and power to negotiate prices and conduct foreign trade, limited progress had been made but then reversed by the retrenchment measures introduced in early 1981. In the area of financial power, however, the principle and practice of profit retention had been established and reformers sought to defend and consolidate this achievement. But the overall impact of the enterprise autonomy movement was relatively shallow and disappointing: state enterprises were still harnessed to state planning targets and the allowed level of commercialization in procuring supplies and marketing products was still low.

While the initial economic benefits of greater enterprise autonomy seemed to vindicate reformers' convictions of its necessity, the problems which emerged in 1979–80 were serious enough to demand careful study and re-thinking. Greater enterprise autonomy had brought certain problematic results in its train: pressure towards price instability and inflation, unplanned investment and uncoordinated production, financial pressure on the state, bottle-necks in supply of raw materials and energy, and so on. In retrospect, and particularly if one puts the reforms in a comparative context, these effects were hardly surprising. Chinese economists familiar with reform processes in Eastern Europe, notably Poland, Hungary and Yugoslavia, were not slow to draw parallels and the analyses of reformers such as Brus became powerfully relevant (e.g. Brus, 1979). The basic lesson is that certain economic and therefore ultimately political problems are *inherent* in reform policies (rather than merely the result of, say, bureaucratic or political opposition) and that these have to be foreseen and counteracted in future reforms. The experience of 1979—80 suggested more caution and coordination. Ironically, this implies a greater need for *planning* a reform strategy, with a much more precise understanding of several key relationships: between macro and micro changes, between different areas of policy at each level (particularly the link between greater enterprise autonomy and wage/price reform) and between different stages of the process. It is in this spirit that Hu Yaobang announced in September 1982 at the 12th Party Congress that the period of the Sixth Five-Year Plan (1981—5) would be one in which 'we must consolidate and perfect the initial reforms in economic administration and work out an early overall plan in economic administration and the measures for its implementation'.[21]

In working out such a strategy, the reasonably successful Hungarian experience in introducing the New Economic Mechanism is instructive (Hare *et al.*, 1981).

Inherent problems aside, however, the experience of 1979—80 also revealed the ideological, institutional and social obstacles to reforming enterprise behaviour. Two decades of central planning and one decade of Cultural Revolution had implanted attitudes inimical to enterprise autonomy and markets among state and enterprise cadres. For many industrial workers, moreover, the reforms threatened to betray the basic socialist values of equality and job security. The complex network of state bureaucracies, at central and local levels, posed a double hindrance: on the one hand, as a matrix within which opponents could marshal their forces, on the other hand by virtue of their inherent organizational sluggishness and conservatism. Either way, conservatism and obstruction hardened into active opposition when greater enterprise autonomy threatened to undermine the revenue basis of the state. At the enterprise level, managerial cadres were often *de facto* state officials, obeying an administrative logic of hierarchical bargaining and compliance rather than the entrepreneurial economic logic defined by the reformers. Indeed, one could argue that the 1979—80 reforms had outrun their social base, i.e. that the new type of cadre so necessary to their project — professionally trained, technocratically oriented, economically motivated and entrepreneurial in spirit — did not yet exist in sufficient numbers. In fact, far too many factories were 'no-go areas' for both reforms and reformers, particularly those who stood to lose out to stronger competitors if the reforms really began to bite.

The policy atmosphere of late 1982 and early 1983 shows a much greater sensitivity to these problems and constraints — to this extent, 1979—80 was sobering but salutary for the reform-mongers. They now approached the future with greater clarity and caution — the reform process was reconceived as a gradual war of attrition rather than a dramatic offensive.

But there are no obvious reasons for optimism. Schemes for the national coordination of 'plan' and 'market' are more easily put on paper than into practice; the problems of policy coordination in any comprehensive reform are enormous; the bureaucratic and attitudinal constraints are daunting. Clearly *reform has to be engineered at several levels*: at the policy level, through greater precision, flexibility and coordination; at the institutional level, through improved planning techniques and thorough-going reform of state bureaucracies and enterprise management systems; at the social level, through the creation or promotion of new strata sympathetic to the reforms and adequate to its demands. But the Chinese state's grip on the economy is a strong one, reinforced by millennia of imperial tradition and decades of Stalinist state socialism — it will not be loosened without a prolonged struggle.

ABBREVIATIONS

CREA: Joint Publications Research Service, *China Report: Economic Affairs*.
FBIS: Foreign Broadcasts Information Service, *China: Daily Report*.
GMRB: *Guangming Ribao* (Glorious Daily), Peking.
JJGL: *Jingji Guanli* (Economic Management), Peking.

JJYJ: *Jingji Yanjiu* (Economic Research), Peking.

PD: *People's Daily* (Renmin Ribao), Peking.
XH: *Xinhua* (New China News Agency), Peking.

NOTES

1. I have not located a text of these regulations, but commentaries on them can be found in *Caiwu yu Kuaiji* (Finance and Accounting), No. 10 (20 October, 1979), in *CREA* 59 (1 May, 1980) and *Beijing Review* 12 (24 March 1980), p. 25.

2. *XH*, domestic service, 19 February 1980, in *FBIS*, 20 February.

3. *XH*, domestic, 10–11 April 1980, in *FBIS*, 14 April.

4. *XH*, domestic, 6 September 1980, in *FBIS*, 9 September.

5. *PD*, 17 January 1979, in *FBIS*, 23 January.

6. *XH*, domestic, 5 March 1981, in *FBIS*, 11 March.

7. *XH*, domestic, 20 April 1980, in *FBIS*, 22 April.

8. *Nanfang Ribao* (Southern Daily), Canton, 25 April 1980, in *CREA* no. 69, (14 July), pp. 6–9.

9. This circular and an accompanying report are translated in *Issues and Studies*, Taipei, XVIII, 4 (April 1982).

10. *PD*, 24 February 1981, in *FBIS*, 26 February.

11. *XH*, domestic, 30 March 1982, in *FBIS*, 1 April.

12. 'Enterprise consolidation must be stepped up', *PD* editorial, 12 October, 1981, in *FBIS*, 20 October.

13. For example, see 'Seriously straighten out the enterprises', *Tientsin Daily,* 28 July 1981, in *FBIS*, 20 August.

14. *XH*, domestic, 30 March 1982, in *FBIS*, 1 April 1982, p. K5.

15. *JJGL*, No. 12 (15 December 1980), pp. 29–32, in *CREA*, No. 124 (26 March 1981), pp. 23–32.

16. *Ibid.*, No. 2 (25 February 1981), pp. 11, 29, in *CREA*, No. 131 (20 April 1981), pp. 8–10.

17. *XH*, domestic, 28 July 1981, in *FBIS*, 29 July.

18. *Wen Hui Bao*, Hongkong, 25 September 1981; *XH*, domestic, 6 November 1981, in *FBIS*, 13 November; *Hongqi* (Red Flag), No. 5 (1 March 1982), pp. 32–36, in *FBIS*, 2 April 1982.

19. *XH*, domestic, 13 April 1982, in *FBIS*, 14 April 1982.

20. 'Restructuring administrative organisations is a revolution', *Hongqi* (Red Flag), No. 6 (16 March 1982), in *FBIS*, 8 April 1982, p. K2.

21. Cited by Robert Delfs, 'Mixed from the centre', *Far Eastern Economic Review*, 15 October 1982, p. 56.

REFERENCES

Brus, W., 'The East European reforms: what happened to them?', *Soviet Studies*, **XXXI**, 2 (April 1979), pp. 257–267.

Cai, Yanchu, 'On expanding enterprises' autonomy', *GMRB* (1 March 1980) in *CREA*, No. 55 (15 April 1980), pp. 10–15.

'Draft Decisions Concerning Some Problems in Speeding Up the Development of Industry' (the '30 points'), translated in *Issues and Studies*, Taipei, **XIV**, No. 11 (November 1978) and **XV**, No. 1 (January 1979).

Fujimoto, Akira, 'The Economic Responsibility System in China's industrial sector', *China Newsletter*, JETRO, No. 41 (November–December 1982).

Gao, Wenxiang, 'Several problems on the trial implementation of the profit retention system by commercial enterprises', *JJGL*, No. 1, (15 January 1980) in *CREA*, No. 62 (20 May 1980), pp. 51–54.

Hao, ZhiYan, 'Support a planned economy and intensify planning', *Dazhong Ribao* (Great Masses Daily) (11 February 1982).

Hare, P., H. Radice, and N. Swain, (eds.) *Hungary: A Decade of Economic Reform* (London: Allen and Unwin, 1981).

He, Jianzhang, 'Problems in the planned management of the economy owned by the whole people and the orientation of reform', *JJYJ*, No. 5 (20 May 1979), pp. 35–45, in *CREA*, 5 (3 August 1979).

Hu, Qiaomu, 'Observe economic laws, speed up the Four Modernisations', *Peking Review*, Nos. 45, 46 and 47 (1978).

Ji, Chongwei and Wenzuo Rong, 'How are we to reform the system of industrial administration?', *JJGL*, No. 6 (25 June 1979), pp. 8–12, in *CREA*, No. 14 (17 September 1979), p. 13.

Jiang, Yiwei, 'The theory of an enterprise-based economy', *Social Sciences in China*, No. 1 (1980), pp. 48–70.

Lee, Hong-yung, 'Deng Xiaoping's reform of the Chinese bureaucracy', *Journal of Northeast Asian Studies*, **I**, No. 1 (June 1982).

Li, Dehua, 'Another discussion of enterprise decision-making power and its objective foundations . . .', *Jianghan Luntan* (Jianghan Forum), No. 1 (January 1980), in *CREA*, 87, pp. 1–12.

Li, Zhisheng, 'On the relationship between corporations, centralisation and unification', *PD* (9 November 1981) in *FBIS* (16 November 1981).

Liao, Jili, 'A talk on structural reform in terms of horizontal and vertical integration', *PD*, Peking (26 August 1980) in *FBIS* (11 September 1980), L50 ff.

Lin, Qingsheng, 'How to understand correctly the objective foundations of the autonomy of enterprises', *JJYJ*, No. 12 (20 December 1980), pp. 42–48 in *CREA*, 124, pp. 23–32.

Lin, Zili, 'A beginning for restructuring China's economic system – experiments in increasing the decision-making power of enterprises in Sichuan, Anhui and Zhejiang studied', *PD* (4 April 1980) in *CREA*, No. 64, (17 June 1980) pp. 1–10.

Liu, Guoguang, Jinglian, Wu and Renwei, Zhao, 'The relationship between planning and market as seen by China in her socialist economy', *Atlantic Economic Journal*, No. 31 (1979), pp. 11–21.

Lu, Qikang, 'Exploring several questions concerning "enterprise funds" ', *Caiwu yu Kaiji* (Finance and Accounting), No. 7 (20 July 1979), in *CREA*, No. 30 (28 November 1979), pp. 26–30.

Ma, Hong, 'On several questions of reforming the economic management system', *JJYJ*, Peking, No. 7 (20 July 1981), pp. 11–24.

Meisner, Mitch, 'The Shenyang Transformer Factory – a profile', *China Quarterly*, No. 52 (1972), pp. 717–737.

Mun, Kin-chok, 'China's management system and state enterprise behaviour', *Journal of Contemporary Business*, **10**, 3 (1981), pp. 29–45.

Ren, Tao and Hongqing Zheng, 'A brief discussion of synchronisation in reforming the economic system', *GMRB* (23 January 1982), in *FBIS* (10 February 1982).

Reynolds, Bruce L., 'Reform in Chinese industrial management: an empirical report', in Joint Economic Committee, U.S. Congress, *China Under The Four Modernizations*, Part I (Washington: 1982), pp. 119–137.

Sabel, Charles F. and David Stark, 'Planning, politics and shop-floor power: hidden forms of bargaining in Soviet-imposed state-socialist societies', *Politics and Society*, 11, No. 4 (1982), pp. 439–475.

Su, Lian and Rong Shi, 'Carry out enterprise consolidation in a down-to-earth manner', *PD* (12 October 1981) in *FBIS* (29 October 1981).

Tian, Fang *et al.*, 'Initial investigation on trial points in enlarging the autonomy of Chongqing's enterprises', *JJYJ*, 3 (20 March 1981), in *CREA*,

Watson, Andrew, 'The management of the industrial economy: the return of the economists', in Jack Gray and Gordon White (eds.) *China's New Development Strategy* (London: Academic Press, 1982), pp. 87–118.

White, Gordon, 'Urban Employment and Labour Allocation Policies in Post-Mao China', *World Development*, **10**, No. 8 (1982), pp. 613–632.

Wu, Jinglian, Shulian Zhou and Haibo Wang, 'Establish and improve the system of retaining earnings for enterprise funds', *PD* (2 September 1978) in *FBIS* (19 September 1978).

Xue, Muqiao, 'A probe into the question of changing the economic system', *JJYJ*, No. 6 (20 June 1980), pp. 3–11, in *CREA*, 81 (3 September 1980), pp. 1–19.

You, Lin, 'Planned production is primary, free production is supplementary', *JJYJ*, No. 9 (20 September 1980), pp. 3–9.

Zhang, Xiang, 'A summary of the discussions of the problem of expanding enterprise autonomy', *Wen Hui Bao*, Shanghai (12 May 1980) in *CREA*, No. 70 (21 July 1980), pp. 9–11.

Zhou, Shulian and Jinglian Wu, 'Rectification should be put in the position it deserves', *PD* (6 May 1981) in *FBIS* (13 May 1981).

Trends in Chinese Enterprise Management, 1978–1982

MARTIN LOCKETT and CRAIG R. LITTLER*

Imperial College of Science and Technology, London University

Summary. – Economic reforms in relation to industry have passed through three phases, centred on (i) expanded autonomy for experimental enterprises in 1978–80, (ii) 'economic responsibility systems' in 1981–82, and (iii) 'consolidation' particularly of large enterprises from 1982. While limited in scope, the reforms to date have had a significant impact on management practices. In addition there have been moves towards greater industrial democracy, involving the election of managers and workers' congresses. In practice, however, the degree of democracy is limited and varies widely between plants and regions. Another aspect of change has been a greater emphasis on the smaller urban collective enterprises. Overall reform policies face substantial inertia, a half-way house which may lead to worse long-term economic problems than either more rigid planning or further reform.

1. INTRODUCTION

Since 1978, there have been a number of policies designed to reform the way in which industrial enterprises operate in China. These are associated with more general ideas of 'economic reform' similar to those undertaken from the 1960s in various Eastern European economies, notably Hungary, and to some extent in the USSR. Such economic reform is primarily concerned with relationships between enterprises, and between enterprises and the state, and attempts to provide a method to overcome the problems of central planning, particularly in a more advanced industrial economy. So one aspect of enterprise management which this article considers is the context of economic reform in the industrial sector as a whole which has taken place since 1978.

But we are also concerned with intra- as well as inter-enterprise relationships as these are essential to an understanding of how enterprise management has changed in China. After our initial examination of general economic policy towards industrial enterprises, we therefore turn to the impact of economic reforms on the structure and process of management. We then focus more specifically on one aspect of these questions — that of the demo-cratization of industrial management. This is because part of the overall 'package' of reform (which Chinese economists and others have proposed) consists of measures to increase the degree of 'democratic management' in Chinese industry. We have therefore examined both the extent of any democratization of industry and the links between this and economic reforms at the inter-enterprise level — the latter being a controversial question amongst a number of analysts of contemporary China. Our focus is on two policies in particular: the election of managers and the creation of elected workers' congresses in industrial enterprises.

Next, the changes in the role and management of smaller-scale urban 'collective' industry are analysed, as most of the paper concentrates on the larger-scale state-owned enterprises. Finally, we draw some conclusions regarding

* The research on which this paper is based is supported by a project grant from the Social Science Research Council, as well as being assisted by the British Academy/SSRC exchange scheme with the Chinese Academy of Social Sciences. We are grateful for the help of the Institute of Industrial Economics, Beijing, and the Guangdong, Sichuan and Shanghai Academies of Social Science in 1981 and 1982. Our thanks also go to Joan Wright for typing the article and conference paper on which it was based.

the state of economic reform and industrial management in China today: to what extent has there been a genuine process of reform or is the system in a state of inertia while reform remains just an idea? To what extent are the overall economic reforms linked with democratization of industrial enterprises? Can reform provide an answer to the short- and long-term problems of Chinese industry?

2. THE EVOLUTION OF POLICY TOWARDS INDUSTRIAL ENTERPRISES: 1978–1982

Looking at recent economic policy in China, 1978 is a key date, in particular the December 1978 Party Central Committee 'Third Plenum'. For it was at that meeting that economic reforms were given a top-level go-ahead and assigned high priority. Since then economic reform has been on the agenda as a policy goal. However, its relative importance and immediacy in policy terms has changed over the last five years, as we show below. In fact it is possible to identify three phases of policy: first, reform through *experimental enterprises* with expanded autonomy; second, a focus on the setting up of *'economic responsibility systems'*; and third, emphasizing the *'consolidation'* of industrial enterprises. These phases are not distinct, for since 1979 they have all fallen under the general policy slogan of 'Readjustment, Reform, Consolidation and Improvement' (*tiaozheng, gaige, zhengdun, tigao*). Rather, these phases show how the emphasis in policies towards industrial enterprises has differed from 1978 to 1982, although it would be mistaken to see each phase as totally replacing the policies of the previous one.

(a) *Phase one: experimental enterprises, 1978–1980*

From 1978, various pilot schemes expanding enterprise autonomy began in the state sector. The most well known is the 'Sichuan experiment' which started with six of the province's enterprises in October 1978, giving them a variety of new powers over production, marketing, management and finance (Shehei Kexue Yanjiu (1980); Chen, 1982). Another less well-known experiment was in Qingyuan County, Guangdong, which started at the same time and by November 1978 involved all 17 local state enterprises in the county (Zeng, 1980). These experiments soon expanded to cover more enterprises and other areas of the country. Thus in Sichuan, the number of enterprises involved grew to 100 at the start of 1979 and to over 400 in 1980. Other areas were slower to start experiments, but by 1980 experimental enterprises had been created in nearly all areas of the country. National figures showed that 1300 enterprises were involved in early 1979, growing to 2600 in October that year, 3358 in April 1980 and 6600 at the end of 1980. Although this figure only represents under 10% of the number of state-owned enterprises in China, the experimental enterprises were by no means randomly chosen as these 6600 enterprises accounted for about 60% of total output value and 70% of profits.[1] In short, they tended to be the larger, more profitable and better-managed enterprises.

There were considerable regional variations in the form of experiments. Some provinces were slower to start than others, while the powers given to enterprises also differed. This was a result of the combination of national policy guidelines with provincial and lower-level implementation. In particular the powers given to enterprises in Sichuan from 1978 were greater than those in the national guidelines published in 1979. However the key features were similar and included:

(a) *Profit retention*

At the heart of the experiments was the right of enterprises to retain and utilize part of their profits. Previously state enterprises' profits were handed over to the state more or less *in toto*. The experimental enterprises were able to keep a percentage of their profits for (i) re-investment for production and technical innovation, (ii) workers' and staff individual bonuses, (iii) collective welfare, such as housing and nurseries, and (iv) reserve funds.

In practice there were a number of schemes. The main ones have been: (i) *progressive profit retention*, in which a basic sum is more or less guaranteed in line with past policies if the enterprise meets its main targets, but a larger proportion of the increase in profits from one year to the next is retained by the enterprise; (ii) *simple profit retention*, in which the enterprise retains a fixed percentage of all profit made; and (iii) a *tax system*, in which enterprises formally assume responsibility for their own profit and loss. Instead of retaining a proportion of profit they change to a system of retaining all their profit but paying various taxes to the state, in particular 'income tax' on their value added, a 'revenue equalization tax' to adjust for the differing profitability of the sector in which they operate, and a 'fixed assets tax' which is a percentage of the book value of their fixed assets. This tax system is a fairly radical change, as it implies that the enterprise is no longer assured of, say, being able to pay its wage bill if its performance is bad. As a result it must be seen as a more radical reform than the first two types.[2] However, it still applies only to relatively few enterprises — nationally only 191 out of the 6600 experimental enterprises were involved in it at the end of 1980 (*SWB*/FE/W1154/A/3).

The implication of these schemes is that enterprises have increased incentives to raise profits and hence to improve efficiency in the use of both human and natural resources. However, the use of profit as the indicator in a system with planned prices means that to some extent profit is realized as a result of the price system rather than efficiency. For example, in textiles until early 1983 natural cotton had a lower price than artificial fibres. This meant that two Shanghai textile factories with apparently similar size and efficiency could have profits differing by a factor of about 5 (Zhou, 1982, p. 20). The exact form of the incentives differs between the types, with, as Reynolds (1982) argues, the 'progressive' type giving the greatest incentive but also the largest scope for negotiation and gamesmanship in deciding targets.

(b) *Extension of planning and marketing rights*

Once enterprises have met the targets of the state plan, they can decide what to produce next. However, they also have to obtain the raw materials and other goods needed as inputs in many cases. Some guarantees were given that plan quotas would not be increased so that the motivation to innovate and reorganize would not be stifled, though it is unclear how much these have been respected. More significant has been the reduction in plan quotas in many areas of heavy industry as part of readjustment policies to shift the balance of production towards light industry. Some factories had state plan targets cut by as much as 50% leading to great freedom very suddenly!

Alongside these extended production planning powers have come more rights to market an enterprise's products. The extent of these again varies by sector. Thus the Sichuan No. 1 Cotton Mill can only market about 2% of its production outside state distribution channels as cotton cloth is a product for everyday use and thus in heavy demand. Other factories market more — for example the Chongqing

Clock and Watch Company marketed 15–20% of its output. In sectors of heavy industry this ratio is even higher (interviews, September 1981).

Parallel to these changes came greater rights to conduct foreign trade and to retain a proportion (around 5%) of foreign exchange earnings for importing foreign machinery etc., though Reynolds (1982, p. 133) states that often these rights were not honoured. In other cases, rights of direct marketing by enterprises have not been respected as in the case quoted by Lee (1981, p. 40) in Sichuan: 'A cannery . . . produced sixty tons of cans and requested the commercial department to absorb it but they did not give (an) answer. However, when the cannery succeeded in distributing the product and earned 40,000 dollars, the commercial department took 20,000 . . . without even giving a formal receipt. The cannery did not dare challenge the commercial department since it was afraid that the commercial department would make trouble for them.' Even when these new rights have existed, they have not always been adequately protected.

(c) *Increased flexibility in labour management*

So far, this has been a contentious area and changes have been on a limited scale. Theoretically, enterprises were given greater rights to recruit, promote and demote both cadres and workers as well as the power to sack workers on disciplinary grounds and to determine their own pay and incentive systems.

One aim here was to break the 'iron rice bowl' of workers and cadres in the state sector, i.e. the situation of each having a job for life with stable or increasing pay and little or no chance of losing one's job. However this new policy of restricting job security has met with resistance from government departments, economists and workers (see White, 1983). The result is that actual dismissals appear to have been rare and quotable cases hard to find. An example in 1980 was that the Sichuan No. 1 Cotton Mill dismissed only two workers and these were punished for long periods of absenteeism; this decision was approved by the mill's workers' congress. Most examples of dismissal on disciplinary grounds seem to have been extreme, although the picture is different at enterprises in China's 'Special Economic Zones' for foreign investors. However, some factories have reduced their workforce substantially, as in the case of the Shandong Experimental Plastics Factory which made about a third of its workforce redundant in 1982 because it was 'overstaffed and suffered a long term deficit' (*SWB*/FE/7199/BII/10, quoting *Dazhong Ribao*, 8/11/1982).

In fact, the 'flexibility' in labour management has been largely a matter of paying higher bonuses to workers. Wages seem to have increased significantly since the experiments began, and many of the experimental enterprises we visited were paying bonuses up to the maximum allowed by state directives — usually an average of two months' basic wage a year.

To sum up, the system of experimental enterprises has spread to most of the relatively large and successful state enterprises and has made some impact on the way they are run. The most important change is that of right to profit retention and the funds (and incentives) this gives to enterprises. But it is important to bear in mind that those promoting economic reform in China see it only as a first step in the right direction. While few Chinese economists today seek Yugoslav-style 'market socialism', something more along the lines of the Hungarian economic reforms *is* seen as desirable. This would mean increased separation of enterprises (as economic units) from direct state and Party control;[3] the replacement of detailed centralized planning at all levels by planning of the main features of the overall economy combined with direct inter-enterprise contracting; and a reform of the price system such that profitability more accurately reflected efficiency, thus increasing the role of the 'law of value' — a Marxist concept with an ambiguous meaning in current Chinese economic debates.

Whilst intended to have beneficial short-term effects, the reform strategy is essentially a major effort to increase the importance of intensive growth rather than extensive growth in the Chinese economy, i.e. to achieve economic growth by using resources (e.g. labour, capital goods and energy) more efficiently rather than by using more and more of them. In implementing this policy the aim is to stimulate technical innovation, both product and process, in existing enterprises rather than to rely upon

building new factories, perhaps using imported 'turnkey' plants. This is to some extent reflected in the tax concessions given to those enterprises making innovations (especially in Sichuan) and in the rights given to market new 'trial' products. For example, while the Sichuan No. 1 Cotton Mill had little control over most of its marketing (see above) it could market all of its own 'trial' products. To achieve this shift from extensive to intensive growth, the reforms made in the experimental enterprises needed both to be maintained and extended — with reform of the price system usually mentioned as constituting the major block by many 'reformers' in our discussions with them in autumn 1981. However, since late 1980 industrial enterprise policy has evolved in a different, though not entirely contradictory way. To see why that happened we need first to analyse the results of the experimental-enterprise phase.

(b) *Results from the experiments in enterprise autonomy*

What were the economic results of the enterprise autonomy schemes? As the reforms in Sichuan have been the most advanced, we will begin there with financial figures from the Provincial Economic Commission (interviews, September 1981) and Shapiro (1981, p. 7) as shown in Table 1.

The results for 1979 are clearly impressive, as (in general terms) were those for other areas (Lockett, 1981, Table 2). The performance of the experimental enterprises in both 1979 and 1980 were better than others according to all three of these criteria. The fact that profit growth exceeded that of output indicates some increased efficiency, presumably as a result of the incentive to reduce 'slackness' in the enterprise, though it could also be a result of changes in product mix (see below) or in accounting techniques. The increase in profits remitted to the state (after the enterprises

Table 1. *Results of enterprise autonomy experiments in Sichuan* (1979–1980)

	1979	1980
Output value	+14.9% (+3.2%)	+9.7% (+6.8%)*
Total profit	+33.2% (+6.9%)	+7.9% (?)
Profit remitted to state	+20.2% (+14.2%)	−0.7% (?)
No. of enterprises	100 (6000)	417 (5600)

Note: Figures in brackets are for enterprises *not* in the experiment, except * which denotes all enterprises.

retained their share) supported the reformers' contention that *both* state finances and enterprises could be better off as a result of the new incentives. However, the 1980 figures look less good, with profits remitted to the state actually decreasing. In part this was a result of various price adjustments in fuel and other inputs, as well as the impact of readjustment policies. In part due to severe flooding, the 1981 figures would look worse again, as industrial output in Sichuan grew by only 2% (Chen, 1982).[4] Thus the pattern seems to be one of diminishing effectiveness in the short term, a situation like that in the USSR in the mid-1960s where similar reforms were implemented (Lockett, 1981). It is still too early to judge their long-term effectiveness in stimulating innovation, but in the short term these disappointing results began to give ammunition to political critics of enterprise autonomy.

The explanation lies partly in prevailing economic conditions, particularly those flowing from the implementation of readjustment policies, and in the impossibility of getting rapid results indefinitely from simply taking up 'slack' in enterprises. But it also arises from the methodology of such experimentation, as the enterprises have not been selected randomly but purposively — they have been chosen because they are expected to do well by those favouring reform.[5] As a result, expansion of the experiment typically means reducing the 'bias' towards exceptionally good results, making the experiment appear less successful. However, other problems were even more important.

Some of these were clearly the result of the partial nature of the reforms achievable through experimental enterprises. There is no doubt that the present price structure is irrational if enterprise profitability is to be the key criterion for judging performance and distributing funds. Previously fixed prices were usually maintained, given the lack of price reform, meaning that enterprises seeking to maximize profits would often gain more by switching the product mix to profitable lines than by increasing efficiency. Differences between sectors could to some extent be adjusted for by using different profit retention rates, with all the ensuing problems of negotiating these. But within an enterprise (given that many of them are in a 'sellers' market'), the state plan acted as the major constraint on concentrating on high-margin products, and some enterprises ignored the plan. As a result, there was a contradiction between encouraging profit-maximization and satisfying social needs, with stricter planning being seen

as the alternative to a thoroughgoing price reform.

Associated with this was inflation. Since the early 1950s China has had a remarkable degree of price stability — with official consumer price indices showing increases of the order of 30% between 1950 and 1979 (*Zhongguo Jingji Nianjian*, 1981, VI-23), an average inflation rate of under 1% per annum. However, in 1980 prices began to 'shoot up' in Chinese terms with retail price inflation of 6% (Yao, 1981, p. 15). Given the emphasis placed on price stability in the past, such inflation was likely to lead to dissatisfaction, particularly amongst those whose incomes had not increased as a result of bonuses and other measures. While acceptance of higher inflation rates is a more or less inevitable consequence of reform, such problems were exacerbated by the 'irrational' price structure and the excess level of popular demand for consumer goods, particularly those of higher quality.

Another problem which a more complete reform could be expected to solve was the relationship between the state and enterprises. The lack of an effective legal framework meant that there was no stable boundary between enterprises and state industrial bureaux. As a result, managers experienced *ad hoc* changes of production-targets as well as the administrative transfer of machinery, equipment and staff disregarding the formal rights of the enterprise (Lee, 1981, p. 39).

Other problems relate to the lack of skills and experience in Chinese industry in such areas as auditing and accounting. This has given rise to a greater potential for corruption or the development of 'grey' areas where economic advantage is gained from breaking the spirit (if not the letter) of economic policies. For example, one of Sichuan's showpiece experimental enterprises, the No. 1 Cotton Mill, was accused of ¥ 2.4 million (£3/4 million) worth of tax evasion, mainly by inflating costs (*Jingji Guanli*, 1981, pp. 11 and 59). Nationally, economic crimes such as corruption seem to have increased dramatically with a total of 136,000 recorded in the first three-quarters of 1982 (Zhao, 1982, p. 23).

Within enterprises concern has been expressed that bonuses have been paid in a 'disorderly way', not being linked to productivity or other formal criteria. The State Council issued national regulations limiting the amount that enterprises can use for bonus funds in 1981, though these were relaxed a little later that year. But the extent of inequality of bonuses both within and between enterprises posed problems. If bonuses were to be limited, the incentives for workers in successful experimental enterprises would be reduced, and if bonuses were less constrained, those workers not in these enterprises would become dissatisfied. While the problem of income inequality is a continuing one, the new experiments threatened to upset the existing situation.

Perhaps the crucial factor in the evolution of policies towards industrial enterprises was the national impact of the reforms on the state budget. In the late 1970s about half the state revenue came from its share of enterprise profits, and much of the rest from 'industrial and commercial tax', a form of turnover tax on industrial and agricultural products. Between 1978 and 1980 the revenue from the profits of state enterprises had dropped by almost a quarter. Even though tax revenue rose, the state was faced with falling income and rising expenditure as a result of large-scale capital projects, increased wages, agricultural subsidies and employment-creation efforts. The result was a large budget deficit in 1979 of ¥ 17 billion and another of ¥ 12 billion in 1980. Though enterprise autonomy and profit retention did reduce the need for state expenditure, it could not be guaranteed that profits handed over to the state would increase as the experiments were generalized. Thus there was a need for policies which could guarantee that the state obtained revenue from increases in profit, as well as a choice of whether to extend reforms to make a more coherent overall system or to try to reimpose more centralized control.

Reformers around the end of 1980 saw the experimental enterprises as 'only an initial and transitional step in the reform of the whole economic system' (Tang, 1981, p. 58). However, others saw the dangers posed to the reform project by the problems associated with the experiments. Among these was the future premier, Zhao Ziyang, who had initiated the Sichuan experiment. In March 1980 he argued that 'We must not commit the same mistake as in the past when "a free rein leads to chaos, chaos forces us to rein in and once we rein in the thing becomes dead"' (Zhao, 1980, p. 2).[6] But opinion amongst top Party and state leaders was shifting away from giving priority to reform towards more short-term problems. The state budget crisis analysed above was one of these, while the other *main* question became that of 'readjustment'. The readjustment of the national economy was argued to be necessary in order to shift the balance away from concentration on heavy industry towards consumer goods, from high rates of accumulation to more moderate ones, and from productive towards non-productive investment. Those seeing readjustment as a priority saw the decentralization of decision-making powers to enterprises undermining the ability to pursue the readjustment policies determined by the centre. During 1980 the view that readjustment had to be given priority over reform gained ground, with the conclusion that only those reforms which promoted readjustment should be allowed. By December 1980 this had been discussed and approved by a Party Central Committee 'Work Conference' and became official policy (see Solinger, 1982). Thenceforth, enterprise autonomy experiments were to be limited to the 6600 already involved, and the phase of reform gave way to a new one in the industrial field.

(c) *Phase two: economic responsibility systems, 1981—1982*

One major aspect of these shifts in policy in 1980 was a shift back towards more centralized control, especially for major investment projects. Another was a cutback of heavy industry to such an extent that its output actually declined by almost 5% in 1981. But from the point of view of industrial management, the most important was the widespread introduction of 'economic responsibility systems' during 1981. This idea was put forward at the April 1981 national conference on industry and communications as a parallel to the 'responsibility systems' being adopted in agriculture. By July (at a State Economic Commission symposium) it was being presented as a 'breakthrough' in enterprise reorganization (Lu, 1981, p. 29), and especially during the second half of 1981 'responsibility systems' spread rapidly amongst state enterprises. What were they, and how did they work?

A first point to note is that the word 'system' implies more coherence than is in fact justified. As in agriculture, such 'economic responsibility systems' in industry tend to differ considerably, though essentially based on the definition of responsibilities and benefits through some form of contracting. Sun (1982, p. 1) defines an 'economic responsibility system' as one 'in which clearly defined responsibilities must be borne between the state and the enterprises, between enterprises among themselves, between various sectors within the enterprise and by workers in their productive activities. In simple terms, there is to be a sound system of economic responsibilities at all levels and for each person.'

Thus the idea of an 'economic responsibility system' is that it covers both inter- and intra-enterprise organization, and in both of these areas sets up rules to be followed. In practice, this has centred around contracts stipulating the enterprise's responsibility for its profit and loss in the inter-enterprise field and for payment systems within enterprises.

These contracts have typically been profit-sharing ones, with enterprises 'contracting' with the state to provide a certain volume of profits. If this target is exceeded, the above-quota profits are divided in fixed proportions between the state and enterprise funds. If there is a shortfall, the enterprise must hand at least a proportion of this to the state from its own funds. Broadly this resembles the 'progressive' form of profit retention in the 'experimental' enterprises, though it is tougher on enterprises not meeting profit targets. Enterprises involved here may not have some of the other rights of experimental enterprises. On the other hand, they can include loss-making enterprises, as they are given a target figure for losses, rather than a profit target. It seems that in many such schemes it was guaranteed that the system would remain unchanged for a period of two to four years.

Such 'economic responsibility systems' can be analysed in different ways, reflecting the alliance which agreed to their rapid diffusion:

(i) From the viewpoint of reforming the economic system, these changes maintained the status of the 6600 experimental enterprises. They also increased the scope of profit retention and enterprise profit and loss responsibility. So they can be seen as a disguised method for spreading economic reform, albeit at a reduced rate and under a different name.

(ii) From the viewpoint of improving the state's financial position, they give clear incentives to increase profits and hence to increase state revenue, as the state was guaranteed most of the profits above a quota (usually based on existing profit levels). In addition, it could tackle those loss-making enterprises largely ignored in the experimental enterprise schemes. As well as the incentive to reduce losses, a number of measures were taken to increase the control of state organization over loss-making units. For example, in Liaoning Province a set of eight regulations was formulated to try to eliminate loss-making commercial enterprises. These regulations included monthly reporting to province-level bureaux, cuts in managers' wages if 'mismanagement' led to losses in two successive years, the dismissal or transfer of incompetent managers, and the closure or merger of persistent loss-makers (*SWB*/FE/W1127/A/5–6, also Harris and Fine, 1981).

(iii) From the viewpoint of those advocating improved techniques of centralized planning rather than focusing on reform, the emphasis of policy shifted away from experimental enterprises towards 'industrial specialization and integration'. This meant creating industrial corporations with some powers over previously separate enterprises, aiming to cut down on duplicated production. So in 1980 over 5% of state enterprises underwent mergers or integration with others, and in 1981 even more were affected (*SWB*/FE/6878/BII/11–13). A nationally publicized example was the Chongqing Watch and Clock Factory which became the centre of a corporation involving 14 more factories employing a workforce of 11,000 and divided into specialized subgroups (interviews, 19 September 1981; Tang, 1981). To some extent such specialization was in line with reform ideas, but these policies are probably more in line with the type of economic policies pursued in the GDR which has maintained a more centralized planning system than, say, Hungary.

So aspects of 'economic responsibility systems' could be seized upon by those in favour of different strategies for longer-term economic development. In part this was because 'economic responsibility' was more a set of *ad hoc* measures than a coherent policy. While it was pushed strongly in many areas, it was not until November 1981 that the State Council issued a circular on the subject.[7] In the meantime, the picture that had emerged showed that the effects were not quite as had been intended. In the first place, it did not reverse the downward trend in profit remittances to the state budget, which fell again in 1981 to approximately 60% of their 1978 level, largely as a result of the severe impact of readjustment policies on heavy industry.

The profit-sharing aspect of 'economic responsibility' also led to problems. Compared with the care taken in calculating retention ratios for experimental enterprises, less was used in this phase, given the short time and large numbers of enterprises involved. The aim of getting quick results led to a tendency to make retention ratios for enterprises high. According to Sun (1982, p. 7) the system 'had neither objective foundations, nor was it based on detailed calculations'. So in practice the retention rates were probably higher than necessary to provide an adequate incentive for enterprises, leading to lower state revenue than would have been possible.

At the same time, the concentration on enterprise profit retention led to the same problems as were associated with experimental enterprises, but on a wider scale. Given the price system, some enterprises (as could be expected) went 'against the objectives of socialist production' by switching to more profitable product lines, reducing quality, raising prices and so on (Xu, 1982, pp. 4–5). Tax evasion was another problem, accentuated by inefficiency in tax collection agencies, with a nationwide investigation turning up ¥ 1.3 billion of tax evasions[8] (*Zhongguo Caimao Bao*, 1982). Other enterprises practised more creative forms of fraud, for example, unofficially making highly taxed products such as fridges on their welfare budget and making them available cheaply to their workers (see e.g. Liu, 1981, p. 85). Here again the limited economic reforms made such practices more possible than in a more rigidly controlled planning system while the incomplete nature of reforms made them more profitable than in a 'fully' reformed economy.

At the inter-enterprise level, therefore, 'economic responsibility' was a label for profit-sharing contracts between enterprises and the state. To implement the theory behind it, responsibility would have had to be extended both to inter-enterprise contracts and to more aspects of the state/enterprise relationship, as was subsequently realized by more perceptive Chinese economists and politicians who began to emphasize the importance of such measures as production costs and productivity (e.g. Gu, 1982; Xu, 1982, pp. 5–6). The logic of such analysis was that 'economic responsibility systems' could be 'merely a temporary emergency expedient' (Sun, 1982, p. 12) and not a substitute for either reform or more effective centralized planning.[9] By 1982, the problems of 'economic responsibility' had been recognized and the focus of policies again shifted to a new phase of 'consolidation'.

(d) *Phase three: consolidation, 1982 to date*

Given the problems of industrial management associated with the economic reforms and responsibility systems, and the widespread concern about the growth of corruption and other forms of economic crimes, the focus of attention shifted again — to the 'consolidation' of industrial enterprises. This was signalled by the State Council in late 1981 when it approved a set of proposals from the State Economic Commission designed as 'the most realistic method for tapping the potential of . . . enterprises, achieving better economic results, and increasing revenues' (*SWB*/FE/6877/BII/1). So what was this 'enterprise consolidation'?

The first point to make is that it was not a completely new policy, as two other 'consolidations' were already supposed to have taken place since 1976, though these were said to have been more limited (Xie, 1982, p. 2). A second is that it was aimed at the internal working of the enterprise, in particular its top managers, though covering many different aspects of its operations. Thirdly, its main method was generally to try to tighten up on these operations and to replace less competent leaders with more competent and younger ones. The State Economic Commission's 'six criteria' for consolidation covered a huge range of tasks, the most important of which were as follows (according to *Qiye Guanli*, 1982):

(1) reorganize enterprises' top management bodies;
(2) strengthen economic responsibility systems, especially those within enterprises rather than concentrating on profit sharing;
(3) consolidate basic management work, practising overall economic accounting and quality management (the latter being a priority in experimental enterprises);
(4) 'strengthen political and ideological work', especially 'directed at the widespread phenomenon of slack labour discipline existing in enterprises' and 'consolidating factory regulations';
(5) 'strengthen democratic management' (see below);
(6) 'consolidate financial and economic discipline', in other words to tackle such problems as corruption and dubious deals by enterprises.

What this has meant in practice is the sending into enterprises of teams, composed of officials from provincial and municipal industrial and Party organizations, to look at the way the enterprise is organized as well as to check up on its performance. As before, major elements of the policy are to raise state revenue and industrial efficiency, but the priorities now differ as the consolidation process has concentrated heavily on large enterprises. This concentration is based on the fact that (according to 1980 statistics) a mere 369 enterprises produce over 40% of the profits and tax handed over to the state while the top 1000 produce around 50% of state revenue from industry (*SWB*/FE/7180/BII/19—21). In terms of effort, concentrating on these large enterprises makes sense from the viewpoint of increasing state revenues, though less strongly from the viewpoint of *production* as these 1000-odd enterprises produce just under a third of output. For example, in Sichuan the province's governor made it clear that in 1982 consolidation would cover only '40 enterprises which pay high taxes or turn in high profits' and that the criteria for consolidation were to be quality, output, 'economic result' and 'the magnitude of . . . contribution to the state'. Further, 'Any enterprise failing to pass the examination will have to be reorganized again' (Lu, 1982, pp. 35—36).

Thus the focus had shifted from inter-enterprise and state-enterprise relations to the internal management of factories as the key to industrial growth and efficiency — as well as to solving the continuing problem of the state budget.[10] This involved changing the top management to make it more skilled in technical and business issues as well as tightening up labour discipline and organization. It is too early to judge the results of this policy, in part due to the fact that it is scheduled to be implemented over a two to three year period (1982—1984). But like the 'economic responsibility system' phase, concentration on 'consolidation' is more of a temporary policy than a coherent plan. That it could be agreed to so fast indicates that it can be backed by those supporting conflicting long-term strategies of economic development, by both 'economic reformers' and proponents of central planning. In this respect, it cannot be seen as a long-term solution and concentration on 'consolidation' tends to obscure long-term strategic questions. But the aim of improving the standard of management is probably a necessary precondition for the success of any strategy, while the need for such improvement has become more acute with the limited reforms implemented so far. We will therefore turn our attention to this question of the changing demands on management.

3. CHANGING DEMANDS ON MANAGEMENT

The process of economic reform poses a number of problems for those managing an enterprise. It requires a variety of new skills, notably in the areas associated with determining inputs and outputs (sales and marketing, and to a lesser degree buying), economic calculation (e.g. accounting and enterprise planning), and technology (especially in feasibility and similar studies for innovation). It also implies changes in other areas of management, for example, labour management. In short, according to Wan Xiang (1980), it implies a transition 'from bureaucrat to manager', and poses major problems for existing managerial personnel. In concrete terms the educational and professional level of many Chinese industrial managers is relatively low, as recent surveys have shown.[11] In addition, the more technically competent managerial and technical personnel may not be in senior positions within the factory, as they tend to be younger and more recently trained. These problems are compounded by the relatively centralized system of cadre allocation, through which factories may find, say, technically incompetent ex-PLA cadres put in senior production management posts.

Thus, both enterprise-level experiments and wider economic reforms pose problems both of the level and type of managerial expertise at enterprise level, and the way in which managers are allocated to jobs. The great expansion of enterprise management training for existing managers since 1977, the formation of the Enterprise Management Association, the publishing of texts on management and the establishment of management courses in higher education, are all attempts to raise the managerial and technical level of Chinese enterprise management. Combined with increased attention to workforce training these may contribute to reducing the problems of shortage of qualified and experienced management personnel. However, this shortage has always existed, and it will be a relatively long time before a significant impact can be made. In the short term, therefore, even the limited economic reforms have exacerbated existing shortages of managerial skills by both increasing demand for these skills and posing new and unfamiliar demands on enterprise management. Thus the problem of an inadequate level of management skills will be a constraint both on the extension of economic reforms and on successful industrial performance for some time.

So a crucial part of the context of Chinese industrial management is a gap between the level and type of management skills available and those which economic reforms would 'ideally' require. A technocratic view of Chinese industrial management would see this gap (combined with questions of appropriate forms of management organization) as the key to industrial progress. Whilst these are clearly important issues it is also vital to consider relations between managers and the workforce. For past Chinese policies, notably one-man management in the 1950s, ran into substantial resistance from the workforce whilst a reliance on material incentives in the form of bonuses in the early 1960s gave rise to a number of conflicts which were not easily resolved. In addition the policies pursued during and after the Cultural Revolution called into question many aspects of these relations between workers and managers, for example, the emphasis on the 'two participations' — workers in management, and cadres in manual work. The Cultural Revolution had a major impact on the Chinese working class. On the one hand, it gave workers a limited say in some areas from which they had previously been excluded and led to the airing of many critical ideas as well as reducing managerial control in areas such as labour discipline, which has resulted in greater problems of managerial legitimacy than in many socialist countries particularly amongst younger workers. On the other hand, the wages and other material benefits of workers broadly stayed the same for over 10 years (for example, average earnings in state enterprises were ¥ 595 in 1957 and ¥ 602 in 1977), reducing the material incentives for better work at either an individual or collective level. Thus, dissatisfaction with wages and incentives, and the problem of how to deal with the divisions within the workforce over the fairness of new material incentives, posed constraints for enterprise management.

These problems have been exacerbated by the switches in policy over the last two decades as well as the changing nature of the industrial workforce. The policy changes reduce the potential for incentive schemes to work as people are always suspicious of their permanence. Also, although reliable figures are not available, it does appear that absenteeism and other forms of labour 'indiscipline' increased substantially during the 1970s. Generally, the current supply of younger workers does not have the experience of older ones, particularly those who worked before Liberation or even the 1950s and early 1960s. In particular, they do not have experience of emphasis on economic efficiency and also, in some cases, of fairly strict managerial control to achieve this aim. In Shanghai surveys indicate that the number of workers with pre-1949 experience is only 4% and that young workers who began working in factories in the 1970s are now a majority of the workforce (*Jiefang Ribao*, 1981). This has been accentuated by recent policies designed to solve youth unemployment, which have 'replaced a large number of skilled old workers with unskilled young ones' (Yang, 1982, p. 23). In practice this has created problems for managers concerning their own legitimacy as these younger workers are less likely to passively accept management orders, while their lack of skills and experience may make previous forms of managerial control less effective.[12]

For these reasons, a number of Chinese economists and reformers began to see the relations of managers and workers at the enterprise level as a key issue. It was argued that without greater commitment from the workforce, economic reforms would not succeed — or at least would be impeded. As a result, reform of enterprise management systems was needed. As well as general questions of the relationship between the CCP and economic organizations, the potential role of democratization of enterprises was discussed.

Thus, Ling (1979) saw 'democratic management' as one of the five conditions for success in economic reform. For Ling argued (1979, p. 8),

> The expanded financial powers of the enterprise . . . must be based on an expansion of the democratic rights of the employees; otherwise petty bureaucratism will supplant big bureaucratism, a command mentality on the part of factory heads and [Party] secretaries will replace the command mentality on the part of administrative leadership, and the system reform will turn out to be a reform in name only.

Such views have been put forward by other economists, who have also noted trends to worker-participation in advanced capitalist economies (e.g. Wan, 1980; Jiang, 1980) and criticized Soviet industrial management for its lack of democracy (Wan, 1980; Liu, 1979). Democracy in management was also seen as a guarantee against the type of degeneration of socialist enterprises noted in earlier Chinese criticisms of self-management (Jiang, 1980, pp. 69–70; see also Lockett, 1981). Generally, in the conception of economic reform held by a number of influential economists, some form of democratization of management was seen both as a means of resolving problems and conflicts (e.g. in the area of labour discipline) and as a means of realizing socialist ideals of making workers the 'masters of enterprises'.[13] The question of the methods by which this could be done was a complex one, as well as being subject to the decision-making structures of the CCP. In practice, the approach adopted was, to a large degree, a return to the policies of the mid-1950s, and was first outlined in late 1978 by Deng Xiaoping, who announced policies to promote the election of managers and the formation of workers' congresses. These reforms have, at least in theory, been the basis of changes towards a more democratic form of industrial management and will be examined in the next section.

4. DEMOCRACY AND ECONOMIC REFORM

(a) *Election of managers*

At the Ninth National Congress of the All-China Federation of Trade Unions in October 1978, Deng Xiaoping announced that 'workshop directors, section chiefs and group heads in every enterprise must in the future be elected by the workers in the unit' (*Beijing Review*, 20 October 1978, p. 7). From 1978 official CCP policy was to start a process of encouraging the election of managers (below the level of factory directors) which constituted a new development in industrial democracy in China. From the point of view of the leadership, what are the advantages of advocating this form of shop-floor democracy?

A preliminary analysis suggests that election of managers appears to solve some of the problems of managerial legitimacy, a legitimacy which had been seriously eroded by the impact of the Cultural Revolution and other factors outlined in the previous section. However, whilst pressures for democratization and problems of workforce motivation were significant factors behind the new policy-line, we would argue that the crucial factor was the desire of the CCP and State leadership to improve the efficiency of management and to reform the cadre system.

The objectives of the new leadership were to create a technically skilled managerial stratum, removing, as far as possible, the cadres who owed their position to political manoeuvring and patronage rather than competence. Such a policy objective faced a number of problems: first, despite the upheavals of the Cultural Revolution years, the system of lifetime tenure for cadres was so deeply entrenched that removal of managers was likely to be bitterly resented and would increase middle-level opposition to the reform programme as a whole. The new regime did not feel able to override such resentments by a process of new appointments from above because there was a second general problem, namely the credibility of the

Party. As Gray (1982, p. 302) points out, the Party had destroyed much of its own moral authority in the Cultural Revolution with young workers being particularly disillusioned. But beyond the general problem of the position of the Party lay the third difficulty: the new leadership had a deep distrust of many of the local and factory-based party committees who would be responsible for implementing a top-down 'rooting-out' of incompetent managers.

Faced with these problems of the mechanisms of legitimating an intended change in the management of enterprises, the appeal of factory elections was obvious. Whilst opposition to an election process did exist, it was intrinsically more difficult to justify resistance to removal of cadres by the workforce, who, in the official ideology of the CCP are 'masters of the enterprise'. Moreover, there was good reason to hope that the outcomes of elections would be, from a technocratic viewpoint, as good or better than appointments from above. Given the constraints on enterprises, the pressure for profits (or the reduction of losses) and the moves towards linking workers' incomes to economic performance, managers with inadequate technical training and administrative ability are unlikely to prove popular with workers. Thus it was hoped that the main target of an intended shake-up of management would be hit by democratic elections, especially as in all cases higher level state and Party organizations have the right to vet elected candidates.

To what extent has this election of managers been implemented? The available data is summarized in Table 2 which makes it clear that, although the system of elections still does not cover the majority of enterprises, nevertheless (on the face of it) the shift towards the election of shop-floor managers has proceeded remarkably quickly. However, we know of no explanation for the apparent decline in the election of workgroup leaders. This may be because of the usual problems with Chinese statistics, such as different methods of data collection, or it may reflect a real decline in elections at grassroots level. Certainly there have been problems concerning elections, and we encountered one case (the Chongqing Clock and Watch Company) where the election of workgroup leaders had been abandoned after a brief trial in 1980 for reasons that were far from clear (Interviews, 19 September 1981). More generally, there has been a significant degree of managerial opposition to elections, with a variety of objections to control-from-below expressed in terms of the supposed

Table 2. *Election of managers*

	June 1980	% of state ind. enterprises	June 1982	% of state ind. enterprises
Workgroup and section leaders	33,200	40	29,400	35
Workshop directors and deputy directors	11,000+	13	14,800	18
Factory directors and deputy directors	1000 approx.	1	8900	11

Sources: *SWB* (14 March 1981); *SWB* (12 June 1981); Interview with ACFTU (8 September 1981); *Beijing Review* (28 June 1982). The base for the percentages in 84,000 — see Lockett, 1982, p. 226. Percentages are rounded. The June 1980 figures were said to be based on 'incomplete statistics'. It is not clear when the 'June 1982' figures were actually collected.

need for secrecy in management work and the possibility that the workforce will not make the 'right' choice (e.g. see Xinhua, 1980). Moreover, the spread of elections has not been uniform. In Guangdong Province it proved unusual for us to find a factory which had *any* form of elections during a research trip in 1982. For example, at the Guangzhou No. 2 Cigarette Factory there were no elections of any kind and the factory director was definite that there were no such plans for the future (Interview, 29 September 1982).

Table 2 also indicates that the extension of elections to senior managers and especially factory directors has been a more limited process. This was certainly our impression in Sichuan Province where it was stated in 1981 that only *one* of the 400-odd experimental enterprises had an elected factory director. In Guangdong Province, representatives of the Economic Commission stated that they knew of only a handful of firms (out of 5280 state enterprises) where the factory director was elected (Interview, 5 October 1982). By contrast, at the end of September 1982, 447 enterprises in Beijing had elected their directors (*SWB*/FE/7204/BII/16).

Despite the obvious slowness of some provinces in changing over to the election of factory directors, the views of the top Party leadership were clarified by the 'Provisional Regulations on the Work of State Factory Directors' issued in 1982. These stipulate that in all state enterprises workers' congresses should elect their directors who are then approved by higher authorities (*SWB*/FE/7204/BII/16; see also the views of Feng Wenbin, 1980, p. 20). Presumably it is such high-level support which has resulted in a particularly rapid advance of election of factory directors from 1981 (when a figure of around 1000

was still being quoted) to the 1982 total of 8900.

Apart from the diffusion of factory elections, there is the question of methods. In general, the method of election has not been standardized. Indeed, as with the local government elections at county level, there seems to be a good deal of confusion and ignorance about representative democracy (Goodman, forthcoming). Some of the elections have been contested ones, and some not; some of the elections have involved secret ballots, e.g. the Zigong Steel Casting Plant in Sichuan (Su, 1982, p. 105), whilst others have involved votes at public meetings, for example, the Beibei Glassware Factory, Sichuan (Interview, 20 September 1981). In relation to factory directors, some of the elections have been direct, whilst most have been limited to the representatives of the workers' congress (Interview with the Beijing Municipal Trade Union Council, 10 September 1981). Perhaps most crucially, the pattern of nomination has varied from factory to factory. Generally, most of the argument goes on *before* the election, so the process of nomination is crucial. In some cases the trade union collects opinions amongst the workers and produces a list of names — as at the Beibei Glassware Factory; in other cases, standing committees of the workers' congress perform this task, e.g. the Guangzhou Linen and Silk Company (Interview, 28 September 1982), whilst at other enterprises the Party plays a significant role.

The Beijing Leather Products Factory provides an interesting indication of the development of factory elections. It was stated that most of the top factory management including the director himself were 'elected'. Detailed questioning made it clear that the present factory director having taken up his post in

1978 was elected by the workers' congress in 1981. There were no other candidates. Having been elected, the factory director submitted a list of five other deputy directors to the congress for discussion and approval. These nominations were then accepted by congress and the managers duly 'elected' (Interview, 5 September 1981). This example illustrates some of the problems in talking about democratic elections in China: the potential for manipulation is considerable, and even where this does not occur, higher administrative levels and the Party may still exert considerable influence. Candidates may not be nominated or voted for if it is known that their election would not be approved.

In sum, since 1978 there have been extensive moves towards the election of lower-level managers and surprisingly large steps towards the election of factory directors. However, elections have faced problems of obstinate opposition from middle-level cadres, who see their power and privileges being challenged if they are subject to control from below. Moreover, even if elections do occur, industrial democracy in China takes place subject to a higher-level veto power on the outcomes.

(b) Workers' congresses

Workers' congresses consisting of elected representatives of the workers and staff of an enterprise are not new: they have existed at various times in Chinese industry. They were abandoned in the Cultural Revolution, although various other types of representative bodies (usually excluding staff members) did play a significant role especially in the late 1960s and early 1970s. However, since 1978, workers' congresses have been promoted more systematically than in the past and their powers have been extended. An indication of this continuity, broken by the Cultural Revolution, is provided by the Guangzhou Linen and Silk Company: their congress was first set up in 1958 and ran through until 1966. It was re-established in 1975 and has continued to function since then (Interviews, 28 September 1982; also see *Beijing Review*, 8 June 1979).

Our research data (covering 29 factories) indicates that workers' congresses re-emerged between 1975 and 1979, although there was no formal national framework for their operation until June 1981, when the 'Provisional Regulations Concerning Congresses of Workers and Staff Members in State-Owned Industrial Enterprises' were promulgated. These regulations make it clear that the congresses are not to be seen as simply consultative or advisory bodies, but are the 'organs of power' through which workers and staff are to take part in decision-making to supervise cadres (Article 2). The main powers of the workers' congresses set out in Article 5 are:

(1) to scrutinize the directors' production plans and budgets;

(2) 'to discuss and decide on the use of the enterprise's funds for labour protection', welfare (including housing allocation), and bonuses;

(3) to decide about any proposed changes in the structure of management, the payment system or training;

(4) to supervise leading cadres, to the extent of making reports to the higher authorities;

(5) to arrange the elections of leading cadres.

The power (on paper) of workers' congresses is therefore wide-ranging, but other clauses in the 1981 Regulations make it clear that this is no charter for workers' control. In particular, Article 3 spells out that decision-making powers of the congress must be exercised in accordance with the Party's principles and policies.

Apart from the leadership of the enterprise Party committee, the other centre of power within the post-Mao factory is the management hierarchy. What happens if there is a policy difference between congress and management? The answer to this question is not clear in the Regulations, but if the factory director obtains the support of higher officials in, say, the industrial bureau then Article 7 would come into play:

> When a workers' congress differs with a decision or directive from the higher organ of the enterprise, (*qiye zhuguan jiguan*), it may put forward its own suggestions. If the higher organ decides to uphold the original decision or directive after discussing and examining the congress' opinion, the workers congress *is obliged to carry out the decisions or directives*.

Clearly workers' congresses are a *limited experiment in participation*. Moreover, as Saich (1982) underlines, the power of the congresses are further restricted by the fact that they are not permanent bodies. Article 11 specifies that congresses will not have a standing committee; instead, the enterprise trade union undertakes administrative work before and after a congress is convened and is its 'working organ' (Article 16). However, it is intended that meetings will be convened at least every six months (Article 12).[14]

According to the Regulations, representatives are elected by the workers and staff (including managers) for a two-year term of office and are subject to recall. These rules are similar to those prevailing in Yugoslavia in relation to workers' councils. In addition Article 8 of the Chinese regulations specifies that workers must constitute at least 60% of representatives with 'appropriate representation' guaranteed to technical and administrative staff, young workers and women workers. However, as the Yugoslav experience indicates, numerical representation does not necessarily lead to significant influence (e.g., see Ramond, 1979).

The general picture across China seems to be that the institutionalization of workers' congresses has been more successful than that of the election of managers. Indeed, the growth of workers' congresses has been fairly rapid since the introduction of new management policies in late 1978. This was partly a result of imitation of the *forms* of workers' congress which had existed in the 1950s and 1960s. Table 3 gives some indication of the spread of workers' congresses by autumn 1981.

Table 3. *Extent of workers' congresses in certain areas*, 1981

Area	% of state enterprises
Beijing	88
Shanghai	80
Sichuan	60
Shandong	60
Guangdong	40

Sources: Interviews, 1981; Harris and Fine, 1981; *Nanfang Ribao*, 26 October 1981.[15]

From the end of 1981 there have been concentrated efforts to introduce workers' congresses to all large and medium enterprises and achieve a near-total coverage in all the major industrial cities (*Beijing Review*, 28 June 1982). For example, representatives of Guangzhou Trade Union Federation claimed that by October 1982, 90% of all industrial and communication units in Guangdong has established workers' congresses (Interview, 4 October 1982), a 125% increase over the previous year. Of course there are still areas (primarily the outer, less industrialized provinces such as Guangxi) which are reporting a lower density of congresses.[16] Even in the Special Economic Zones some efforts have been made to set up workers' congresses, though not in the foreign-owned or foreign-dominated enterprises (Interviews, September/October 1982).

The rapidity of the diffusion of such congresses raises questions about their effectiveness in providing workers with channels of influence and communication. Some early reports of workers' congresses indicated that they were just consultative bodies and their influence was low (e.g. *FBIS*, 7 December 1978). This lack of influence was reflected in Chinese criticisms of some of them being 'held . . . only for the sake of formality' and so not gaining 'the wide attention of the masses of workers' (Lin, 1980, pp. 6 and 8), or as 'nothing but rubber-stamp organizations without real power' (Qian, 1980, p. 16). Even in February 1982, *Gongren Ribao* was urging workers and managers to 'Make a success of this year's workers' congresses', and warning against formalism:

> If we hold a congress for the sake of holding a congress, without adequate preparations and without laying the situation before the masses and presenting them with the facts, the congress will merely be a formality to give workers' representatives the chance to raise their hands. This kind of formalistic workers' congress is a completely futile exercise. (*Gongren Ribao*, 22 February 1982, p. 1.)

Apart from Chinese criticisms and exhortations, some Western observers have viewed the re-emergence of workers' congresses with scepticism, arguing that beyond the ritualized performances 'the powers of workers to intervene directly in the running of enterprises either through assertion of their economic rights or in political criticism of management was to be substantially reduced and henceforth channelled through the Party' (Henley and Chen, 1981, p. 90).

Detailed evidence with which to assess the above arguments is still lacking. Analyses by the Chinese trade unions in 1981 led to statements that only a quarter of congresses were performing their job well, 60% were 'not so effective' and 15% were in a dormant state (Interview with the ACFTU, 8 September 1981). Another small piece of evidence can be provided by asking shop-floor workers two questions: 'Do they know who their workers' congress representative is?' and 'Do they know what was discussed at the last meeting of the congress?' As most readers will be aware, asking such questions on a Chinese factory floor hardly amounts to survey conditions. Nevertheless, the results are interesting. Out of 25 workers interviewed in nine different factories in Guangdong, only five knew the identity of their congress representative, whilst only two knew what had been discussed at the last meeting of the congress. For example, a young apprentice working at the Guangzhou Watch Company in the final assembly shop had no idea about the workers' congress. It could be argued, and was argued by the factory director, that this young worker had not been in the factory for very long. However, in the Guangzhou No. 2 Cigarette Factory an experienced worker who had been there for ten years and who was working on a British-made Molins cigarette machine tool proved to be equally ignorant. In the Shenzhen Printing Factory, which was a model experimental plant with a workers' congress electing the factory director, a worker on a German Web offset machine in the Printing Shop not only knew nothing of the workers' congress but did not know that the election of the plant director had taken place. (Interviews in 1982 in nine enterprises in Guangdong Province including two factories in Shenzhen Special Economic Zone.)

Given the low rates of participation and low degree of knowledge shown by many British workers about various industrial democracy schemes, perhaps the results above should not surprise us.[17] Nevertheless, it does suggest that the Chinese criticisms concerning 'formalism' should be taken seriously, and that any claims to have achieved widespread grassroots industrial democracy in Chinese factories should be treated sceptically.

The above argument does not necessarily mean that all congresses are 'rubber-stamp' operations: a group of activists may provide a significant check on managerial decision-making. Is there any evidence that this is happening? So far the evidence suggests that workers' congresses have achieved some influence over the areas of factory housing and collective welfare. The funding and allocation of housing has been one of the main areas of the congress's activities. In a number of cases they have taken over responsibility from management for the allocation of housing to workers, as the housing shortages in many areas make this a particularly contentious issue.

Beyond the areas of housing and welfare it is still unclear whether workers' congresses are generating policy alternatives and actively monitoring the performance of management. Investment and budget decisions are, of course, crucial long-term policy decisions and it should be remembered that in the 6600 experimental enterprises it is the workers' congress which formally decides the division of *retained profits* between reinvestment, collective welfare and bonuses.[18] In practice this power is limited by various local and state regulations. Neverthe-

less, within these regulations (and sometimes outside of them) the congresses have seemed to be a pressure point towards increased bonus provision as well as increased welfare spending.

Some economists, notably Ma Hong (1980) and Jiang Yiwei (1980) have put forward the radical proposal that the workers' congress replace the Party committee as the main policy-making body in the enterprise – a move towards the Yugoslav type of system within enterprises. The issues involved here are not just those of industrial democracy, perhaps more important is that of the appropriate role for the Party. The advocates of self-management are seeking to extricate the Party from day-to-day management and the detailed aspects of production so that any failures to achieve economic or production success are not laid at the door of the Party. This policy-line did lead to a small-scale experiment approved by the State Council and involving 44 enterprises beginning in 1980. However, some of these factories have suspended this experiment in self-management, and during 1982 there was little debate over the proposals to make the workers' congress the policy authority. (For a fuller account of this debate, see Lockett, 1983, pp. 244–248.) Indeed, the emphasis of economists seems to have shifted, with, for example, Xue Muqiao warning in May 1982 that such self-management can degenerate into 'departmentalism' and,

> Therefore, the workers' autonomy in the State-owned enterprises is only allowed to be relative and not absolute. The leaders of the enterprises should not be responsible only to the workers' congresses of their enterprises. They should also be responsible to the organs at a higher level. This is especially true for the party committees. They should represent the common, long-term interests of the people of the entire country and should supervise the implementation of the state plans and the policies and decrees of the state in their enterprises. (*Guangming Ribao*, 19 May 1982, p. 3.)

So, although ideas of substantially expanding the role of workers' congresses have been proposed by influential economists and government advisers, the general climate of opinion now does not favour these, while the actual performance of workers' congresses as agents for industrial democracy is still limited.

5. CHANGES IN THE COLLECTIVE SECTOR

So far this paper has concentrated on changes in management in the state sector of industry.

To complement this, this section will look at how the situation of the urban collective sector has changed. First, some of the changes of views about the collective sector and how it should be run in theory are discussed, followed by an analysis of what has actually happened in the last two years. The urban collective sector is a significant part of the economy of China's towns and cities, particularly in terms of employment. In 1981 it had 25.68 million workers and staff — almost one-quarter of the national total (State Statistical Bureau, 1982). It also produces many 'daily use' consumer goods and services, as well as playing a role in new sectors such as electronics. As Table 4 shows, it is divided up into two main parts, both of which have substantial direct links with the local state apparatus, despite formally being owned by the workers in an individual enterprise or group of enterprises.

collectives faced discrimination in terms of labour, materials and energy allocation. 'Small' collectives, in which pay and benefits are lower, probably had greater variety in terms of the way they were run. However, some argued that the performance of 'small' collectives was better than 'big' ones as there was a smaller chance of subsidy and a closer link between economic performance and rewards. These were supported by case studies, for example, of enterprises which had made the transition 'upwards' from 'small' to 'big' and whose performance dropped sharply (Liang, 1980; Zhu, 1980). A further conclusion from the debates was that although in theory workers in collective enterprises had the right to elect managers and exercise ultimate control, actual practice was different (Li and Huang, 1979; Zhao, 1979).

From this debate came both an important

Table 4. *State and urban collective sectors* (*late* 1970s)

Type of enterprise	Formal ownership	Administrative superior body	Theoretical level of profit and loss responsibility (before economic reform)
State	Whole people	Specialized Municipal Bureau (or central Ministry)	All state enterprises
'Big' collective	Members of group of enterprises	Municipal Second Bureau of Light Industry (or specialized Municipal Bureau)	Group of enterprises
'Small' collective	Members of individual enterprise	District or Neighbourhood Management Bureau (under local government)	Individual enterprise

Theoretically, the suspicion of collective ownership and the assumption that it was inferior to state ownership has been challenged. In a debate which started around 1978 a number of research reports and more theoretical articles have seen advantages in collective ownership and have suggested that the state sector can learn from it (e.g. Liu *et al.*, 1980). One major aspect of this was an attempt to characterize the collective sector in terms of the reality of its operation rather than an idealized theoretical view. The broad conclusion was that 'big collectives' were operated in a similar way to state enterprises, except in the area of financing (e.g. *Guangming Ribao*, 1979; Xiao *et al.*, 1980, pp. 221–222) since the group of enterprises in a particular area was effectively self-financed. Also workers had lower pay and welfare than in state enterprises, and 'big'

theoretical question and a number of more concrete policy proposals. The theoretical question was whether it was correct to see a transition to state ownership as the long-term future for collective enterprises. While the past orthodoxy that this was 'correct' was implicitly or explicitly adopted by some, others such as Zhu (1980) began to challenge this, arguing that it was better to see both state and collective ownership moving towards a third form of 'direct social ownership'.[19]

In terms of more concrete policies, it was argued that there should be:
    (a) elimination of systematic discrimination against collective enterprises, e.g. in materials allocation;
    (b) increased effective profit retention by enterprises;
    (c) improved wages and conditions, with

removal of barriers to collective workers earning more than state sector ones, and restoration of year-end profit-sharing bonuses;

(d) reduction of direct control by state bodies, and greater separation between the local state apparatus and collective enterprises;

(e) greater independence in supply and marketing;

(f) more democratic management through implementing workers' theoretical rights;

(g) changes in the profit/loss responsibility system of 'big' collectives towards individual enterprise responsibility.

Most of these appear to have been accepted in principle by those involved in the debates, and have been emphasized in press reports and policy statements. There was, however, particular controversy over item (g) at the 1980 Conference on the Theory of the Urban Collective Economy in Shenyang, with critics of the 'big' collective system arguing that it was 'equalitarianism and indiscriminate transfer of resources' (*ping tiao*) rather than further progress towards socialism (*Zhongguo Baike Nianjian*, 1981, p. 401). Thus the changes advocated in the urban collective economy were broadly similar to those in the state sector, although they represented more the restoration of existing theoretical rights to collective enterprises and their workers than a new path of development. But in doing so, the importance of the collective sector had been re-emphasized, particularly in the development of smaller cities and towns where 'big collectives' linked with agriculture and other industrial enterprises were seen as a desirable model for development, as in Changzhou (Wu and Li, 1979) and Weihai (Xiao *et al.*, 1980).

In the area of increased autonomy and profit retention, some moves were made in Sichuan from about 1977 in the form of reduced taxes, although it seems that Liaoning was the first province to try to shift 'big collectives' systematically over to individual enterprise responsibility for profit and loss starting in mid to late 1979 (Zhu, 1980; Tian, 1980; *SWB*/FE/W1084/A/17; Zhuang *et al.*, 1981), a reform which has been followed elsewhere to a more limited extent. The proportion of after-tax profit retained by individual enterprises has also generally been increased, although there are regional differences in the systems used as well as differences between 'big' and 'small' collectives. In mid-1981, for example, in Shanghai 'small' collectives and an experimental group of 17 'big' collectives retained 40% of profits, while most 'big' collectives retained only 20%. In Sichuan in contrast 'big' collectives under the Second Light Industry Bureau retained 70% of after-tax profit.[20]

Some of the systematic discrimination against collective enterprises has been relaxed (for example, explicit rules that collective workers could not be better-off than state sector ones), although continuing complaints make it clear that it has by no means disappeared. One aspect of this is in payment systems, as bonuses have been reinstated including ones from profits at the end of the year. However, at least in Shanghai, changes in this area seemed to be slower than in the state sector with most collectives having standard bonuses not related to enterprise performance. Yet the relative wage level of collective sector workers did appear to be improving, particularly that of 'small' collective workers who are on basic wage scales fixed by the Shanghai Municipality. They had received an increase of over 10% as part of a shift from daily to monthly wage rates, and there were plans for further increases. Although these might be comparable to state or 'big' collective wages, the lack of welfare benefits and a low maximum for workers (¥ 42 or ¥ 45 in mid-1981 plus ¥ 3 bonus) still makes them an unattractive place for the longer term.

Democratization of the collective sector has been taking place but (as in the state sector) not as fast as might appear from policy statements. Some of the newer youth cooperatives may well be more democratic than more established ones, although no systematic information exists. But in many places such aspects of democracy such as elections of managers have only been implemented on a trial basis so far.

Finally, more general questions of management, the reforms in the collective sector as well as more general economic reforms, and the readjustment policies have a number of implications. One is that increased autonomy does pose new challenges, both to enterprises and to the local bureaux in charge of, or guiding, collective enterprises. Changing market conditions have led to greater pressure on less efficient units as well as competition on quality grounds. Even in expanding sectors such as small electrical consumer goods, which used to be a sector in which it was easy to survive even with low quality products, economic life has become tougher, due both to more enterprises producing goods and to price changes. Also, the economic readjustment and reforms increasing the extent of market allocation of raw materials and intermediate products have eased the supply problems of collective enterprises. To take an example, the very successful Shanghai Hongkou District 'Baihua' Electric Fan Factory has expanded not only by taking on new workers but also through 'takeovers' of less successful local collectives. The impact of reform and readjustment has been to change the main problem for management, from trying to obtain raw materials supplies from unused stocks in state enterprises and other unofficial means, to the marketing of the finished product.[21]

One can see the changes in industrial managements in the collective sector as broadly similar to those in the state sector, although specific features of its position in the economy do affect its development: In the course of these changes, one can see a reduction in the divergence between a theory of collective economy of democratic independent enterprises and the reality of the way they have been run in the past.

6. CONCLUSIONS

The evolution of industrial enterprise policy since 1978 has not been the smooth progression towards some form of market socialism based on quasi-independent production units envisaged by some reformers as well as some Western observers (e.g. see Watson, 1982, pp. 116–117). Indeed, some analysts argue that the economic reforms in industry are so marginal that 'the Chinese industrial enterprise today remains more tightly bound within a web of bureaucratic central planning than in most East European countries' (Reynolds, 1982, p. 119). But such a conclusion overstates the degree of inertia. It is true that there are severe obstacles to the reform process such as a lack of a legal framework, economic laws and institutions. As we have said, this has resulted in a lack of a stable boundary between enterprises and State bureaux, which could be exploited by those agencies (such as the State Bureau of Materials Supply and the Ministry of Foreign Trade) who appeared to resist economic changes. Moreover, bureaucratic inertia can be justified by (i) the financial problems created by the reforms, such as the threat of inflation after an era of price stability and the disastrous decline in central state revenues; and (ii) the apparent ideological problems, particularly the concerns about economic corruption. However, despite the obstacles to reform, our research indicates that the reforms have had a significant impact

in changing managerial behaviour in many provinces and that, for the moment at least, fundamental reform is still possible. Though the policies of economic responsibility in 1981 and enterprise consolidation in 1982 represent some concessions by market reformers to the widespread concern about inflation, economic crimes and profiteering, nevertheless China is now probably at the juncture which the Soviet Union reached in the late 1960s — the reforms can be swallowed up in a mire of political and financial difficulties or re-emerge as a major force in the mid-1980s.

The economic reforms in Eastern Europe (with the exception of Yugoslavia) left the internal organization of enterprises largely unchanged. The relations between managers and workers, and the respective positions of managers, party committee and trade union committee persisted in the same mould. This raises the point that there is no necessary link between economic reform and democratization. In practice, the Chinese leadership has linked the economic reforms to increased enterprise-level democracy. The enlargement of an enterprise's power to manage its own affairs has been seen to require a change in the system of leadership, but it is not yet clear how deep-rooted a linkage this is. At present the consolidation policy seems to shift emphasis away from democratization, partly because democratic ideas threaten certain segments of both Party and management.

In China at present it appears that the forms of democratic self-management may be diffused more rapidly than economic reform. But as we have argued above, there is a major gap between the form and the content of democracy in Chinese enterprises. The current powers of workers' congresses and the scope for electing managers are limited, although we did find that workers' congresses were often not just 'rubber stamp' bodies. It would require more research and more time to establish whether in China developments will be similar to those in Yugoslavia and elsewhere. It may well be the case that the emerging pattern is one where the workers' congress does exert some degree of control over issues relating to workers' welfare but is less influential in the area of business policy. In this latter area economic reforms tend to increase the need for managerial and technical expertise, and to reduce apparently powerful democratic bodies to the role of approvers of management policies.

Another issue raised is whether democratization would be possible without economic reforms above the enterprise level. Brus (1975) has argued that enterprise autonomy is a necessary precondition for the exercise of effective influence by workers. In the past the Chinese arguments had been like those of Bettelheim who argued that only with democratic planning could workers as a whole have control over industry. Our research indicates that there is a 'trade-off' as a result of economic reform in which the increased autonomy of enterprises does give rise to problems of, for example, inequality in wages (which are not seen as fair), yet centralized planning creates similar – or worse – results. Thus if Chinese industry were to be democratized further it will still require strong but limited elements of planning which are themselves responsive to the workforce.

The final question which we raised in the Introduction was whether the economic reforms provide any solution to the pressing problems of Chinese industry? The pushing of blame onto the 'Gang of Four' and much of the discussion of economic reform has ignored the fact that to a large extent China's problems are those of success rather than failure (see e.g. Xue, 1980, p. 37). Over the past 30 years China has succeeded in establishing an industrial base which makes it one of the world's leading producers of many industrial goods. Even in the so-called 'ten-year period of chaos', industrial production more than doubled. It is in the context of the *success* of this pattern of extensive growth (using large amounts of labour and capital) that current problems of poor product quality, productivity, technical level and lack of fit between supply and demand must be seen. In the longer-run, therefore, it is likely that a fairly full implementation of the economic reforms would lead towards a switch to a more intensive pattern of growth.

But there are two problems. The first, which has not really been encountered yet, is the social and economic cost of such a reform programme in such areas as inequality and competition as well as the possibility that price stability will be replaced by at least limited price inflation. This is clearly a political choice which has not been clarified. The second problem – the main one at present – is the cost of transition from the current situation to that envisaged by the reformers. The present state of *partial* reform is in many ways worse than either the alternatives of better planning or more reform. Many of the current problems attributed to reform are actually those either of transition or the lack of progress in areas like price structure. Thus the problems of the present state of limited reform are being used to discredit reform as a whole. Our view is that while there clearly are problems with the reform 'programme', its opponents do not recognize so clearly the problems of the Chinese economy and the management of industrial enterprises and do not provide a coherent alternative strategy for intensive growth to achieve the planned target of 7.2% increases in industrial output per year for the rest of the century.

Given the political divisions in China, it is possible that what appeared to be a decisive movement towards reform in 1978 and 1979 will turn to inertia. In the short-term this situation may appear beneficial but is likely to be harmful in the long run. The increased incentives to enterprises are offset by irrationalities such as those resulting from many enterprise 'economic responsibility systems'. Advocates of economic reform in China not only have to do more work on the nature of the balances between plan and market, and between democracy and direction, but also need to be able to show how the transition to this state can be achieved.

NOTES

1. This is similar to the reforms in the USSR in the 1960s, and in fact the initial results were more or less identical (see Lockett, 1981, p. 104).

2. See Tang (1981); also information from visits, 1981. Reynolds (1982) argues that the 'simple' type of profit retention is more advanced than the 'progressive' one, but in practice it seems that they have been implemented as alternatives rather than as a progression.

3. This aspect was emphasized by a number of reformers concerned with what they saw as too much direct Party intervention in the management of industry. Instead they wished to shift to more indirect forms of control. For example, Jiang Yiwei (1980, p. 63) argued that,

> The State organs of political power should be separated from economic entities. The State would exercise leadership over economic entities and supervise them from without, and should not direct their daily activities as a superstructure within them.

4. In Shapiro (1981, p. 7) the 1981 figure is given as 24.2% which appears to be a printing error as a variety of sources give the figure of 20.2% (e.g. Chen, 1982), although Kasper (1982, p. 166) quotes 24%.

5. This has been noted both by Western analysts such as Oksenberg (1982, p. 167) and by Chinese economists. For example, Yang Jisheng (1982, p. 23) noted that '. . . the enterprises selected for experimentation are not representative because they possess some favourable conditions which ordinary enterprises never have'. More generally the weakness of some statistics and the lack of either controlled experiments or detailed analysis of the results is a feature both of assessment of economic results and of investigations into industrial management. While in part this reflects the desire to get things done and shortages of resources for more rigorous studies, it is also a result of the politically sensitive nature of experiments in the industrial sphere.

6. A similar statement was made by Jiang Yiwei (1980) in a paper circulated to the State Council. In this he argued that unless reform was carried out thoroughly there would be 'a recurring cycle' in which 'centralization leads to rigidity, rigidity leads to complaints, complaints lead to decentralization, decentralization leads to disorder, and disorder leads back to centralization' (1980, p. 55). For 1980 one might see the incomplete reforms putting China in the fourth stage of the cycle.

7. Three months before then, we had been told that all enterprises in Sichuan Province were using some form of 'economic responsibility system' or other form of reform (interview, Sichuan Economic Commission, 16 September 1981). Other areas have reported 100% coverage, for example, Shanghai (Zhou, 1982, p. 26).

8. This included (but was not limited to) industrial enterprises and was on a national scale. Other local cases in Yunnan and Liaoning provinces are given by Liu (1981, p. 85).

9. This section has largely ignored the intra-enterprise aspects of 'economic responsibility'. Broadly it involved further shifts towards payment systems based on output or similar measures. These have ranged from forms of piecework to more limited production bonuses. Just as concern was expressed over profit retention ratios, the lack of connection between bonuses and actual output has been a subject of concern for economists concerned with increasing productivity. Other aspects of responsibility systems in some enterprises have included various forms of internal contracting between workshops, and the setting up of detailed systems of internal regulations down to the level of individual workers (see e.g. SWB/FE/7177/C/1–5 and 7180/BII/21–23; Shu, 1981).

10. A parallel shift has been to recognize the importance of improving the performance of existing enterprises rather than relying on new ones for technical innovation. A report in December 1982 (SWB/FE/7203/C/10) indicated that such analyses had been accepted by the State Council which had ordered the relevant bodies to 'put forward concrete plans' to achieve this aim.

11. For example, according to Wan (1980) the Shanghai Number One Machinery and Electricity Bureau surveyed 2000 'production management cadres in 64 enterprises' and found that only 1.6% were graduates or equivalent. Another survey of leading cadres in over 2000 enterprises in the machinery industry showed 14.3% had university level education, 21.4% senior middle school or college level, and 64.3% primary or junior middle school education. He concluded (unfairly in our view) that 'The bureaucratic system of economic management in China is the worst and most backward in the world'.

12. It should be noted that the great majority of these young workers will be better educated than their predecessors, even if they have fewer industrial skills. Also, while Chinese commentators place most of the blame on the continuing influence of Cultural Revolution 'leftism', to a large extent these problems result from broader social changes in such areas as demography.

13. Another major area covered was the role of trade unions themselves. Due to space constraints these changes have not been included in this paper, but are outlined in Littler and Lockett (1982) and Lockett (1983).

14. Though there are provisions under Articles 14 and 15 for the congresses to set up working committees for investigation, collecting proposals and monitoring the implementation of congress decisions.

15. Like many Chinese statistics the accuracy of these figures is not clear. In addition, though all these figures were published or given to us around the same time (September/October 1981), the date of their collection is also unclear.

16. It was reported in December 1981 that only 14.2% of all grassroot units had established workers' congresses in Guangxi 'according to incomplete statistics'. (FBIS China Report (Econ. Affairs) 198 (21 January 1982), JPRS 79916, pp. 57–58.)

17. It should also be noted that Guangdong Province may not be typical of the whole of China. According to Nanfang Ribao (26 October 1981, 'Guangdong Enterprises Institute System of Workers' Congress'), 'on the whole, democratic management of enterprises is still backward in our province'.

18. Apart from the 6600 experimental enterprises, the State Council decided in late 1978 that enterprises fulfilling over half of their plan targets would get additional funds for collective welfare and 'rewarding oustanding workers'. The use of these funds had to be approved by the workers' congress (see Lockett, 1983, p. 242).

19. See also Yu (1980, p. 15) and Wang et al. (1981). One can see a shift in this direction by Xue Muqiao between his 1981a and 1981b. A view similar to Zhu

Chuan's but coming instead from the unofficial 'democracy movement' is given by Siwu Luntan (1979).

20. Information from discussions with Liu Gang

on Shanghai, and representatives of Sichuan Second Light Industry Bureau (September 1981).

21. Information from visit (25 September 1981).

REFERENCES

Brus, W., *Socialist Ownership and Political Systems* (London: Routledge & Kegan Paul, 1975).

Chen, C., 'Sichuan de Shiyan' (The Sichuan Experiment), Paper to 3rd Conference of the International Association for the Economics of Self-Management (mimeo, Sichuan Shehui Kexue Yuan, Chengdu, 1982).

FBIS (Foreign Broadcast Information Service), 'Hopei Plant Democracy', *People's Republic of China Daily Report* (7 December 1982), p. 236, K2.

Feng, W., 'On questions of socialist democracy', *Beijing Review*, No. 4 (1981), pp. 17–20, 28.

Goodman, D., 'The direct election campaign of 1979–81: responsibility without power', *China Quarterly* (forthcoming).

Gray, J., 'Conclusions' in J. Gray and G. White (eds.), *China's New Development Strategy* (London: Academic Press, 1982), pp. 289–310.

Gu, Z., 'Urgent solutions sought for some problems in perfecting the economic responsibility system in Guangdong industrial enterprises', *Yang Cheng Wanbao* (16 June 1982), in *China Report (Economic Affairs)*, No. 266, pp. 31–33; JPRS 81834.

Guangming Ribao, 'Pay serious attention to the study of the theory of an urban collective economy' (19 December 1979), No. 3 in *FBIS Daily Report* People's Republic of China, 1 (008) (11 January 1980), pp. L9–L10.

Harris, L. and B. Fine, Research Trip Notes 1981. (We would like to thank Laurence Harris and Ben Fine for making available their research material.)

Henley, J. S. and P. K. N. Chen, 'A note on the appearance, disappearance and re-appearance of dual functioning trade unions in the People's Republic of China', *British Journal of Industrial Relations*, Vol. 19, No. 1 (1981), pp. 87–93.

Jiang Y., 'The theory of an enterprise-based economy', *Social Sciences in China*, Vol. 1, No. 1 (1980), pp. 48–70.

Jingji Guanli, Sichuan No. 1 Cotton Mill 'evades over ¥ 2.4 million income tax' — what is it actually all about?, No. 2 (February 1981), pp. 11 and 59.

Kasper, W., 'Note on the Sichuan experiment', *Australian Journal of Chinese Affairs*, Vol. 7 (1982), pp. 163–172.

Lee, P. N.-s., 'The Revival of Pragmatic Alternatives in the Post-Mao Era: the Case of the Enterprise Autonomy Scheme 1978–1980' (mimeo, Public Affairs Research Centre, Chinese University, Hong Kong, 1981).

Li, S. and Y. Huang, 'Several questions which urgently await solution in the development of collectively owned industries in cities and towns', *Jingji Yanjiu*, Vol. 9 (1979), pp. 27–32 in *China Report (Economic Affairs)*, No. 28, pp. 1–12, JRPS 74598.

Liang, J., 'Profit distribution system of major collective enterprises must be reformed', *Jingji Guanli*,

No. 1 (1980), pp. 21–23 and 50 in *China Report (Economic Affairs)*, No. 83, pp. 1–8, JPRS 76396.

Lin, P., 'Establish and perfect the system of workers' congresses', *Renmin Ribao* (6 March 1980), tr. in *SWB*, 6403/B11 (24 April 1980).

Ling, C., 'State-owned enterprises must actively and systematically test the system of retention of a percentage of profits', *Jingji Guanli*, No. 12 (25 December 1979), pp. 15–19 in *China Report (Economic Affairs)*, No. 52, JPRS 75423, pp. 1–9.

Littler, C. R. and M. Lockett, 'What role for the unions?', *China Now*, No. 102 (May/June 1982), pp. 5–8.

Liu, G., 'Views on several fundamental issues of economic restructuring', *Jingji Guanli*, No. 11 (25 November 1979), pp. 12–17 in *China Report (Economic Affairs)*, No. 46, JPRS 75219, pp. 1–11.

Liu, G., G. Wang and Y. Xing, *Shanghai Chengshi Jitinoyouzhi Gongye Yanjiu* (*Research on Shanghai Urban Collective Industry*) (Shanghai: Renmin Chubanshe, 1980).

Liu, Y., 'Retransformation of the system of ownership – a new trend in China's economy after the 6th Plenary Session', *Zhengming* (1 September, 1981), pp. 20–23 in *China Report (Economic Affairs)*, No. 181, JPRS 79430, pp. 81–88.

Lockett, M., 'Self-management in China?' *Economic Analysis and Workers' Management*, Vol. 15, No. 1 (1981), pp. 85–114.

Lockett, M., 'Enterprise management – moves towards democracy?' in S. Feuchtwang and A. Hussain (eds.), *The Chinese Economic Reforms* (London: Croom Helm, 1983), pp. 224–256.

Lu, D., 'Report on government work', *Sichuan Ribao* (3 March 1982), pp. 1–3, in *China Report (Economic Affairs)*, No. 235, JPRS 80898, pp. 23–48.

Lu, Q., 'Why do we adapt the system of economic responsibility for industrial production?', *Wenhui Bao* (22 October 1981), p. 3, *China Report (Economic Affairs)*, No. 194, JPRS 79807, pp. 29–31.

Ma, H., 'Tentative study on reform of leadership system in industrial enterprises', *Jingji Guanli*, tr. in *China Report (Econ. Affairs)*, No. 116 (1980), JPRS 77359, pp. 28–44.

Oksenberg, M., 'Economic policy-making in China' *China Quarterly*, Vol. 90 (June 1982), pp. 165–194.

Qian, J., 'Eliminate feudal vestiges in economic work', *Beijing Review*, No. 23 (29 December 1980).

Qiye Guanli (*Enterprise Management*), 'Guojia Jingwei tichu diaozheng shiqi zhengdun qiye de liu tiao biaozhun' (The State Economic Commission puts forward six criteria for consolidating enterprises in the readjustment period) (1981), pp. 5 and 19.

Ramond, J., 'Workers' self-management and its constraints: the Yugoslav experience', *British Journal of Industrial Relations*, Vol. XVII (1979), pp. 83–94.

Reynolds, B. L., 'Reform in Chinese industrial management: an empirical report', in US Congress Joint Economic Committee, *China under the Four Modernizations*, Part 1, (Washington, D.C.: US Government Printing Office, 1982), pp. 119–137.

Saich, T., 'Workers participation in China', *China Now*, No. 104 (1982), pp. 4–6.

Shapiro, S., *Experiment in Sichuan* (Beijing: New World Press, 1981).

'Shehui Kexue Yanjiu', *Sichuan Guangda Qiye Zizhuquan Shidian Jingyan* (*The Experience of Experiments in Enlarging Enterprise Autonomy in Sichuan*) (Chengdu: 1980).

Shu, B., 'Problems of economic contracting system within plants discussed', *Caiwu yu Kuaiji*, No. 12 (1981), pp. 28–29 in *China Report (Economic Affairs)*, No. 217, pp. 17–21, JPRS 80478.

Siwu, L., 'On collective ownership and its future', No. 12 (1979), pp. 1–8 in *China Report (Political, Sociological and Military Affairs)*, No. 47, pp. 22–35, JPRS 74909.

Solinger, D. J., 'The Fifth National People's Congress and the process of policy-making: reform, readjustment and the opposition', *Issues and Studies*, Vol. 18, No. 8 (August 1982), pp. 63–106.

State Statistical Bureau, 'Communique on fulfilment of 1981 National Economic Plan', *Beijing Review*, Vol. 25, No. 20 (1982), pp. 15–24.

Su, W. (ed.), *Economic Readjustment and Reform?*, (Beijing Review, 1982).

Sun, X., 'Problems arising in the process of implementing the system of enterprises' responsibility for their own profits and losses', *Jingji Lilun yu Jingji Guanli*, No. 25 (June 1982), pp. 1–6, in *China Report (Economic Affairs)*, No. 269, pp. 1–12, JPRS 81886.

Tang, F., 'A further step in expanding the autonomy of state-owned enterprises', *Social Science in China* Vol. 2, No. 1 (1981), pp. 157–168.

Tian, Y., 'Handicraft industry: trends of development', *Beijing Review*, No. 23 (1980), pp. 16–26.

Wan, X., 'From bureaucrat to manager', *Jingji Guanli*, No. 11 (15 November 1980), pp. 3–8 and 40 in *China Report (Economic Affairs)*, No. 110, pp. 15–26, JPRS 77198.

Wang, Y., Y. Du and S. Wang, 'What is meant by "ownership of the whole people"?', *Social Sciences in China*, Vol. 2, No. 2 (1981), pp. 5–14.

Watson, A., 'The management of the industrial economy: the return of the economists' in J. Gray and G. White (eds.), *China's New Development Strategy* (London: Academic Press, 1982), pp. 87–118.

White, G., 'Urban employment and labour allocation policies' in S. Feuchtwang and A. Hussain (eds.), *The Chinese Economic Reforms* (London: Croom Helm, 1983), pp. 257–287.

Wu, J. and W. Li, *Changzhou Gongye Fashan de Daolu* (*Changzhou's Road of Industrial Development*) (Beijing: Renmin Chubanshe, 1979).

Yang, J., 'Theories, blueprints, experiments and conditions: investigation and research on the problems of reforming the economic structure', *Jingji Yanjiu*, No. 4 (1982), pp. 18–22 in *China Report (Economic Affairs)*, No. 236, JPRS 80929, pp. 19–26.

Yao, Y., 'Report on the readjustment of the 1981 National Economic Plan and state revenue and expenditure', *Beijing Review*, Vol. 24, No. 11 (1981), pp. 14–20, 27.

Yu, G., 'The basic approach to socialist ownership', *Beijing Review*, Vol. 23, No. 49 (1980), pp. 13–15.

Xiao, L., Z. Tang and T. Zhang, 'Weihai Shi de "da jiti" gongye' ('Big collective' industry in Weihai Municipality), *Zhongguo Shehui Kexue*, No. 1 (1980), pp. 213–224.

Xie, D., 'Questions concerning the system of economic responsibility in state enterprises', *Jingji Yanjiu*, No. 12 (1982), pp. 3–8 in *China Report (Economic Affairs)*, No. 199, pp. 1–10, JPRS 79935.

Xinhua Ribao, 'Have complete respect for the masses' democratic right to recommend worthy and capable people', (18 August 1980), in *China Report (Political, Sociological and Military Affairs)*, No. 134, JPRS 76736, pp. 52–55.

Xue, M. *Dangqian Woguo Jingji Ruogan Wenti* (*Current Problems of the Chinese Economy*) (Beijing: *Renmin Chubanshe*, 1980).

Xue, M., *China's Socialist Economy* (Beijing: Foreign Languages Press, 1981a).

Xue M., 'Addendum to "China's Socialist Economy" ', *Beijing Review*, Vol. 24, No. 49 (1981b), pp. 14–16.

Zeng, M., 'Zai yige xian de fanwei nei shixing jingji tizhi gaige de jingyuan' (The experience of implementing economic system reform within the limits of one county), *Zhongguo Shehui Kexue*, 1980(2), reprinted in *Qingyuan Jingyan* (*The Qingyuan Experience*) (Guangdong Shehui Kexue Yuan Jingji Yanjiu Suo, Guangzhou, 1982).

Zhao, Y., 'Restore independence to municipal collective enterprises', *Beijing Ribao* No. 3 (18 October 1979), in *China Report (Economic Affairs)*, No. 30, pp. 47–51, JPRS 74665.

Zhao, Z., 'Report on the Sixth Five-Year Plan', *Beijing Review*, Vol. 25, No. 51 (1982), pp. 10–35.

Zhongguo Baike Nianjian, 'Quanguo chengzhen jiti suoyouzhi jingji lilun de taolun' (The discussion on the theory of the whole nation's urban collective economy) (Beijing: Zhongguo Da Baike Quan Shu Chubanshe, 1981).

Zhongguo Caimao Bao, (*China Finance and Trade Paper*) 'Tax evasions totalling 1.3 billion Renminbi found' No. 1 (6 March 1982), *China Report (Economic Affairs)*, No. 265, JPRS 81810, p. 42.

Zhongguo Jingji Nianjian, (*Chinese Economic Yearbook*) (Beijing: Jingji Guanli, 1981).

Zhou, Y., 'Developing a responsibility system in industry', *China Reconstructs*, Vol. 31, No. 9 (September 1982), pp. 19–22, 26.

Zhu, C., 'Collective ownership in cities and towns and several questions on economic policy', *Jingji Yanjiu*, No. 2 (1980), pp. 3–11 in *China Report (Economic Affairs)*, No. 62, pp. 20–35, JPRS 75735.

Zhuang, Q., X. Liu, Y. Zhu and K. Sun, 'An investigation of urban employment in Liaoning Province' *Jingji Yanjiu*, No. 12 (1982), pp. 25–31 in *China Report (Economic Affairs)*, No. 199, pp. 47–59, JPRS 79935.

Agriculture Looks for 'Shoes that Fit': The Production Responsibility System and Its Implications

ANDREW WATSON*

Centre for Asian Studies, University of Adelaide, Australia

Summary. — By the end of 1981 problems clearly recognized within the communes included low productivity, the failure to accumulate funds for modern inputs, inefficient and corrupt cadres, hidden unemployment, inability to stimulate growth in other than major crops and disappointingly low levels of peasant incomes in many counties. In north China, peasants in 1980 began to divide up the collective fields of communes into smaller plots for cultivation by households and labour groups. Since then the face of China has been altered — physically, politically and organizationally — by the creation of the 'responsibility system' largely outside party control and influence. 'Document 75' of September 1980 sanctioning some form of 'production responsibility system' was itself overtaken by events, as a bewildering variety of forms emerged, swamping the cadres. Practice was rapidly expanding beyond the theoretical discussions, or pronouncements of officials like Du Runsheng The paper describes each of the many forms of contracting between peasant groups and the State now current in China, with estimates of the relative proportions of the accounting units involved in each type (Table 3). New contradictions are already emerging in the changed rural set-up, partly because farm management problems bear similarities to those that confronted the open-field strip farming of the European Manor, while the incentive to have more hands on family farms contradicts official Chinese population policy.

1. INTRODUCTION

The growth of the production responsibility system in the Chinese countryside since 1979 has brought about fundamental changes in the operation of the rural economy.[1] These changes have been as profound in their implications as the formation of cooperatives and communes in the 1950s. Initially conceived as a reform in the methods of labour management, the system has, in all but the richest areas, reduced collective organization to its most skeletal form and decentralized most farming activities to the family unit. As a result, the people's commune is no longer seen as the sole model for rural development or even as the most appropriate. Its structure is being revised to separate its governmental and economic functions, and experiments with alternative forms of organization are taking place. Even more significantly, the production responsibility system has led to the creation of new types of 'economic associations' (*jingji lianheti*). These are owned and operated by peasants quite independently from the existing administrative and Party structure. Although still very much at a formative stage, such associations are now seen by some Chinese to offer an entirely new basis for a process of agricultural modernization guided by 'objective' economic stimuli. In many parts of China these changes have been dramatically symbolized by the physical transformation of the landscape as the large collective fields have been subdivided into strips of various sizes for farming by individuals and households. China's agriculture is thus set to embark on a radically different path of development from that which characterized the twenty years between 1958 and 1978.

These changes have taken place at the same time as similar but independent developments

* This paper is based on work being undertaken jointly with Dr Greg O'Leary of the South Australian College of the Arts and Education, supported by grants from the Australian Research Grants Scheme. It has also benefited from the comments of participants in the 'China in Transition' Conference held at The Contemporary China Centre, Queen Elizabeth House, Oxford, September 1982, especially Peter Nolan and Mark Selden.

have occurred in Vietnam.[2] As has been the case there, two types of arguments have been made to explain the reasons for a radical revision of the collective system. First, there has been the growth of a form of economic rationalism with stress being laid on the observance of 'objective' economic laws, on the need to use the market to help regulate the economy, and on the use of economic levers such as pricing, credit and taxation to implement central policies. Second, there has been acknowledgement of many internal structural problems in the operation of collective agriculture and the planned economy. In China, these considerations have not only brought about changes in commune operation. They have also led to reform in such things as methods of marketing, pricing policy, banking, credit regulations and planning methods. The production responsibility system must therefore be seen alongside many other developments which have combined to transform the established system of collective agriculture. Given the political, social and economic advantages that many once ascribed to the commune model, this extensive retreat from collective farming has both forced a re-evaluation of previous claims and also raised many new questions about the value of collectivization for development in peasant countries.

It is not only outside China that these events have been interpreted as the abandonment of collective agriculture in favour of family farming. As abundant discussion in the Chinese media has made clear, many within China also regard them as a retreat to the forms of organization that existed in the early 1950s and before. They feel that 'more than twenty years of socialism have been all for nothing'.[3] Such views are countered by the claim that so long as the collective ownership of land is not abandoned the situation is not the same as individual farming, and that 'the production responsibility system characterized by contracting output to households is not a negation of collective agriculture but a rational form of management of collective agriculture for the real situation in China at the current stage'.[4] This position is justified in ideological terms by the argument that in large areas of the Chinese countryside the relations of production embodied in the commune system had exceeded the level of development of the forces of production. Turning Mao's criticism of people who opposed cooperativization in the 1950s as 'women with bound feet'[5] against him, it is now argued that 'leftist' policies in advance of the forces of production had made agriculture

'put on shoes that were too big so that she couldn't move' and that it is necessary to find 'shoes that fit'.[6]

Whatever the merits of such arguments, ultimately a variety of political and economic factors have contributed to the retreat from collective farming that has taken place. In what follows, it will be argued that one of the most basic has been the failure of the communes to improve the level of rural incomes which has led to a loss of peasant support for the existing collective system. In part this has been the result of the price structure for industrial and agricultural products which has worked to the disadvantage of agriculture over a period in which the use of modern inputs has greatly increased. In part it has been the result of the failure to raise the productivity of agricultural labour significantly while at the same time providing alternative employment for the growth in the rural labour force. Thus while the productivity of some peasants has gone up and the total number of days worked per year has also increased, large numbers of rural labourers have remained relatively underemployed. Although many of the causes of these problems were outside the control of the communes, poor management and low incentives within the collectives contributed significantly to the difficulties faced. Having examined these issues as factors forcing change in the collective system, I shall then trace the evolution of the production responsibility system and analyse the nature of the different forms it has taken. This, in turn, will lead to a consideration of the new organizational and economic problems that the system has brought with it. Finally, I shall briefly look at the new kinds of economic associations that have emerged in response to some of these problems. I shall conclude by summing up the overall impact of these developments and their implications for the future development of Chinese agriculture.

2. RELATIVE PRICES AND RURAL INCOMES

Despite considerable efforts to keep the costs of modern inputs down, the growth in the use of such things as machinery, fertilizers and plastics in the Chinese countryside over the twenty years from 1958 to 1978 substantially increased production costs per unit of output. Given the low prices for agricultural products, the high yields already achieved in the most productive areas and the general policy of stressing grain production even on relatively marginal land, this led to a decline in the returns from investment in agriculture and to a situation where collectives produced high grain yields but still had low incomes. At the same time the low agricultural prices and the high profit and tax rates set for light industrial goods meant that the overall terms of trade between industry and agriculture tended to work against agriculture. While this enabled the state to accumulate substantial funds from the agricultural sector, the net result was that increases in agricultural production were ·not matched by equivalent improvements in peasant incomes and living standards. The collective system thus worked to channel modern inputs into agriculture and to meet the demands of the state, but it did so at the cost of peasant support by failing to raise peasant incomes significantly except in a minority of communes where locational advantages of investment in subsidiary undertakings provided a basis for increased distribution.

According to the *1981 Zhongguo Jingji Nianjian*, the level of modernization in Chinese agriculture rose substantially over the period from 1957 to 1975.[7] The total horsepower of agricultural machinery increased from 1.65 to 181.91 million, while the machine-ploughed area grew from 2.636 million hectares (2.4% of cultivated acreage) to 33.203 million hectares (33.3%). During the same period the machine-irrigated area increased from 1.202 million hectares (4.4% of the irrigated area) to 22.889 million hectares (52.9%). In addition, fertilizer application went up from 3.3 to 53.8 kg per hectare. Clearly not all of this machinery was continuously available for use and there were considerable problems of poor serviceability, bad management and shortage of fuel, spare parts and integrated sets of equipment.[8] Nevertheless, there was a significant improvement in productivity per unit area. In terms of sown acreage, grain yields rose from 1.46 tonnes per hectare in 1957 to 2.35 tonnes per hectare in 1975 and cotton yields from 284 to 480 kg per hectare.[9] Since sown acreage includes double-cropping, the growth in the value of output per unit of cultivated land was substantial.

Despite the above achievements, however, the returns measured in terms of the growth of collective income were much lower. As Zhan Wu has pointed out, from 1965 to 1977 the motive power of agricultural machinery increased by 830% and the supply of chemical fertilizer by 260%. Over the same period, however, production costs went up by 130% and the gross income from agricultural production only grew by 80%.[10] This meant a decline in the returns from investment in modern inputs. A survey of 2163 units in 23 provinces, for example, revealed that during the same years grain yields increased by 36% but production costs went up by 54% and the value of the labour day declined from ¥0.70 to ¥0.56, a reduction of around 20%.[11] One commune reported that machine transplantation of seedlings could save 7660 labour days at a cost of ¥120,000, equivalent to ¥1.57 per day saved. Since the value of the labour day was under ¥0.80, however, the costs were higher than if hand labour had been used.[12] Similarly, Su Xing reported a survey from Hebei province which showed that both production costs and labour costs had increased. In 1965, production costs for 100 *jin* of cotton and wheat were ¥64 and ¥13, respectively. By 1976 these had risen to ¥112 and ¥15. As a result, production costs had grown from 26.5% of output value to 40.2%. The reason was increased expenditure on fertilizers, pesticides, irrigation and machinery. Furthermore, the amount of labour used per *mu* of wheat had gone up from 19.1 to 33 days and per *mu* of cotton from 42.6 to 49.8.[13] In this situation, it is not surprising to find that some peasants in the suburbs of Beijing in 1981 referred to their small 12 h.p. tractors as *'beng-beng qiong'* (pop-pop poor), meaning the more the engine sounded, the poorer they became.

The same case is made by Zhang Liuzheng who notes that between 1965 and 1977 the gross income of basic accounting units went up by 83.6% (a more precise figure than Zhan Wu's) while income distributed to commune members rose by only 24.3%. Taking price inflation into account, he argues that 'in reality there was no improvement in living standards and in some areas there was a decline'.[14] Despite this limited growth in distributed income, Zhang goes on to argue that between 1957 and 1977 the value of the labour day itself declined by 33%.[15] He attributes this to the combination of increased collective expenditure on welfare, education and health, reduced state support as more activities became locally financed (*min ban*), larger administrative levies, and increased production costs with the lack of a corresponding rise in the purchase prices for agricultural products. While there may be uncertainties about the statistics behind this argument which, in any case, discounts the value of collective services to peasants, any decline in the value of a day's work may be expected to have had a significant impact on incentives for peasants to work hard and on peasant support for the collective generally.

The general issue of the relationship between industrial and agricultural prices is more complex, given the acknowledged problems in the structure of prices in China. Certainly in terms of prices it is possible to show that over the period since 1949 the 'scissors' gap between agriculture and industry has steadily closed. Li Bingkun, for example, quotes figures to show that between 1950 and 1978 the purchase price for agricultural products rose by 107.3% while the rural selling price for industrial products rose by only 9.8%. In addition the exchange value per 100 *jin* of wheat, paddy, rapeseed, ginned cotton and fat pig in terms of salt, refined sugar, cotton cloth, matches and kerosene all rose substantially.[16] Other authors quote similar figures.[17] Nevertheless, as efforts at price reform since 1978 have shown, it is generally accepted that the price structure does not fully reflect the costs of production and the relative productivity of industrial and agricultural labour. Su Xing states that between 1952 and 1977 labour productivity in industry went up around 50%. He argues that the drop in industrial prices has not reflected this relative change.[18] Li Bingkun estimates that if allowances are made for differences in productivity, agricultural prices in 1977 were at least 34% below 'value' and industrial prices at least 19.6% above. He concluded, therefore, that compared to 1952 and 1957 the 'scissors' gap had widened.[19] While statistical calculations of this kind are problematic given the unreliability of many reported figures in China, it is clear that a major problem in calculating agricultural prices is the value to be assigned to agricultural labour.[20] Furthermore, as Liang Wensen has pointed out, there were fewer price adjustments between 1966 and 1978 than between 1950 and 1965.[21] In the recent period state procurement prices for agricultural products rose by only 11.9% while the retail prices of industrial goods sold in the countryside dropped by 7.2%. Thus the rate of improvement in price differentials slowed down over a period when the rural consumption of industrial products increased.

In effect, therefore, the price differences between industrial and agricultural products have been an important factor in state accumulation from the agricultural sector. This is clearly acknowledged by Dong Fureng,

> This historical 'scissors' gap between agricultural and industrial prices cannot be closed overnight and its existence has provided a way of concentrating agricultural accumulation in the hands of the state. The major mechanism has been the high profit made on light industrial products manu-

factured using agricultural raw materials. The amount accumulated in this way has been much greater than that accumulated through taxation.[22]

The same point is also forcefully made by Su Xing who states that around two-thirds of light industrial products are sold in the countryside. Since both profit rates and tax rates in light industry are fairly high, a large proportion of state accumulation has to come from agriculture. In the 1950s, for example, a cigarette factory with a production capacity of 280,000 boxes per year could recoup its invested capital within two months, a sugar factory with a capacity of 30,000 tonnes would take ten months and a cotton textile factory with 100,000 spindles and 3500 looms would take fifteen months.[23] Li Bingkun estimates that as a result of these factors, between a third and a half of state financial income in 1977 was derived from the agricultural sector.[24]

While state accumulation from agriculture has been substantial, it has not been matched by direct state investment back into agriculture. Liang Wensen states that between 1952 and 1979 just 12% of some ¥630,000 million accumulated investment went to agriculture.[25] Furthermore, this only represented a limited proportion of total investment in agricultural production. According to Zhang Liuzheng, statistics from one province indicate that of ¥15,000 million invested in agriculture from 1949 to 1979, 24% came from the state and the remainder came from within the collectives.[26] Agriculture, therefore, not only contributed to accumulation for industrial development but also had to rely on its own resources for most of its own investment. Inevitably this also restricted the extent to which peasant incomes could grow.

Despite the various weaknesses in the statistics quoted above, the evidence put forward demonstrates that in terms of production costs, relative prices and levels of accumulation the burden on agriculture was considerable. While most of these factors were outside the control of the collectives, they combined to restrict the extent to which peasant incomes could be increased. It is reasonable to assume that this contributed significantly to the loss of peasant support for the collective system.

3. LABOUR PRODUCTIVITY AND RURAL LIVING STANDARDS FROM 1958 TO 1978

Despite the initial problems when the commune system was established and the subsequent fluctuations in policy towards such things as private plots and rural markets, throughout the period from 1958 to 1978 there was never any indication that the socialist development of Chinese agriculture could be other than a steady progression in terms of ownership, management and accounting up through the three-level structure. It was never accepted that differences in endowment, location and structure of production might require differences in the nature of economic organization. Still less was it accepted that poor areas practising subsistence farming might benefit from a less collectivized system. On the contrary, the opposite position was taken and it was argued that where material conditions were poor, the collective organization of the peasants could provide the means for economic growth and social change. In the absence of capital, therefore, the mobilization of labour to start the process of accumulation lay at the heart of the commune as a model for rural development. It was assumed that using a combination of inspirational leadership and a reasonably egalitarian distribution of the benefits of economic growth, the commune would ensure a steady increase in the productivity of rural labour.

In practice, the results have been less clear-cut. The evidence suggests that there has been considerable regional variation in the rate of improvement in labour productivity. Furthermore, any improvement that has taken place in communes has been partially offset by the large increase in the size of the agricultural labour force over the period from 1957 to 1978 (see Table 1). Despite the achievements in agricultural modernization and in raising yields noted above, the effective use and expansion of labour-saving machinery in the countryside has been hampered by the need to develop alternative employment both for the labour displaced by mechanization and for the new additions to the labour force. While increased multiple-cropping might have been expected to absorb some of that labour, it was estimated in 1979 that complete mechanization would displace some 90% of the then labour force of approximately 300 million.[27] The difficulty in dealing with such a large reserve of labour was a major factor contributing to the reassessment of mechanization policy that took place during 1978 and 1979 and led to the switch in emphasis away from the mechanization goals originally put forward for 1980 and 1985, towards agricultural technology that

Table 1. *The productivity of agricultural labour in terms of grain output (1957–1978)*

Year	Total agricultural social labour force (millions)	Total grain output (million tonnes)	Grain output per labourer (kg per person)
1957	193.10	195.5	1010.1
1958	154.92	200.0	1290.9
1959	162.73	170.0	1044.7
1960	170.19	143.5	843.7
1961	197.49	147.5	746.8
1962	212.78	160.0	751.9
1963	224.68	170.0	756.6
1964	228.03	192.5	844.1
1965	233.98	194.5	831.2
1966	242.99	214.0	880.7
1967	251.67	217.8	865.4
1968	260.65	209.5	802.1
1969	271.19	210.9	777.8
1970	278.14	239.9	873.3
1971	284.00	250.1	880.8
1972	282.86	245.0	850.0
1973	288.45	264.9	918.5
1974	291.91	275.2	942.9
1975	294.95	284.5	967.2
1976	293.87	286.3	974.2
1977	292.67	282.7	974.2
1978	294.26	304.8	1035.6

Source: Yang Jianbai and Li Xuezeng, see note 30. The figures for grain production are the same as those in *Zhongguo Nongye Nianjian 1980* (Beijing: 1981), p. 34.

increases yields rather than saves labour.[28]

It is now evident that with the exception of a minority of well-led and well-endowed communes there have been only limited gains in labour productivity. The issue has been stated in its simplest terms by Su Xing who pointed out that between 1957 and 1978 grain output went up by 50% while the total agricultural labour force also grew by the same amount.[29] The detailed figures presented by Yang Jianbai and Li Xuezeng (see Table 1) effectively demonstrate this point.[30] While many of these statistics are obviously unreliable, being based on 'upward-reported' figures of questionable value,[31] the order of magnitude indicates the seriousness of the problem. Similar evidence can also be found in terms of the per capita output of other crops such as cotton, oil and aquatic products.[32] Furthermore, though the evidence in Table 2 is not conclusive in relation to the prices of its constituent elements, since there is no indication how it was constructed, the fact that there was no large-scale change in the composition of the gross value of agricultural production between 1957 and 1975 suggests that there were only limited opportunities to transfer labour from crop production to other activities and thereby raise the productivity of those that remained behind.

Not surprisingly, much of the evidence used to show the benefits of the introduction of the production responsibility system has sought to prove that there has indeed been considerable underemployment of peasant labour. One commune in Anhui, for example, reported that before the system was adopted the labour engaged in farming accounted for 81.3% of its total labour force. After the change this declined to 45.1% in 1980 and 37% in 1981.[33] A similar report from three communes in Henan recorded that there was now a surplus of 42.3% of their original labour force.[34] While examples such as these cannot be generalized to the whole of Chinese agriculture, it is estimated that, given the new incentives for peasants to work harder under the production responsibility system, there is currently a surplus of as much as one-third of the total rural labour force.[35] Even if only a proportion of that amount is actually available, the failure to mobilize it in the past represents a considerable waste. Given that such a reallocation of labour power was one of the major goals of the commune system, it is a failure which has seriously undermined the basic rationale behind the commune model. It has also inevitably meant that the average standard of living in the countryside has not appreciably improved. It is now claimed that until 1978 as much as one-eighth of the rural population did not have enough grain to eat and average rations were much the same as in 1957.[36] While once again many of the factors leading to an improvement in labour productivity were outside commune control, to the extent that the communes have been forced to develop by encouraging a growth in the rural labour force rather than an improvement in its quality, they have exacerbated the problem.

4. THE QUALITY OF COMMUNE MANAGEMENT

In the light of these external factors, it is not correct to place all the blame for the failure to raise incomes and productivity on 'blind leadership, mobilization tactics and egalitarianism caused by erroneous methods of manage-

Table 2. *The composition of the gross value of agricultural output (%)*

Year	Crop farming	Forestry	Animal husbandry	Subsidiaries	Fish
1957	80.6	1.7	12.9	4.3	0.5
1962	78.9	1.7	10.3	7.3	1.8
1965	75.8	2.0	14.0	6.5	1.7
1970	75.7	2.2	12.9	8.7	1.5
1971	75.1	2.5	14.8	6.2	1.4
1972	73.2	2.8	15.4	7.1	1.5
1973	74.0	2.8	14.5	7.3	1.4
1974	73.7	3.0	14.1	7.7	1.5
1975	72.5	2.9	14.0	9.1	1.5
1976	69.3	3.3	13.9	12.0	1.5
1977	67.5	3.2	13.1	14.1	1.5
1978	67.8	3.0	13.2	14.6	1.4

Source: Yang Jianbai and Li Xuezeng, see note 30.

ment' as some writers have.[37] Nevertheless, the methods of commune management have contributed to the problem. In this respect, two issues have been particularly important: the quality of leadership and the method of income distribution.

In view of the key role that the mobilization of labour played in the commune model, the need for effective and inspirational leadership at the lower levels is obvious. Almost all the models of collectivization publicized during the period from 1958 to 1978 placed great emphasis on this aspect. In many cases successful team and brigade leaders combined their technical and organizational skills with an established position in their community often dating back to the time of Land Reform or even earlier. In discussions with researchers rural cadres invariably stress the role of leadership as a crucial factor in development.[38] In practice, however, such leadership is not easily provided. Basic level cadres are now widely criticized for their inefficiency, their inability to interpret central policy flexibly according to local conditions, their preference for simplified methods of management and their corruption.[39] It is alleged that many of them used their position to avoid taking part in labour, to increase their personal income, and to gain advantages for their family members. It is also generally acknowledged that there has been considerable peasant resentment against their cadres. This has been true even in relatively good collectives and one agricultural economist reported a rice transplanting song in which the peasants complained that most of their work went to support the hierarchy of cadres above them. As a result, it is claimed, one of the major reasons for the rapid growth of the production responsibility system has been that it requires cadres to work in the fields to produce their own income.[40]

In reality, some of this criticism reflects the fact that rural cadres were subject to the rigidities of the planning system and, as discussed above, they are being blamed for aspects of the system as a whole outside their control. The success of many model collectives shows, however, that the problems were not always insurmountable. Nevertheless, in as far as the criticisms *are* true, it makes sense to reduce the extent of dependency on bad leadership and to introduce more direct income incentives to individuals in order to increase output.

The major criticisms of the work point system of distribution have centred on its excessive egalitarianism. It is argued that in practice it did not embody the principle of 'payment according to work done' and did not reflect the differences in the quality and amount of work each peasant performed. Instead, everyone 'ate from the big pot' and there was little incentive for them to improve the quality of their work. To some extent such criticisms are misleading. The work point system was clearly not egalitarian in regional terms or even in terms of redistributing income from rich teams to poor teams in the same commune.[41] The value of the work-day has always varied considerably between accounting units. Furthermore, since the basis of work point distribution was work done, the level of family income was to a large extent determined by the amount of labour it possessed. Families with few labourers and many dependents were inevitably poorer than families in the opposite position and many collectives had 'leaky ladle' households[42] whose income from work points was insufficient to cover their basic grain distribution. In most provinces the extent of such inequalities was restricted by the placing of top limits on per capita cash and grain distribution.[43] Rich collectives, however, still distributed more to their members through such things as free housing, free medical care, old-age pensions and a variety of other collective benefits.[44]

Nevertheless, the system did require considerable managerial skills if it was to work properly.[45] The fixing of a peasant's labour quotas and labour norms was, in effect, the same as determining his or her income. To ensure that labour was correctly measured and rewarded, cadres had to calculate the relative value of the work done during each stage of production, allow for the different levels of mechanization in each process and measure the input of each labourer. The larger the group of peasants working together as a unit and the greater the diversity of activities carried out, the more complex the issues became. Errors might have a considerable impact on the incentive for each peasant to work and could lead to considerable disputes over relative incomes. It is not surprising, therefore, to find that the administration of the work point system formed a major aspect of the work of basic cadres and that 'disputes over work evaluation, arguments over work points, and hunting for easy jobs in the fields'[46] were an inherent part of the system. The temptation for less capable cadres to muddle through by a combination of average historical norms, standard labour quotas and simplified methods of recording work points must have been very strong.

In reality, of course, there was considerable

variation in the way each brigade or team administered its work point system and established its labour quotas. The Dazhai system clearly attempted to be more egalitarian than many others.[47] By contrast, there are reports of teams and brigades resisting egalitarian methods of distribution in favour of contracting systems with a greater incentive effect.[48] In practice, therefore, the work point system was not necessarily egalitarian in its impact in all places. However, in as far as it did not directly relate work done to the proportion of the end product received, encouraged standardized measurement of work so that a 'ten point' peasant received ten points for a day's work regardless of the quality of that work, and did not repay extra effort by individual peasants with increases in their income, it did act as a disincentive to improve productivity.[49]

In sum, therefore, in a situation where production costs were rising, the level of accumulation was high and the possibilities for raising incomes were limited, the operation of the work point system failed to provide incentives for peasants to work harder. Given the primacy now given by the officials to the forces of production and the fact that simple manual labour is still predominant in the Chinese countryside, the conclusion is drawn that 'the key issue in the development of the forces of production is the improvement of the productivity of labour. And the improvement of the productivity of labour is determined by the enthusiasm of the individual.'[50] The introduction of the production responsibility system has been primarily aimed at solving this problem. It has done so by relating income more directly to output and by providing bonuses for surplus production. In achieving this it has, in the majority of communes, resulted in a decentralization of labour management and income determination to the family unit. This has also entailed accepting greater differentials in income levels. While such differences also existed under the old system, they are now seen as an important stimulus to development under the slogan 'let some get rich first'.

5. THE EVOLUTION OF THE PRODUCTION RESPONSIBILITY SYSTEM[51]

The production responsibility system originated at the Party's third plenum in December 1978.[52] At first known as the 'post responsibility system' (gangwei zerenzhi), it involved the fixing of quotas for such things as the number of peasants, the task, the quality of work, and the payment, reward and penalty associated with each item of farm work. The fixing of output quotas on a household basis and the division of land for family farming were both forbidden. Subsequently known as the 'three-, four- or five-fixed and one reward system' depending on the nature of the work performed, this method was widely promoted during 1979 and 1980. Under it, work groups (zuoyezu) contracted for farming work according to the quotas established for them by their teams. All accounting, planning and farm management was still carried out by the team but the problems of recording each individual's work points and dividing up the income for the work done was transferred downward to the group. In addition the peasants could obtain a bonus if they overfilled their quota. Although the transfer downwards of a part of the team's power over income distribution was involved, the system did not involve any fundamental reorganization of the collective and it was believed capable of providing incentives to increase output. In some ways it revived methods that had been used in communes and collectives at earlier stages.[53] With some modifications and a different name it has remained part of the production responsibility system until the present.

Until the circulation of Document 75 in September 1980,[54] this was the only officially sanctioned form of the production responsibility system. However, even as the Third Plenum was meeting in 1978, experiments with alternative forms of organization were under way in some parts of the country. These experiments progressively led to the introduction and expansion of contracting to individuals and contracting to households which have now become the most dominant forms of the system as a whole. It was subsequently revealed, for example, that household contracting was introduced in 400 teams in Anhui in 1978, expanded to 16% of all teams in 1979 and to 90% in 1980.[55] Despite the fact that most discussions of the quota system at that time still denounced the notion of contracting output to households, practice in the countryside already had begun to diverge from official policy at an early stage. Furthermore, the pressures came from below and proceeded to force the pace of change thereafter. Anhui Provincial Committee, for example, affirmed that the contracting of output to households was a form of the production responsibility system in January 1980, nine months before central approval was given in Document 75.[56]

As outlined in Document 75, the production responsibility system was seen to consist of three types: those for rich collectives where various forms of specialist contracting to work groups could be practised based on collective accounting and management; those for intermediate areas where unified accounting and management could be maintained but contracting to work groups or individual labourers could be less specialized and for longer periods of time; and those for poor areas that had to 'buy back grain from the state, borrow funds for production and rely on relief for survival', where contracting output or land to households could be used. This rehabilitated a wide variety of labour management forms that had been practised in the 1950s and early 1960s.[57] Even though household contracting was now approved, it was still regarded with considerable suspicion, which is not surprising considering the criticism it had received during the cultural revolution. Many local cadres initially resisted it and some retained their dislike at least until the middle of 1982.[58] Initially, much public discussion regarded it as temporary and only suitable for the poorest of collectives because of their low level of development of their forces of production. It was 'the method to use where no method would do' (*meiyou banfa de banfa*)[59] and would give the peasants a breathing space to improve their standard of living and restore production. In contrast to earlier claims, therefore, this view argued that collective farming could not succeed in the most backward areas and it immediately raised the problem of how to decide which collectives should use contracting to work groups and which should use contracting to households.

During late 1980 and most of 1981, there was considerable discussion of this issue. In terms of both ideology and the existing structure of authority the key question was whether household contracting contradicted the socialist system and would lead to the break-up of the communes. This concerned both theoretical economists and administrators in the countryside. Initially, analysis of household contracting was negative and guarded, but it rapidly became more positive in the light of evidence of the success of the system in some areas and of the speed with which it was spreading through the countryside. One of the first commentators, Yu Guoyao, suggested that household contracting might be used in around 10% of collectives and that, once these began to develop, they would adopt the more specialized forms of contracting as used in richer areas.[60] Because the ownership of land remained with the

collective, he did not see it as the same as individual farming which would lead to class polarization. Nevertheless, he did consider it to be a form of 'individual management' which could create difficulties. It should not be indiscriminately lumped together with the other forms of the production responsibility system since this would lead people to neglect the problems involved.

This cautious position contrasted with the views of those reporting on developments from the countryside such as Ma Biao writing in the February 1981 issue of *Jingji Guanli*.[61] He praised the system for the way it embodied the principle of payment for work done, eliminated bad leadership, reduced egalitarianism and improved output. Although he conceded that there were new problems for collective accumulation and management, he concluded that contracting to households 'cannot lead to a departure from the socialist track'. Thereafter, many articles dwelt on the kinds of problems household contracting created for collectives in terms of accumulation, water control, management and welfare provision. The majority concluded that such problems could be overcome and that the collective economy as a whole was not threatened, because there remained the collective ownership of land and the overall dominance of the planned economy. Meanwhile, it was also necessary to persuade rural cadres that, on the one hand, they should not resist peasant demands for the introduction of the system and on the other they should not abandon their work once it was introduced.[62]

By the middle of 1981, however, practice in the countryside was rapidly extending beyond the theoretical discussion. This was particularly the case with the contracting of everything to the household (*bao gan dao hu* or *da bao gan*).[63] This involved the assignment of land, animals and other assets to households in return for tax and sales quotas, a collective levy and some labour service. It also did away with all aspects of collective management including work points. The situation was thus the same as if the peasants were simply paying tax, land rent and labour service while functioning as individual farmers. They also had the right to accumulate by themselves and to own all the means of production except the land. Clearly this presented considerable problems to analysts wishing to prove that it was a form of the production responsibility system and part of socialist collective agriculture. In theoretical terms, therefore, two positions had to be adopted. First, it had to be accepted that the key issue was the ownership of land. Provided that remained with the collective, socialism was secure. Second, the primacy of the forces of production had to be acknowledged so that 'any system which matches the current level of the forces of production and of management in a locality and is capable of arousing the enthusiasm of the cadres and masses and developing production is advanced. Advanced and suitable are complementary aspects.'[64]

Inevitably, the establishment of these positions required a considerable period of time, despite the fact that they were in accord with the general trend of economic policy. Given the continued suspicions about household contracting at the basic levels,[65] they are still not fully accepted. The considerable shift in position involved can be illustrated by the contrast between the argument made by Wu Xiang in the fourth issue of *Zhongguo Shehui Kexue* and the official position adopted by Du Runsheng, Deputy-Director of the State Agricultural Commission in a speech at the central Party school later in the year. Wu argued:

> Although (contracting output to the household) is not the same as individual farming and the collective ownership of the major means of production has not changed, if there are no precise boundaries to policy and no specified administrative methods, it will easily obstruct the development of the collective economy and slide towards individual farming. That is, there is the latent possibility of the system of collective ownership degenerating into individual ownership.[66]

By the October issue of *Hongqi*, Du was able to take a more positive line:

> Today's system of contracting output to households and contracting everything to households differs from the small-holding private economy that existed before Liberation and during the period between Land Reform and co-operativisation. We cannot equate them. Because it is kept within bounds, the system cannot of its own accord lead to polarisation and therefore cannot leave the socialist path. It remains a component part of the rural socialist structure.[67]

Despite this official endorsement, however, the theoretical analysis remains unclear and articles still discuss to what extent household contracting is or is not socialist and how it relates to a commodity economy.[68]

As pointed out above, this process of theoretical adjustment and explanation was a belated effort to adjust to developments that had already occurred in the countryside. As Xu Dixin put it, 'it would be impossible to bring (the rapid growth of household contracting and specialist contracting) to a halt and it would be wrong to try to do so'.[69] Du, for example, had estimated that the three types of production responsibility system defined in Document 75 might each apply to about one-third of collectives. In fact it was already acknowledged that household contracting was spreading into the intermediate areas and was even found in 'relatively well-off teams'[70] and that 'practice has already exceeded the stipulations of Document 75 and it is necessary for the centre to issue a new document in the light of the new situation'.[71] Despite occasional reminders that household contracting was not the only form of the production responsibility system and that rich collectives should use more collective forms of management,[72] it was eventually conceded that household contracting might be used flexibly in rich collectives.[73] Not surprisingly, within a short time of this concession being made, it was shown how Fenghuo Brigade, a highly collectivized model unit, now also incorporates household contracting for some of its less productive land.[74] Throughout the period of the growth of the production responsibility system, therefore, the central authorities and theoreticians have been in the position of reacting to and sanctioning developments that had already taken place. This progressively required adjustments in analysis and relaxation of guidelines.

In sum, the evolution of the production responsibility system has involved changes in five dimensions. First, it has grown from simplicity to complexity with the original concept of work group contracting developing into a wide diversity of forms. Second, it has gone through a process of geographical expansion with household contracting and other less collectivized forms of management spreading from poor areas to richer ones. Third, it has become steadily more comprehensive and, after an initial period when it was limited to particular crops or particular seasons, it has expanded to apply to all farming activities.[75] Fourth, it has grown from placing many restrictions on individual decision-making and using limited incentives to giving the peasants almost complete freedom in production and considerable incentives.[76] Finally, it has changed from being a short-term solution to immediate problems into a system that will last for a considerable length of time.[77] In the following section, therefore, the diversity of forms that have developed and their different implications will be examined.

6. THE DIFFERENT FORMS OF THE PRODUCTION RESPONSIBILITY SYSTEM

Although often discussed as if it were a single entity, in practice the production responsibility system encompasses a wide diversity of forms. It ranges in a continuous hierarchy from highly organized systems of labour management with planning, accounting and distribution carried out by the collective, to completely independent farming, distinguishable from private farming only by the fact that the family does not own the land. Furthermore, even when teams report that nominally they are using the same form, there are often considerable variations in the details of such things as methods by which quotas are worked out, standards are set, and land is divided. Differences of this kind can have a significant effect on production and the relative strength of the private and collective economy. Part of the problem of coming to grips with these differences has been due to the inexact way in which the names of the different forms have been used. Many writers, for example, have considered contracting everything to households as simply a variant of contracting output to households.[78] Despite the differences between them, they are often referred to collectively as 'double contracting' (shuang bao). In other cases, lower level cadres have been reporting one form while practising another.[79] Such confusion of terminology can occur even when no deceit is intended. One agricultural economist at Hubei College of Finance, for example, stated that in October 1981 most teams in a county in northern Hubei reported that they were implementing a form of contracting output to labourers. On investigation, however, the system they were using was more-or-less the same as contracting to households.[80] In addition, several different types of contracting may be used simultaneously in the same unit, or the choice of type used might change through the year according to the work to be done and the nature of the crop.

Leaving aside consideration of the subtle differences between the many variants of each type, six main forms of the production responsibility system can be identified.[81] These are specialized contracting with payment reckoned according to output (zhuanye chengbao, lian chan ji chou); unified management with output contracted to labourers (tongyi jingying, lian chan dao lao); contracting output to work groups with payment reckoned according to output (bao chan dao zu, lian chan ji chou); contracting short-term work tasks with payment reckoned by quota (xiao duan bao gong, ding'e ji chou); contracting output to households (bao chan dao hu) and contracting everything to households (bao gan dao hu, or da bao gan). In addition there are variations on these types used for handicraft and service trades, and also forms used for cadres which give them bonuses according to the fulfilment of set targets.[82] In the following paragraphs the key features of each form are briefly outlined.

Specialized contracting is usually found in the minority of rich collectives.[83] It reflects a level of development where division of labour and specialization have become important and where the technical level of farming is relatively advanced. It is commonly adopted in collectives where diversified farming and subsidiary undertakings provide a large proportion of total income so that collective distribution is higher than families might obtain from simple crop farming. Based on unified planning, management and accounting, the system involves dividing the work force of a collective into specialized groups, individuals and households according to the needs of production and the available skills. Each group then signs a contract with the collective to complete particular tasks according to agreed production and cost targets and in return for a work point payment which is sometimes expressed in a minimum cash value. Bonuses are paid when the contract is overfulfilled and penalties are deducted for underfulfilment. In addition, savings on cost targets can be retained by the group.

When applied to crop farming, specialized contracting bears some similarity to the 'four-or five-fixed' system used in contracting output to the work group (see below). There is, however, less direct identification between groups of peasants and particular plots of land. There is also greater specialization between groups to perform different items of work. In the Fenghuo model this now involves the circulation of internal credit coupons.[84] At the beginning of the year each contracting unit is issued with coupons to the cash value of its cost targets. It can then use these coupons to 'buy' the services of the ploughing group or the watering group and to obtain fertilizers and pesticides from the brigade. Any surplus coupons at the end of the year are divided among the group as a bonus. In the case of those providing services or carrying out particular handicrafts, such as the village barber or the vinegar makers, the production target may be expressed in terms of a cash target to be handed over to the team by the end of the year. In return they are paid work points of a guaranteed minimum value.

The contractor then provides the service to the village at fixed prices. In the case of tractor drivers, targets might be expressed in terms of ploughed acreage and maintenance costs or, as in the example of Fenghuo, in terms of a cash (coupon) target to be earned from the specialist farming groups. In addition, if the tractor driver or the skilled artisan is able to earn extra income from work done in addition to his or her collective tasks, such as providing transport or doing repairs, the surplus is divided between the collective and the individual.

Initially there was a surge in the number of units adopting specialized contracting which reflected the fact that it is generally considered to be the most collectivized form of the production responsibility system. Subsequently the number declined, probably because it is a fairly complex method to use and requires a careful calculation of the various targets and payments and a high level of managerial skills. Where it is the dominant form, it underlines the success of the collective concerned. Even in less well-off units, tractor drivers and other specialists are organized on similar principles despite the fact that the rest of their collective is using a different system. Ultimately, therefore, this form of the production responsibility system does not radically challenge the established collective model, though it does add a greater element of material incentives than used to be present.

Contracting output to labourers and contracting output to work groups are much the same in concept but are distinguished by the fact that, in the latter, work point income has to be further subdivided among the members of the group according to agreed criteria for measuring the quality and quantity of each peasant's labour. In general, both forms are also associated with collective planning, management and distribution. The degree to which this is realized, however, varies considerably. In some cases it might approach the level achieved in specialized contracting and in other cases it might be little different from the complete decentralization of household farming with the collective doing little more than fixing contract quotas at the beginning of the year and then leaving the group or the labourer to operate independently thereafter. In fact, according to some reports, the peasants in some areas regard contracting output to labourers and contracting output to households as 'the same in all but their name'.[85]

Both forms are usually typified as maintaining the 'three constants' (*san bu bian*), the 'four unifieds' (*si tongyi*) and the 'five-fixed

and one reward' (*wu ding yi jiang*). The 'three constants' mean no change in collective ownership, in distribution according to work done and in the basic unit of account. The 'four unifieds' refer to unified farming and planning, unified use of collective assets, unified use of water resources, and unified accounting and distribution. The 'five-fixed' defines the contract between the collective and the group or the individual. It usually involves fixing the amount of labour, the plot of land to be farmed, the cost target, the output target and the work point payment to be received upon completion of the targets. In addition arrangements are made for rewards or penalties where they apply. The system is thus directly related to the original post responsibility system proposed in December 1978.

Of the two forms, contracting to the labourer has tended to increase and contracting to work groups has tended to decline. Essentially this is because the latter merely transfers some of the work point and labour management problems of the team down to a smaller group. In doing so a number of additional problems are generated.[86] The work groups attempt to become self-sufficient like miniature teams and compete for shares in the team's resources. Their levels of achievement and income also vary according to the quality of their leadership and the type of work they perform. Since the potential for disputes to arise in this situation is very large, the general trend of development has been towards forms which simplify procedures and relate individual income directly to output. There is thus little incentive to maintain and develop the work group form. Needless to say, contracting to labourers may also generate conflicts over the use of collective assets.

The extent to which either of these forms affects the collective structure depends on how faithfully the 'three constants', 'four unifieds' and 'five fixed' are followed. As noted above, this can vary considerably. Even in places where collective management is retained, much of the day-to-day activity is decided by the labourer or the small group. Furthermore, since a large proportion of surplus production accrues to the individuals, they have a larger influence on the prospects for future development.

Short-term work task contracting has long been commonly used in communes for small jobs or seasonal work where a specified payment can be made in return for the completion of a set task and sometimes for all items of farm work.[87] Instead of the quantity of output determining the level of payment, work points are awarded when the task is performed to the required standard. Often no time limit is set so that peasants who work quickly are able to perform more tasks and thereby earn more income. Usually the collective inspects the work to see that it is done to the proper standard. If it is not, it has to be repeated without any extra payment.

The effectiveness of this system depends on the quality of the work standards set and the payment quotas adopted. Since it is the only system which does not relate income directly to output, its use has declined rapidly since the introduction of the other forms of the production responsibility system.

Contracting output to households bears many similarities to the contracting of output to work groups and individuals. Although retaining some collective management and some distribution through work points, it has the effect of making the household the basic unit of production and allows it to retain a major proportion of total output. Under this system, the household contracts to the team to farm a particular area of land and to hand over a proportion of the production in return for an agreed work point payment. The land is allocated according to the number of people in the family, often weighted according to the number of labour powers. Usually each family receives a share of good, average and poor land so that the fields are divided into family strips, physically resembling the strip fields of the medieval manor system. Surplus production above that contracted for supply to the team is retained by the family which in most cases also has to bear the costs of production. Draught animals, machinery and other large implements may still be collectively managed or they may be divided among the families or groups of families.

As in the case of contracting to labourers and groups, the extent to which collective assets are maintained and collective management is carried out varies considerably between units. In some cases, for example, land allocations are also made to cadres, local teachers, 'barefoot' doctors and families where the male labour is absent through military service or employment in the cities. This not only reduces the scale of collective services but also leads to families without sufficient labour power either neglecting their plots or hiring labour to help farm them. In other cases, some collective accumulation is maintained to ensure basic services and welfare. By and large, this form reduces collective management to a minimum and establishes a direct relationship between particular families and particular plots of land.

Not surprisingly, therefore, there have been warnings in the Chinese media that families should not revive claims to pieces of land that they owned before collectivization. Even where some system of collective planning and allocation is maintained, the difference between it and the contracting of everything to the household is very slight. The collective accounting may be little more than a book transfer since the family's contracted production target to be handed over to the team is not much different from the grain ration which the team agrees to pay back in return.[88] Ultimately, therefore, the line between this form and independent family farming is very narrow and, given the management problems entailed, the number of teams using it has declined as they have abandoned it in favour of the following.

Contracting everything to the household is the most radically decentralized form of the production responsibility system. Virtually all aspects of collective management are abandoned and there is no work point distribution. Although during late 1981 and early 1982 some discussion of the system called for the reintroduction of some unified planning and management,[89] it remains essentially based on the household unit as a form of family farming. Although the ownership of land is retained by the collective, land, animals and implements are divided among the households. In some cases draught animals might be shared among several families and in other cases each household pays for its own. The household is then completely free to farm its land in the manner it wants. It agrees to pay a tax and sales quota of a particular crop and to hand over a levy to the collective to help maintain some services and such things as the water supply. The remaining production is retained and there is no collective distribution. The household has to pay for its own inputs and any services that it receives. It therefore plans its production according to its sales quota (which is seen to represent planning), its consumption needs and its ability to produce a surplus for sale to the state or on the free market. In some cases families also agree to provide a number of days of free labour to maintain some basic collective assets. This is called 'obligatory' labour (*yiwugong*). Collective cadres have their own plots but get some payment from the collective levy in return for the reduced management tasks that they perform. While in theory control over sales quotas, collective assets such as irrigation and other resources could still give the collectives considerable powers to direct production, in most cases the collective is only a shell of its former self and the household economy becomes the basic unit.

The methods used to divide the land and animals are much the same as those used when contracting output to households. Similar problems arise over the maintenance of collective assets and the extent of support available for cadres, teachers, doctors and families with little or no labour power. Although under this system all families have strong incentives to increase output and income, differentials between families will inevitably grow according to the amount of labour they have and their ability to accumulate and to improve their farming skills.

While it is conceded that this system will slow the growth of the collective and has changed the system of distribution so that family income is obtained both from labour and from assets under its control, it is still argued that this is not a complete retreat to family farming. In response to those who point out that families now control land, direct production and have the initiative in distribution, it is claimed that collective ownership of land still exists and redistribution can take place at some future date, production is coordinated through the contract with the collective, and the tax quota and surplus levy is 'not a negation of the team's power in distribution but a special form in which the initiative remains with the team'.[90] Ultimately, however, such rationalizations do not disguise the extent to which the family has become the key unit.

Given the simplicity of the system and the strong demand for its implementation by peasants who have 'lost faith in the collective', contracting everything to households has rapidly become the most dominant form of the production responsibility system and it has spread far beyond the poor areas for which it was initially intended. At first, it was believed that as the economy developed, the system would be replaced by more specialized forms of contracting. It is now argued, however, that there is no hierarchy of forms leading from backward to advanced but that each form is advanced in as far as it matches the local forces of production. Furthermore, as new types of economic associations have begun to emerge among peasant households, an entirely new course of development is becoming possible, based on household contracting and following a path completely separate from the old teams and brigades which would then become redundant.[91] As such, the system profoundly undermines the commune model.

7. THE PROPORTIONAL DISTRIBUTION OF EACH FORM

Many problems arise when one attempts to measure the proportion of accounting units using each system. As noted above, there are many instances of basic level cadres disguising what they are really doing by reporting something else or of simply not being sure which name to use. One clear example comes from Henan.[92] In autumn 1980 the Zhenping County figures for each system based on upwards-reported statistics were: over 70% contracting to the labourer and less than 20% contracting everything to households. Over the winter as the official sanction of household farming began to take effect, the county Party committee requested the basic level cadres to make a truthful report and the figures changed to 67.1% household farming and 32.3% contracting to the labourer. While some of this change reflected the rapid shift to household farming which was acknowledged as extremely attractive and welcomed by the great majority of peasants, some of it represented the truthful reporting of what was already happening in the first place. Similar rapid changes in numbers can be found in Shanxi and Hebei.[93] When this lack of accuracy is combined with the speed with which change has taken place, the reliability of the reported figures must be seriously open to doubt. Furthermore, an analysis in terms of output value or population may be more revealing than simply in terms of accounting units. With these caveats in mind, however, some indication of the extent of the changes that have taken place and the general trend of development can be found in the statistics that are available.

The most complete set of figures available at the time of writing are those in Table 3. These demonstrate quite clearly the extent to which contracting of land to the household has become the most dominant form. They also show the rapid decline of the short-term work task system. The overall trend appears to be towards a three-tier structure consisting of specialist contracting, contracting output to labourers and contracting everything to households. Of the three, specialist contracting can be expected to occur in a minority of rich collectives in suburban areas, accounting for much less than 10% of all units. Contracting output to labourers will probably be retained in places where a reasonable amount of collective management is maintained, perhaps around 20%. Household contracting, principally in the

Table 3. *Changes in production responsibility systems* 1980–1981*

Type of production responsibility system	Proportion of accounting units at			
	Jan. 1980 (%)	Dec. 1980 (%)	June 1981 (%)	Oct. 1981 (%)
Specialist contracting (*Zhuanye chengbao*)		4.7	7.8	5.9
Contracting to work groups (*lian chan dao zu*)	24.9	23.6	13.8	10.8
Contracting to labourers (*lian chan dao lao*)	3.1	8.6	14.4	15.8
Short-term work tasks (*xiao duan bao gong*)	55.7	39.0	27.2	16.5
Contracting output to households (*bao chan dao hu*)	1.0	9.4	16.9	7.1
Partial contracting output to households (*bufen bao chan dao hu*)	0.026	0.5		3.7
Contracting everything to households (*bao gan dao hu*)	0.02	5.0	11.3	38.0
Total of forms relating income to output	29.0	51.8	64.2	81.3
Total, all forms	84.7	90.8	91.2	97.8
Total accounting units	5,154,000†	5,611,000‡	5,870,000‡	6,000,000†§

Source: *All figures except final row, *Jingjixue Zhoubao*, No. 2 (11 January 1982).
†*1981 Zhongguo Jingji Nianjian*, p. VI-9 (figure for teams).
‡*Quan Guo Jingjixue Tuanti Tongxin* (10 August 1981).
§Su Xing, 'The production responsibility system in the Chinese countryside', paper delivered to the Asian Studies Association Conference, Monash University, Melbourne (May 1982). A revised version of this paper can be found in *Jingji Yanjiu*, No. 11 (1982).

form of contracting everything to households, will then account for over 70%. In late 1981 it accounted for around 45%,[94] by early 1982 it was already estimated that it was 50%, and by mid-1982 it was reported in 74% of units.[95]

Apart from these major forms, it is interesting to note that figures for June 1981 also record some residual categories including unified assignment of work with base work points and flexible evaluation (*you dui tongyi pai gong, si fen huo ping*) 0.9% of units, division of grain ration fields (*huafen kouliang tian*) 0.5%, division of land and individual farming (*fen tian dan gan*) 0.7% and others 4.2%.[96]

Given the speed with which change has taken place and the spread of household contracting into intermediate and rich areas, it is difficult to draw any conclusions about the regional distribution of different forms. Those figures available for mid-1981 suggest that at that time the least collectivized forms did predominate in the poorest areas, though not exclusively.[97] This to some extent appeared to bear out the theoretical analysis that the forces

of production determined the system adopted. The generalization of household contracting since that time has, however, undermined this analysis unless one takes the position that the bulk of Chinese agriculture is at a level of development which precludes the use of more collectivized forms.

Ultimately it may be redundant to discuss the proportional and geographical distribution of these forms as a means of measuring the level of collectivization. As discussed below, the household contracting system has generated new forms of economic associations completely separate from the three-level commune model. If these do represent a basis for entirely different forms of cooperatives, the issue of whether or not a particular form of the production responsibility system contradicts the commune model is no longer important. The fact that the draft state constitution of April 1982 talks of 'communes, agricultural producer cooperatives and other types of cooperative economies'[98] suggests that the potential diversity is already recognized.

8. NEW CONTRADICTIONS

As might be expected, a large number of claims are made for the success of the production responsibility system.[99] In terms of management, four major achievements are canvassed. First, management by administrative command has been replaced by peasant initiative in farming. This has not only simplified procedures but has put an end to the situation where 'the sense of responsibility and the quality of leadership of the team leader has a decisive influence on total team production and the living standards of the commune members'.[100] The much-criticized shortcomings of 'blind leadership', corruption and 'leftism' are all thereby brought to an end. Second, mobilization tactics (*da hulong*) have been abandoned. The summoning of large numbers of people to work together is no longer equated to socialism and it has been replaced by making everyone responsible for their own work. Third, the work point evaluation problem has disappeared. The old framework of labour—work points—distribution has been replaced by labour—output volume (value)—distribution. Finally, the management of distribution has been simplified. Instead of products being managed by the team, work points accruing to the peasant and calculations of value and distribution taking place, everything is predetermined in the contract between the collective and the group, individual or family.

In economic terms there are widespread reports of increased output and improved living standards. There can be little doubt that there has been a substantial rise in peasant incomes. The increase in agricultural prices alone would have ensured that. However, since so much of production is now controlled within households and it is difficult to measure the income of peasants from private activity, reliable figures are becoming difficult to generate. In terms of labour productivity, a number of claims are made. First, it is argued that the composition of the labour force has improved. The number of adult males working in the fields has increased as their time spent on administration and other activities has declined. The alleged major reliance on females, the young and the old has disappeared.[101] Second, labour time has been saved because people work harder to fulfil their contracts and earn a bonus. Finally, waste of 'materialized labour' has been reduced since people now strive to lower costs and to take care of machinery and implements. In addition, it is claimed that financial administration has improved and there has been a large

reduction in management costs and expense account losses. There have also been reports of peasants developing a new interest in scientific farming and appropriate-scale mechanization in order to increase yields and use their labour more effectively.

Despite these and other claims, however, the question immediately arises whether they are short-term gains which cannot be sustained in the longer term.[102] Furthermore, the solution to one set of problems inevitably gives rise to new ones as is now being recognized, and the full impact of these problems has yet to be felt. Apart from the difficulties of reconciling what is happening with a general theoretical framework which has been used to support quite contrary policies over the past twenty years, there are many practical issues to be dealt with. These include such things as new problems of management, greater income differentials and potential social polarization and the difficulties of accumulation and welfare provision in small-scale family farming.

In many ways, the new problems of farm management facing the Chinese bear considerable similarities to those that confronted the open-field strip farming of the European manor.[103] The physical similarity is striking, with collectively owned land divided into a multitude of family strips for independent farming. At the same time the requirements of crop rotation, double-cropping, irrigation and crop management demand much coordination if problems of production are to be avoided. It is thus necessary for the household farmers to work reasonably closely together. As Vinogradoff described the problem for medieval Europe, 'the seasons for the commencement and the interruption of work, the choice of crops to be raised, the sequence in which the different shots and furlongs had to be used, the regulations as to fencing and drainage, etc., were not a matter for private concern and decision, but were to be devised and put in force by the community'.[104] In Chinese terms this is seen as a question of unifying (*tong*) what should be unified and dividing (*fen*) what should be divided. It is thus reported that the contracting of land to the household has gone through a process of moving from 'no unity to several unities',[105] whereby some of the key processes such as the planting plan, (machine) ploughing and watering and the management of machines and irrigation are unified but most other activities are decided at the household level. Given the density of population, the nature of production and the division of land into small strips, development in this direction would seem to be inevitable and the issue has been promoted in a number of ways during 1982.[106] Nevertheless, the line between asserting some unification and reverting to the former collective structure is a fine one and some participants in a major conference on the production responsibility system held in December 1981 stressed that excessive emphasis on unification at this stage would tend to stifle developments that have taken place.

> Some comrades consider that the development of the production responsibility system has gone through a process of from unity to contracts and from contracts back to unity. Currently the general trend in the development of the production responsibility system is evolving towards a combination of unity and contracts. Such a form corresponds to the present developmental needs of China's agriculture. Furthermore, at the moment the crucial issue in the consolidation and perfection of the production responsibility system is to handle the relationship between unity and contracts so that both are used appropriately, peasant enthusiasm for production is mobilised and the superiority of the collective economy is brought fully into play . . .

> Other comrades consider that it is unsuitable to raise the issue of unity too early and too emphatically. Twenty years of unity has not succeeded and instead contracting has worked well. Its advantage is its liveliness. If unity is raised too early and mishandled it would lead back to the deadness in the old economy.[107]

In practical terms a large number of new problems have confronted basic level cadres.[108] If the household strips are too finely divided, how can machine ploughing be used? Should the strips be consolidated with families on poor land paying lower rates or getting larger areas? How should draught animals be looked after? Should they be divided among the peasants? How should collective machinery be managed and maintained? Can any major land management projects be planned and carried out? What should be done about water management and conservancy? What should be done about collective orchards and afforestation work? How can diversification and subsidiaries be organized? How should contracts be drawn up and supervised? What are the duties and functions of team and brigade cadres now? Who pays and organizes local teachers, doctors and other welfare workers? How should 'five-guaranteed' households, martyrs' families and households with difficulties be cared for? Who should run the collective shops? How should finances be administered? The list is a long one and the need to reform a large number of established methods of operation is obvious.

Increasingly, however, the nature of these problems is transformed as people are encouraged to step outside old concepts and 'the theory of "permanent patterns" for the collective economy' is broken down.[109] If the old model no longer applies, completely new ways of dealing with these issues must be found, including the use of market forces and 'user pays' principles. Nevertheless, the problems still exist and require urgent solution. It is not surprising, therefore, to read frequent warnings against the waste or neglect of collective assets and resources and discussions of the need to arrange for accumulation, welfare and care of the needy.

One issue which has already attracted considerable attention is the impact of developments on population policy. It is acknowledged that one of the major factors stimulating population growth in the countryside is the relationship between the amount of labour available within the family and the level of family income.[110] The production responsibility system has not changed this and appears to have intensified the problem by rendering the old collective controls obsolete. The need for at least one male child in each family is now obvious. At the same time, parents are becoming more concerned to ensure that they have someone to look after them in their old age.[111] By late 1981, it was already admitted that the system had led to an upturn in birthrates.[112] During 1982, therefore, greater emphasis was placed on the urgency of maintaining population control,[113] and in February publicity was given to new regulations adopted in Anhui to integrate family planning into the contract system. Those families who promised to raise only one child were to be given extra land. Those who had too many children would not get extra land allocation and may even lose some of the land they have. The changes were to take place at the time when the general adjustment in land contracts was made.[114] While this solution sounds simple enough, the problems of adjusting land when the contracts are supposed to remain stable for many years, the fact that some peasant families may use their surplus labour to expand non-farming income and therefore not worry about having less land, and the general problems of policing the issue all suggest that many pitfalls still remain.

As regards the issue of income differentials, it is admitted that increases will happen but it is denied that this will result in social polarization. Wang Guichen and Wei Daonan report that in one survey after the introduction of household contracting, the general differential for per capita incomes was in the region of 200–300%, in a minority of cases it was 500–600% and in some cases even larger.[115] They claim, however, that this will not lead to polarization since the differentials are largely the result of differences in labour power, levels of skill and amount of family investment in the means of production, and that no exploitation is involved. Nevertheless, even if presently true, this view is a static one based on the current situation. As some families accumulate and others face problems, the differences may well grow and change character. Certainly some rural cadres interviewed in October 1981 felt that potentially the system could lead to a new growth of 'landlords, rich peasants and poor peasants'.[116] They were able to point to family strips lying side-by-side in which the wheat had been planted too early, too late and just right. They also underlined that after the previous harvest some families were in a position to buy fertilizers and other inputs while other families were not. Differentials could thereby grow.

Whether this is or is not a divisive social issue will to some extent depend on peasant perceptions of inequality and justice. If all are growing more prosperous, then greater differentials may be more tolerable. Furthermore, as has been pointed out above, the pre-existing situation was not all that egalitarian.[117] However, some developments do indicate that new kinds of social relationships are incipient in the system. Despite the fact that the hiring of labour is officially forbidden, it is admitted that it takes place.[118] Residents in Xi'an in late 1981 pointed out that families in rural areas with members in the army or working in the city had no alternative but to hire people to help work their land, and one described how he had to persuade his relatives to help him out in this way. In other cases the land might be rented out to those able to farm it. The growth of family subsidiaries employing apprentices and labourers and peasant investment in commercial activity will add further dimensions. In general the position being adopted in the face of these issues is one of 'wait and see'. There is no indication that potential problems of this kind are considered sufficient to halt the changes. Indeed, there is a pragmatic approach of solving problems as they arise through such things as maintaining a reserve of land for making adjustments and providing special relief for families in difficulties.[119]

In practice, it is hard to imagine that nothing will be done in the villages to maintain essential educational and welfare services and to ensure that important productive assets are preserved. The importance of many of these things is self-evident and one suspects that efforts will be made to keep them. As many reports stress, China's countryside is currently going through a process of change and development. The production responsibility systems are continuously evolving and growing. As a result the 'single-cut' model of rural social organization is rapidly disappearing and the ways in which the new problems are solved are likely to be different from past approaches. Of these, the most significant trend has been the growth of the new types of economic associations. These not only confront some of the problems outlined above but also lead to a completely new type of rural development strategy.

9. 'NEW SHOES FOR OLD': THE NEW ECONOMIC ASSOCIATIONS

The emergence and rapid development of new economic associations during 1981 have followed hard on the heels of the growth of contracting land to the households.[120] In the view of many, they 'extend the advantages of household contracting and make up for its shortcomings'.[121] Although still in their early stages and not formally adopted as central policy, they have now been reported from many provinces and appear set to expand rapidly, taking over many of the functions and activities once associated with communes. An indication of the nature and range of undertakings involved can be found in a survey of 34 communes in Jiashan County, Anhui, which was carried out in August 1981. The details of the associations and their rate of development are set out in Tables 4 and 5.

Clearly, the bulk of these undertakings are small-scale and seasonal in character, attempting to make up for the lack of resources within the individual households. Some take the form of alliances to provide the means of production or to accumulate capital to invest in such things as hand tractors and animals. Others are centred on particular skills and help diversify production. Still others are based on organizing labour to provide services. Many of them take the familiar form of mutual-aid teams and, according to Xu Dixin, it is not uncommon for these to be organized along kinship lines with related families pooling land and labour and sharing the results equally.[122] Others are formed in traditional ways by households taking out equal shares or contributing various combi-

Table 4. *Economic associations in Jiashan County, Anhui, August* 1981

Type	Number of associations	Number of households participating	Number employed
(1) Directly associated with agricultural production			
Tractors	812	8731	1732
Plant protection	3	2637	42
Tobacco curing	6	39	29
Seeds	7	266	263
Seedlings	908	5195	2101
Fish rearing	1676	2776	965
(2) Manufacturing and processing			
Grain and cotton processing	236	581	510
Flour mills	34	81	84
Beancurd	33	84	112
Oil pressing	24	62	65
Kilns	40	569	681
Phosphate manufacture	1	8	16
Cement manufacture	1	4	4
Quarries	14	66	107
Smiths and carpenters	25	72	79
Construction teams	3	17	32
Peizhichang	1	6	12
(3) Services			
Trade warehouses	1	4	4
Shops	35	89	86
Restaurants	27	73	86
Hotels	4	13	8
Transport teams	17	35	38
Film teams	1	3	3

Source: Zhang Musheng *et al., Nongye Jingji Wenti*, No. 12 (1981), p. 10.

Table 5. *The development of economic associations, Jiashan County, Anhui,* 1981

	April 1981	August 1981	Percentage increase
Number of associations	1078	3900	262.6
Number of households participating	4415	21,411	385
Number employed	2556	6094	138.4

Source: Zhang Musheng *et al., Nongye Jingji Wenti*, No. 12 (1981), p. 10.

nations of shares, skills and labour. The majority are established on an equal basis between independent households but some, particularly those requiring land (e.g. kilns) or large equipment, are joint ventures where the team supplies some of the resources and the households provide the skills and organization. Payment to the participants takes the form of wages for work done and a dividend for capital invested.

Several reasons are put forward to explain the rapid development of these associations. First, the increase in incomes of the past few years has meant that there is a lot of extra cash and grain in peasant hands. Generally this is too fragmented to be useful and the formation of shareholder cooperatives is one solution to the problem. Second, the production responsibility system has released a lot of surplus labour which can be usefully employed in subsidiary undertakings either within the family or in the new associations. Third, the increase in incomes and the relaxation of the markets has created a large demand for products of all kinds so that there are strong incentives to establish shops and services and to produce for the market. Fourth, the household is too small to provide and maintain many of the resources needed for efficient farming. It therefore makes sense to pool resources in order to buy and use large machinery and other modern inputs. Finally, the reforms of banking and credit and the relaxation of many rules have now begun to make it possible for individuals to take out loans and to buy machinery and raw materials. Many reforms of this kind are still required so that all restrictions on private activity are removed. Pressures for further developments, however, are coming not only from the peasants but also from the industrial enterprises making the products.

The advantages ascribed to these associations are remarkably similar to those ascribed to the collectives and individual enterprises now permitted in urban areas.[123] They absorb fragmented capital and surplus labour in a productive way. They are small and develop flexibly according to market demand. Unlike the previous collective subsidiaries, they are not artificially established according to administrative command (*guan ban*) but are spontaneous and voluntary, thereby having a strong inner vitality. They also compete with collective subsidiaries and force them to be efficient. They are autonomous units which are responsible for their own profits and losses. Since their members depend on their success for income, people work hard and there is careful accounting and a strong incentive to be efficient. Peasants are able to join and withdraw freely so they are organizations which 'associate but don't combine' (*lian er bu he*),[124] that is, they must be clearly distinguished from the cooperatives of the 1950s. Functionally, they encourage the growth of specialization and diversification in the rural economy and enable the peasants to develop particular skills and products. Although it is still necessary for most households to farm some land to ensure their basic grain ration, it is envisaged that as some families specialize they may want to abandon farming altogether. Provided they are able to buy grain, they can disassociate themselves entirely from the old collective and not contract for any land. In addition, such specialization can be the basis of new technical and scientific development as some peasants devote themselves to providing technical services or to plant protection, seed production and the like. The enthusiastic description of such advantages gives the impression of a strong commitment to the role of individual or shareholder entrepreneurs reacting to market forces to meet economic needs while at the same time earning a profit. This is not seen to conflict with

socialist beliefs, however, because the economic associations are collectively owned and implement the principle of payment according to work done. Once again, this view is static rather than dynamic.

In the longer term, these developments are not considered to be a 'simple repetition of the collectivization implemented in the cooperatives and communes'.[125] Instead they are seen to offer a new opportunity to reform both the structure of agricultural organization and the structure of agricultural production. It is envisaged by some that, based on the stable continuation of the household contracting system, the new economic organizations 'will become the major organizational form in the countryside'.[126] They may develop out of the existing teams and brigades, or as a combination of the teams and brigades and the new associations, or as entirely new organizations which have broken out of the existing framework. Such associations, therefore, grow directly out of the household contracting system and further serve to undermine the commune model.

Given that the communes were also intended to develop local resources and subsidiary undertakings and, in some cases, have done so successfully,[127] the criticism of leaden management, lack of efficiency, and general failure at first glance appears unwarranted. It may be, however, that the overall structure of agricultural organization did prevent the collectives from succeeding as well as they might. It is noticeable, for example, that the bulk of the communes which have successfully developed subsidiary undertakings are in suburban areas and can respond to urban demand or form contracts with urban industry to process parts. Since the market in remoter areas was depressed, many communes did not have this kind of stimulus. More importantly, the administration of the rural economy was subordinate to the territorial and hierarchical divisions of the governmental and Party structure. While this enabled the government to extract surplus from agriculture for its overall goals and to direct agricultural production towards certain targets such as grain production, it effectively precluded the possibility of rural development taking place flexibly in response to stimuli beyond those coming from the administrative hierarchy. This removed much initiative from the unit of production, made agriculture subservient to administrative priorities and limited the potential for economic growth. The fact that the new associations cross the administrative boundaries of teams, brigades, communes and districts may therefore provide a clue to an underlying structural problem. In effect, the People's Republic inherited the administrative boundaries of the old empire. While many of these were subsequently modified, it did proceed to locate economic decision-making power in that hierarchy, making economic contacts across administrative boundaries more difficult.[128] Given the territorial misalignment between administrative and economic hierarchies traced by Skinner,[129] it may well be that this formed a structural obstacle to development. The decentralization of many economic decision-making powers to the household, the establishment of the new associations and the relaxation of controls over marketing inevitably imply a growing divergence between economic and administrative structure which may well stimulate the economy while making it less responsive to administrative controls.[130]

10. CONCLUSION

Although many of the reforms discussed above are still in the process of changing and developing, it is clear that the agricultural economy in China is undergoing fundamental change. As I have argued, there were a number of major problems in the economic structure within which the commune operated which contributed significantly to the pressures for these reforms. Problems of pricing, production costs and productivity combined to prevent adequate growth of average rural incomes. When these factors were exacerbated by poor quality management within communes, a tendency to place administrative convenience over economic efficiency and a system of income distribution which lacked incentives, it is not surprising to find that peasant support for collective agriculture declined. Once collective control over labour began to relax and peasants were able to develop alternative sources of income, tremendous pressures came from below to force the pace of change faster and further than the central leadership had at first envisaged. At each stage, the Party had to sanction and justify changes that had already taken place. Whether collective agriculture might have been more successful if levels of accumulation had been allowed to improve more rapidly and the private sector had not been so limited and controlled remains an open question. Certainly the emergence of the new forms of economic associations outside administrative control show that there are strong reasons for some forms of economic cooperation in a peasant economy based on households where the possibilities for accumulation are severely restricted. If the collective is no longer in a position to accumulate and the government fails to do so through taxation and such things as extension services, the small entrepreneur can be expected to fill the gap.

Whether the reforms will, in fact, solve the problems remains to be seen despite the early claims of success. Furthermore, new problems will inevitably be generated and not all peasants will benefit equally. Nevertheless, the acceptance of greater diversity and experiment suggests a flexibility that was not possible when development was seen principally in terms of a 'two-line struggle'. This flexibility has required substantial adjustments in the theoretical analysis that is being made. The antecedents of that theoretical analysis can be found in the writings of people like Fei Xiaotong[131] and Chen Yun[132] in the 1950s and early 1960s. The fact that their emphasis on such things as the need to develop family sidelines and to use market forces has re-emerged, underlines the extent to which the commune has not solved the problems they observed at that time.

There are many major questions raised by the above arguments which I have not explored and which merit further consideration. Not the least is the political dimension. I have argued that the pace of change has been forced by pressures from below and that peasants have pushed the reforms further than was originally envisaged at the central level. Nevertheless, it seems reasonable to assume that some of China's leaders were sympathetic to and encouraged the trend. The fact that Anhui emerged as an early model suggests that provincial leaders there and perhaps central backers such as Wan Li[133] may have swum with the tide for political reasons. There is also the problem of the position of the lower level cadres. Doubtless many were committed to the collective commune model and have tried to resist the reforms. Others may have been more concerned with the loss of power that the down-grading of their administrative roles brings with it. Furthermore, there is a new political dimension in the countryside in terms of the relationship between the existing cadres and the new group of successful families and entrepreneurs that is emerging. Will economic power outside the control of collective organization give rise to new types of political influence? Questions such as these have now acquired an important significance.

Ultimately, therefore, the old model is disappearing and a more complex structure is evolving. While the commune system still exists and is found in the majority of areas, it is unlikely that this will continue to be the case. As the constitutional reforms to establish the new Xiang level of government are implemented and the commune loses its administrative role, the agricultural sector will consist of a great diversity of forms. Successful communes and brigades with a high level of per capita income are likely to remain committed to the collective model and will be able to use their advantages of scale and organization to benefit from the reforms in marketing and planning. Alongside these, there will be a great variety of collectives, cooperatives and independent associations, each associated in some way with the peasant households who farm their allocated land with varying degrees of independence. The interrelationship between these forms is likely to become dominated by a combination of contract planning and market forces. Agriculture as a whole will thereby become less responsive to administrative demand.

(December 1982)

NOTES

1. For a discussion of the evolution and nature of the various forms of the production responsibility system, see Greg O'Leary and Andrew Watson, 'The production responsibility system and the future of collective farming', *The Australian Journal of Chinese Affairs*, No. 8 (July 1982), pp. 1–34.

2. Christine White, 'Reforming relations of production: family and co-operative in Vietnamese agricultural policy', paper presented at the Association of Southeast Asian Studies Conference, Hull (March 1982).

3. Wang Kezhong *et al.*, 'Some problems of contracting land to households', *Nongye Jingji Wenti*, No. 3 (1982), p. 16.

4. Xu Dixin, 'On the agricultural responsibility system', *Nongye Jingji Wenti*, No. 11 (1981), p. 6.

5. Mao Zedong, 'On the co-operative transformation of agriculture' (1955), *Selected Works*, Vol. 5 (Beijing: 1977), p. 184.

6. Wang Yuzhao, 'Contracting output to households is a new breakthrough in the management of the rural collective economy', *Nongye Jingji Wenti*, No. 5 (1981), pp. 4–5.

7. *1981 Zhongguo Jingji Nianjian* (Beijing: 1981), p. VI, 12–13.

8. Problems of this kind have been extensively discussed in the Chinese media. See, for example, *Hongqi*, No. 2 (1978), pp. 54–57; *Jingji Yanjiu*, No. 3 (1978), pp. 29–36; and *ibid.*, No. 5 (1978), pp. 42–47.

9. *1981 Zhongguo Jingji Nianjian*, p. VI, 11.

10. Zhan Wu, 'Take a Chinese path to agricultural modernisation', Part Two, *Jingji Guanli*, No. 9 (1979), p. 7.

11. *Ibid.*

12. *Ibid.*

13. Su Xing, 'The problem of agricultural product prices', *Shehui Kexue Zhanxian*, No. 2 (1979), p. 105.

14. Zhang Liuzheng, 'Develop agricultural production, improve the peasant's standard of living', *Nongye Jingji Wenti*, No. 1 (1980), p. 34.

15. *Ibid.*, p. 35.

16. Li Bingkun, *Gong-nongye chanpin jiage jiandaocha wenti* (Nongye Chubanshe, 1981), pp. 35–43.

17. See, for example, Yao Jinguan, 'A preliminary discussion of several problems in the "scissors" gap between agricultural and industrial product prices', *Jingji Yanjiu*, No. 12 (1978), p. 33; and Su Xing, *Shehui Kexue Zhanxian*, No. 2 (1979), p. 103.

18. Su Xing, *ibid.*, p. 105.

19. *Op. cit.*, p. 49

20. For a discussion of the problems associated with defining the 'value' of the labour-day in agriculture see 'Forum on cost accounting for agricultural products summoned by the Ministry of Agriculture', *Jingjixue Dongtai*, No. 11 (1979), pp. 9–11.

21. Liang Wensen, 'Balanced development of industry and agriculture' in Xu Dixin *et al.*, *China's Search for Economic Growth* (Beijing: New World Press, 1982), p. 71.

22. Dong Fureng, 'Relationship between accumulation and consumption', in Xu Dixin, *ibid.*, p. 97.

23. Su Xing, *Shehui Kexue Zhanxian*, No. 2 (1979), p. 104.

24. Li Bingkun, *op. cit.*, p. 50.

25. Liang Wensen, *op. cit.*, p. 63. This figure probably ignores the fact that much investment in industry also

ultimately benefits agriculture through the production of modern inputs.

26. Zhang Liuzheng, *op. cit.*, p. 35.

27. Zhan Wu, 'Take a Chinese path to agricultural modernisation', Part One, *Jingji Guanli*, No. 9 (1979), p. 7.

28. The argument is outlined in Zhang Fushan *et al.*, 'Give agricultural mechanisation the position it should have in agricultural modernisation', *Jingji Yanjiu*, No. 11 (1979), pp. 22–29. The change in mechanization policy is reflected by the decline in the production of tractors and hand tractors after 1979.

29. Su Xing, 'Some problems in the improvement of the productivity of agricultural labour', *Jingji Yanjiu*, No. 2 (1979), p. 37.

30. Yang Jianbai and Li Xuezeng, 'On the historical experience of the relationship between agriculture, light industry and heavy industry in China', *Jingji Yanjiu Cankao Ziliao* (3 May 1980). A modified version of this internal distribution report was published in *Social Sciences in China*, No. 2 (1980), pp. 182–212.

31. The most glaring example of the unreliability of China's agricultural statistics is the figure for cultivated acreage which is officially 99.5 million hectares but is acknowledged to be under-reported and is likely to be in the region of 120 million hectares. See *Zhongguo Nongye Nianjian 1980* (Beijing: 1981), p. 2.

32. *1981 Zhongguo Jingji Nianjian* (Beijing: 1981), p. VI, 12.

33. *Renmin Ribao* (26 November 1981).

34. *Jingji Guanli*, No. 8 (1981), p. 3.

35. *Renmin Ribao* (1 September 1981), and *Nongye Jingji Wenti*, No. 8 (1981), p. 11.

36. 'Decision of the Central Committee of the Chinese Communist Party on some questions concerning the acceleration of agricultural development (draft)', December 1978 in *Issues and Studies* (July 1979), pp. 105–106.

37. Ou Yuanfang, 'Production responsibility systems related to output seen in terms of their economic results', *Nongye Jingji Wenti*, No. 4 (1981), pp. 23–24.

38. This has been the case in all the communes visited by Greg O'Leary and myself in 1979–80 and 1981.

39. Xu Dixin, 'On the agricultural production responsibility system', *Nongye Jingji Wenti*, No. 11 (1981), pp. 3–4.

40. Zhan Wu *et al., Hongqi*, No. 17 (1981), p. 15.

41. E. B. Vermeer, 'Income differentials in rural China', *The China Quarterly*, Vol. 89 (March 1982), pp. 1–33.

42. The nickname is given by Gao Xiaosheng to the hero of his cycle of peasant stories, Chen Huansheng, who was chronically in debt to his collective. See '*Chen Huansheng shang cheng*' in *Renmin Wenxue*, No. 2 (1980).

43. Interview at Daminggong Commune, Shaanxi, in September 1981 reported that such restrictions had been lifted in that area.

44. This was strikingly apparent at Dayudao Brigade in late 1979.

45. Detailed discussion of the technical issues involved can be found in many Chinese journals published during 1979 and 1980. See, for example, *Jingji Guanli*, No. 1 (1979), pp. 1–32; *ibid.*, No. 4 (1979), pp. 31–34; *ibid.*, No. 5 (1979), pp. 27–30 and 30–33; *ibid.*, No. 7 (1979), pp. 35–37 and 38–39 and *Jingji Yanjiu*, No. 6 (1980), pp. 45–48.

46. Wang Yuzhao, *Nongye Jingji Wenti*, No. 5 (1981), p. 8.

47. W. L. Parish and M. K. Whyte, *Village and Family in Contemporary China* (University of Chicago Press, 1978), pp. 62–71.

48. Ou Yuanfang reports that one team in Anhui used household contracting for twenty years despite the criticism of the Cultural Revolution; *Nongye Jingji Wenti*, No. 4 (1981), p. 23. Dayudao and Shijiazhuang Brigades in Shandong also claimed in 1979 that they had maintained incentive schemes while reporting upwards that they were using 'communist systems of distribution'; interviews, December 1979.

49. One example quoted by an agricultural economist told of peasants applying manure to the fields but only carting it a short way from the truck, secure in the knowledge that their work points would be paid even if the manure was spread unevenly.

50. Wei Xian and Gan Zhiyong, 'A form of the production responsibility system suitable for mountain areas', *Nongye Jingji Wenti*, No. 10·(1980), p. 20.

51. The following discussion draws heavily on Greg O'Leary and Andrew Watson, 'The production responsibility system and the future of collective farming', *The Australian Journal of Chinese Affairs*, Vol. 8 (July 1982), pp. 1–34.

52. Draft regulations on work in the rural people's communes (The Sixty Points), in *Issues and Studies* (August 1979), pp. 100–115.

53. See *Jingji Yanjiu*, Nos. 7–8 (1960), pp. 62–69; *ibid.*, No. 1 (1961), pp. 1–10; *ibid.*, No. 2 (1961), pp. 16–24.

54. *Zhonggong Nianbao 1981* (Institute for the Study of Chinese Communist Problems, Taiwan, 1981), pp. 7/50–7/53.

55. Xu Shiqi, 'A debate that has aroused widespread attention', *Nongye Jingji Wenti*, No. 3 (1982), p. 3.

56. Wang Yuzhao, 'Contracting output to households is a new breakthrough in the management of the rural collective economy', *Nongye Jingji Wenti*, No. 5 (1981), p. 5.

57. Some of the precedents are mentioned in Xu Dixin, 'On the agricultural production responsibility system', *Nongye Jingji Wenti*, No. 11 (1981), p. 3.

58. *Renmin Ribao* (13 July 1982), quoted in *Summary of World Broadcasts*, FE/7083/BII/3.

59. Xu Shiqi, *op. cit., Nongye Jingji Wenti*, No. 3 (1982), p. 4.

60. Yu Guoyao, 'How to regard contracting output to the household', *Hongqi*, No. 20 (1980), pp. 12–15.

61. Ma Biao, 'A survey of contracting to households in the Anhui countryside', *Jingji Guanli*, No. 2 (1981), pp. 19–22.

62. *Renmin Ribao* (4 and 30 October 1981).

63. The term used to translate this in *Beijing Review*, 'allotting work to households' (No. 24, 14 June 1981, p. 22) understates the nature of the system. The word *gan* is to be read in the first tone and means 'everything', not in the fourth tone meaning 'do'.

64. 'Summary of the National Symposium on the System of Production Responsibility in Agriculture', *Nongye Jingji Wenti*, No. 2 (1982), p. 4.

65. *Renmin Ribao* (13 July 1982), in *Summary of World Broadcasts*, FE/7082/BII/3.

66. 'The three major forms of agricultural responsibility systems', *Zhongguo Shehui Kexue*, No. 4 (1981), pp. 70–71.

67. 'Agricultural responsibility systems and the reform of the structure of the rural economy', *Hongqi*, No. 19 (1981), p. 24.

68. Wang Kezhong *et al.*, 'Some problems related to contracting land to households', *Nongye Jingji Wenti*, No. 3 (1982), pp. 13–18.

69. *Nongye Jingji Wenti*, No. 11 (1981), p. 17.

70. *Quanguo Jingjixue Tuanti Tongxin* (25 August 1981).

71. 'A summary of the national symposium on agro-economic problems', *Nongye Jingji Wenti*, No. 10 (1981), p. 3.

72. *Renmin Ribao* (24 November 1981).

73. 'Persist in the socialist direction, perfect the agricultural production responsibility system', *Nongye Jingji Wenti*, No. 12 (1981), pp. 30–31.

74. *Renmin Ribao* (23 January 1982). For more details on Fenghuo see O'Leary and Watson, *op. cit.*, pp. 21–27. At the time of our visit there in October 1981, the cadres were very critical of household contracting and did not report that it was used in their brigade at all.

75. Ma Renping, 'New development of the agricultural production responsibility system', *Nongye Jingji Wenti*, No. 7 (1981), p. 26.

76. *Ibid.*

77. Xu Shiqi, *Nongye Jingji Wenti*, No. 3 (1982), p. 4.

78. Wu Xiang, *Zhongguo Shehui Kexue*, No. 4 (1981), p. 69.

79. Zhao Xiu, 'A survey of the agricultural production responsibility system in Henan', *Nongye Jingji Wenti*, No. 8 (1981), p. 9 describes cadres in intermediate areas practising contracting land to households but reporting contracting to labourers for fear of being criticized for backsliding.

80. Interview, 17 October 1981.

81. See Liu Xumao, 'A simple introduction to several major forms of the production responsibility system implemented in China's countryside', *Jingji Guanli*, No. 9 (1981), pp. 12–14.

82. Yan Chuanxin *et al.*, 'A new problem in agricultural management', *Nongye Jingji Wenti*, No. 1 (1981), pp. 12–16.

83. Zhan Wu and Wang Guizhen, 'On specialised contracting with payment reckoned according to output', *Jingji Yanjiu*, No. 4 (1981), pp. 55–59.

84. The article 'Specialised contracting with payment reckoned according to output as practised in Fenghuo Brigade', *Nongye Jingji Wenti*, No. 4 (1981), pp. 32–33, makes no mention of the coupon system. The report on the brigade in *Renmin Ribao* (23 January 1982) stresses its importance.

85. *Nongye Jingji Wenti*, No. 8 (1981), p. 8.

86. Zhang Cheng *et al.*, 'Xinghuo Brigade actively solves the new problems that have appeared with contracting work to groups', *Nongye Jingji Wenti*, No. 10 (1980), pp. 16–17.

87. W. L. Parish and M. K. Whyte, *Village and Family in Contemporary China* (University of Chicago Press, 1978), pp. 62–65.

88. Yu Guoyao, *Hongqi*, No. 20 (1980), pp. 12–15.

89. Miao Yuyou *et al.*, 'The system of "contracting everything to households while retaining some collective management" is deeply welcomed by the peasants', *Nongye Jingji Wenti*, No. 12 (1981), pp. 32–35.

90. Xu Dixin, 'On the agricultural production responsibility system', *Nongye Jingji Wenti*, No. 11 (1981), p. 5.

91. See the discussion below.

92. Zhao Xiu, 'A survey of the agricultural production responsibility system in Henan', *Nongye Jingji Wenti* No. 8 (1981), p. 9.

93. See O'Leary and Watson, *op. cit.* (July 1982), p. 20.

94. *Nongye Jingji Wenti*, No. 12 (1981), p. 29 clearly bases itself on the figures in Table 3 and quotes 45%.

95. *Nongye Jingji Wenti*, No. 2 (1982), p. 3 estimates 'around 50%' and *ibid.*, No. 10 (1982), p. 12 reports 74%.

96. *Quan Guo Jingjixue Tuanti Tongxin* (10 August 1981).

97. *Ibid.*, gives the highest rates of household contracting as Guizhou (95%), Gansu (72.2%), Anhui (69.3%) and Ningxia (57.9%). These are among the provinces with the greatest concentrations of poor areas listed by Vermeer for the period 1977–79, *The China Quarterly*, Vol. 89 (March 1982), p. 25. The provincial distribution figures for spring 1981 are quoted in O'Leary and Watson, *op. cit.* (July 1982), p. 19.

98. *Renmin Ribao* (28 April 1982).

99. The following is based on Wang Yuzhao, *Nongye Jingji Wenti*, No. 5 (1981), pp. 7–8; Xu Dixin, *Nongye Jingji Wenti*, No. 11 (1981), pp. 3–9; and Ou Yuanfang, *Nongye Jingji Wenti*, No. 4 (1981), pp. 23–26.

100. Wang Yuzhao, *Nongye Jingji Wenti*, No. 5 (1981), p. 7.

101. Xu Dixin, *Nongye Jingji Wenti*, No. 11 (1981), p. 6.

102. It is recognized, for example, that there are limits to the rate at which grain output can go on increasing under this system. 'New problems in agricultural development', *Zhongguo Shehui Kexue*, No. 3 (1982), pp. 94–95.

103. See, for example, Sir Paul Vinogradoff, *The Growth of the Manor* (Allen and Unwin, second edition, 1911), especially pp. 165–199.

104. *Ibid.*, p. 182.

105. Miao Yuyou *et al.*, *Nongye Jingji Wenti*, No. 12 (1981), p. 32.

106. 'Several conceptual problems in perfecting the agricultural production responsibility system', *Renmin Ribao* (27 April 1982) and *Renmin Ribao* (6 July 1982) reported in FE/7090/BII/9–14.

107. *Nongye Jingji Wenti*, No. 2 (1982), p. 4.

108. Rural Work Department of Gansu Provincial Committee, 'How to handle the new problems that have emerged after the introduction of contracting to household', *Nongye Jingji Wenti*, No. 5 (1981), pp. 9–15.

109. *Renmin Ribao* (6 July 1982), in FE/7090/BII/12.

110. Chen Du, 'On reproduction of the rural population', from *Jingji Yanjiu*, in FE/7086/C/1–8.

111. Xu Tianqi, 'An academic conference on rural birth rates', *Xinhua Wenzhai*, No. 4 (1982), p. 13.

112. Zhao Ziyang, 'The present economic situation and the principles for future economic construction', *Beijing Review*, No. 51 (21 December 1981), p. 29.

113. Xu Xuehan, 'Resolutely implement the rural population policy', *Renmin Ribao* (5 February 1982).

114. New China News Agency, Hefei (19 February 1982).

115. Wang Guichen and Wei Daonan, 'On contracting output to households', *Jingji Yanjiu*, No. 1 (1981), p. 67.

116. Interview, Fenghuo Brigade (October 1981).

117. *Zhongguo Shehui Kexue*, No. 3 (1982), pp. 97–98 argues that in fact differentials have not yet increased and that peasants do not worry about the issue.

118. *Ibid.*, p. 97, and *Renmin Ribao* (19 September 1981).

119. *Zhongguo Shehui Kexue*, No. 3 (1982), pp. 96–99.

120. Some of the most interesting articles discussing these associations are Ma Renping, 'A new development of the agricultural production responsibility system', *Nongye Jingji Wenti*, No. 7 (1981), pp. 25–30; Zhang Musheng *et al.*, 'A preliminary discussion of cooperation and association based on the contracting of land to households', *Nongye Jingji*

Wenti, No. 12 (1981), pp. 9–18; Wang Guichen, 'Some thoughts on the new economic associations', *Nongye Jingji Wenti*, No. 4 (1982), pp. 17–19; Ouyang Junpin *et al.*, 'How to treat the new economic associations in the villages', *Nongye Jingji Wenti*, No. 5 (1982), pp. 21–25; and 'New problems of agricultural development', *Zhongguo Shehui Kexue*, No. 3 (1982), pp. 102–106.

121. *Zhongguo Shehui Kexue*, No. 3 (1982), p. 104.

122. Xu Dixin, *Nongye Jingji Wenti*, No. 11 (1981), p. 8.

123. Hong Yuanpeng and Weng Qiquan, 'On collectively owned industries in urban areas', *Jingji Yanjiu*, No. 1 (1980), pp. 62–67.

124. *Zhongguo Shehui Kexue*, No. 3 (1982), p. 103.

125. Ma Renping, *Nongye Jingji Wenti*, No. 7 (1981), p. 29.

126. Ouyang Junpin *et al.*, *Nongye Jingji Wenti*, No. 5 (1982), p. 24.

127. Model suburban communes and integrated areas like Wuxi typically generate more than half their total income from non-agricultural undertakings.

128. A similar problem in industry is cited as part of the rationale for developing trusts.

129. G. William Skinner, 'Cities and the hierarchy of local systems', pp. 341–344 in Skinner (ed.), *The City in Late Imperial China* (Stanford University Press, 1977), pp. 275–346.

130. This development is not limited to agriculture but is also found in industry and other aspects of the Chinese economy. See A. Donnithorne, *Centre-Provincial Economic Relations in China*, Contemporary China Papers, No. 16 (ANU, 1981), pp. 33–36.

131. Fei Xiaotong, 'A return visit to River Village', *Xin Guancha Zazhi*, No. 11 (1 June 1957) and No. 12 (16 June 1957), reprinted by Fenghua Press, Hong Kong.

132. Chen Yun, *Selected Manuscripts of Comrade Chen Yun (Renmin chubanshe*, 1981). A translation with introduction by N. Lardy and K. Lieberthal will be published during 1982 or 1983.

133. One is reminded of the popular saying of 1980: *Yao chi fan, zhao Ziyang. Yao chi mi, zhao Wan Li. Yao jiefang, zhao Hu Yaobang.* (If you want to eat, seek (Zhao) Ziyang. If you want to eat rice, seek Wan Li. If you want liberation, seek Hu Yaobang.)

Peasant Labour for Urban Industry: Temporary Contract Labour, Urban–Rural Balance and Class Relations in a Chinese County

MARC BLECHER*

Oberlin College, Ohio, USA

and

Institute of Development Studies at the University of Sussex, UK

Summary. — Urban–rural relations in China have a dual character: while a higher level of urban–rural economic *balance* than most other countries has been achieved, a sharp structural *cleavage* between workers and peasants has been maintained, based mainly on strict household registrations. Peasants are prevented from migrating to towns and gaining employment there, except under specially approved contracts arranged to resolve local shortages of industrial labour. Contract labour has complex and important effects on rural and urban industrial development. It also embodies the duality of urban–rural relations in China: at the same time as it redistributes wage funds from urban to rural areas, it reinforces the class cleavage between workers and peasants (including contract workers). It also opens up a complex web of inequalities and cleavages among those peasants with contract work and those without. Contract workers have been placed in a contradictory class position which has been a flashpoint of political conflict. The relationships of contract labour to urban industrial and rural development, urbanization, urban–rural balance and structural cleavage, class structure and political conflict are examined through a study of Shulu County, an ordinary rural area with a growing industrial centre in which over half of the industrial labour force is comprised of peasant contract workers.

1. INTRODUCTION

To the extent that such generalizations can ever be advanced in the face of formidable conceptual complexities and methodological problems, Chinese economic development since 1949 has by all accounts been quite successful in maintaining a good urban–rural *balance*.

Suzanne Paine finds no pattern of 'urban bias' — in the Liptonian sense of planning decisions and resource allocations which, by favouring urban areas, actually have sub-optimal results for the development of the economy as a whole — from 1949 to 1976.[1] William Parish and Martin Whyte speak of real progress in reducing the urban–rural gap in income, orien-

* This paper is based upon collaborative research carried out by Phyllis Andors, Stephen Andors, Mitch Meisner, Vivienne Shue and me in China in 1979. Our field trip was arranged at the invitation of the Chinese People's Association for Friendship with Foreign Countries, co-sponsored by the Chinese Academy of Social Sciences and funded by generous grants from the National Endowment for the Humanities and the Ford Foundation. Oberlin College generously provided me with a Powers Travel Grant. In particular we wish to thank the officials and citizens of Shulu County for their extraordinary cooperation during our stay there. This paper was drafted by me alone, but it draws upon material contained in chapters of *Town and Country in a Developing Chinese County*, a forthcoming collaborative book on our trip, which were drafted by other members of the group and me.

The interpretations and analyses in this paper as well as any errors therein are my responsibility alone. I owe a debt of gratitude to the organizers and participants of the September 1982 Conference on 'China in Transition' (Contemporary China Centre, Oxford), who provided a stimulating few days of study and discussion regarding some of the issues raised here and many others relating to them.

In describing the temporary contract labour system, the present tense is frequently used. In fact, the paper describes the system as it was in 1979. There is no reason to think that it has changed significantly since then, but also no reason to think it has not; unfortunately, subsequent research on the more recent situation has not been possible. Readers are urged to keep this in mind.

tation of production, education and public health.[2] By the 1970s the urban—rural income differential was somewhere between 2:1 and 3:1,[3] low in comparison with most other developing countries.[4] Urban—rural terms of trade have been moving in favour of the latter, and the present leadership is striving for even more progress in this area.[5] Rhoads Murphey, having chosen India as the most appropriate standard of comparison, writes: 'It would appear . . . that the Chinese have been more successful than the Indians, or than most other countries . . . perhaps, in distributing the benefits of growth more adequately to all regions of the country and to the rural areas'.[6]

Yet, in China the structural *cleavage* between urban and rural still remains formidable, in no small part due to the actions of the very same political leadership which has been so successful at reducing the differentials around that cleavage. Town and countryside have been subject to very different forms of political and economic organization ever since the earliest post-liberation days: for the former there have been mainly state-run enterprises supplemented by urban collective ones under close state supervision and regulation; while for the latter there have been rural collectives with certain (though of course variable) degrees of juridical, administrative, economic and political autonomy, supplemented by elements of household economy. In the post-Mao era, reforms have pushed the rural areas very far in the direction of reducing the role and scale of the collective economy, while planned reforms of the state sector economy in the urban areas have met with considerable resistance; so the gap in terms of socialist productive relations may have even grown. Experiments designed to reduce the social cleavage between town and country people — such as 4 May Cadre Schools, rustication of urban youth and reorientation of education and social services toward rural needs — met with mixed results and have now been utterly abandoned. Perhaps the most vivid material manifestation of the urban—rural cleavage in China — the registration of the citizenry into categories of 'rural householders' (*nongye hukou*) and 'non-rural householders' (*fei nongye hukou*) — remains intact and as difficult to cross as ever. It continues to determine into which of the two major constellations —rural or urban — of employment opportunity, social services and political and economic organization a Chinese citizen may be incorporated. Most fundamentally, it means that rural Chinese cannot migrate freely to towns and cities to set up residence and hold employment.

Townward migration has been shown to have major macro-level consequences for economic development, demographic change, labour market operation, social structure and political change in developing countries. In micro-analytical terms, it has tremendous impact on the rural and urban people and the communities to and from which they migrate. The general question of townward migration is, therefore, a very significant one from a number of perspectives. The specific question of townward migration — or the absence and regulation of it — in China is important both because of its direct relationship to key aspects and processes of Chinese development, and also because China's rather unique experience in restricting and controlling townward migration is of comparative interest to those concerned with development and urban—rural relations more generally.

Tremendous pressures exist in China for townward migration. In much of rural China, very high levels of population density prevail, leading to under-employment and depressed incomes and standards of living. Other parts of the countryside — the vast areas which suffer from poor natural conditions (relating to soil quality, terrain, climate and weather) or sheer remoteness — have the interrelated problems of very low population density and poverty: the poverty of the area can support few people, and this poverty is reproduced by the absence of a critical mass of population which could command the political and economic resources or mobilize the labour power to undertake the major investments needed to. promote a breakthrough to meaningful development. People tend to want to move away from both kinds of places in China, and they have done so when the opportunity presented itself.[7] Added to the 'push' factors in the countryside are those relating to 'pull' toward the cities: the significantly higher standard of living in urban China, the locus of political power and advantage there, and the relatively greater opportunities for social and economic mobility in a country whose already high level of agricultural development but relatively lower level in industry make the urban areas far more dynamic for the foreseeable future in terms of economic growth and occupational upgrading (not to mention social life). Finally, these 'push' and 'pull' factors operate within structural conditions highly conducive to migration: China's historically well-developed commercial and transport networks, the relatively high level of incorporation of rural China into urban-centred political, social and economic systems,[8] and the generally high level of exchange of information between village and city through official media and informal social networks. In China, then, there are a lot of villagers with good reasons to want to move to towns and cities, and a lot of information and other conditions facilitating such migration.

There are also a lot of reasons why such migration is a matter of deep concern to China's political leaders and economic planners. It goes without saying that China has a serious problem feeding itself. Agricultural development goals such as the present one of raising factor productivity and overall efficiency may be worthy, but maintaining and raising total output to keep up with population growth remains the very highest priority, a constraint within which other developmental goals must operate. Hence any flight of labour with even the lowest marginal productivity out of agriculture may be a potential source of alarm. On the other side, some of China's cities, especially its larger, more developed (and therefore more attractive) ones, are already very heavily populated and have serious unemployment; migration of even a small percentage of the massive peasantry to them would cause political, economic and social problems of potentially explosive proportions. It is not at all surprising, then, that a serious commitment to regulating and controlling rural-to-urban migration has been evinced by China's political leaders and economic planners of the right and the left; in fact, it is one of the few continuous themes of an otherwise radically shifting Chinese development policy since 1949.

China's leaders have approached this problem with high imagination and broad vision. They have met with success: rural-to-urban migration is probably lower in China than in any other developing country.[9] One set of reasons is the effects, intended or unintended by political leaders and planners, of seemingly unrelated or only indirectly related aspects of Chinese development: for example, rural collectivization has promoted a high level of intra-village economic equality,[10] which Lipton has identified as a major deterrent to rural outmigration.[11] But certainly another important factor accounting for the low rate of townward migration in China has been the administrative controls preventing 'rural householders' from moving to urban areas to live and work.

In some cases, in fact, China has been too successful in restricting migration. In many places there has been an excessive buildup of rural labour and in others there have been shortages of industrial labour. Shulu County,

the subject of this study, is such a place in both respects.[12] There, as in many other parts of China, the sluices of townward migration have been opened, but only in a closely regulated and partial way — partial because urban employment has been permitted but change of permanent residence has not. Specifically, peasants have been employed in urban industry and commerce as 'temporary contract workers' (linshi hetonggong), while remaining tied to their rural village homes and collective units in fundamental ways.

This discussion describes the practice and terms of temporary contract employment in Shulu County, and analyses it in relationship to several problems, some of which have already been mentioned: what has its role been in fostering industrial growth? What effect has it had on urban–rural developmental balance? Has it helped to reinforce or overcome the structural cleavage between town and countryside, which has been so tenacious despite China's successes in achieving greater urban–rural balance? How can it be understood in terms of China's changing social structure? Concomitantly, what political tensions has it produced?

2. TEMPORARY CONTRACT WORK: DEFINITION, RATIONALE AND MAGNITUDE

'Temporary contract workers' are peasants who have been hired by urban state/collective sector industrial enterprises through contracts with their rural collectives. Although 'temporary contract work' is often not very temporary at all — in Shulu most contract workers had been so employed for many years — the contract workers retain the official status of 'rural householders', and maintain their permanent homes in their villages. Their families remain behind there, and the contract workers visit home periodically — in Shulu usually weekly or monthly — living the rest of the time (indeed, most of the time) in factory dormitories; only those lucky ones hailing from suburbs of the town in which they are employed may be able to live at home and commute to work daily. The families of contract workers also, of course, remain 'rural householders', which means they have no claim on urban employment, housing or education.

Contract workers also remain members of their rural collective units (sheyuan), which means that their rural units — in practice, usually their production teams — retain the ultimate claim over allocation of their labour. In formal terms, then, contract workers continue to be employed by their production teams, which assign them to urban employment under the terms of the contract which the team has made — often through the brigade or commune — with the factory in town. This is no *mere* formality: the team has the power to decide which of its members will be assigned to contract employment, and it can substitute one of its members for another if it wishes. Originally, the teams also controlled part of the contract workers' salaries, paying them like other team members in the form of work points (which in turn were financed by a part of the workers' salaries which were paid by the employing unit directly to his/her production team under the terms of the contract).[13]

One of the most important operative differences between rural and non-rural householders is that the latter receive their allocation of foodgrain from their rural collective units, whereas the former get theirs — known as 'commodity grain' — from the state grain bureau through its local outlets. Shulu officials said that the major reason for requiring contract workers to maintain their rural household registrations — which lies, after all, at the very heart of the contract labour system itself — was to relieve the state of the burden of supplying commodity grain to them. This would put new pressure on the distributive capacity of the state grain bureau, but more importantly, would require an increase in state grain procurement from the rural collective sector, through purchase (which the state could ill afford, since it has already been subsidizing urban grain supply) or through higher taxes or quotas (which would prove politically risky). Apparently a system under which production teams supply their own contract workers with grain (charging the workers by deducting work points) has been preferred by peasants and/or rural cadres to one under which the state would supply them with grain by raising its rural procurements.[14]

In any event, Shulu officials said that they (specifically, it appears, the County Planning Commission) operated under a very strict quota from higher level state agencies on the size of the regular urban industrial labour force, and that it had not been revised upward for quite some time, because of the state's unwillingness to increase the number of people depending on commodity grain supplies. Yet Shulu industry had been growing and was continuing to do so, and for this it had required

and continued to require more workers. Expansion of the contract labour force was the answer. Between 1964 and 1978, the industrial labour force at the county level in Shulu trebled, from 5150 to 15,034; 7475 of these new workers (76%) were contract workers. By 1978, contract workers comprised over half of Shulu's county industry labour.

Though the grain supply problem was given as the major — in fact the only reason for the reliance on contract labour, it is quite likely that other factors were operative as well. Contract workers cost less to employ; as we shall see, their average wages are significantly lower than regular workers', and they draw fewer fringe benefits. By housing them in dormitories and keeping their families in the village, pressure on scarce urban housing and land has been reduced. Employing enterprises and the planning and administrative agencies which supervise them have gained managerial flexibility by using contract labour, which is easier to dismiss (simply by failing to renew the contract) than is the regular labour force, which is used to its 'iron rice bowl' and is in a better position than rural contract workers to threaten the state politically should its security come under attack. Moreover, employment of peasants as contract workers in urban industry provides the state with a way of reducing rural underemployment or unemployment *in a planned way*, avoiding the risks of massive desertion of the rural collectives, which would endanger not only agriculture but also (as it has in the past) China's rural socialist project.[15] The contract labour system, then, has strong attractions for Chinese industrial managers and administrators, for urban government officials, and for rural cadres in areas like Shulu where excess rural labour is a problem. Little wonder that it has grown so quickly and become so important in Shulu.

Perhaps that is also the reason for the firm policy to deny official status as regular workers to the contract workers. Prior to 1972, there was a policy to change the classification of contract workers to regular workers, perhaps as a result of the obstreperous agitations by contract workers during the Cultural Revolution. In 1972, Shulu factories received a 'general guideline' to convert their contract workers to regular workers by changing their rural household registrations to non-rural ones, and it was in fact adopted in at least one Shulu plant: the locally and historically important Fur and Leather Tannery. But apparently this was so controversial that it was soon dropped. Since 1972, contract workers have specifically been denied the opportunity to become regular workers. The outlines of this controversy were not made clear, though it is easy to see how converting contract workers into regular workers would be opposed both by the regular workers (who feared the dilution of their privileged position by its extension to peasant contract workers) and by factory managers and industrial administrators who benefited from the lower wages and potentially more flexible terms on which the contract workers could be employed. In any event, contract labour continues to be a source of controversy and of discontent, as we shall see.

3. REMUNERATION: METHODS AND INEQUALITIES

While regular industrial workers received their monthly salaries in full from the factories that employed them, before 1972 contract workers were paid only part of their salaries directly, with the rest coming indirectly in the then-standard rural form of work points awarded by their production teams. This method reflected, and was one of the most important material embodiments of, the contract workers' ambiguous status between the rural collective sector on the one hand and the urban state/collective sector on the other. Under it, Shulu contract workers received half of their salaries directly from their employing units in cash. The other half was sent by the employers to the contract workers' production teams,[16] which deposited it in their own cash accounts and in turn awarded the contract workers 10 work points for each day the worker had been employed in the contracting factory. The workers then used the work points just like their fellow production team members: to pay for distributions of grain and other items from the team, and, if the worker's

account still had a balance after doing so, to draw cash income from the team at the end of the year.

From the workers' and peasants' point of view, this method had several important implications. First, only contract workers from very well-off teams received all of their salary as paid by their factories. Most others received only a portion. Precisely how large a portion they did receive depended on the value of their production team's work points. Those from more prosperous teams with higher work point values received a greater portion of their salaries than those from less prosperous teams with lower work point values. Table 1, which displays hypothetical examples based on the situation in Shulu, indicates the magnitudes involved. It calculates the monthly salaries of Shulu contract workers from teams with 1978 work point values that in Shulu were considered low (¥ 0.03), average (¥ 0.05) and high (¥ 0.07). (The table may overstate *all* contract workers' salaries, if work point values before 1972, when this system was changed, were lower than in 1978.) In each example, the worker received half of the ¥ 38 average monthly salary of Shulu contract workers (¥ 19) plus work points for 26 days. The differentials were not inconsiderable; indeed, the worker from the ¥ 0.07 team received almost 40% more than the one from the ¥ 0.03 team.[17] Of course, to some extent these inequalities would exist anyway in the absence of contract work.

In fact, the second point that emerges from the hypothetical example is that contract work actually *reduces* the inequality among workers of teams with unequal work point values. The income inequalities among contract workers, though significant, were still less than the inequalities among members of the same rural collectives who were not contract workers. The contract worker from the ¥ 0.07 team may indeed have been receiving

Table 1. *Hypothetical incomes of contract workers and regular team members of production teams with various work point values*

Team work point value	Contract workers' monthly income				Regular team members' monthly income (= 26 days' work points = 260 points)
	Value of 26 days' work points (= 260 points)	+	Cash salary received from factory	= Total	
¥ 0.03	¥ 7.80	+	¥ 19	= ¥ 26.80	¥ 7.80
¥ 0.05	¥ 13.00	+	¥ 19	= ¥ 32.00	¥ 13.00
¥ 0.07	¥ 18.20	+	¥ 19	= ¥ 37.20	¥ 18.20

almost 40% more than the one from the ¥ 0.03 team, but the regular team member (engaged full-time in collective agriculture) of the ¥ 0.07 team was receiving 133% more than his/her counterpart in the ¥ 0.03 team.

But this leads directly to the third point: the reduction of this inequality is more than matched by the creation of a new one between the contract workers and regular team members of the same team. Each contract worker in the example received ¥ 19/month more than the regular team worker. In quantitative terms, this creates the *largest* inequalities in the system. In the ¥ 0.03 team, the contract worker was receiving almost 250% more than the regular team worker. No wonder that contract work has been so prized among peasants. But, and this is the fourth point, this intra-team inequality is lower in the higher-income teams: where the work point value was ¥ 0.07, the differential between contract and regular team workers was only (!) around 100%.

But fifth, for all of their economic advantages over their fellow team members left behind in the countryside, contract workers were at an economic disadvantage in comparison with the regular workers alongside whom they worked, usually doing the identical task. Looking simply at wages for the moment, Shulu contract workers averaged annual salaries of ¥ 455, compared with the regular workers' ¥ 571. It may be that some of this differential derives from the contract workers' lower levels of skill or experience; in other words, the wage differential between regular and contract workers doing the same jobs or having the same length of job tenure might be less than the aggregate averages suggest. But the fact that intra-factory differentials between regular and contract workers in two Shulu plants were also around ¥ 120/year points clearly to the existence of a generally lower pay scale for contract workers.

Of course, any comparison of the economic situations of contract and regular workers must go beyond the simple wage differential. We learned little about bonuses in Shulu, though officials did state that both regular and contract workers were eligible to receive them. Another complication is that contract workers pay around ¥ 60/year less for their and their families' grain than do regular workers, by virtue of the fact that they can buy it at low rural prices.[18] But this must be weighed against other factors which put contract workers at a relative economic disadvantage. First, they incur some additional expenses for travel to and from home. Second, they do not receive the 'fringe' benefits enjoyed by regular workers, such as free medical insurance, accident insurance (workers' compensation), pensions and sick leave. The cash value of these items is hard to estimate. But even if they roughly balance out with the grain cost differential, the income gap between the contract and regular workers has still exceeded the simple wage differential of 1.25:1, because as we have seen the contract workers were (before 1972) only receiving part of their wages, with the rest being retained by their teams. Returning to the hypothetical example for a moment, the gap between regular workers and those from a team with a work point value of ¥ 0.07 (assuming that other factors cancel each other out) would be 1.28:1, since these workers were receiving nearly all the wage paid by the factory (i.e. the production team was keeping very little); but for the worker from the ¥ 0.05 team, the gap was 1.49:1, and for the one from the ¥ 0.03 team 1.78:1.

When it is recalled that these are inequalities among workers who are usually doing similar or identical work under the very same factory roofs their seriousness and political explosiveness is not hard to understand. Nationally, contract workers tended to join radical factions during the Cultural Revolution, in the context of which they vociferously protested not only their lower wages but also their less secure job tenure which placed them at a disadvantage in expressing their discontent over a range of issues.[19] While we could learn little about the contours of political conflict during the Cultural Revolution in Shulu, there are strong suggestions that contract work had created political pressures which came to a head in 1972. We noted above that before that year it was possible, at least in terms of official policy, for contract workers to have their rural household registrations changed, which would entitle them not only to all the benefits of employment enjoyed by regular workers but also urban housing, education for their children, medical care, proximity to commercial services and cultural opportunities, and so forth. This policy was no doubt partly a response to discontent which had been building up among contract workers against their subordinate status. But it was controversial, facing opposition from regular workers, factory managers and urban agency officials. One attempt to implement it in Shulu's Fur and Leather Tannery was quickly put to a stop in 1972.

Perhaps as part of a compromise solution, the method according to which contract workers were paid was changed in that same year, and was still in effect in 1979. While the old method of payment was still offered to workers, they were also offered a new option of receiving all of their salaries in cash, except for a monthly amount of ¥ 3 or ¥ 4 — around 10% of their salaries — which was sent directly to their production teams. The teams got this free and clear, with no responsibility to award work points to the workers in turn. The contract workers still purchased their grain from their production teams at the lower rural price. For most contract workers, the new system would leave them with more income: the average contract worker could now clear around ¥ 34.50 per month, about the same as a contract worker from a team with a work point value of ¥ 0.06 in our hypothetical example had cleared under the old system. But the average work point value in Shulu in 1978 was more like ¥ 0.05, and therefore in many teams it was quite a bit less. So the new system must have gone far toward raising the incomes of many, and probably most, Shulu contract workers. (This effect was reduced somewhat by the effects of a policy, adopted to compensate poorer teams for the revenues they lost under the new system, by which poorer teams received a slightly higher percentage of the contract workers' wages than richer teams. In Shulu's Chengguan Commune, the poorer teams received 15% while the richer ones got 10%.) Moreover, contract workers from more prosperous teams, whose work point values were so high (in the hypothetical example, over ¥ 0.06) that they would actually lose from the new system, could still opt to be paid under the old one.

4. TEMPORARY CONTRACT LABOUR AND URBAN–RURAL FINANCIAL AND DEVELOPMENTAL FLOWS

Temporary contract labour involves a complex set of relationships between urban and rural, involving economic inequalities, financial transfers, redistributive effects, developmental dynamics, class structure and political tension. The complex and cross-cutting web of income inequalities which it sets up among peasants, contract workers and regular urban industrial workers, discussed above, are but a part of the picture. Here we look into some of the other implications of temporary contract labour for urban–rural relations.

In 1978 there were 7779 temporary contract workers employed in Shulu industry.[20] This comes to only 3.5% of the rural labour force

— clearly a small amount, though a potentially important group if they are drawn from among the 'best and brightest' of the rural labour force, a possibility which will be addressed below. But if small by rural standards, contract labour made up a very large part — indeed, over half — of the industrial labour force in the urban state/collective sector. Moreover, most of this labour was recruited starting in the latter half of the 1960s, when Shulu industry experienced some of its greatest growth and achieved levels of sophistication that have made it the premier industrial county of Shijiazhuang Prefecture. It is no exaggeration to say that the latest and most advanced stage of Shulu's industrialization has been achieved on the basis of an increment to the labour force comprised predominantly of peasants hired on a contract basis.

(a) Advantages for urban areas and for the urban state/collective industrial sector

Use of peasant contract labour has had several major advantages for Shulu's urban areas and urban state/collective industrial sector. First, it has reduced wage costs in urban state/collective industry considerably, by around ¥ 900,000 in 1978, which amounts to about 12% of the total payroll in that year.[21]

Second, it has transferred a large part of the social reproduction costs of the industrial labour force onto the rural collective sector and the individual households that comprise it. Contract workers' housing in town is paid for by the factories that employ them, but this can be done relatively inexpensively in dormitories, usually located on factory grounds; moreover, housing for the workers' families need not be provided at all, since they stay home in the countryside.[22] This means in turn that education too need not be provided by urban factories or city governments for the children of these workers. Contract workers are expected to rely for their health care on rural paramedics, doctors, clinics, hospitals and cooperative health care plans (although they are provided first aid in the factory clinic if necessary). They are paid no pensions and provided no retirees' services. The precise cash value of these savings is difficult to estimate, but certainly it is large, especially when it is remembered that we are talking about all these services for over half of the urban industrial labour force.

The third point is simply another aspect of the second: the pressure on urban land, institutions and services is significantly reduced by contract labour. Indeed, because of it, Xinji is a far less congested place, its schools and hospitals are far less crowded and pressurized, its housing is far more available and comfortable, and its budgets far less strained than they otherwise would be without contract labour.

Fourth, urban employers are given the flexibility in labour force matters which they are denied by the various restrictions on hiring and firing of regular urban labour. On the one hand, by 1979 the state had not permitted any expansions of the regular labour force in Shulu for many years. On the other, the 'iron rice bowl' policies had made firing workers almost impossible. While it does not appear that there was much need for industrial employers in Shulu to reduce their labour force in any significant numbers (since industry was expanding apace), the *power* to fire can be a major lever in the hands of employers seeking to enforce greater discipline over their workers and of planners seeking to move workers around among enterprises. Indeed, the major arguments advanced by proponents of restoring the employers' right to fire workers in China have been the presumed salutary effects on labour discipline and allocative flexibility. As well, contract workers complained during the Cultural Revolution that almost all the flexibility which factory managers had in labour matters was achieved at the contract workers' expense; this included not only hiring and firing but also transfers, job allocations and even wage negotiations.[23] Not surprisingly, we could not find out anything in Shulu about how employers and planners made use of the leverage afforded them by the institution of contract labour, but it is hard to imagine that they would not prefer having it, particularly coming into a period like the present one when efficiency and profitability are being stressed in national policy, and when planners' and managers' own careers may well be tied to such matters.

Of course the urban sector's gains in these matters — especially relating to wage differentials and the shunting off of social reproduction costs of the labour force — are the rural sector's losses. The fact is, though, that while the rural collective sector is in effect being forced by the institution of contract labour to bear some of the costs of industrialization in Shulu, it is also benefiting from industry's use of contract labour in some very concrete ways, at least compared with where it would be without it.

(b) *Advantages for rural areas and for the rural collective sector*

First of all there is the economic transfer from urban to rural which is effected by contract labour. This includes the monies which rural collective units appropriate as a share of the contract workers' salary (under either of the payment systems that have prevailed in Shulu) as well as the remittances which contract workers send to their families back home. The first can be estimated, both for 1972 (the last year of the old payment system) and 1978 (under the new one), as amounting roughly to a third of a million *yuan* per year, an amount whose magnitude to the rural collective sector can be appreciated when it is noted that it about equalled 1972 total state budgetary support for agriculture (¥ 357,500) and 1978 state budgeted relief for poor communes (¥ 345,000).[24] (The figure would be higher if the 2215 contract workers engaged in commerce were included.) The second is harder to estimate, but if each contract worker were remitting only one-fourth of his or her net income (after paying the fee to the team) back home — probably a conservative estimate since these workers were getting free housing in town, so their only expenses were self-maintenance and travel) — this would still amount to around ¥ 100 per year, or another ¥ 800,000 per year.[25] Therefore, the total amount of money brought into the rural collective sector by Shulu industrial contract workers in 1978 was, all told, in the vicinity of ¥ 1,000,000. To put this figure into context, it amounts to the entire contribution of the rural collective sector to the massive water conservancy project carried out in southern Shulu in 1977—78.

Of course this is only the one-way flow; it does not take into account the output and income lost to the rural collective sector by the loss of these contract workers. If average per capita collectively distributed income (¥ 88.20 in 1978) were taken as a surrogate for net per capita income in the rural collective sector (after deducting for taxes, direct costs of production, allotments for further accumulation and collective income expenditures), each contract worker would have been making a net contribution to the rural collective sector of only ¥ 50 or so per year (¥ 42 fees + ¥ 100 family remittances – ¥ 88 lost net income), rather than the estimates of ¥ 140–170 worked out above. But in fact there is every reason to believe that the net income which each contract worker would have contributed to the rural collective sector in the absence of contract employment would be significantly lower than ¥ 88 per year. First, the ¥ 88 figure includes as a component the relatively high net income per worker in commune and brigade sidelines, but it is not at all likely that contract workers are being recruited at the expense of this enterprise labour. In this densely populated part of the North China plain, there is a problem of excessive labour on the land, i.e. in agriculture. Employment in commune and brigade industries is one attempt to solve the problem, and contract labour another. It makes more sense, then, to compare the value of income produced by contract workers against that produced by agricultural workers, which is where they would otherwise be employed; and the net income per worker is no doubt lower than ¥ 88, probably by quite a bit. Second, comparison should be made not against *average* but rather against *marginal* net income per worker; here again the marginal figures, especially in agriculture are probably quite low in Shulu in view of the fact that low marginal productivities (in land but especially labor) are among the major problems facing Chinese agriculture. All in all, then, the net income lost to the rural collective sector in Shulu because of the assignment of a portion of the rural (and, we have argued, specifically agricultural) labour force to contract work in industry is in all likelihood quite low. Most of the revenues brought into that sector by contract workers, therefore, are probably net gains for the rural collective sector.

A second kind of benefit which the rural collective sector can gain from contract labour has to do with the skills and contacts which contract workers bring back with them upon their return to the villages. This is always a difficult matter to measure, even with complete information, and the problem is compounded by the dearth of information we could collect on it in Shulu. Given the rapid expansion of the contract labour force there, it does not appear that many contract workers have been returning home anyway, at least in the aggregate. But it is possible that the aggregate figures mask turnover of those who are returning only to be replaced by other peasants, either under some rotation scheme or because of demographic reasons (e.g. young women returning home to bear and nurture children or returning home when their children who may have been with them in town start school in the countryside). It also should be noted that even in the absence of a significant return rate, the contacts and information which contract workers can supply to their home villages

through visits, phone calls and letters can be of enormous importance to the rural collective units in helping them identify markets for industrial and sideline products which they are already or could start turning out, and in helping them to obtain needed inputs for industry, sidelines or even for agriculture.

Third, the rural collective sector is spared by the institution of contract labour from suffering the very serious losses that can and indeed in recent history have been visited on it by the uncontrolled outflow of peasant labour to towns in search of employment. Of course the extent of labour outflow, and the precise effects which it has upon the rural economy, vary depending on the marginal demand (or, perhaps more appropriately in a socialist system, utility or even need) for labour in a given locality, on the extent of remittances, on the length of stay away and so forth. The experience of the Great Leap Forward, in the wake of which peasants deserted many villages *en masse*, may be instructive of the possible effects. Here the effects on the rural economy and the socialist transition in the countryside, though obviously related, need to be distinguished. In terms of the former, many villages which were poor from the outset, particularly because of low labour densities or lack of infrastructure, lost the very workers whose labour, organized into farmland construction projects under the then-new communes, was the best hope for recovery. A downward spiral was set into motion, in which the desertions of some — and usually it was indeed the 'best and brightest' peasants who left first — only exacerbated the crisis of the rural economy, which increased the pressure (or, if you will, the incentive) on others to leave, which worsened the crisis further, etc.[26] In terms of the latter, the rural crisis was simultaneously a crisis for the rural socialist institutions, whose development was always predicated on a growing rural economy.[27] Inversely, as peasants, especially poor peasants, left the countryside, the capacity of the rural collective units to redeem themselves and prove their worth and viability by organizing the recovery through collective projects in farmland reconstruction, was diminished, and for a time the only way out was to retreat to less collectivist and even pre-collectivist forms of productive relations in agriculture.

It is certainly no accident that the outflow of labour from the countryside after the Great Leap coincided with the appearance of household contract production and other forms of individual or small collective sub-contracting;

nor were these purely parallel responses to the crisis brought on by the Great Leap. (It is also not accidental that an essential element of recovery when it did come was the recall of peasant labour to villages which had been victimized by its outflow.[28]) In the absence of the labour power which could be mobilized collectively for recovery, many localities were forced to retreat on the collectivization front. That this was a welcome development to many former rich and upper-middle peasants adds a dimension of class conflict to the matter.[29]

In sum, the uncontrolled outflow of labour after the Great Leap contributed in many localities to developments which can appropriately be seen as struggles between rural collectivist and pre-collectivist modes of production, and between rural classes as well. The contract labour system was born partly as a response to these problems. By placing the flow of labour out of the rural sector under the regulation of state and rural collective sector authorities, the risks posed by uncontrolled outflow to the health of the rural economy, the prospects for socialism, and the rural class conflict (perhaps the latter two are not yet moot) are reduced.

There is a fourth benefit from contract labour which accrues at least to a part of the rural areas — namely, its poorer part. This has to do with the redistributive effects (among rural *units*, not individuals) of contract labour. Under the pre-1972 payment system in Shulu, poorer teams benefited more than rich ones from the portion of the contract workers' wages which they received, since they paid out to the workers less valuable work points than did the richer teams. Even under the post-1972 payment system, the poorer teams were to receive a larger fee than the richer ones. It was also claimed in Shulu — and this claim is hardly unique — that in allocating contract labour slots preference is given to poorer communes, brigades and teams. Of course, this redistributive effect must be balanced against the significant inequalities among peasants, contract workers and regular workers which contract labour opens up, which quantitatively are probably greater overall than the redistribution effected at the unit level.[30]

5. CONTRACT LABOUR, CLASS STRUCTURE AND URBAN—RURAL CLEAVAGE

The general conclusion of the previous two sections is that temporary contract labour, though still providing for certain inequalities between peasants who take contract work on the one hand and regular urban workers and peasants on the other, nevertheless promotes some degree of urban—rural *balance* in the areas of financial flows, developmental possibilities and even, in some respects, individual income. Yet, at the same time it also rests upon and may even serve to reinforce the structural *cleavage* between urban and rural people, economies and institutions. Contract labour is built around the household registration system, which divides the Chinese people into categories of rural and urban (technically, 'non-rural') householders. People in these categories face entirely different prospects for employment and advancement, structures of income and social services, and social and cultural life. Peasants in Shulu County and much of China accept — indeed, they vie for — urban contract work, despite its more unfavourable terms compared with regular urban workers, precisely because the urban—rural cleavage, and the household registration system which is used to enforce it, pose such severe obstacles to upward and townward mobility in any other way. In this sense, contract labour is based upon the urban—rural cleavage. Moreover, by permitting state regulated movement of labour from countryside to city in places where it is needed, contract labour prevents the state from having to dismantle the household registration system. In this sense, contract labour may actually be seen as reinforcing or at least preserving the urban—rural cleavage at its point of greatest vulnerability.

Yet, at the same time, contract labour may, in dialectical fashion, be producing new class forces which will bring pressure against the household registration and contract labour systems themselves. Contract workers form a distinct stratum of the peasantry. They remain tied to it by the rural collective units' continuing claim on their labour, their occupational futures and a portion of their income, as well as by the fact that their families usually stay at home in the village. Yet their non-agricultural occupations, their opportunity in many cases to reside in a town (albeit on an irregular or subaltern basis) and their higher incomes set them clearly apart from the peasantry. These same factors bring them within the closest possible proximity to the urban working class, yet they are denied equal status with members of that class in terms of income, job security, fringe benefits, housing and access to opportunities for upward mobility for themselves (like job promotions) and for their children (like superior schooling and assignment to urban employment). Contract workers' objective situation engenders a clear interest in removing the restrictions embedded in the household registration and contract labour systems, so that they can become regular workers. In Shulu, they acted on this interest by trying to change their household registrations; though this failed, they did manage to alter their payment system, reducing significantly the share of their income going to their rural collective units. Throughout much of China, contract workers proved to be among the most radical participants in the Cultural Revolution. In short, the system of contract work, intended originally to reinforce the household registration system and through it the peasant—worker cleavage, has created a stratum which strongly opposes continued maintenance of the cleavage and the regulatory systems associated with it.[31]

6. CONCLUSIONS

Six main points have emerged in this discussion. First, in Shulu County temporary contract labour has made a very significant contribution to industrialization. Shulu had built a solid industrial base by the mid-1960s, but it was only in the latter half of that decade and on into the 1970s that Shulu really grew into the premier industrial county of Shijiazhuang Prefecture, developing a wide range of industries including some rather modern, sophisticated lines of production. This development was based predominantly on the employment of peasants on a temporary contract basis, to the point that by 1978 these workers made up a majority of the workforce in county-level industry. Contract workers also helped subsidize Shulu industry by virtue of their lower wages compared with the regular urban industrial workforce.

Second, this heavy use of temporary contract labour enabled Shulu to minimize permanent townward migration during its period of rapid industrialization. In other words, urbanization has proceeded at a much slower rate than the county's rapid industrialization would otherwise have caused. Xinji, the county capital, would have had around twice its 1978 population if the temporary contract system had not prevented the contract workers' families from setting up residence there.

Third, the system of contract labour has helped promote urban—rural balance in a number of ways, but also set limits to that

balance. It enabled rural collective units to appropriate significant amounts of funds which could be used to finance rural development. It also directed significant funds into the rural household sector by paying contract workers far more than they would have made in their villages. Had the contract work system not existed, these monies would have reached the workers anyway of course, but as members of an urban rather than rural household sector. By tightly regulating the labour market, the contract system may also have kept wages higher than they would have been if peasants had been permitted to flood the labour market, although this is a highly speculative, counterfactual matter and also one subject to other possible interventions by the state to maintain wage levels. Whatever the size of the gains in urban—rural balance resulting from contract labour may be, they must be weighed against other imbalances built into the system. The most glaring of these were the continuing inequalities between contract and regular workers in the areas of wages and benefits. Then there is also the intangible factor of the burden placed on contract workers (and their families) by virtue of separation from family and the rigours of periodic travel home.

Fourth, contract labour had complex effects in terms of distributional questions within the rural areas, increasing equality in some respects but opening up new inequalities in others. Specifically, it increased equality among rural collective units in various ways, but it also increased inequality among peasants within given collective units.

Fifth, it helped to reinforce the structural class inequality between workers and peasants in China. Most discussions of rural—urban relations address the question of balance in the distribution of particular resources or utility values, such as investment funds, knowledge, capital goods or income. A more structural perspective is also needed, paying attention to class relations and differences in terms of incorporation into a particular mode of production which may exist in the social formation, questions about occupational structure and opportunity that flow directly from this, and other matters which may or may not also flow from it such as incorporation into a specific structure of political organization, social status and culture. In this general area, *temporary contract labour has had the effect of reinforcing the worker—peasant cleavage in Chinese society, even while it may be redistributing resources in a somewhat more balanced way across that cleavage line.* Thus, while paying contract workers more than they would make as peasants, it also prevents them and their families from becoming workers and urban dwellers. By putting peasant contract workers in the closest possible proximity to the urban-based working class, it drives home ever more forcefully the class inequality between them.

This leads directly to the final point. The contract work system creates a social stratum — the contract workers and their families — which threatens the very basis of the worker—peasant class cleavage that the contract labour system was designed to or at least served to maintain. Contract workers have already expressed their opposition to the class inequalities between themselves and the working class in the form of political protests during the Cultural Revolution (in China generally) and in some, perhaps more measured, form of political action in Shulu County up to 1972. While the details of the 1972 dispute remain unclear — itself an indicator of their seriousness, perhaps — what is clear is that the workers gained economic concessions for themselves at the expense of their rural collective units (and therefore also at the expense of their fellow peasants), but that they lost in their effort to remove the structural barrier dividing them from the working class: their demand for a change in their household registrations to 'non-rural' was not met. The class cleavage still remains, therefore, and while its effects have been ameliorated by economic concessions, there is no reason to expect the class conflict embodied in, engendered by, and perhaps even reinforced by contract labour to go away by itself. Contract labour will continue to be part and parcel of the dynamics of socialist China's changing class structure and the political changes which they in turn effect.

POSTSCRIPT: CONTRACT LABOUR AND THE CHINESE RURAL REFORMS — SOME SPECULATIONS

Temporary contract labour has never received very much attention in Chinese published media, and it has not been possible to return to China since 1979 to study the issue further. Therefore, the effects of the massive changes in rural organization under the recent reforms on contract labour in Shulu remain adumbrated. While there is little to report, therefore, it may not be inappropriate to speculate on the possible developments given what is already known about pre-reform days.

The major changes in rural political and economic organization which will bear upon contract labour are two: first, the reduced capacity of rural collective units, especially at the grassroots levels (the teams but particularly the brigades) to regulate economic activity; and second, the general freeing up of labour markets in the towns and rural areas. The contract labour system always depended for its operation upon a double enforcement: by the rural collective units below, which kept peasants employed in the rural areas and regulated contract arrangements by which a select few could undertake urban industrial employment; and by the urban factories and labour bureaux above, which restricted and regulated the labour markets on the urban side. As the general administrative and political capacities of the rural collective units have declined under the recent reforms, control of rural outmigration will become harder to enforce. Specifically, now that rural cadres are not calling upon peasants to show up for work each day on collective fields, peasants will be freer to leave the countryside on their own to seek urban employment. And since rural cadres have seen their political role decline under the recent reforms, even if such migration is formally made illegal or frowned upon in policy and propaganda, there will be less that rural officials will be able to do to enforce such laws or policies.

In addition, as freer and more informal labour markets open up in towns, peasants are likely to respond by coming to town in greater numbers in search of employment. Even if more jobs do not actually open up in a given area, townward migration may grow as peasants now find it easier to leave hoping they can find or even create such jobs. Hence, townward migration can be expected to grow, and to do so in ways which are less subject than before to state regulation and control. Moreover, with the possible opening up of private and informal housing markets in towns (the rise of privately run inns has been reported in the Chinese press, and it is certainly not beyond the capacity of Chinese urban dwellers to try to make some money by renting out space in their homes if they have any to spare), the increased townward migration may take on a broader and more permanent character, as peasants bring all or part of their families with them and stay longer.

If this set of developments begins to take place, a number of effects can be imagined. Factory managers under pressure to maximize profits may prefer to hire these migrants rather than rural contract workers (or even regular urban workers), since they could probably get them on better terms. This could further undermine the contract labour system, while also possibly driving down the level of industrial wages across the board. For the rural areas, this would mean a loss of the intra-rural redistributive effects of contract labour, as well as of the urban-to-rural economic transfers that it had effected. For the peasants who obtain urban jobs, falling wages on the more competitive labour market may mean a loss of income relative to what they would have received under contract labour. For urban workers there may also be downward pressure on wages and increased capacity for factory managers to enforce all manner of labour discipline on them. And for town dwellers and urban governments, there would of course be the increased pressure on urban services, amenities and space.

Of course, none of the elements of this grim scenario is beyond the capacity of the Chinese state to regulate should it choose to do so. The question may rather be to what extent, and in what ways, it chooses to do so. The set of possibilities outlined here would go far toward overcoming the class cleavage between peasants and workers which contract labour embodied and reinforced. But in doing so, it might well make both classes worse off in economic terms, while also pitting both against the interests and power of the Chinese socialist state and its plans for China's economic development.

NOTES

1. Suzanne Paine, 'Some reflections on the presence of "rural" or "urban" bias in China's development policies 1949–1976', *World Development*, Vol. 6, No. 5 (May 1978), pp. 693–707.

2. William Parish and Martin Whyte, *Village and Family in Contemporary China* (Chicago: University of Chicago Press, 1978), pp. 52–54.

3. *Ibid*.; Benedict Stavis, 'The Standard of Living in Rural China, 1978–1979', unpublished paper, Department of Agricultural Economics, Michigan State University (November 1980), p. 60; William Parish, 'Egalitarianism in Chinese society', *Problems of Communism* (January–February 1981), p. 41.

4. Michael Lipton, *Why Poor People Stay Poor: Urban Bias in World Development* (Cambridge: Harvard University Press, 1976), p. 150.

5. Nicholas Lardy, *Economic Growth and Distribution in China* (Cambridge: Cambridge University Press, 1978), pp. 175–178; Xue Muqiao, *China's Socialist Economy* (Beijing: Foreign Languages Press, 1981), pp. 146–154.

6. Rhoads Murphey, *The Fading of the Maoist Vision: City and Country in China's Development* (New York: Methuen, 1980), p. 22.

7. For an example, see Tang Tsou, Marc Blecher and Mitch Meisner, 'Organization, growth and equality in Xiyang County, Part II', *Modern China*, Vol. 5, No. 2 (April 1979), pp. 140–154, and *passim*.

8. G. William Skinner, 'Marketing and social structure in rural China (Parts I–III)', *Journal of Asian Studies*, Vol. 24, Nos. 1–3 (November 1964–May 1965), pp. 3–43, 195–228 and 363–399.

9. Michael Lipton, 'Rural development and the retention of the rural population in the countryside of developing countries', *Canadian Journal of Development Studies*, Vol. 3, No. 1 (Summer 1982), p. 18.

10. Marc Blecher, 'Income distribution in small rural Chinese communities', *China Quarterly*, Vol. 68 (December 1976), pp. 797–816.

11. Lipton, *op. cit.* (1982), pp. 20–22.

12. Shulu County is located approximately 70 km by paved road to the east of Shijiazhuang Municipality, which is the capital of Hebei Province. It is therefore a rural rather than suburban area, situated well out into the North China Plain. It is about average for its area in agricultural development, but relatively advanced industrially; in fact, it is the most industrially advanced county in the prefecture. Though industrial output value made up 55% of total output value by official count (and actually 65% if the output of brigade-level industry is included), still only 4% of the county's population were classified as 'non-rural householders'. With 6.94 persons per cultivated hectare, it is densely populated. For further description of the county, see Marc Blecher *et al.*, *Town and Country in a Developing Chinese County: Government, Economy and Society in Shulu Xian*, forthcoming; and Marc Blecher, 'Balance and cleavage in urban–rural relations: the case of Shulu County', in William Parish (ed.), *Problems in Chinese Rural Development* (forthcoming).

13. This method of paying contract workers was changed after 1972. The change, along with other features of the payment system, is discussed below.

14. It would be very interesting to try to understand to what extent this preference was rooted in concrete calculations of short-term utility and to what extent in a more general and traditional distrust by peasants of the state.

15. Outflow of rural labour has been characterized by some Chinese as part of the country's class struggle. See Tsou, Blecher and Meisner, *op. cit.* (1979).

16. It appears that the contract was actually made between the urban factory and the people's commune or production brigade acting on behalf of the team. The payroll transfer may, therefore, have gone through the commune or brigade. But it does not appear that either of these kept any significant amount of the funds -- perhaps a minor fee was charged.

17. In the hypothetical example, a contract worker's team would have to have a work point value of ¥ 0.073 for him/her to break even. Though we cannot be certain, it is probable that contract workers from teams with work point values higher than this would not receive any more, since this would amount to a subsidy from their teams, which were, after all, receiving only ¥ 19/month (or ¥ 0.73/day = ¥ 0.073 per work point based on 10 points per day) to cover the work points awarded to the contract workers. In other words, above a certain work point value there was an upper limit to the income increments which contract workers could receive just by virtue of being from higher-income teams.

18. This estimate was constructed by using the rural figure for average annual per capita distributed grain (229 kg) as a figure for both rural and urban consumption, and multiplying that by the ¥ 16/kg urban–rural grain price differential prevailing in mid-1979, which produced a per capita annual differential of ¥ 36.64. But workers have to purchase grain for their families as well as themselves. In Shulu the urban and rural dependency ratios were around 2:1 (see below), so the grain cost differential must be doubled, to ¥ 73.28. A further correction is also necessary, to account for the fact that rural residents, including contract workers, receive unhusked grain while urban residents purchase it already husked. The differential between husked and unhusked grain is around 20% by weight. If the grain cost differential is deflated by this same percentage, the final figure comes to ¥ 58.62. (The urban dependency ratio was calculated by summing the numbers of regular urban industrial workers [7225], commercial workers [4767] and county government staff [586] at 12,608, which when divided by the number of urban residents [around 25,000] gives a ratio of about 2. For the rural areas, the labour force participation rate in the rural collective sector in 1979 was 45.6% which when inverted yields a dependency ratio of 2.19.)

19. Hong Yung Lee, *The Politics of the Chinese Cultural Revolution* (Berkeley: University of California Press, 1978), pp. 130–132.

20. Contract workers were also an important part of the labour force employed in state commerce, comprising 2215 (46.5%) of the 4767 commercial workers employed at the commune level and above.

21. These are calculations from Shulu data. Average wages for regular workers in the urban/state collective industrial sector were ¥ 571, compared with an average of ¥ 455 paid to contract workers employed there. If the differential of ¥ 116 is multiplied by the total number of contract workers employed in urban state/collective industry (7779), the total saving is ¥ 902,364, which is 11.7% of the total wage bill for contract and regular workers of ¥ 7,682,050. (The total payroll figure was calculated by multiplying the average contract worker wage [¥ 455] by the total number of contract workers [7779] and adding the product [¥ 3,539,445] to the product of the average regular wage [¥ 571] and the number of regular workers [7255], which was ¥ 4,142,605.)

22. The only exception is that pre-school children of mothers with contract work could remain with them in town, housed in their mothers' dormitories and cared for during the day in factory crèches. But when the children reached school age they had to return to their parents' home villages. (Often this was also the time for their mothers to resign from contract work to move home too.)

23. Lee, *op. cit.* (1978), p. 132.

24. The figure of one-third of a million *yuan* was derived from the following calculations and assumptions: (1) *for the pre-1972 payment method*, production teams were appropriating about half the contract workers' wages, or ¥ 227.50 per year on average. In turn, they were awarding work points to these workers, which in the roughly average Shulu team (with a work point value of ¥ 0.05) came to ¥ 13/month (see Table 1) or ¥ 156/year. Subtracting this figure from the ¥ 227.50 appropriated from salary, it can be estimated that the average team appropriated ¥ 71.5 per year from the average contract worker. Though we lack data on the size of the contract labour force in industry in 1972, assuming linear growth from 1964 to 1978 produces an estimate of 4575 contract workers in Shulu industry in 1972. Their teams would therefore have been appropriating ¥ 327,113 (¥ 71.5 per workers × 4575 workers) in 1972. (2) *post-1972 method used in 1978*: each team was appropriating around ¥ 3.5 ('three to four *yuan*' we were told) per month from each industrial contract worker, or ¥ 42/year or so per year, amounting to ¥ 326,718 for all of the 7779 contract workers in 1978.

25. One-fourth of average net (after fee) income (¥ 413) was ¥ 103.25, which when multiplied by 7779 contract workers comes to ¥ 803,182.

26. Tsou, Blecher and Meisner, *op. cit.* (1979)

27. Vivienne Shue, *Peasant China in Transition* (Berkeley: University of California Press, 1980).

28. Tsou, Blecher and Meisner, *op. cit.* (1979).

29. Ann Thurston, 'The Revival of Classes in Rural Kwangtung: Production Team Politics in a Period of Crisis', paper presented to the Workshop on the

Pursuit of Political Interest in the People's Republic of China, Ann Arbor, Michigan (August 1977).

30. Still, it is interesting to note that in rural China inter-unit inequalities have, at least up to the time when the responsibility systems were introduced starting around 1979, been greater than intra-unit ones. The contract labour system effects redistribution precisely where it is needed most (at least from an egalitarian point of view).

31. It may be that the peasantry as a whole shares this opposition to household registration and maintenance of the peasant—worker cleavage. Their lower income and standard of living and their more toilsome conditions of work provide an objective material base for such opposition. Yet it is not at all clear that most peasants would have an objective interest in eliminating the contract labour system. In view of the high rates of urban unemployment in China, most peasants seeking urban work would have difficulty finding it; many of those who did might end up in an informal labour market doing periodic, insecure, low-paying work. Of course many might still want to

be able to take their chances. But for those staying behind (excluding family of those who found lucrative urban employment), eliminating the contract labour system would mean the loss of collective revenues accruing from the collectives' share of contract workers' wages, and also loss of a claim on the contract workers' labour in emergency situations. Certainly this would be opposed by those most committed to and dependent on the rural collectives, such as some of the poor and the rural collective unit cadres. The precise lines of cleavage on this issue of course have a subjective component which cannot be discerned from even the most precise analysis of the objective conditions. My point here is simply that there is no necessary reason to suppose that the peasantry as a whole would favour the elimination of the contract labour system and its replacement by unrestricted movement of rural labour to urban employment. Much more likely, the question would be controversial within the peasantry, one possible line of cleavage being between the strata of contract workers and some, but only some, of those who continue to be employed in agriculture.

The Single-Child Family: The First Five Years

ELISABETH J. CROLL*

Contemporary China Centre, Oxford

Summary. — Family planning has been seen as part of economic development in China since the 1960s. Its success did not lead to any slackening of campaigns in the 1970s, when new impetus to interest in holding down population growth was given by the adoption of the four modernizations and new problems posed by the production responsibility system. Reproduction, like production itself, became an object of planning. The single-child family policy is seen in official circles as an emergency measure lasting thirty years. Recent changes in emphasis include rules, bans and penalties for those ignoring official pressure to accept a single child family, although there are a number of very particular conditions under which the birth of a second child is permitted. Dissent continues on this question both as to penalties and exceptions permitted, while substantial rewards are given to those who conform to official policy. Heavy financial losses can be imposed on transgressors, as well as demotion and compulsory abortion. All of this represents a unique case of State dominance over the reproductive unit, the family. The State has been driven to act by looming unemployment, the high investment costs of population growth and the desire to achieve minimum per capita income.

One of the most momentous of the policies introduced by the present government and far-reaching in its implications for China's economic development and future social fabric is the single or one-child family programme. Family planning as such is not a new policy in China in that planned birth programmes had previously recommended late marriage, a four-year interval between births and fewer children per family. Moreover family planning clinics and techniques to facilitate birth planning were already more comprehensive and widespread than in most societies and were certainly the envy of many an international planned parenthood body. As a result of a decade of such policies, the 1970s had been marked by a sharp decline in the birth rate[1] from somewhere around 30 per thousand to about 19 or 20 per thousand with only 30 per cent or so of births made up of a third or additional children per family.[2] Despite this decline, family planning became the focus of new policies and campaigns in the late 1970s. Both the new Construction and the new Marriage Law of 1980 included the injunction that 'husband and wife are bound to practise family planning', and simultaneously the government embarked on a new and radical family planning policy which demanded that only in exceptional circumstances should couples have more than one child. A major reason for the introduction of this ambitious policy is to be found in the present government's ambitious plans for development and modernization.

By 1979 the post-Mao government had already embarked on a new and much heralded phase of socialist modernization the general aim of which was to turn China into a powerful and modern socialist society by developing four sectors of the economy: agriculture, industry, science and technology and defence. Although statements on the goals of socialist modernization referred to a new 'Long March' in the development of China, in 1978 the pace of economic development was designed to be rapid. To this end individual policies emphasized the importance of production, professionalism, skills, scientific and technological research, profitability and the operation of economic incentives in the planning, management and expansion of production. Of course, plans and indeed ambitious plans to promote development and increase production are not new in China, but what is novel is the degree to which plans to develop and modernize China are thought to be equally contingent on China also taking drastic steps to reduce her population.

* The research and writing of this paper was made possible by a grant from the Leverhulme Foundation.

The basic problem according to the present government is that unless the population to be fed, housed and clothed is reduced, the goals of any development strategy in China are bound to fail. The official concern with population and its relations to development in the late 1970s reflected the increasing alarm of the present government over the total sum of the population of China, more than one billion persons, and present and projected rates of population growth. Because of the age structure of China's population with some 65% and 50% of the population under 30 and 20 years of age respectively, growth rates were expected to be unprecedentedly high in the near future. As a result of birth peaks between 1954 and 1957 and subsequently between 1967 and 1972, it was expected that some 20 million persons will enter marriageable and child-bearing age between 1979 and 1982 and again in 1987 through to 1996 which amounted to some ten million more annually than is normal for other periods. If the government based its calculations on the present average birth rate of 2.3 children per couple, the total population would reach some 1.3 billion after 20 years and 1.5 billion after 40 years[3] (see Table 1). Demographic projections and their correlation with material and social resources showed that land ratios, per capita grain rations and the demand for facilities to feed, clothe, house and educate such a growing population were formidable and a barrier to accumulating the necessary capital for economic development and modernization.

In 1978 the government did not alter its emphasis on production so much as redefine production to include both production of material goods as well as the reproduction of human beings themselves. The government constantly quoted Engels in support of its two-fold definition of production:

> Social production itself is of a two-fold character: on the one hand, the production of the means of subsistence of food, of clothing, and shelter and the necessary tools; and on the other the production of human beings themselves, the propagation of the species.[4]

Current slogans thus directed cadres and the population to 'grasp the two kinds of production' and be aware of the consequences of allowing the population to increase out of step with China's productive capacity.

> If we do not implement planned population control and let the population increase uncontrollably, rapid population growth is bound to put a heavy burden on the state and the people,

cripple the national economy, adversely affect accumulation and State construction, the people's living standard and their health and slow down progress of the Four modernisations.[5]

On this basis, 'planned and proportionate' development not only called for the planned development of the production of material goods but also for planned development of the production of human beings. The potential for simultaneously achieving these twin goals was conceived to be one of the unique strengths of the socialist mode of development and again one long ago identified by Engels.[6] He had forecast that because the public ownership of the means of production already subjected the production of goods to State planning, it was but a natural consequence to take planning one step further and if necessary include reproduction within national economic plans. This analysis, simple as it is, offered an immediate explanation for the apparent lack of development in China in the past decades when the 'unchecked growth of population' and the resulting imbalance between the 'two kinds of production' had been allowed to violate the socialist principles of a planned economy. It also offered a plan for the future achievement of planned and proportionate development. Five-year national economic plans began to include twin targets and quotas for both production and reproduction. To fulfil the current national population targets of reducing rates of growth to 1% by the end of 1979, 0.5% in 1985 and zero population growth by the turn of the century, the present government felt it had no alternative but to adopt the rule — only one child.[7]

1. THE SINGLE-CHILD FAMILY POLICY

The single-child family policy is viewed as an emergency measure perhaps lasting twenty to thirty years, and it is defined in terms of a 'social payment' to make up for the lack of population control of the previous years.[8] Presently three factors distinguished this new policy from its predecessors. Firstly there is its novel, universal and singular recommendation — one child — which was deemed to be the 'fairest' means of reducing the birth rate. However, any success in promoting the one-child family is determined by the accompanying policies and measures to reduce the number of second and additional parity births. The published sets of rules and regulations on family size uniformly advocate the birth of one child and categorically 'prohibit', 'eliminate' or 'ban' the birth of a third child. That is, there are no conditions under which the birth of a third child is officially permitted in either rural or urban areas. What is not yet so clear or so uniform throughout China are the policies towards the birth of a second child. Yet it is precisely the acceptability or otherwise of a second child which will be the key determinant of the success of the single-child family policy. Official policies towards second parity births include programmes which aim to 'control' and 'regulate' the birth of second children in order to 'reduce' their number. The slogans range from 'no second child' to 'no more than two', and there is a range of circumstances, by no means uniform throughout China, under which a second child is allowed. Such regulations usually read:

> Among government cadres, workers and urban residents each couple shall have only one child, with the exemption of those who for special reasons have obtained permission to have more than one child. In rural areas, couples should limit themselves to a single child, but some couples may be given permission to have a second child if their requirements can be justified on account of practical difficulties which can be examined and approved. No one is allowed to have a third child no matter what.[9]

There are a number of very particular conditions under which the birth of a second child is permitted and these usually include situations in which (a) the first child is diagnosed as suffering from a non-hereditary disease and is not expected to grow into a normal able-bodied person; (b) one partner of a re-married couple is childless; and (c) after years of marriage, a woman who has been certified as sterile becomes pregnant after adopting a child.[10] These conditions apply equally to urban and rural couples, but there are in rural areas additional circumstances under which a second child might be born. These usually allow a second child 'if an individual commune member is having true or real difficulties'; a state which is to be defined and approved by county government officials and can therefore be variously interpreted throughout China. These conditions can be quite narrowly defined or, as in the most recent set of regulations published for Shanxi province, 'true difficulties' may embrace quite a range of circumstances. There couples are permitted to have a second child in the following situations:

1. after marriage the husband settles in with the family of an only daughter;
2. people who have long been living in sparsely populated mountain villages disadvantaged by inadequate transport facilities and natural conditions;
3. only one of three brothers or more is fertile;
4. the only son of a revolutionary martyr;
5. one party of a couple has a first degree deformity;
6. families which have only one son for three generations in a row;
7. both parties are an only son and an only daughter.[11]

So far the regulations enacting the single-child family policy are contained in provincial and municipal sets of regulations, and there is no national family planning law applicable throughout the entire country. It seems that a family planning law was drafted and was originally intended to be presented to the Fifth National People's Congress when it met in late 1980. That it has not yet appeared is apparently due to the 'lack of consensus' surrounding certain of its provisions.[12] It is a fair guess that much of the dissent centres around the conditions under which a second child is permitted and the severity of the penalties to be attached to the birth of a second child.

The second distinguishing feature of the single-child family policy is the degree to which punitive economic sanctions are to be taken against those not adhering to the national birth plan. Official regulations on the single-child family published by various provincial and municipal authorities include lists of incentives and disincentives which reward those couples with one child who pledge to have no more and penalize households not limiting family size to one child.[13] Over the past three years or so, rewards have gradually become more standardized over much of China, so that in all provinces and cities, couples with one child who apply for a single-child family certificate can now expect to receive a cash health or welfare subsidy. This is paid to the parents by their units of employment either as a monthly or annual subsidy or in rural areas is payable at each periodic distribution after the harvest. In many of the municipalities and most of the provinces the subsidy in 1982 amounted to 4 to 5 yuan per month until the child reached fourteen years of age; and within the rural production team the subsidy is frequently measured in terms of work points or between 3 to 6 labour days, which is the equivalent of 40 yuan or so per year.

In addition to the cash subsidy, there are a number of other privileges and subsidies to which the single-child family is entitled. The single child has priority of admission to nurseries, schools, hospitals, clinics and in job allocation. All educational and medical fees from birth onwards are to be waived or at least reduced. The single child is to receive an adult grain ration and a private plot allocation equivalent in area to that normally due to 1.5 to 2 children. The single-child family should receive priority in allocation of housing or housing plots and be allotted space due to a two-child family. The parents of a single-child will receive on retirement a subsidy additional to their pensions which amounts to 5% of the value of their last annual wage and which rises to 10% if they have no children to provide for their support in old age. The rewards are to be paid directly by the husband's and wife's unit of employment and the exact proportion paid to each parent depends on the level of ownership of their unit. For instance where both are employed at the same level the payments are to be equally shared, but if one member is employed in a State-owned enterprise and the other by either a rural or urban co-operative, then the State factory is likely to pay the whole subsidy. Potentially the economic rewards can be quite considerable, and in one commune it has been calculated that a couple with one child could augment its total collective income by a quarter or even a third through the benefits and rewards available to the single-child family.[14]

The economic penalties for a subsequent or additional child are the reverse of the incentives. An 'excess child levy' is to be made on the income of couples as a form of economic compensation to the State and the collective for the extra burdens caused by the birth of those children. Thus the regulations provide for a 5 to 10% deduction from the total income of a couple for somewhere between ten to sixteen years after birth. In some areas, the levy is graduated so that the parents of a fourth or fifth child pay higher levies — these are mostly set at 15% of their total income for a fourth or 20% for a fifth child. The wages of couples are directly debited by their units of employment while in the rural areas a production team may retain an equivalent portion of their distributed income. In a few regions there are alternative arrangements and the single levy or fine, which may amount to 300 or 400 yuan, is payable at the time of birth. In addition, the offending family must bear all the costs of the birth and subsequent medical and educational expenses incurred by the extra child, and it enjoys no priority in admission to any educational or medical institutions. The grain ration for the excess child is either reduced or available at a higher price,

and any coupons or rations for other items are not to be distributed to additional children below the ages of fourteen or in some cases eighteen years. The family with more than one child is not to be eligible for additional housing space in the urban areas or for new housing sites and additional private plots in rural areas. Finally, parents who reject the single-child family policy are not to be eligible for promotion or for a bonus for a number of years and cannot apply for subsidies in cases of hardship.

Potentially, then, the economic sanctions are quite considerable and what makes them even more exacting is the requirement that, in addition to these sanctions, the value of the rewards received for the first and single child are with few exceptions also to be paid back on the birth of a second child. What is not clear, however, is the extent to which penalties have been exacted on the birth of a second child. There have been no such cases reported in the media and it seems that local responses range from those where a second pregnancy is not permitted to proceed to term to those where local authorities take a softer line, allow the birth of a second child and do not exact any penalties. In the media, most of the cases where penalties are reported to have been exacted apply to the births of a third, fourth, and fifth child among cadres and Party members who are supposed to be setting an example. In these cases the couples have been demoted, their salaries reduced and an abortion or sterilization ordered. The operation of the penalties could amount to a financial loss of several hundreds or even thousands of yuan. In one case reported in the press a couple was charged a 15% excess child fee so that from the period of pregnancy until the child reached fourteen years of age, the salary of the husband was reduced by ¥ 9.21 and the wife's by ¥ 8.4 each month. They were ordered to pay all hospital fees and expenses of child birth, the wife forfeited her salary for maternity leave and her bonus for three years and the husband lost his bonus for one year. In all, the penalties in this case amounted to the staggering sum of ¥ 3000.[15] However, it does seem that intervention in second and third parity births may take place at an earlier stage and that the pressures brought to bear on offending couples are such that they may well be more likely to terminate the pregnancy rather than proceed and be penalized.

The third distinguishing feature marking out this policy from its predecessors is the degree of State intervention in family affairs which it represents. It can be said to mark a third phase in the relations between State and the reproductive unit. In the first phase, in the 1950s and 1960s, the State made available the means and techniques to limit family size, but left the decision to limit births up to the couple themselves. Then, in the late 1970s, there were some more flexible negotiations between State and family over the number of children, and family birth plans were supposed to be the subject of local administrative quotas — only so many births allowed each year — with some agreement effected between the collective and family as to who should give birth in a particular year.[16] From the late 1970s onwards, family plans were not to be subject to negotiation, and birth planning became a decision which the present Chinese leadership now thinks is too important to be delegated to the reproductive unit, the family:

> The population plan of the whole country is based on the reproductive activities of individual families and the family birth plan must be co-ordinated with the national population plan.[17]

The incorporation of family plans into a national population plan means that the control of births and family size becomes a matter of State planning and for State intervention in the reproductive plans of individual couples. It is no exaggeration to suggest that the population planning policies of the present Chinese leadership may represent an almost unique attempt by the State to acquire an exclusive measure of control over reproduction, family planning and family size. Indeed as the following quote suggests the policy is also seen as an extreme measure or instance of State interference in family affairs within China itself. A city newspaper reported that people in China still think

of the bearing of children as a private matter and thus say of the government: 'You are in charge of the earth and the sky and now you still want to take charge of child bearing.'[18]

The single-child family policy has been reckoned by observers of China to be the most unpopular policy in contemporary China, and it is by any standards a radical solution to the problems of modernization and development. The present government is thus faced with the considerable task of seeking the co-operation of the Chinese people to implement this policy.

2. ONE-CHILD CAMPAIGNS

In 1979 the government embarked on a massive educational campaign designed to publicize and popularize the idea of the one-child family, and all aspects of the media have been marshalled in its support.[19] The main aim of the educational campaign has been to convince the present population of China that it is the 'objective' conditions of China, rather than the Communist Party or the present leadership, that do not permit the birth of more children. To this end, the government has taken great pains to identify and explain the dimensions of the problem to the population at large. The government has calculated the projected population totals for China in the year 2000 on the basis of number of children per couple in order to establish a direct link between family size and population totals (see Table 1). It has also emphasized the costs of educating, training and employing the younger generation and the costs of providing basic needs for an ever-expanding population, which both reduce the resources available for accumulation and modernization and for

Table 1. *Projected Population Growth*

Average Birth Rate of every married couple[2]	Population Figure Year 2000[1]	Number of Increase Over 1979
3	1,414 million	444 million
2.3	1,282 million	312 million
2.0	1,217 million	247 million
1.5	1,125 million	155 million
1.0[3]	1,050 million	80 million

Notes: 1. Population Figures do not include Taiwan and Overseas Chinese.
2. Presumed from 1979 that the birth rate is maintained without variation.
3. Presumed from 1979 that the birth rate will decline and from 1985 be maintained at average of one child per couple.
Source: Zhongshan Daxue Xuebao Zhekue Ban (Zhongshan University Journal, Philosophy and Social Science Edition).

increasing standards of urban and rural livelihood.

To encourage a decrease in family size the government has drawn attention to the costs entailed in raising new generations of children which are borne by both family and state. The total cost of nurturing and educating a child to sixteen years (not including college) and according to the general standard of living in China is estimated to be ¥ 1,600 in the countryside (87% of the population), ¥ 4,800 in the small towns (4.2%) and ¥ 6,900 in the cities (8.6%). On the basis of these rough estimates, the government reckons that it has cost more than 1000 billion yuan to bring up the 600 million children born since 1949.[20] Given that 30% of this cost was borne by the State, the government estimates that upwards of 30% of the national income has been spent on reproducing the labour force and that if present birth rates continue it will cost the country dearly in the future. An additional and major problem identified by the government is that of providing employment for an ever expanding labour force. In the 1950s, one million young persons entered employment annually, now jobs have to be found for 6 to 10 million each year. To employ these young people, large capital investment in the means of production, amounting to billions of yuan annually, is necessary.[21]

The second set of arguments employed by the government to encourage a decrease in number of births per couple relate to the difficulties in providing basic needs for such a large and growing population. Here again the present government has published much data to show the difficulties which China has faced and will face in feeding, clothing and sheltering her large population. For instance the last thirty years have already seen a decline in cultivable land from 2.6 to 1.5 mu per capita[22] and it can be expected to decline further in the future. Again, although grain production has more than doubled in the same period from approximately 110 million tons in 1949 to near 318 million tons in 1980, the population has also nearly doubled — from 500 million to 1,000 million.[23] There has consequently been little change in the average grain output per capita between 1956, when it was about 307 kg, and 1980 when it was still around 307 kg.[24] Government reports estimate that for grain production to keep pace with the present population growth, the total grain output would need to be 480 million tons by the end of the century, 50% more than the total output for 1980.[25] Similar calculations have been made for the provision of housing and cotton which both show a decline in production per capita. It is reported that a survey in 190 cities in 1978 revealed that each person had an average of 3.6 square metres of housing space compared to 4.5 square metres in the 1950s.[26]

As Table 2 illustrates the government has correlated the number of children born per couple with the projected demands on resources by the end of the century. Indeed the general aim of all these calculations is to directly link

Table 2. *Family size and basic needs in year 2000*

Average Births[1] per couple	Average arable land[2] (mu per person)	Average Jin of Foodgrain[3] per person per year	Average No. of children entering primary school annually 1996–2000 (millions)	Total nurturing expenses incurred[4] (100 million yuan)
3	1.05	618	1.8	9768
2.3	1.16	682	1.4	6864
2	1.22	718	1.3	5434
1.5	1.32	777	0.9	3410
1	1.42	833	0.7	1760

Notes: 1. See Table 1.
2. Calculated on the assumption that by the year 2000 the country's arable land can be maintained at 1.49 billion mu.
3. Calculated on the basis of a progressive yearly production increase of 10 billion jin.
4. Calculated on the basis of an average of 2,200 yuan in nurturing expenses for each person born between 1979 and 2000 AD.
Source: 'One Married Couple, One Child Seen as Necessity', Zhongshan Daxue Xuebao-Zhexue Shehui Kexue Ban (Zhongshan University Journal), 1980 No. 4.

the responsibility of the individual couple with the welfare of the collective and the nation. According to the present government, one of the problems in the past was that all too often couples were only acquainted with the circumstances of their own family, and made their individual decisions on family size without reference to national conditions and constraints.

To communicate and popularize the objects of the new policy, the Department of Family Planning has taken special responsibility for the nation-wide administration and implementation of the single-child family programme. It already had a national network providing comprehensive services throughout China which could be activated in support of the new policy. To persuade families to accept new norms and take practical steps to implement the policy, each family is visited individually by members of the local family planning committees of the urban neighbourhood, factory enterprise or rural production team. Their task is to ascertain the couple's attitudes towards the new policy, their contraceptive practices and birth plans and to provide contraceptive services.[27] The degree of pressure applied to couples varies very much. In some areas, individual women, their husbands and their mothers-in-law may be visited time and again until all sources of resistance are worn down. Once a couple decides to sign the single-child family pledge or to have no more children then their decision may be publicized immediately on the local noticeboard or in the local newspaper and by publicly celebrating and rewarding them, and thus they are left with little opportunity to retract the decision. But in other areas the new policies, once expounded and explained, are not followed up with quite the same vigour.

The single-child family policy has been propagated in most regions of China — except for national minority areas — and by mid-1981 it was reckoned that some 12.5 million or so couples out of 22 million with one child had taken out single-child family certificates.[28] Of course those already having more than one child in 1979 were not eligible, and some single-child families had already decided to have but one child long before the current policy. It is probably too soon to ascertain in any detail the response of different sections of the population to this policy, but the data already available does suggest certain trends. First of all, there is a great deal of variation in response to the policy. In some model areas such as Changchow city it is reported that couples dare not have a second child, while in other areas multiple births are still common. In some

urban areas the number of couples with one child who are certified as single-child families may reach a high 80 to 90%, while in other areas, chiefly rural, the proportions may fall to below 20%. It is clear that the largest single factor determining the response of an individual couple to the new policy is the location of the household — primarily whether it be urban or rural.

3. THE CITIES

In urban districts of the main cities such as Beijing and Shanghai, it is reported that around 90% of couples with one child have pledged to remain single-child families. These proportions also include numbers of cadres and intellectuals who had already opted for one child long before the policy was introduced. A first-hand survey of 39 single-child families in Beijing and Shanghai in 1980 found that 40% or so of the parents were more than thirty-five years of age.[29]

Two detailed studies have been undertaken in China in the last three years which give some indication of contemporary responses of the urban population to the new policy. In an urban residential district of Beijing, the Family Planning Office undertook a detailed population survey in July 1980.[30] This survey showed that 92% (3,535) of the married women of child-bearing age with one child had taken out one-child certificates. The remaining 8% (290) had not yet applied for a one-child certificate. The high proportion of certified single-child families was the result of a campaign by the local family planning office in early 1980 which had worked very hard to persuade women of the benefits of the certificate. Many had needed lengthy persuasion, although the survey does report that 60% of those who had taken out the certificate had done so 'with little persuasion' because they said they had only wanted one child anyway. Most of the women in this category had experienced higher education and they were now cadres and intellectuals with demanding careers. They were also more likely to have had a son as their first child. Another 30% of the respondents said that they had hesitated and had really had to be persuaded. Indeed, they had only taken out the certificate to conform to the new policy, and indicated that if there were a change in the policy they would change their minds immediately. Some of this group felt they could not really afford to have a second child in the near future so they were willing to wait until their economic conditions improved, by which time they might change their minds and proceed to have a second child. A third group of 10% were unsure of their decision, and had only belatedly, 'under extreme pressure', agreed to take out a certificate. These women had largely done so because they feared discrimination at work, denial of promotion and the pressures of their colleagues, who, as a work group, would themselves be criticized and penalized for not meeting birth quotas. In contrast to that reluctant 30%, a minority of 8% of all women with one child had refused to take out a certificate, because they still wanted to keep open the option of having a second child, most often a boy. They did not think that the economic rewards were so valuable as to close that option, and some feared something might happen to their only child. Interestingly a very few, only 7 out of 290, had withheld their pledge as a weapon with which to bargain for better housing or promotion at work. Generally this group of 8% of those surveyed felt that the policy was itself unpredictable and might well change, and at this stage they preferred to adopt a 'wait and see' attitude.

A second survey undertaken in Hefei city in Anhui province where the success rate was only 62% is probably far more representative of city patterns.[31] In a Hefei district covering eight city blocks of factories and university and college institutions, there were 5,032 single-child families of whom 3,102 were certified. A survey of 1000 of those with certificates and a 1000 without certificates showed that parents of boys and parents with a higher education and higher than average incomes were more likely to have signed a certificate. The non-holders wanted to have more children (or more particularly a son) and saw no reason to believe that the rewards or economic incentives would actually materialize. They expected that in the future the policy might again be extended to allow for two children. The survey suggested that the chief source of dissatisfaction and tension among both holders and non-holders was the shortage of housing. Indeed, those conducting the investigation suggested that the establishment of a direct link between housing and family size would both be of benefit to the welfare of city families and assist family planning programmes. They also suggested that the family planning policies should be coordinated so that rules, penalties and incentives were standardized in order to counter dissatisfaction with the differentials between areas and units and the hesitation and

fear generated by uncertainty about the future of the policy:

> During the survey, we have heard complaints from a large number of parents as well as our fellow workers in family planning that the present policies are not unified and always changing and cause much instability in the thinking of the people . . .

In their report investigators also note the discrepancies in the distribution of rewards and incentives for single-child families. They cited examples of factories and enterprises which provided bonuses for single-child families amounting to as much as ¥ 100 in cash or its value in woollen blankets, transistor radios, or brocade sheets; while in neighbouring units such as administrative organizations, with no profits from which to draw special funds for family planning and which could only take money out of general welfare funds, the rewards might be as low as ¥ 10 or ¥ 12 in cash, or constitute a couple of towels, a thermos flask, some toys or an enamel wash basin. In some cases there were no rewards at all.

The government had undertaken elaborate calculations to show how the cost of making economic rewards might be met, but these usually rested on the savings made for the country by each child *not* born because of the new policy. These savings were estimated to range from ¥ 2000 per child in cities, ¥ 1000 per child in the towns and ¥ 400 per child in the countryside.[32] However in real cash terms these savings were somewhat hypothetical, and this makes an interesting contrast with the policies on production in the national and economic plan which are backed by a large budget and the allocation of material resources. As in the past, policies to do with reproduction and the family are allocated no such equivalent material base. Thus it is not surprising to find that the investigators in Hefei conclude their report by urgently recommending the national allocation of funds on a stable basis to uniformly reward the single-child family and the single child. However, in comparison to the countryside, the problems of implementing the single-child family policy in the cities are considerably less.

4. THE COUNTRYSIDE

Although the birth rate in the rural areas is estimated to have declined significantly, from 2.3% in 1971 to 1.2% in 1979,[33] neither the decline in the birth rate nor the number of single-child families in rural areas is as great as in the towns and cities. Estimates of the proportion of couples with one child who are certificated as single-child families range between 20 and 50%. From 1981 onwards, however, reports suggested that the birth rate was again rising and that there were increasing difficulties and problems associated with implementing the single-child family policy in the rural areas.[34] One of the main reasons for the more recent rise in the birth rate is that national production and reproduction policies make quite different, even contradictory, demands on the peasant household, which is at one and the same time the reproductive unit and, increasingly, the productive unit. On the one hand, State reproduction plans demand that peasant couples have only one child and on the other, State productive plans demand that peasant households have considerable access to labour resources. Current policies to expand production in the rural economy increase the opportunities for domestic production, the family organization of the labour process and encourage greater productivity by members of the peasant household. Many of the new incentives to expand production are designed to encourage family rather than collective labour. In the past five years, two new programmes have been particularly designed to achieve these ends. The first is the rural production responsibility system and the second is the expansion of domestic sidelines.

The rural responsibility system was designed to remedy several defects in agricultural production and especially the low rates of productivity which were attributed to a number of inter-related factors, but chiefly to poor management and insufficient incentives. The general aim of the new rural responsibility system was therefore to reduce the size of the labour group and link reward more directly to performance, and thus simultaneously both to promote production and increase peasant incomes.[35] It is primarily a system whereby the production team enters into a contract with a small labour group or a labourer, which imposes a set of rights, obligations and responsibilities on both parties. Although there are many varieties in responsibility systems, it is apparent that the contracting out of land to peasant households, the assignment of maximum responsibility for the entire production process to peasant households and payment according to output has taken place over much of China and is increasingly the norm. Recently the government conceded that in the main the household rather than the collective had become the basic unit of production.[36] A second marked characteristic of current rural economic policies has been the promotion of household or domestic sideline production (which refers to the production undertaken by the household on an individual basis either for its own subsistence or for exchange).[37] This production may be based on the cultivation of the private plot, the raising of domestic livestock, the cultivation of wild plants and the production of handicrafts, all of which rely exclusively on family labour. In the current search for every available means to expand the economy the government has encouraged the growth of domestic sidelines, which have the advantages that the labour and capital are chiefly provided for by the household, they offer quick returns and they rapidly increase supplies of foods and consumer goods for local markets and for export as well as raw materials for industry.

Recent reports from China suggest that there has been a great deal of satisfaction with these two new rural policies. It seems that production has been initially boosted in many communes and especially in the poorer regions and that peasant incomes have risen substantially as a result.[38] However, the degree to which a peasant household can assume a greater degree of autonomy and share in the rise in incomes is very much dependent on its resources and particularly its labour resources. As the government itself has recognized, the degree to which peasant households will benefit from the responsibility system is linked to their available labour power and their technical and managerial skills. It confidently expects that over the next few years 30 to 40% of peasant households will become rich, 40 to 50% will achieve considerable improvements while 15 to 20% of peasant households (with little or no labour power, no technical specialities, and no business acumen) will still encounter difficulties in meeting basic needs.[39] Thus the income of a peasant household is increasingly dependent on the organization and distribution of its labour resources to produce a surplus over and above the output quotas for which it has been made responsible by the collective and in the expansion of its domestic sidelines.

The correlation between the economic livelihood and immediate welfare of the peasant household and its labour resources is not a new characteristic in rural communes. Although the policies of collectivization had the effect of reducing the land component of the individual family estate and the economic base of the individual household, the economic organization of rural China had continued to require that the peasant household mobilize its resources in order to find solutions to a number of organizational problems, namely collective and domestic production and the provision of basic needs. In any society where labour forms the major part of the total means of production, where control over labour resources is a major source of socio-economic differentiation and where the private hiring of labour is prohibited, the reproduction of family labour becomes the major means of expanding the labour resources of the household and necessary for increasing its production. In China the reproduction of labour power had replaced landed property as an important source of wealth and the chief source of differentials between households within the rural commune before 1978.[40] Since 1978 many of the current rural policies have exacerbated this trend and intensified demands on the labour resources of the household, thus increasing their value to the peasant household. That parents still perceived there to be a direct correlation between the size of family and its income and welfare was reflected in the persistence of many an old folk saying linking 'more children, more income'. Recent surveys and reports also correlate size of family and income and currently suggest that most of the '10,000 jin households' and 'thousand yuan households' which have emerged in the rural areas over the last two years are 'big' families.[41] The conflict in the State's demands on the peasant household, as both a unit of production and of reproduction, has probably never been greater.

5. PRODUCTION VERSUS REPRODUCTION

From 1981 onwards the government has very much linked the rise in rural birth rate and increasing problems in implementing the single-child family policy with the introduction of the rural responsibility system. It has attempted to resolve the contradiction between the two sets of policies by three means: ideological, economic, and exemplary — by the example of good leadership. The emphasis on ideological means in implementing the single-child family policy, and the emphasis placed on education and establishing a new norm of behaviour reflects the official belief in China that ideology and organization can introduce and maintain the momentum of social change. The government believes that if the population can be persuaded to accept the new norms in the long-term national interest then change will be possible even if it directly counters their family interest in the short-term. However,

present attempts to persuade the peasant household by employing a new ideology may well prove to be more difficult to implement in the coming decade than in the past. This leadership faces a central problem in that the credibility of the government in implementing an ideological campaign to convince peasant households to alter their short-term birth plans (in the interest of long-term societal goals) has been made more difficult by repeated and substantive changes in official policies over the past twenty-five years. These have generated cynicism, and reports since the late 1970s suggest that some peasants had felt themselves to be duped by past counterposing of material interests against levels of political consciousness.[42] The power of any government to utilize political campaigns (such as a Socialist Education Movement) to adjust policies which then reduce the standard of living of peasant households may have been irretrievably weakened. There is clear evidence that the new rural economic policies and the current strength of the peasant household as a unit of production have increased the bargaining power of the peasant household *vis-à-vis* collective and State and shifted the balance of power. As peasants themselves have argued:

> We cultivate our own land, eat our grain and bring up all our children on our own.[43]
> We have taken responsibility for the land and there is no need for you to bother about our child birth.[44]

The response of the government to this alteration in the balance of power is to make greater use of economic rewards and sanctions in support of the single-child family policy.

To reduce the link between more children and more income, the government introduced a system of rewards and penalties, but several factors suggest that these are more difficult to implement in rural areas. As in the towns and cities, the value of the incentives and subsidies are very much dependent on the wealth of individual units or in the case of the rural areas, of the collective unit in which the peasant household is located. The cost of the economic benefits are supposed to be met by a unit's public welfare funds and in many areas there are just not enough funds to meet demand. Again, as in the cities, in the absence of nationally allocated funds there is a wide range in the value of rewards and incentives for single-child families. However, it has to be said that even if economic rewards and sanctions were fully implemented, the economic sanctions may be less of a deterrent to the peasant household which can tap many resources, including its own private plot, domestic livestock and sidelines, to counter the effects of food and cash penalties. Moreover, the cost of raising children in the countryside is much less than in urban areas, and a child of a peasant household can contribute to the family budget from an early age. Yet the economic penalties have been designed on the assumption that the peasant household is only a unit of consumption; they fail to take into account that it was always (and is increasingly) a unit of production which exercises a certain degree of autonomy and control over the produce of its own labour. Rural housing is also privately owned, and because health and education facilities are not as well developed as those in the urban areas, many of the penalties to do with admission to institutions or allocation of housing and job privileges are of less relevance in the rural communes.

Throughout 1981 there was a growing awareness on the part of the government that the responsibility system had rendered its economic penalties irrelevant. The replacement of collective control of produce and surplus by that of the peasant household meant that the collective no longer had unified control of food and income and resource distribution and was therefore not in a position to reward and penalize its member households. If the single-child family policy was to be successful, new ways had to be found to relate the system of production responsibility to birth responsibility and this has been the main aim of the government since 1981. In some areas supplementary regulations on birth control have recently been introduced which directly link the distribution of land and output quotas to family size so that the smaller the family size, the larger the size of the responsibility plot of land and the lower the fixed output quotas levied by the collective.[45] If and how this new policy, linking the 'two types of responsibilities', will work out is not yet clear.

There is a singular incentive that might have some effect on the birth rate and family size and that is the introduction of a pension system for retirement in rural areas similar to that which already operates in the cities. In rural areas without a real pension system, the labour of children remains one of the only forms of insurance to which the elderly have access. Recent surveys of family size, and the factors determining family structure in rural areas, suggest that 45% of women of child-bearing age still wanted three or more children and that for the large majority, children constituted a form of insurance in their old age.[46] Again, a recent survey of 775 peasant households

revealed that 50% of their inhabitants wanted to reside in households of three generations in order that they might maximize their labour resources and provide mutual economic support.[47] This is also the reason why couples prefer to have a son who, because of post-marital residence patterns, will remain with them in the same household (or at least within the same neighbourhood after marriage) and are therefore more likely to provide greater support for aged parents. In a recent survey of peasant households published in 1982, a mere 2.2% of peasant households wanted a daughter as an only child,[48] and again in a number of peasant households with two children, recently surveyed, one third of those with two sons wanted a third child compared to 62% of those with two daughters who wanted a son.[49] Where only one child is allowed, the desire for boys is so great that it has led to an unforeseen reappearance of female infanticide and violence against women who bear daughters.[50] If a peasant household has only one daughter and the rules of patrilocal residence continue, then half of all peasant households foresee a situation in which they will have no direct economic support and young married couples will between them have to support seven persons — two sets of grandparents, themselves and one child.

There have been some attempts in the richer communes to make provision for the retired and elderly, but pensions are only available in a few privileged units and it is likely that the future decline in communal welfare funds as a result of the responsibility system may make further attempts elsewhere more difficult. Although the government has itself promised to provide pensions some time in the future, the recent changes in government policy have done little to convince peasants of their long-term ability or will to do so. The fact that the birth rate in three-generational households is higher than in two-generational households may suggest a correlation between number of children and the proximity of grandparents.[51] It is apparent that many grandparents and especially younger grandparents are reluctant to encourage their children to limit their families, either because they fear the government will not be able to fulfil long term obligations to support them or, indeed, because by that time a new policy will be in operation and they will be deprived of all support.

A key factor which determines village response in rural areas is the quality of local planning cadres responsible for the operation of the policy. It has not been uncommon in the past for the government to hold basic level cadres responsible for the tardy implementation of national policies within the local socio-political arena, and many a failure has been attributed to faulty leadership. Current reports throughout the country all stress that one of the central factors determining the success or failure of the single-child family policy will be the quality of local leadership and there are numerous official complaints that cadres either underestimate the importance of the population problem or do not give enough attention to birth control work in the villages.[52] There are a number of reasons why local cadres may find it difficult to operate this policy in the villages. First, they have no legal backing and are not able to act on the basis of State law. The power of rumour that the policy is operated differentially in other areas and that it is likely to change in the near future should not be underestimated. Secondly, the achievement of production quotas and output targets has always taken priority over policies of reproduction and welfare within the village, so that it is a radical change for cadres to attribute equal importance to the two sets of targets. Moreover, the single-child family policy has been introduced into the villages at the same time as the introduction of the responsibility system and has caused numerous extra demands on the organizational capacity of local cadres. Many of the cadres themselves have now been allocated contract lands and output quotas and they have thus relinquished administrative and collective responsibility in favour of individual production.

> Positive and negative experience indicates repeatedly that the success of planned parenthood still depends heavily on leadership. At present the most serious problem is that some party organisations in the countryside have abandoned leadership in planned parenthood after the implementation of the production responsibility system.[53]

Finally, the population policy is not a popular one and basic level cadres themselves are both members of local kin and village primary groups as well as representatives of the government. Where cadres have attempted to enforce rules strictly there is evidence of local hostility and it is not unknown for family planning cadres to be attacked by irate peasant families. Indeed, there is bound to be some tension between an older generation of cadres who already have their children and the younger generation who are being asked to forfeit their right to decide their own family size. One enquiry into the birth rate of cadres found that 68% of the cadres had three or more children and in one

county 10 had 7, 53 had 6, 101 had 5, 164 had 4 and 166 had 3.[54] The cadres themselves are frequently accused of not setting an example, and in the face of local hostility it is not surprising to find that many have preferred not to intervene in such a potentially explosive area.

To encourage cadres to intervene, the government has recently attempted to link cadre responsibility for both production quotas and reproduction targets. In many areas they are now required to meet both production quotas in their areas of administrative responsibility and to keep to birth quotas. In a few locations there is known to be a reward and penalty scheme attached to the operation of these quotas, and cadres may be rewarded by as much as ¥100 for meeting birth quotas or alternatively be penalized by ¥10 for every unplanned birth.[55] Placed in such a position, it is not surprising to learn that cadres have employed coercive tactics to keep within their quotas. There are enough instances of the forced termination of pregnancies reported throughout the rural area of China to suggest that this is no small problem despite the strongest warnings against the use of force by the government. The question in rural areas is: Can there be any alternative to the employment of coercion, given the conflicting demands on the peasant household which current economic and family planning policies have engendered? Can an ideology placing primacy on national and collective interests, a system of rewards and penalties and leadership-by-example resolve this contradiction in favour of the single-child family and against the immediate material interests of the peasant household?

6. A PROGNOSIS

To proceed further with reducing family size to one child, the present government has a number of alternative strategies at its disposal and elements of several of these can be identified in 1983. The first option is that the government can continue to promote the single-child family policy, despite all the problems associated with its implementation and its major conflict with current economic policies. The more recent tightening of regulations, the expressions of determination to succeed and current campaigns concentrating on the rural areas in 1983 all suggest that the government perceives the problems of population growth to be too serious to allow any relaxation of the single-child family policy.[56]

Alternatively, the government could either

modify the new rural economic policies or the single-child family policy to lessen the conflict between the two. These are some signs that this is also a possible strategy, although it seems unlikely that the government will want to modify the responsibility system and reduce domestic sidelines or indeed that it would be in a position to do so. But it has pondered the problem of labour supply, and at present there is some debate about the possible hiring of labour by peasant families as an alternative to reproducing its own labour supply.[57] Already it seems as if there may be the beginnings of an informal hire system in operation in some villages which could be formalized and legitimized. This would be a major departure from past policies and perhaps more than any other factor, the very presence of this debate suggests the determination of the government to implement the single-child family policy. At the same time there are also signs that some elements of the leadership think that the single-child family policy will not succeed in rural areas and it would be better to lower the targets and allow say 1.5 to 2 children per peasant couple or aim for a 50% success rate in establishing one-child families in rural areas.[58] Indeed, there are precedents in which national policies to do with the family which have met with an apathetic or hostile response in rural villages have been subsequently modified.

In the past new national policies have not uncommonly passed through a sequence of stages which have often resulted in the institution of new patterns of social behaviour in the villages which represent a significant departure from past customs, a concession to the new ideology, and very importantly, an adjustment to contemporary economic policies. Frequently these modified forms of social behaviour instituted at the local level in turn have their effect on the national policy itself and cause some modification in a new ruling ideology or in some cases even cause the original policy to be dropped altogether. Whether the single-child family policy will be modified by the lack of response within the local socio-political arena or whether the government will persevere with the single-child family policy as originally conceived and formulated in 1979 has after only five years of implementation to remain an open question.

NOTES

1. Editorial on 'Planned Parenthood', *Renmin Ribao*, 3 February 1979.

2. 'China's Population Growth', *Jingji Yanjiu*, 20 May 1979, Editorial, 'Control of Population Growth', *Renmin Ribao*, 11 August 1979; 'Controlling Population Growth', *Zhongguo Qingnian*, 14 August 1979.

3. For a lengthy discussion in English on the characteristics of China's population, see Liu Zheng *et al.*, *China's Population: Problems and Prospects*, New World Press, Beijing 1981.

4. Liu Zheng, 'Problems of China's Population Growth', in *Jingji Yanjiu*, 20 May 1979.

5. Editorial, *Renmin Ribao*, 8 July 1978.

6. Chen Zhongli, 'An Analysis of the Large Population Policy', *Gongren Ribao*, 4 October 1979.

7. 'Population Control and Modernisation', *Jiefang Ribao*, 30 July 1979; Liu Zhang *et. al., op. cit.*

8. 'Development Trends in Chinese Population Growth', *Beijing Review*, 11 January 1981, p. 25.

9. 'Central Committee and State Council Urge Better Family Planning', *NCNA*, 13 March 1982.

10. E.g. Shanghai Planned Parenthood Regulations, *Jiefang Ribao*, 10 August 1981, SWB, 31 August 1981 (FE/6815/B11/1).

11. Shanxi Planned Parenthood Regulations, *Shanxi Ribao*, 17 November 1982 in SWB, 16 December 1982 (FE 7210/B11/3).

12. Xinhua, 13 September 1980.

13. For example see 'Sichuan Regulations in Family Planning', *Survey of World Broadcasts* (SWB) 16 March 1979 (FE/6068/B11/9).

14. Ashwani Saith, 'Economic Incentives for the one-child family in rural China', *China Quarterly*, September 1981.

15. 'Problems in Family Planning Work in Zhejiang', *Renmin Ribao*, 11 April 1980.

16. See Pi Chao-chen, *Population Growth and Policy*, Occasional Monograph Series No. 9, Interdisciplinary Communication Programme, Smithsonian Institute, Washington 1976; Orleans, L. (ed.) *Chinese Approaches to Family Planning*, M. E. Sharpe, New York, 1979; H. Yuan Tien, *Population Theory in China*, M. E. Sharpe, New York, 1980.

17. Liu Zheng, 'There must be a Population Plan', *Renmin Ribao*, 2 June 1980.

18. 'Take Urgent Action to Reduce the Birth Rate', *Tianjin Ribao*, 4 August 1979.

19. For full discussion of arguments in support of the policy, see Gui Shixin, 'Population Control and Economic Policy', Shanghai Teachers' Journal, *Zhexue Shehui Kexue Ban* (Philosophy and Social Science), 25 April 1980 (Translated JPRS May 1980).

20. Chen Muhua, 'Population Control', *Renmin Ribao*, 11 August 1979.

21. 'Population Situation: Theory Studies from an Economic Angle', *Jingji Yanjiu* 20 May 1979; 'Population Control Important to Economic Planning', *Renmin Ribao*, 2 June 1980.

22. Chen Muhua *op. cit.*

23. Li Shiyi 'Development Trends in Chinese Population Growth', *Beijing Review*, 11 January 1982.

24. *Ibid.*

25. *Ibid.*

26. 'Change in Population Growth, Economic Development Ratio Urged', *Renmin Ribao*, 31 March 1980.

27. See 'Family Planning in Tianjin', *Tianjin Ribao*, 22 July 1979; 'Family Planning in Shanghai', *Wenhui Bao* (Shanghai), 18 January 1980.

28. Beijing Center of Communications and Family Planning, *Topics in Population Theory* (Renkou Li Lun Xuan jiang), p. 40.

29. Elisabeth Croll, *The Chinese Household and its Economy: Urban and Rural Survey Data.* Queen Elizabeth House Contemporary China Centre, Mimeographed Resource Paper, 1982.

30. 'One-Child Family Becoming Norm in Beijing West District', *Renkou Yanjiu* (Population Research), 1 January 1981.

31. *A Survey of Single-Child Families in Hefei, Anhui Province*, by Population Research Office, Anhui University, 1980.

32. Gui Shixin, *op. cit.*

33. Xu Xuehan, 'Resolutely Implement the Policy on Rural Population', *Renmin Ribao*, 5 February 1982.

34. *Ibid*; Sichuan Provincial Radio Service, Chengdu 2 January 1981 *SWB* 22 May 1981 (FE 6730/B11/13); Editorial, *Renmin Ribao*, 29 September 1981; *SWB* 21 October 1981 (FE 6859/B11/5).

35. For articles on the rural production responsibility system see 'Quota Fixing at Household Level', *SWB*, 28 December 1979 (FE 6305/B11/7–8); 'Discussion on the Systems of Responsibility for Output Quotas by Production Terms in Rural People's Communes', *Jingji Yanjiu*, 20 October 1980; 'Fixing Output Quotas for Individual Households', *Ibid*, 20 January 1981; 'Communist Party Central Committee Discusses Agriculture', China News Analysis (NCNA) 19 May 1981; 'Prospects for Development of Double-Contract System', *Renmin Ribao*, 9 March 1982 *SWB* 19 March 1981 (FE/6982/B11/5–8).

36. 'The Leadership Role of Rural Basic-Level Organisations', RMRB, 19 February 1982; also in *SWB* 4 March 1982 (FE/6969/B11/3).

37. For discussion on Domestic Sidelines, see: Croll, E. 'The Promotion of Domestic Sideline Production in Rural China 1978–79' in Gray J. and White, G. (ed) *China's New Development Strategy*, Academic Press, London, 1982; 'Defence of Domestic Sideline Production', in *SWB*, 27 April 1978 (FE/5799/B11/9); 'The Encouragement of Domestic Sideline Production', *Jingji Yanjiu*, 20 August 1979, pp. 28–32.

38. 'Sideline Production and Rural Income', *SWB*, 24 June 1981 (FE/W1139/A/1); 'Peasants' Income and Savings', *SWB*, 19 August 1981 (FE/W1143/A/1).

39. *NCNA*, 9 March 1982.

40. For an expansion of this argument see Croll, Elisabeth, *The Politics of Marriage in Contemporary China*, Cambridge University Press 1981.

41. Zhang Huaiya, 'Population, Economy and Population Control in Rural Areas' in *Jingji Yanjiu*, 20 December 1981; 'Analysis of Reproduction of Rural Population', *Ibid* 20 June 1982.

42. Croll, E. 'The Promotion of Domestic Sideline Production', *op. cit.*

43. 'Rural Population Policy', *SWB*, 18 February 1982 (FE/6957/B11/4).

44. 'Population and Education in Family Planning Work', *Renmin Ribao*, 29 September 1981 (Editorial).

45. *SWB*, 21 October 1981 (FE 6859/B11/5); *SWB*, 30 October 1981 (FE/6867/B11/12); Hunan Provincial Service, Changsha, 5 February 1982.

46. *Jingji Yanjiu*, 20 June 1982, *op. cit.*

47. *Ibid.*

48. *Ibid.*

49. *Ibid.*

50. Yangfan 'Save the baby girls', *Zhongguo Qingnian*, 9 November 1982; *SWB*, 16 December 1982 (FE/7210/B11/12).

51. *Jingji Yanjiu*, 20 June 1982, *op. cit.*

52. Zhang Huaiya *op. cit.*

53. Editorial, *Shanxi Ribao*, 12 April 1982.

54. 'Problems of Family Planning Work in Zhejiang Province' *op. cit.*

55. *SWB*, 5 November 1981 (FE/6872/B11/15).

56. 'Family Planning', in *NCNA*, 17 August 1982; Editorial *Renmin Ribao* 23 August 1982; *Guardian* (Manchester) 3 November 1982.

57. *Ibid.*

58. Xu Xuehan, *op. cit.*

Middle-Level Education in Contemporary China

PAULINE KEATING

University of Melbourne, Australia

Summary. — Serious problems are emerging within the rural areas of China concerning secondary education. The underdeveloped school network is not responding well to intolerable strains placed on it by post-1977 educational and agricultural reforms and agricultural responsibility systems concerning production. Many teenagers are working on family farms instead of going to school. Rural secondary schools have problems in getting girls to attend classes. Prejudice in attitudes and the benefits of more family members working land to peasant households are major causes. Prejudice now includes not only a sceptical view of the value of educating females but the new Rightist view that in the past collective funds used for education promoted the now despised 'egalitarianism'. The low status afforded secondary teachers is an obstacle to improvement, reinforced by the variable quality of the teachers and official demands for longer courses as part of agricultural modernization.

1. INTRODUCTION

The elimination of illiteracy remains the first aim and strategy of rural education in the Chinese countryside; there is little debate on this point. Questions about the functions and purpose of literacy, however, questions about the goals of middle-level schooling in the countryside, are likely to produce a variety of responses. Some educationalists will talk loftily of the 'civilizing role' of education, of how 'enlightenment' will rid the countryside of barbarism and feudal darkness.[1] But, people closer to rural realities worry about the damage done to people in their districts by a blind application of national education strategies; they are saying that their secondary schools are not serving the needs of the local area or their young people, and they call for a flexible, creative adaptation of policies to local conditions.

The appearance of increasingly serious and blatant problems in rural secondary schools is giving strength to the arguments for reassessment and radical reform. Like the village primary schools, secondary schools are suffering from the general rural tendency to devalue education while 'responsibility land' is being distributed and the new systems made to work. There are also the special problems of Commune and County secondary schools which must try to enrol teenagers from a number of different, perhaps scattered, villages and must look even further afield for teaching staff.

Finally, the anomalies and contradictions created by the restored examination system, the competitiveness, elitism and rigidly narrow curriculum which are worrying parents and teachers throughout the country, are producing specially urgent problems for rural secondary schools. This is now frequently acknowledged in official commentaries on educational developments. The underdeveloped secondary school network in the countryside is not coping well under the strains created by post-1977 agricultural and educational reforms, and there are growing demands for a complete restructuring and overhaul in the rural areas of what is called 'middle-level education'.[2]

2. SECONDARY SCHOOLS AND THE RESPONSIBILITY SYSTEMS

In many cases, it needs a special enthusiasm for education on the part of peasant parents to send their children to full-time secondary school. A child must have first completed five years of primary school and qualified for junior secondary; that, in itself, entails considerable parent commitment and sacrifice. Then, it is possible that there is only one post-primary school in the Commune, and going to school means leaving the home village; a prosperous peasant might be able to allow his child the daily use of a bicycle; a prosperous and educationally ambitious Commune might provide dormitory accommodation for secondary school children.

Given the need for special commitment and effort, it might be assumed that peasant parents with children in secondary school would do their best to keep them there. It seems, however, that enrolment and attendance rates in rural secondary schools have been affected almost as severely as primary schools by the new need for labour hands at home. Newspapers are reporting successful efforts by some Communes and Counties to get teenagers back to school: teachers visit the students' homes and try to convince parents of the long-term advantages of education; Commune enterprises (factories and workshops) are announcing that, in future, they will recruit junior secondary graduates only, and job applicants will be asked to take an exam first; special classes are being organized for the returned dropouts to help them catch up on the work they missed; and, school curricula are being reformed to make them more relevant to the needs of rural youth.[3] NanShenZao Commune in DongTai County, Jaingsu Province, claims that 700 primary and secondary school children have returned to school as a result of the solving of 'ideological problems among parents and students'. A Commune cadre found that Old Zhu, fat and prosperous, had taken his 13-year-old daughter away from school just so that she would qualify for a piece of 'responsibility land'; the cadre pointed out that regulations now disallow extra land for the family in the daughter's name and 'Anyway, Old Zhu, are you so poor that you have nothing left in the pot? You mustn't just look at what's in front of your nose and ruin your daughter's whole future'. This made Old Zhu 'wake up', says the report, and his daughter was at school the next day.[4]

Rural secondary schools also share with village primary schools the problem of getting girls to attend classes. The vigour and commitment required to tackle this problem is evidenced in a report from QuanShang Commune of NingHua County, Fujian; in order to remove the obstacles to girls coming to school, Commune cadres tackled prejudiced attitudes among the peasants by publicizing the achievements and public contributions of young girls in the district, gave special consideration to girl students when deciding cases in which school fees would be lowered or waived, arranged that the schools run kindergarten annexes so that girls would not be encumbered with younger brothers and sisters in class, and ruled that basic lessons be clustered around the middle of the day so that girls could arrive at school late and leave early.[5] However, many of the reports suggest that the 'responsibility systems' have created a situation in which the peasants will value the schools only if they teach agricultural skills to their children; it is one thing to persuade peasant fathers to leave their sons at school to learn scientific farming, and quite another to persuade them that their daughters need this kind of knowledge.

Another development which demonstrates the declining prestige of educational enterprises in the countryside is the frequently unchallenged theft of school property, appropriations of school land, and violence towards rural teachers. A 1982 vicious beating, by the Brigade bully and his cronies, of three young women teachers (in JiShi Commune of the Peking municipality) was given broad publicity in the national papers,[6] provoked a series of top-level Education and Legal Bureaux meetings, and is being used as a catalyst to draw both official and popular attention to the difficulties being experienced by teachers, especially rural teachers. The cause of the incident is attributed to a persisting attitude of contempt for intellectuals fostered during the 'Gang of 4 period', but also to the failure to promote educational policies forcefully and to the confusion among some rural cadres and commune members about the meaning and extent of new agricultural policies.[7]

Some people have interpreted post-1979 rural reforms as the abandonment of policies which promote and develop education. Some Brigade and Commune cadres claim that to use the collective's funds for educational enterprises would be to commit the mistake of 'egalitarianism and the indiscriminate transfer of funds'[8] (using the people's money on nonproductive enterprises and, presumably, against their will). With the dividing up and distribution of land to responsible units there has been something of a land scramble in many places, and it is the schools which most frequently lose out. The Education Bureau of HeChi District, Guangxi, reports that more than 1,150 mou of school land (used by the district schools for experimental farming) has been seized by local people.[9] Of the 3,019 mou of land farmed by schools in XinTian County, Hunan, only 555 mou is left. During the QingMing 'Sweeping of the Graves' in April this year, more than 60 peasants dug ancestral graves on the playing field of MaoJia secondary school, also in XinTian County.[10] Some Brigades are issuing certificates which, in defiance of policy, allow Commune members to use school land for forestry, fruit-growing or for grazing their animals.[11] A way of countering the arbitrary appropriations of school land is the issuing to the schools themselves of 'property rights' certificates; this is beginning to happen in some places.[12]

Not only land but school furniture, even the fabric of school buildings, is being carried off by those who dare and who can get away with it. The newspapers lament that an extraordinary number of people *are* 'getting away with it', that local officials are turning a blind eye to the dismantling of the schools or even actively participating in the sabotage. In Guangxi's ChiDi District, more than 300,000 *yuan*'s worth of school property was lost through theft or vandalism during the last summer and winter holidays. A whole set of tables and chairs was carted away in a tractor in broad daylight.[13] In XinTian County, Hunan, people took advantage of a shopping expedition by teachers to strip the school of 7 doors, 1 doorframe, 5 windows, 4 tables, 3 blackboards and all of the teachers' cooking utensils.[14] In HuangPi County's BaoLong Commune, Hebei, the HengXin Brigade Accountant dug up the school's playground to make mud bricks for his new house, filled one of the classrooms with his bricks, and hurled insults at the teachers when they complained about the loss of the classroom and the devastated playground.[15]

Teachers have been abused, even beaten, when they attempt to defend school property against these lootings. They are also abused and beaten for no apparent reason; we can guess, however, that people who are strangers to a district and who pester the local people to send their children to school when they don't want to, will have prejudices to battle with. The problem has become so serious that rural Party Branches are beginning to devise measures which will counter negative and resentful attitudes towards the teachers in Commune schools. Brigades in JingHai County of Guangdong's Hainan Island formulated a 'Respect the Teachers, Cherish the Schools' pact, and used it as a propaganda tool for cultivating public respect for the teachers in the area.[16] In other places, leaders hope that ostentatious solicitude for the local teachers, solicitude in the form of Spring Festival Tea Parties and 'Teacher Here' Meetings,[17] will raise teacher prestige in the eyes of the people. It is clear, however, that a solution needs to go deeper than this, that a radical change in the definitions and structures of rural schooling is necessary before school education becomes meaningful and important in the eyes of many of the peasants.

3. RURAL SECONDARY SCHOOL TEACHERS

Stressful work and living conditions for rural secondary teachers predate the responsibility systems; they are related to the underdeveloped condition of middle-level education in the countryside and the fact that, in most cases, most of the teachers are State (not Brigade or Commune) employees and so, when at school, are often living far away from home. The policy of 'universalizing education' applies only to primary schooling in the countryside. Populist enthusiasm has, at various times, tried to make junior secondary schooling 'universal' for rural children, and two or three secondary grades were sometimes tacked on to the village primary schools. This is now regarded as an overstretching of meagre resources and many of the junior secondary 'annexes' have been scrapped. A typical Commune might run just one full-time and complete (5 grades) secondary school (although now it is preferred that these schools be under County management), and one or two junior secondary (3 grades) schools; a select few graduates from village primary schools will pass the entrance exam into a County secondary school; any other children who have qualified for Junior One and whose parents want them to stay at school will attend one of the Commune schools. Because these schools have not (until recently, at least) been the special focus of rural education policy, they are usually poorly equipped, understaffed, uncomfortable and ugly.

The open and fierce resistance by Teachers' College graduates to rural postings, and the recent well-publicized brutal attacks on rural teachers is resulting in deeper enquiries into the conditions of teachers in the countryside, publicity for their problems, and demands that these problems be quickly solved. A basic issue is food; without land for growing vegetables and raising domestic animals, teachers in some places are forced to pay close-to-city prices for vegetables; there are months when some teachers in mountain districts eat nothing but rice flavoured with soy sauce while the children they teach have vegetables and eggs to eat.[18] Away from their families, teachers often do not have access to bicycles; the Teng County Committee in Shandong Province recently bought 100 bicycles to solve the transport problems of the teachers under its jurisdiction.[19] In the past, local authorities have been slow to provide adequate accommodation for live-in teachers.[20] In some places, the school and teachers' dormitories do not qualify for the wintertime coal subsidy that is granted to each household in North China.[21] Teachers' letters to the newspapers beg for quick solutions to difficulties such as inadequate water supply arrangements in the schools, rural teachers' desperate need for refresher courses, the conflict between teaching duties and family pressures to help out on the farm,[22] and the inability of many young teachers away from their home villages or towns to find marriage partners.[23]

When reporting these problems, the newspapers usually describe the measures taken to remedy them. Especially in June and July, when College graduates are waiting for their work assignments, the press vigorously urges young people to serve the Motherland by willingly going to 'Education's Front Line' — the Countryside, and reassures them with evidence that things are changing for rural teachers. The *People's Daily* published a letter from a 1981 graduate (of the Beijing Physical Education College) who has been teaching in a rural secondary school for the last year; she assures her readers that things have changed in the villages, that conditions are not nearly so bad as her classmates had warned. She rejoices in the prospect of even greater rural changes as teachers and peasants work together and concludes her letter with 'Comrade Students, the countryside needs you, the countryside is waiting for you!'[24]

4. RURAL SECONDARY SCHOOL STUDENTS AND WHAT THEY LEARN

Full-time secondary schooling is available to only a minority of rural young people. Many of them are the children of Brigade and Commune cadres, and their parents' purpose in sending them to school is usually to ensure that they will not spend their lives as agricultural labourers. Rural people continue to reach for education as a way out of the villages into the towns and cities, and this is probably one of the reasons why rural secondary schools have grimly persisted with the College Entrance Exam curriculum as the basic curriculum for the great majority of students who will never pass that entrance exam. Of the small proportion of peasant children who go on from primary to secondary school, only 20% to 30% move

from junior to senior secondary school. And, at best, 1% or 2% of those who complete Senior Two in all but the 'keypoint' rural secondary schools will pass the entrance exams and go on to a tertiary college.

A *Guangming Daily* article powerfully describes this disappointment and frustration of rural people whose struggles to get their children to college have repeatedly failed. In 1978, the Education Office of HengLan Commune, in Guangdong's ZhongShan County, decided to make an all-out effort to get some of the Commune teenagers to college. The best students in the Commune's six Senior Two classes[25] were put together in two 'advanced classes' and given the best teachers; all courses and lessons not directly related to the examinations were scrapped; the best students in these two classes came to live at the school and the Commune spent more than 200 *yuan* on electric lighting for evening study; the students were given specially nourishing food; all their travel expenses were paid by the school; scholarships of 100 *yuan* were offered to students who got into college; the twelve brightest students were selected for special coaching and, as a strategy for further stimulating their 'scholarly ambitions', the Commune provided more than 200 *yuan* for a trip by these twelve to visit seven tertiary colleges in Guangzhou, Canton. Not one student from HengLan Commune passed the 1978 College Entrance Examinations.

Not surprisingly, Commune officials were less than happy with the results. Moreover, 'parents were critical of the school's performance, the masses were scornful, and the school principal and teachers could not lift their heads in public'.[26] There is a growing public awareness that this fruitless 'pursuit of higher education' wastes time, resources and energy, it brings little obvious benefit to rural society, it severely damages the morale of the students, it aggravates the elitism and competitiveness in secondary schools, and produces a population of young people qualified for nothing. The failed examination candidates have no choice but to return to their villages where many of them form gangs of discontented layabouts and create youth cultures that challenge old village traditions and harmonies. The calls for radical change in the rural education system are becoming more and more insistent.

5. RESTRUCTURING MIDDLE-LEVEL EDUCATION IN THE COUNTRYSIDE

The decisions to give new emphasis to the

development of 'technical' or 'speciality' schools were made in 1978 and 1979, but the transforming of the existing 'general' secondary schools has been slow. Now, however, as once- and twice-failed examination candidates begin to constitute a bitterly disaffected component of both the urban and rural unemployed, and as the post-1979 agricultural reforms deepen the dilemmas of rural educationalists while creating a new need for skilled farm workers, the demand for the provision of vocational and skills training for the majority of rural youth is becoming more urgent.

Education authorities are recommending that all but a very few full-time secondary schools become Agricultural Secondary Schools and Vocational Secondary Schools; these can offer one, two and three, even four or five-year courses. Most of the remaining general secondary schools are to be 'keypoint schools' and will continue to prepare students for the college entrance examinations. However, for the most part, emphasis is to be placed on developing *junior* rather than senior secondary education. In Guangdong's XinHui County, for example, 13 of its 19 secondary schools have become Vocational Secondary Schools; ZhongShan County has reduced the number of its complete secondary schools from 41 to 31, and 23 of those 31 have been transformed into Vocational Schools.[27] In DeHui County of Jilin Province, 405 senior secondary school teachers have been transferred to junior secondary teaching, and 535 junior secondary teachers have gone to primary schools;[28] this readjustment accords with the policy of giving first place to the universalizing of primary education, and then developing junior secondary schools.

There is the persistent plea that school curricula be relevant and useful to the work students will do when they leave school. It has been suggested that the 'responsibility systems' should not be seen as the cause of drops in school attendance; rather, it is the almost complete irrelevance of what rural children learn in secondary schools which keeps them at home.[29] Setting up Agricultural Schools does not automatically solve the problem; the designing of appropriate curricula and courses and the quality of teaching are of basic importance. Agricultural and Vocational Schools try to offer courses that are appropriate to local needs and must ensure, at the same time, that students continue to develop basic skills of literacy and numeracy. For example, students in ZhongShan County's Agricultural Schools must attend classes in Chinese language, mathematics, soil cultivation, animal husbandry,

the use and maintenance of farm machinery, and may choose one or two electives out of a possible five; these schools aim to have their students skilled in at least one speciality by the time they graduate.[30] It is being recommended that the technical schools also provide classes in 'rural policy' and agricultural management; people who have only had skills-training and know nothing about economics and farm management cannot be reckoned as 'scientific farmers'.[31]

The general full-time secondary schools in rural areas are also to increase the number of agricultural and vocational skills courses in their curricula. In Heilongjiang's NeiHe County, the LaoCai Commune's secondary school, a 'key-point school', expects its students in Junior One to choose one speciality from a possible ten and to work at that speciality alongside the basic secondary school (entrance exam oriented) subjects for the rest of their school lives. This school has set up ten 'experimental teaching bases' in Commune-, Brigade- and School-run workshops and has its senior students writing scientific research reports, four of which have been published in national journals. Since 1977, 103 of the school's graduates (12% of the total) have gone on to tertiary colleges, 158 are working as cadres or as skilled agri-culturalists in Brigades and Communes, more than 360 have become specialists in agricultural machinery, accountancy or health work, more than 180 are working in Primary Schools, and 700 Junior School graduates are doing farm work.[32]

Clearly, school access to farm land for teaching and experimental purposes is crucially important to the achievement of the goal of preparing young people for skilled agricultural work; the schools must be able to reclaim the land they have lost in the recent 'scrambles'. A renewed emphasis on 'labour education' and 'work study activities' is resulting in official support and funds for developing the schools' experimental farms and workshops. When the school-run enterprises begin to earn profits, they support the further expansion of voca-tional education.[33] The 'work-study pro-grammes' also send secondary students into Communes and Brigades for direct work experience; through this means, the rural schools can disseminate and popularize scientific farming methods and give practical, skilled help to local peasant communities.[34] If the help is accepted and welcomed, the teachers and schools are well on their way to being 'respected and cherished' by the peasants.

6. PEASANT INTELLECTUALS OR EDUCATED INTELLECTUAL 'PEASANTS'?

The building, equipping and staffing of a broad network of vocational schools in the Chinese countryside, a network which can accommodate the teenage children among 800,000,000 rural dwellers, is a massive undertaking and one which the national budget cannot possibly support at present. As part of the attempt to push forward the development of vocational education for the majority of rural young people, educational authorities are giving publicity to individual Brigades and Communes which use their own funds to develop new and useful educational facilities; it is hoped, apparently, that significant change will be achieved through local financial contributions and initiatives. Last year, Anhui's YingDing County put up more school buildings than have been built in the area in the previous thirty years; a large proportion of the money came from 'collective funds'.[35] Dilapidated school houses in Hebei's SanHe County have been replaced with attractive wood and brick buildings; the school's 'work-study activities' provided the money.[36] In LuLiang County, Yunnan, the County cadres contributed 3,100 *yuan*, profits over five years from experimental vegetable plots, to buy new desks and benches for school classrooms.[37] These are isolated instances. Willingness to contribute money for educational development will rely on a valuing and seeking of education by rural dwellers. But, while the education offered by the schools is irrelevant, even a nuisance, the peasants will not value it. It would seem that a broad and vigorous educational thrust into the countryside by the central government will be needed if that vicious circle is to be broken.

Many of the educational reformers imply that they want to change people's perceptions and definitions of 'education for the masses'. And, the strategy for implementing the new thinking is to be the restructuring and reform of 'middle-level education' in the countryside. Giving the peasants an education in science and agricultural skills is a way of 'readjusting the relationship between man and nature'; once the peasants have scientific skills 'new productive forces will have formed'.[38] The modernization of agriculture will depend on educated peasants, so of course it is essential that peasants

who are educated remain in the countryside and are directly involved in agricultural work. For the vast majority of rural young people who cannot hope to be admitted to tertiary colleges, secondary school education is not to be seen as a way out of the countryside and into the cities. But, nor is the struggle for an education to be abandoned just because this path is closed. A reformed education system should offer a number of different possible paths to rural students.

At the moment, 'middle-level education' encompasses a variety of forms; as well as the full- and part-time secondary schools, general and vocational, a Commune might run Night School, Winter School, Skills Training Classes and encourage commune members to participate in Radio Correspondence Courses. Sparetime and part-time education is now offered to those who have not been well served, or not served at all, by the rural primary and secondary schools. There is the assumption that, in the future, all rural teenagers will receive in the full-time secondary schools the education they need to prepare them for creative service in rural society. Good schools will give young peasants 'scientific wings'[39] and access, therefore, to a vastly broader world, albeit a rural world. The products of the 'new education' will not be intellectuals, but 'new peasants'.[40]

That is the vision, the future hope, but it is hardly a programme yet. The 'responsibility systems', it is said, are creating widespread peasant enthusiasm for the learning of scientific farming and are providing the prosperity, the material basis for the development of rural education. But, it is not at all clear that the peasants associate 'scientific farming' with 'education'. In the past, both distant and recent, prosperous peasant communities have established schools which provide paths to officialdom for their children and remove them from the world of manual labour. There is a good deal of evidence to show that contemporary peasants perceive education in the same way; newspaper reports admit some strong resistance to the replacing of general secondary schools with vocational schools, and ambitious parents will still struggle to get their children into the 'keypoint' general schools.[41] Precisely how the 'new peasants' are to evolve, and what the nature of their new rural society will be, has still to be determined.

NOTES

1. Lu Shuxiang, 'Why Education Must be Stressed', *Social Sciences* (Shanghai), No. 8, 1982.

2. 'Middle-level education' refers to a variety of educational forms such as Night School, Winter

School, Spare-Time Skills Training as well as full- and part-time general and vocational secondary school.

3. See, for example, 'Rural Education in Shanghai's ShuHe Commune is full of Vitality', *Guangming Daily*, 16 April 1982. 'ChongMing County's ShuHe Commune Takes the First Step Towards Setting up an Education Network', *People's Daily*, 18 May 1982.

4. 'Seven Hundred Drop-Outs Go Back to School', *Peasants' Gazette*, 16 May 1982.

5. 'QuanShang Commune Gives Serious Attention to Raising the Attendance Rate of Girl Students', *Peasants' Gazette*, 16 May 1982.

6. See, for example, *Guangming Daily*, 24, 25, 27 June 1982.

7. 'Reform Rural Education So that it Serves the Construction of a New Socialist Countryside', *Guangming Daily*, 28 August 1982.

8. 'Chongming County's ShuHe Commune Takes the First. . . .' *Ibid, People's Daily*, 18 May 1982.

9. 'Serious Stealing of Secondary and Primary School Property in Guangxi's ChiDi District', *People's Daily*, 18 June 1982.

10. 'Primary and Secondary Schools in XinTian County of Hunan Province Suffer Repeated Damage', *People's Daily*, 18 June 1982.

11. *Op. Cit.*

12. 'Reform Rural Education . . .', *Ibid, Guangming Daily*, 28 August 1982.

13. 'Serious Stealing of Secondary and Primary Education in Guangxi's Chidi District', *People's Daily*, 18 June 1982.

14. 'Primary and Secondary Schools in Xin Tian County of Hunan Province', *People's Daily*, 18 June 1982.

15. *Op. cit.*

16. ' "Respecting the Teachers, Cherishing the Schools" Has Become Common Practice in QiongHai County', *Guangming Daily*, 24 August 1982.

17. 'The Party Committee of TianZhu Commune Makes Efforts to Improve the Social Position of Teachers', *Guangming Daily*, August 1982.

18. 'The Incident in Which Three Women Teachers Were Harassed, Insulted and Beaten', *Guangming Daily*, 24 June 1982.

19. 'Improving the Life of Teachers in the Mountain Districts of Teng County', *Guangming Daily*, 26 October 1981.

20. 'Tianjin Municipality Allocates Special Funds for the Construction of Accommodation for Rural Teachers', *People's Daily*, 1, 2 November 1981.

21. 'Improving the life of Teachers . . .', *Ibid, GD*, 26 October 1981.

22. 'Voices from Secondary and Primary Schools', *GD*, 26 June 1982.

23. 'Helping the Teachers in Mountain Districts Solve the Problem of Getting Vegetables', *Guangming Daily*, 1 December 1981.

24. 'Comrade Students, The Countryside Needs You', *People's Daily*, 3 June 1982.

25. Six Senior 2 classes are a relatively large number; the article describes ZhongShan County as a 'culturally developed' area of the Province.

26. 'Putting Life into Rural Secondary Schooling', *Guangming Daily*, 3 April 1982.

27. *Op. Cit.* (*GD*, 3 April 1982).

28. 'DeHui County Resolutely Grasps the Work of Readjusting Teacher Numbers in Primary and Secondary Schools', *Guangming Daily*, 21 June 1982.

29. 'There Must be a Constant Readjusting of the Relationship Between Man And Nature', *GD*, 9 June 1982.

30. 'Putting Life Into . . .', *Ibid* (*GD*, 3 April 1982).

31. 'Reform Rural Education So That . . .', *Ibid* (*GD*, 28 August 1982).

32. 'Keep Going in Two Directions – Further Education and Vocational Education', *Guangming Daily*, 9 August 1982.

33. 'There Has Been a Rapid Restoration and Development of Work-Study Programmes in Secondary and Primary Schools Throughout the Country', *Guangming Daily*, 19 April 1982.

34. 'Reform Rural Education So That . . .', *Ibid* (*GD*, 28 August 1982).

35. 'There is Plenty of Scope for Activating Social Forces in the Education Area', *People's Daily*, 6 July 1982.

36. 'SanHe County Actively Improves School Conditions', *Peasants' Gazette*, 16 May 1982.

37. 'The Classrooms Built For a Future Generation Stand Tall and Can Be Seen From a Long Way Off', *People's Daily*, 25 May 1982.

38. 'There Must Be a Constant Readjusting . . .', *Ibid* (*GD*, 9 June 1982).

39. 'Be Concerned in Every Way About Rural Youth', *Peasants' Gazette*, 2 May 1882.

40. 'There Must be a Constant Readjusting . . .', *Ibid* (*GD*, 9 June 1982).

41. See, for example, 'Putting Life Into . . .', *Ibid*, (*GD*, 3 April 1982) and 'Reform Rural Education So That . . .', *Ibid*, (*GD*, 28 August 1982).

Party Building since Mao—A Question of Style?

TONY SAICH

Sinologisch Instituut, University of Leiden, Netherlands

Summary: — Party workstyle remains a problem for the CPC leadership, reinforced by rejection of Cultural Revolution methods and re-evaluation of Mao which have confused many cadres. In a number of ways, Mao had destroyed the 'rules of the game' of the Leninist Party-state. Yet the problem is one of structure of power not merely of attitude. Development strategies have been changing; moves have been made towards economic reforms. These call for a different kind of Party than that which existed prior to 1976. For example, in relations with other institutions, the dominating role of the Party will need modification. In combating 'sickness' within the Party, two problems have been diagnosed by the authorities: bureaucratism and feudal hangovers. These lead to corruption, patronage and lack of inner-Party democracy. Earlier ideas of inner-Party struggle by democratic means and a real role for the Constitution have been revived. The latter now includes restrictions on individuals acting beyond the scope of Party policy — a thrust at the personality cult that develops around Party leaders. Life-long tenure for cadres is being abolished, and interpenetration of state and Party organs limited to a degree, though differences continue on how far t' is should proceed and on the amount of freedom to be given to intellectuals to interve. e in the process.

The question of workstyle of a Party in power is one that has a strong bearing on the life and death of a Party (Chen Yun).

1. INTRODUCTION

Perhaps the most enduring and damaging legacy of the Cultural Revolution decade (1966–1976) is the loss of the Communist Party's prestige. The sponsored attacks on the Party which ushered in the Cultural Revolution, the ensuing twists and turns of political line promoted by the Party, the alleged disappearance of intra-Party democracy and the exposés of the corrupt practices of some Party officials have damaged the Party's prestige and 'aroused indignation'.[1] The current view promoted by the Chinese authorities appears to be that what is at fault is not so much the policies but the way those policies have been decided and implemented. The need to build democracy and socialist legality has been a key theme for the present leadership. Since the arrest of the 'Gang of Four' the Chinese press has been littered with articles discussing Party workstyle. Following a meeting of the Central Commission for Inspecting Discipline in early 1982, the campaign to rectify workstyle was stepped up. The seriousness of this problem to the Chinese was indicated in a *Red Flag* article of March 1982. The article stated that although five years had passed since the 'smashing' of the 'Gang of Four', Party workstyle had not fundamentally improved. Following Chen Yun's lead this problem was described as a 'life and death question for the whole Party'.[2] Both Hu Yaobang and Deng Xiaoping, in their speeches to the 12th Party Congress (September 1982),[3] listed the need to rectify Party workstyle as one of the four main tasks.

The emphasis on criticism of workstyle and not structures is reinforced by the public reassessment of Mao Zedong. Although great criticism has been levelled against Mao's economic policies and his 'erroneous' views on class struggle in socialist society, it could well be argued that, for the present leadership, Mao's greatest fault lay not so much with what he did but with the way in which he did it. In this sense Mao's 'crime' was that he destroyed the 'rules of the game' which he, himself, had helped draw up. The result was that genuine discussion within the Party was destroyed as politics became increasingly personalized.

Such a line of argument is enticing. To be sure, the authoritarian political practice of the 'Gang of Four' contrasted strikingly with their espoused democratic principles. However, an excessive concentration on workstyle tends to blind one to major changes which have taken and are taking place. First, there appears to be a realization by some Party members that a concentration on workstyle without making structural changes would be a waste of time. Some of the problems of workstyle are endemic to a system where power is so hierarchically arranged and where 'security of tenure' and access to restricted materials and goods gives unlimited opportunity for corruption and patronage. The notion implied by the concentration on workstyle is that the problem is primarily one of attitude, not one of structure. However, past experience not only from China but also from Eastern Europe and the Soviet Union shows that the problems inherent in a system where power is so unequally distributed cannot be overcome simply by ensuring that those within the system think in the proper way and adopt the correct workstyle. Some in the Party do recognize the need for structural reform. Indeed the Constitution adopted at the 12th Party Congress takes some tentative steps towards structural reform, although clearly they are not as far-reaching as some would have liked. Also, the sterner measures introduced in March 1982 to combat corruption suggest a more widespread lack of confidence in the approach offered. As of March, corrupt cadres were given the choice of 'owning up now' and receiving seven years imprisonment or waiting to be found out and then being taken out and shot![4]

Secondly, an excessive concentration on workstyle can obscure the change which has taken place in the role of the Party in the Chinese system. The development strategy promoted in earnest since the 3rd Plenum (December 1978) calls for quite a different kind of Party than that which existed immediately prior to the arrest of the 'Gang of Four' or, for that matter, to that which existed during the years 1977–1978. The current focus on economic modernization and the exclusion of any 'serious' class struggle from Chinese society requires a different Party to preside over the system than the mobilizational Party of either the 'Gang of Four' or Hua Guofeng.

The main part of this paper will address itself to the Party which has evolved since the 3rd Plenum. It is hoped that the discussion will also highlight different views within the Party about what kind of a Party it should be and what its correct relationship with state and society should be. In part, these views are related to differing approaches to development but, as with the study of all things Chinese, a neat division cannot be made.

2. PARTY REBUILDING BEFORE THE THIRD PLENUM

Before considering the more recent developments it is instructive to consider briefly differing conceptions of the Party since the attacks launched on it in the mid- to late 1960s. Such a consideration not only shows the diverse range of views about the Party and its role but also prevents the later discussion from appearing in a vacuum. Although the changes in the post-Mao era appear to have occurred swiftly some of the trends had already been set in motion from the early 1970s. The inability of the Cultural Revolution to find alternative forms of organization which could gain legitimacy meant that some kind of a Party would be in power. The question remained of what kind of a Party?

The attack on the Party at the start of the Cultural Revolution should have laid to rest the approach of studying the Chinese Communist Party as a monolithic entity. Indeed, the severity of the attacks led some authors to speculate whether the Party would continue to provide the institutional core for political leadership. For a while it appeared as if the future of the Party as an institution was being called into question. Even though the 'radical' alternative of the commune was rejected it appeared that, from the Party's point of view, at worst it would be replaced by the new 'organ of power' — the revolutionary committee — or, at best, it would share power thus losing its uniquely dominant role. Certainly its leadership role had been shattered. There was no possibility that, in Schurmann's words, all members would at any time 'act in a unified fashion throughout the society to carry out policy determined by the top leadership'.[5]

Yet, when it came to the crunch Mao was too much of a Leninist to reject outright the concept of Party leadership. When confronted with the alternative of the commune as set up in Shanghai, Mao rejected it and claimed that 'communes are too weak when it comes to suppressing counter-revolution'.[6] In fact the revolutionary committees set up in early 1967 implied the future reorganization of new and independent Party committees. Notices published by the Heilongjiang and Guizhou Revolutionary Committees looked forward to the re-establishment of provincial Party committees and regarded the jurisdiction of the revolutionary committee over Party affairs as a purely temporary measure.[7] Certainly, with the convocation of the 9th Party Congress (1969) it was clear to all that the Party would return.

This intended return of the Party brought to the forefront of Chinese politics a number of important organizational questions. First, what kind of a Party should it be? Second, what should the correct relationship be between the Party and other institutions — particularly the revolutionary committee and the People's Liberation Army? Third, where should the new revolutionary cadres come from? Before considering these it is worth outlining those ideas of Mao's which are relevant to the programme of Party-building.

Like most people Mao was better at knowing what he did not want than at knowing what he did want. Little of Mao's time seems to have been devoted to working out the precise organizational arrangements which would follow the destruction of the Cultural Revolution. Perhaps like the straw sandals of Hunan they were to shape themselves in the making.[8] In large part it was up to others to put the flesh on the bones which Mao provided, an undertaking which, as later history has shown, was dangerous for those involved.

As was noted above, in the final analysis Mao was unwilling to totally reject leadership by some kind of elite over Chinese society. Hence the suggestions of the Shengwulian to create a system based on the commune were rejected, as were those of Chen Boda who favoured the continuation of the Party as it had been in the radical phase of the Cultural Revolution. For Mao leadership was necessary but those people in leadership positions were the object of suspicion. In particular Mao thought that there was a tendency for leaders to divorce themselves from the masses with disastrous results for the masses. As a consequence leaders were to maintain contact with the masses through, for example, the participation of cadres in labour and by giving the masses the opportunity to supervise and criticise their leaders. Thus, within the Party, institutional controls such as the Commissions for Inspecting Discipline were not considered necessary. Cadres would be kept on the 'straight and narrow' by the vigilance of the masses and by their closer integration with the masses. Naturally this also implied a suspicion of the hierarchical structure of the Party because it could lead to a divorce of leaders from the led and a pursuit of self-interest. This thread of ideas reaches its fruition with Mao's notion that this could provide part of the basis for the emergence of a new class.

In practical terms this concern was reflected in Party and State Constitutions adopted during the 1970s. The Party Constitutions adopted by the 10th and 11th Party Congresses both contained a stipulation enabling individuals to bypass the normal chain of democratic centralism. Party members were given the right to appeal to the Party Chairman himself (Articles 5 and 12, respectively).[9] The State Constitution adopted by the 5th National People's Congress actually gave citizens the right to 'speak out freely, air their views fully, hold great debates and write big-character posters', (Article 45).[10] The growing stress, particularly from 1979, on the restoration of internal monitoring of the Party and the adoption of institutionalized channels of participation for the masses has meant that such references have been dropped from the new Party Constitution and Draft State Constitution.

Another important and related aspect of Mao's ideas was that of the relationship of the Party to other organizations and institutions in society. Without doubt Mao saw the Party as the most important institution. However, as Schram has shown, the Party for Mao was one instrument among many, it was not something unique which, in itself, was the embodiment of legitimacy.[11] The Party was seen as a means towards an end, a view which gave rise to the possibility that other organizations might be equally effective as the means. The practical consequence of this has been that other institutions gain in importance. The 'Gang of Four' have been criticized for their promotion of non-Party organizations as a challenge to Party power. In part this can be interpreted as an expedient given their weakness in the Party but also it derives from Mao's ambivalence over the role of the Party and its relationship to other institutions. This ambivalence over the superiority of the Party and the subordination of mass organizations to it, combined with a suspicion of Party leadership made the operationalization of the system extremely difficult.

Two other aspects of Mao's thought must be mentioned: his view of class struggle, and his approach to development strategy. While building socialism it was important for Mao that not only the end be borne in mind but also that the means of achieving that end be carefully scrutinized. The Party was not only to promote production but was also to ensure that a 'new class' did not come to power in the process. Revolutionary struggle and the struggle for production was inseparable and in the last analysis class struggle was the most important. As Andors has stated, although economic development and technical transformation were seen by Mao as a vital part of building socialism, unless this was accompanied by a struggle to revolutionize production relations 'not only would the transformation of the economy and technology ultimately be limited by the forms these had assumed under capitalism, but also the attempt to revolutionize consciousness or ideology would not succeed'.[12] The Party, then, has a major role in ensuring political and ideological correctness. Also, Mao's faith in the masses meant that a greater role could be attributed to them as a part of the development strategy. In the Great Leap Forward, although the Party was to be in control of the movement, the movement was based on the premise that the enthusiasm of the masses could be harnessed and used for economic growth and industrialization. Such an approach calls for a different type of Party than one which relies on experts and carefully prepared plans.

It was left to others to find the required organizational forms. One problem which arose during this search was that of legitimacy, a problem which has persisted. At the start of the Cultural Revolution the massive attacks on the Party meant that its legitimacy was eroded and legitimacy was transferred to the supreme leader. Although the extremes of the cult of personality were rejected, as was the form of Party organization proposed by Chen Boda to support it, the problem remains in the post-Mao years. The 'Gang of Four' sought to devise new organizational forms which could combine more traditional Leninist concepts with those thrown up by the Cultural Revolution. They did not seek to abandon Leninism and as White has commented the 'Gang of Four' failed to 'make a break with the structural and normative logic of the Leninist form of state socialism'. White writes that they used hierarchical means to bring equality, authoritarian means to bring democracy, and the invocation of obedience to encourage initiative.[13] The models experimented with failed to gain legitimacy. This, combined with their suspicion of the Party and lack of support within its top leadership, meant that they all too readily fell back on the invocation of Mao's name as a source of legitimacy. The breakdown of the Party's authority and the inability to revive it or to produce a substitute created an excessively leader-oriented source of legitimacy.

Despite Hua Guofeng's policy differences with the 'Gang of Four' he, too, was presented with the problem of securing legitimacy. The problem remained of institutionalizing what he perceived to be the Maoist legacy. In terms of development strategy he favoured an approach similar to that of the Great Leap Forward. This approach was to be based on mobilization but was to be conducted with the Party firmly in command. In early 1978 at the 5th National People's Congress, Hua unveiled the economic plans for the future. The basis was the 1976–1985 Ten-Year Plan which set forward a series of ambitious targets. The plan bore resemblances to Mao's Twelve-Year Plan of the mid-1950s which had preceded the Great Leap Forward and the rhetoric began to mirror that which accompanied the Great Leap. In fact, the slogan of the Great Leap of 'going all out, aiming high to achieve greater, faster, better and more economical results in building socialism' was included in the General Programme of the Party Constitution adopted by the 11th Party Congress.[14] Noticeably it is absent from the Constitution adopted by the 12th Party Congress.[15] Hua appears to have wanted to create a 'Great Leap type of Party' — one which was sufficiently flexible and able to use a mobilizational style of politics. However, again the problem of creating legitimacy remained. While trying to restore Party prestige Hua also resorted to the adulation of Mao as the source of legitimacy while at the same time creating his own cult of personality.

Most of the 1970s saw an attempt to institutionalize and operationalize a system which did not reject the fundamentals of Leninism but at the same time incorporated the innovative and new organizational principles of the Cultural Revolution. This is reflected in the Party Constitutions of 1973 and 1977. Although there was a steady erosion of the new and a greater preponderance of the old both Constitutions sought to strike a balance. Consequently, one sees traditional Leninist concepts such as Democratic Centralism and the need for Party discipline alongside emphasis on the rebellious nature of the Cultural Revolution as summed up in the phrase 'going against the tide is a Marxist principle'.[16] The Constitution adopted by the 11th Party Congress reflected the drive to revive traditional Leninism at the expense of innovation introduced during the Cultural Revolution, but not all was thrown overboard. A favourable attitude to the Cultural Revolution was maintained and Hua pointed out that many such political revolutions would be necessary in the future.[17] Although the disciplinary role of the masses was limited they were still expected to 'keep an eye' on the Party.

3. PARTY REBUILDING SINCE THE 3RD PLENUM

Following the 3rd Plenum of the 11th Central Committee (December 1978) a faster and more fundamental change has taken place. For our purposes the Plenum was important in two respects. First, despite the Plenum's exhortations to forget about the past and look to the future, decisions made at the Plenum led to a selectively detailed review of the thirty years of the history of the People's Republic. From the point of view of Party rebuilding the 'reversals of verdict' on two particular people were of great significance. The restoration of Peng Dehuai's good name paved the way for criticisms of the breakdown of traditional Party norms while the reversal of the verdict on Liu Shaoqi aided the reconstruction of those norms.[18] Secondly, the Plenum put China firmly on a new economic path to achieve the goal of the four modernizations. The Great Leap style mobilization strategy was replaced by the more cautious programmes for economic growth favoured by people such as Chen Yun and Xue Muqiao. Although the trend had been visible for a long time the need was clearly for a more predictable Party capable of being an efficient organizational decision-making body.

The Plenum marked the subordination of all other work to that of achieving the four modernizations. The Plenum contended that class struggle was no longer the principal contradiction in Chinese society and *Beijing Review* stated that 'the fundamental change in the class situation in our country is the objective basis for the shift in focus of our Party's work to socialist modernization'.[19] Political work was being seen increasingly in terms of its ability to increase production. The slogan continually put forward was that of 'less empty talk'. This was used to criticise previous campaigns and political objectives. Also politics and economics were being separated into distinct entities. This was combined with the notion that economic work should 'grasp the Laws of Economic Development'.[20]

Economics and the struggle for production are now clearly in command with immediate consequences for the Party. Party work is now to serve and help bring about the realization of the four modernizations. Correspondingly, political and ideological work decline in importance. Consequently, the role of the Party as guardian in these realms diminishes. The role of the Party and its superiority as interpreter of the ideology are still affirmed but it is difficult, in practice, to see what this means other than removing the 'ideological driftwood' which is seen as an impediment to economic work. The new stress on production guided by 'experts' and conducted in an orderly fashion without the unrestrained participation of the masses has meant that Party organizations are now required to be efficient planning institutions, predictable, but not inflexible, in their actions and with a discernible and hierarchical chain of command. As Young has pointed out, what is now required of the integrative functions of the Party is to provide a 'competent administration' rather than to discover and implement a 'correct' political direction.[21]

4. INTERNAL PARTY ORGANIZATION

Criticisms of the Party have concentrated on bad workstyle and only belatedly have structural problems been approached. While criticizing the 'Gang of Four' for their arbitrary methods it is conveniently forgotten that the post-Mao leadership came to power through an act totally outside of the established principles — members of the highest Party body were arrested without consulting the Politburo.

The criticism and re-examination of the past have led to the identification of two different problems as the source of faulty workstyle: problems of bureaucratism and problems of remaining vestiges of feudalism. The term bureaucracy in this derogative sense covers a multitude of sins ranging from the swollen and overstaffed offices to the criticism of cadres who are said to have 'divorced themselves from the masses'. As early as August 1980 Deng Xiaoping identified this as a major problem when he told the Politburo that:

> Bureaucratism is a great problem that exists in the political life of our Party and state . . . Both in our domestic affairs and our international dealings, all this has reached an absolutely intolerable state.[22]

By March 1982 Wang Renzhong was moved to lament that investigation had shown that not a single province could be found which was free from graft, embezzlement, etc.[23]

The continued existence of feudalism is seen to arise not only as a result of 'hangovers' from the past, such as attitudes towards authority, but also because the 'Gang of Four' promoted 'feudal fascism'.[24] One major concern of this thrust of the criticism is the excessive power which such an approach gives to one person. Deification of Mao clearly has not been eradicated. Those who adhered too closely to the principles laid down by Mao were denounced as the 'Whatever' faction. Later, during the campaign to criticise 'leftism' which preceded the 6th Plenum (June 1981) the criticism was extended to include Hua Guofeng.

However, the extent of criticism of the past has varied considerably. Leaders such as Hua Guofeng and Ye Jianying have continually sought, for example, to moderate criticism of Mao and to stem the flood of exposés of Mao's 'mistakes'. Hua in his pronouncements has sought to narrow the focus of those under criticism. Criticisms of Mao undermine Hua's legitimacy to rule as Mao's personally chosen successor, while a broadening of those to be criticized would chip away at his own supporters. At the other extreme within the Party there have been the criticisms of those such as Li Honglin. In March 1979, Li made a scathing attack on the legacy of the Cultural Revolution and he clearly indicated that the source of these faults was the dominance of the individual in the Chinese political system. Li implies that the years of the late 1950s also suffered from the same problem. Clearly these were years when policy formulation was dominated by Mao.[25] Other Party members have been less harsh. Li Xiannian, for example, has pointed out that although, in retrospect, the faults of the Great Leap Forward are apparent, the decision to launch the movement was made by the Party and not by an individual.[26] Dominating the middle ground have been the shifting views of Deng Xiaoping. He has sought to steer a path avoiding the excesses of criticism and the whitewashing of the mistakes committed by Mao. This approach dominated the 'Resolution on Party History' adopted by the 6th Plenum (1981). On the question of Mao the 'Resolution' condemns him for his mistakes but makes it clear that the mistakes were those of a 'great proletarian revolutionary' whose errors were secondary to his great revolutionary achievements.[27]

To right the past wrongs and to suit the demands of the new modernization programme a number of institutions and policies have been revived or created. For the most part these reflect Deng Xiaoping's desire to return to a 'conventional way of doing things'.[28] Measures have been introduced to deal with both work-style and some of the more obvious structural problems, such as the abolition of the lifetime tenure of cadres. The reforms being experimented with do not in any way threaten the stability and integrity of the Party and represent an attempt to modify the excesses of traditional Leninism. Challenges to the right of the Party to rule based on its none too good

'track-record' during the Cultural Revolution decade are rejected with statements to the effect that although the 'Gang of Four' used the Party to implement their 'disastrous' policies, it was the Party which set things to right. Reforms, then, will be carried out by the Party itself. Forces outside of the Party, such as those unleashed during the Cultural Revolution, will not be mobilized. To revitalize the leadership and to restore Party prestige, Party discipline has been re-emphasized. Discipline and good behaviour are to be reinforced by administrative control mechanisms and definitively not by mass supervision.

Within the Party the correct functioning of principles such as democratic centralism and collective leadership are seen as vital. The Constitution adopted by the 12th Party Congress contains a more detailed outline of the principles of democratic centralism than was previously the case. While stressing the subordination of minority to majority and lower levels to higher levels the Constitution also states that higher Party organizations should pay constant attention to the lower organizations and rank-and-file Party members.[29] In terms of the right of Party members to criticize, the stress is on this being carried out in an orderly fashion. Party members, if they disagree with decisions or policies, are still accorded the right to take their views to higher levels including the Central Committee, but not to the Chairperson (the post having been abolished). The Constitution stresses, like the 11th but unlike the 10th, that while this process is taking place Party members must 'resolutely carry out the decision or policy while it is in force'.[30] Also, it is stated that any criticism of other members or organizations should be 'well-grounded'.[31]

If recent practice seems to have stressed the centralist component more than the democratic one, democracy is still seen as important not just for the Party but for society as a whole. However, within the Party, two restraints are placed on democracy. It is limited to those who do not challenge the fundamentals of the Party line and it is not to be seen as an end in itself — it, too, must serve the goal of the four modernizations.[32] To date, two groups have been identified to which the rights of democratic expression do not extend. First, there are those who are said to have mis-interpreted the degree of freedom possible and who have promoted 'so-called democracy'.[33] Second, there are those who have been denounced as the 'Whateverists'. The existence of democracy in the Party is vital both for internal communication and to link the Party with state and society. This will provide the Party leadership with the necessary information to frame the general policy guidelines to suit the changing conditions.

The new Constitution also shows concern for the need for collective leadership and the avoidance of personal rule. This relationship of leader to the Party has been a continual problem. The problem reached its height during the heyday of the Cultural Revolution when, for many, the authority of the Party was replaced by the authority of the individual. The present leadership have tried through a series of measures to bring to bear formal and informal controls over the top political leaders.

The 'Guiding Principles for Inner-Political Life' adopted in 1980 criticized the 'unprincipled glorification of leaders'. The 'Principles' stated that publicity for leading members should be factual and while no museums are to be built for the living 'not too many' are to be built for the dead.[34] The move against the glorification of the leader was set in motion by the now deposed Chairman, Hua Guofeng, in December 1978. Hua, at a Central Work Conference, stated '. . . when the local authorities and various units send reports to the Central Committee for its views, then reports should not be addressed to Chairman Hua and the Central Committee . . . Do not call me the wise leader, just call me comrade'.[35] Such modesty and recognition of his past faults was not enough, however, to save him his job.

In September 1980, Li Honglin wrote a more systematic condemnation of the 'incorrect' relationship between the leader and the led. Li criticized the personality cult of the Cultural Revolution, which he said was only necessary in a feudal society. In a sideswipe at Hua Guofeng, Li suggested that the cult had continued for a while even after 1976. For Li the consequence of the cult was that the leader could not be criticized, a tendency which he traced from the treatment of Peng Dehuai in 1959.[36] While not all the leadership would necessarily support the severity of Li's judgements they do seem to accept the need to play down the role of the individual and to institutionalize collective leadership. Measures have been introduced to reduce the adulation of national leaders[37] and also to prevent individuals from holding too many posts concurrently.[38] The Resolution on Establishing the Secretariat of the Central Committee explicitly stated that the Secretariat would apply the 'system of collective leadership and division of work with individual responsibility'.[39]

When listing the principles of democratic centralism the system of collective leadership with individual responsibility was reaffirmed and 'all forms of personality cult' were expressly forbidden.[40] The abolition of the post of Chairperson is seen as a further check on the abuse of the system by individuals. Hu Qiaomu, who presided over the drafting of the new Constitution, when commenting on the change outlined the difference between a General Secretary and a Chairperson:

He (the General Secretary) is responsible for convening the meetings of the Political Bureau and its Standing Committee and presides over the work of the Secretariat. Obviously, convening and presiding are different roles.[41] Such an organisational system will help prevent the recurrence of over-concentration of personal power and arbitrariness of a single person. Experiences of our own and other countries' organisations show that when a Party has both a Chairman and a General Secretary, often one position is merely nominal. Therefore, it is unnecessary to have these two positions simultaneously. Moreover, there is no reason for the posts of the Chairman and the General Secretary to be held by one person.[42]

Hu may well be right but the 'foreign experience' of the Soviet Union under Stalin shows that the existence of the post of General Secretary is quite compatible with 'overconcentration of personal power' and arbitrary rule.

The restrictions on individuals acting beyond the scope of Party policy are dealt with in Article 16 of the Constitution. The views must be on behalf of the Party organization and the contents must have been referred to that organization first or have been referred to the next higher Party organization for instructions. Party members, no matter what their position, cannot make decisions on major issues by themselves and cannot place themselves above the Party organization.[43]

However, for the system to work effectively responsibility rests on a well-trained and responsive cadre force. Not surprisingly measures have been introduced to remedy the problems with cadres and their work. However, Deng Xiaoping's and his supporters' attempts to reform the cadre system and improve their quality has met with stiff opposition. Following a speech of Deng's in January 1980, the press has stressed the importance of training cadres and has reiterated Mao's statement that 'after the political line has been fixed cadres become the decisive factor'.

Cadres are not only to undergo the education programme for all Party members but have their own specific materials to study and contemplate. The Central Commission for Inspecting Discipline drew up a fifteen-point code of behaviour instructing cadres that they should not act like high officials and overbearing bureaucrats, seek personal gain, become idealistic, act arbitrarily or abuse their power. The new Party Constitution set a number of requirements above those expected of ordinary members. In addition to covering the kind of abuses mentioned above the requirements call on cadres to correctly implement the Party's line, principles and policies; fight resolutely against hostile forces and combat all erroneous tendencies inside and outside the Party.[44]

The new Party Constitution also calls for 'genuine efforts to make the ranks of the cadres more revolutionary, younger in average age, better educated and more professionally competent'.[45] The attempts to replace the older cadres with little formal training by younger, better qualified cadres has met stiff opposition and it was not until late 1981–early 1982 that the policy was pursued in earnest.[46] However, as early as April 1980 *Red Flag* pointed out the poor quality of cadres. The article pointed out that few cadres were really proficient in professional work, that many were laypeople and that some of these people were in leading positions at the provincial level making final decisions.[47] Later in the year the *People's Daily* pointed out the 'evils' which stem from the life-long tenure of cadres:

> Personnel in leading posts tend to be senile . . . it is difficult for talented and erudite people to be recruited to leading bodies and get experience . . . the system does not encourage people to work hard but muddle along . . . nepotism replaces appointment on merit . . . power tends to become highly concentrated until ultimately all powers of the Party and state are wielded by one person alone.[48]

In particular there was resentment that 'excessive stress' was placed on formal educational training which would, of course, discriminate against many of the incumbent cadres. The reaction caused Deng to moderate his policy and by the end of 1980 and early 1981 a more flexible application of age and educational requirements was promised and incumbent cadres were promised retraining opportunities and the possibility of training their successors.[49]

Clearly regulations were needed to persuade cadres to retire voluntarily. Given the power and privileged access to scarce goods that leading Party positions provide this is hardly surprising. In March 1982, the *People's Daily* informed veteran cadres that their 'glorious and sacred duty' was to retire! This, it was stated, was the greatest contribution that one could make in one's old age.[50] Recognizing that such an appeal might not be enough by itself it was also made clear that financial incentives were available for those who did retire.[51] It is hoped that ending the life-long tenure of cadres, in both Party and state, will make cadres more accountable. This, in turn, should make cadres more responsive to both Party and the masses and more liable to dismissal should they be found guilty of corruption or incompetence.

The new Party Constitution tackles this problem but not as thoroughly as was orginally intended. It contains stipulations that cadres, whether elected or appointed, are not entitled to lifelong tenure, and that they can be transferred from or relieved of their posts.[52] However, the Constitution contains no stipulations strictly limiting the terms of office. An earlier draft which was circulated contained greater details concerning both the period of tenure and the average age limit of cadres.[53] Hu Qiaomu stated that 'after repeated discussions' strict limits on the term of office would not be set. The reason he gives is for the need to retain some veteran cadres with experience and high prestige to ensure 'stability and maturity' of leadership.[54] In practice, it seems to be a concession to the large number of cadres who feared their imminent removal from office.

To help with the problem of relieving cadres of their posts while still making use of their expertise, advisory commissions are to be set up at and above the provincial level.[55] It is intended that the members of these commissions will act as political assistants and consultants. Whether this becomes a genuine reform or whether it is a short-term measure to open up avenues for promotion only time will tell. It is difficult to see what the real change would be, apart from the name, if all the oldest Party members simply became advisers. The immediate effect of creating these advisory commissions has been to increase the number of people attending plenary sessions of the Central Committee. The 7th Plenum of the 11th Central Committee (August 1982) was attended by a total of 318 people (297 Committee members and alternates and 21 observers), while the 1st Plenum of the 12th Central Committee was attended by 631 people (347 Committee members and alternates and 284 observers). This 100% increase does not bode well for a régime committed to reducing bureaucracy. Also, this can only give more ammunition to those who believe that the Central Committee is not an important decision-making body in the Party.

However, the creation of the Central Advisory Commission has provided some places for new members on the Central Committee. Of the 172 Central Advisory Commission members 49 were on the 11th Central Committee (Deng Xiaoping is still on the 12th) and 14 were alternates. This provided some of the places for the 211 newly elected committee members and alternates. However, the vast majority of new places was provided by the purge of members and alternates from the 11th Central Committee. Of the new members 140 are said to be less than 60 with a youngest age of 38. The new Committee and its alternate members also reflects the drive to recruit more specialized personnel to leadership positions. Specialized personnel is said to have increased from 2.7% at the 11th to 17% at the 12th Central Committee.[56]

In company with this 'righting of wrongs' and, to a large extent, preceding it, a number of pre-Cultural Revolution institutions have been revived. As we mentioned, the Secretariat has been revived as a collective leadership body to handle the day-to-day work of the Party. This is seen by the Chinese to be a function of the shift of focus of the work to modernization. Concentration on this objective is said to have produced a greater complexity of work.[57] In theory the Politburo and its Standing Committee are freed to concentrate on taking important decisions on national and international issues with the Secretariat becoming the Party's administrative heart. In practice, the Secretariat is placed in an extremely powerful position as its supervises the regional Party organs and the functional departments of the Party, departments which, in theory, should be responsible directly to the Central Committee and the Politburo.

To overcome the impediments of bureaucratism and faulty workstyle a system of internal Party control has been resurrected, the lynchpin of which is the Commissions for Inspecting Discipline. This reflects a more institutionalized method for dealing with discipline, replacing the more arbitrary methods which operated during the Cultural Revolution. The Central Commission for Inspecting Discipline was set up by the 3rd Plenum and has been charged with the resurrection of rules and regulations which the Party feels have been flouted since the late 1950s. Among its most important activities in this respect have been the publication of the aforementioned 'Guiding Principles' and the draft of the educational

materials for Party cadres, providing the findings for the posthumous rehabilitation of Liu Shaoqi, and the recreation of a discipline and control system throughout the Party.

Also, Party Schools have been revived to provide Party members with a proper education in the way that they should behave and the way in which the Party should be run.[58] The influx of new Party members during the years 1966–1976 is said to be a major cause of the faulty workstyle of the Party.[59] Red Flag claims that the Party ranks expanded by 100% during the Cultural Revolution decade.[60] Because this was a time of 'abnormality' in Party life, many of these new members are said to be unfamiliar with traditional Party procedures and hence unqualified to be Party members. Consequently, a programme of education has been launched to instil in members the 'basis knowledge of the Party, its rules, discipline, fine traditions and style of work'.[61] In fact, similar criticisms are made of the basic political knowledge of cadres. According to an article in the mid-June 1982 issue of Red Flag, statistics from some provinces showed that 80% of cadres had no systematic and basic knowledge of Marxism. The article called for those between the ages of 30 and 50 to receive special attention in the training programmes given in the Party and Cadre Schools.[62]

Presumably, those who do not come up to the required standards will be expelled from the Party. In fact, in August 1982 the People's Daily called for 'degenerate elements' to be expelled.[63] Also, Hu Yaobang, in his report to the 12th Party Congress, when talking of the three-year Party rectification to begin in the second half of 1983 mentioned that all Party members would be required to re-register at the end of this period. He explicitly stated that 'those who still fail to meet the requirements for membership after education shall be expelled from the Party or asked to withdraw from it'.[64] Chen Yun, among others, indicated that three categories of people would not be welcome in the future: first, people who rose to prominence in the Cultural Revolution by following the 'Gang of Four' in rebellion; second, people who are seriously factionalist in their ideas; and third, people who indulged in beating, smashing and looting.[65]

Finally, the rehabilitation of Liu Shaoqi by the 5th Plenum (February 1980) was a significant event in terms of the restoration of the norms which had governed Party life in the mid-1950s. His rehabilitation has facilitated the republication and discussion of his major works and theories concerning Party organization and how to conduct Party life. It is expected that a reading of works such as 'How to be a Good Communist' (1939) and 'On Inner-Party Struggle' (1941) will give Party members a clearer understanding of their rights and duties and how debate within the Party should be conducted. The most notable feature of these writings is the preoccupation with organization. Such an emphasis obviously finds more sympathy with a leadership committed to the present approach to development. It helps the attempts to build a more professionalized, traditionally Leninist-style Party aiding the transformation of the Party into an instrument to achieve the four modernizations. The present leadership clearly have a preference for a leadership style associated with Liu than with Mao. As Dittmer has shown, while Liu's style was formal and routinized, Mao's was episodic and provocative; while Liu called meetings, drew up agendas etc., Mao would short-circuit the system, often presenting the leadership with a *fait accompli*; and while Liu's institutional strategy of policy formulation resulted in extremely detailed directives, Mao's directives by contrast were schematic to avoid inflexibility.[66] Now, spontaneous action by the masses, albeit often loosely orchestrated, has been replaced by tight organization and central leadership and a reliance on the ingenuity of the masses is replaced by a reliance on the professional skills of the technical and managerial elite.

5. PARTY–STATE RELATIONS

Like other Communist Party-states, China can be studied in terms of the classic duality of the Party and the state and their inter-relationship. In theory, the Party devises policy and provides political leadership while the state implements and administers the policy. In this section two aspects of recent policy in this area will be considered: first, the attempts to make a clear distinction between Party and state; and second, the consequences of the current resolution of the debate on the decentralization of economic decision-making.

In all Communist Party-states the distinction between Party and state is blurred and in China this distinction has been the least clear. In China there has existed confusion about the division of responsibility between policy formulation and implementation. On occasions, this overlap of Party and state has led to the Party actually implementing policy. Normally, this is condemned but during the

Cultural Revolution it appeared to be positively encouraged. For example, at the beginning of the Cultural Revolution the organs of Party and state, at the non-central levels, were identical. Following the attacks on the old Party and state organs in 1966 they were replaced by the revolutionary committee which, for a while at least, combined Party and state functions in one body. The rebuilding of the Party from 1969 following the total collapse of the distinction between Party and state caused a persistent confusion over the division of responsibilities between Party committees and revolutionary committees. Throughout the early 1970s the press stressed the need for the Party committees to strengthen their leadership over the revolutionary committees, emphasizing that the Party should make the major decisions and that the revolutionary committee must 'consciously accept the Party committee's leadership in exercising power and carrying out its work'.[67] This problem was not helped by the fact that the leadership personnel of the two committees were often identical and Party committees in some factories were criticized for handling such trivial matters as family disputes and water temperatures in bath-houses. The concurrent holding of posts was even more noticeable at the centre of the system. For example, until mid-1980 all the Vice-Premiers of the State Council were high-ranking members of the Central Committee and Politburo.

This penetration of Party into the state and its control of the state sector are reflected in both the 'more radical' Constitution of 1975 and the 'less radical' one of 1978. While Article 3 of the two Constitutions states that 'all power in the People's Republic of China belongs to the people', Article 2 indicates that the real power lies with the Party. In both Constitutions the Article states that the Party is 'the core of leadership of the whole Chinese people' and that the working-class exercises leadership over the state through the Party — its vanguard.[68]

The post-Mao leadership has attempted to recreate the distinction between Party and state which is supposed to exist under 'socialism'. This attempt has gone beyond paying mere lip-service to the distinction as appeared to be the case in the immediate post-Mao years to actually trying to give the theoretical distinction some substance in practice. Direct administration by the Party has been criticized and it has been pointed out that the Party's responsibility for leadership should never have meant direct control.[69] Apart from the theoretical reasons for maintaining Party and state as separate organs there are also practical ones. As Schurmann pointed out, the more an organization becomes a 'command-issuing body' the more it must 'grapple with the concrete technicalities of command'. This would lead to increasing bureaucratism and inflexibility thus thwarting the Party's ability to innovate and adjust to changing circumstances.[70] Also, the new development strategy relies heavily on the experts to implement it and this necessitates a weakening of the Party's grip over both state and society and, especially in the economic sphere, the relaxation of state over society. Finally, by distancing itself from the day-to-day running of the system, the Party can seek to avoid the blame for economic failings. These can more readily be blamed on faulty implementation etc. Particularly at the level of the enterprise this can be important. Management can be held responsible for failings and thus be dismissed if necessary while, in theory, the Party could remain intact.

The dangers in such a course are evident. A corporatist structure could begin to emerge with other powerful groups in state and society challenging Party dominance. The reliance on groups such as the economic planners must afford them increased power. The solution for the Party in this situation, as much of Eastern European experience has shown, is to recruit these groups into the Party to maintain control over the state. However, as White points out, this imports their 'autonomous power and distinct interests' thus, in turn, exerting pressure on the direction of public policy.[71]

The first problem the post-Mao leadership tackled was to try to resolve the continuing confusion between the revolutionary committee and the Party committee. The State constitution presented in 1978 stressed the purely administrative function of the revolutionary committee, referring to it as the executive rather than the permanent organ of the people's congress at the corresponding level and as the local people's government at the various levels. The committee's ubiquity was curtailed by restricting it only to levels of government. The second session of the 5th National People's Congress went even further than this and abolished them altogether. Peng Zhen in making the, by then, largely symbolic announcement stated that the posts of governors, mayors etc. would be restored.[72]

The next problem tackled was that of cadres holding both top Party and state posts which blurred the distinction between Party and state work. At the 3rd session of the 5th

National People's Congress (August—September 1980) Hua Guofeng announced that the common practice of the same person holding the leading Party and state posts at provincial level was to come to an end. According to Hua, the objective of this was to prevent the 'over-concentration of power and the holding of too many posts concurrently by one person'. Its aim was to 'effectively and clearly separate Party work from government work'.[73] Earlier, in July that year, it was announced that the highest posts in the Party and state would again be held by different people — as had been the case up until Mao's death. Hua Guofeng, while remaining Chairman of the Party, 'handed over' the post of Premier to Zhao Ziyang.[74]

This freeing of the state from the grip of the Party is also reflected in the new Draft Constitution for the state. This draft reverts back to the similar one of 1954 when the power of the Party was hidden in the Constitution. The Article of the 1975 and 1978 Constitutions which referred to the Party as the 'core of leadership' has been dropped as has the claim that it is the citizens' duty to support the Party (Article 26, 1975; Article 56, 1978). Now citizens are said to have the duty to 'abide by the Constitution and the law'.[75] Direct Party control is further weakened by dropping the provision that the Party and its Chairperson lead and command the PLA (Article 15, 1975; Article 19, 1978) and also by renouncing the stipulation that the Premier be recommended by the Party's Central Committee (Article 17, 1975; Article 22, 1978). In fact the emphasis on constitutionalism appears to go beyond even that of 1954. Mention of Party control now only appears in the Preamble where its leading role is acknowledged.[76]

The period since the death of Mao has seen the revival of the debate over the decentralization of economic decision-making. As Schurmann has shown, in the debates of the 1950s two main options were put forward. Either powers could be devolved to the provinces (Decentralization 1) or they could be devolved to the units of production (Decentralization 2).[77] Both options have consequences for the Party's role in economic affairs and both options have been experimented with since Mao's death.

Initial policy was along the lines of Schurmann's Decentralization 1. As has been noted, Hua Guofeng sought a 'Great Leap' approach to development with the emphasis on social mobilization rather than on material incentives. This approach was to take place with the Party firmly in command and as a consequence greater powers accrued to the provincial Party apparatus and the Party Committees in the unit of production. Provincial government and particularly Party Committees through their unique coordinating role dominated the process. The individual production units, by contrast, had very little autonomy. As had happened before, this approach was accompanied by announcements that economic zones should be set up for cooperation. Again mention was made in the Chinese press of establishing economic systems in the six big regions. An article by the State Planning Commission on the first anniversary of Mao's death stated that these would have 'their own special features, operate independently, cooperate with one another and ensure a fairly balanced growth of agriculture, light industry and heavy industry'.[78]

More recent policy has produced an emphasis on greater autonomy for the units of production. Such an approach makes the use of material, rather than moral, incentives as a stimulus to development easier. Clearly this approach, too, has consequences for the Party's role. Increasingly since the 3rd Plenum we have seen the dominance of the ideas of Chen Yun in the economic field. The role of the market is emphasized along with that of material incentives, and power in decision-making has been shifted from provincial Party Committees and Party Committees in production units to the ministries and enterprise managers. The Party is forced into a situation where production units, or their managers, can exert considerable pressure on it. The powers of the enterprise Party Committee will inevitably become limited. Similarly, in the countryside the Party's control can be challenged. At present, rural policy favours the wealthier peasants and this should, in turn, increase their power to challenge the Party's authority at the basic levels, a problem which will be returned to later.

6. PARTY AND SOCIETY

The renewed stress on the four modernizations has revived parallels with other periods when the demands of the economy have required the relaxation of the Party's grip over society. As with its relationship with the state, the Party is trying to redefine its position *vis-à-vis* society. To encourage the greater supply of information by experts to the Party less interference is to be tolerated in specialized areas by the Party. Reference is no longer made to the overall leadership of the Party over

the seven sectors in Chinese society and the draft State Constitution does not refer to the Party as the 'core of leadership of the whole people'. Yet, clearly overall leadership is to be maintained as is encapsulated in the emphasis on the adherence to the 'Four Fundamental Principles'.[79] In an interview a 'leading comrade' of the Central Committee's Organization Department implicitly criticized past practice by stating that leadership must not be exercised by issuing orders or by using mandatory administrative means. According to the interviewee, the future leadership role of the Party is to be exercised in three ways. First, Party leading organs are to formulate and implement the correct line, principles and policies. Second, at the different levels the Party is to coordinate the relations: the different fields ensuring harmony in achieving the prescribed goals. Third, Party members themselves are to set shining examples for others to follow.[80]

Similarly, as with other periods of 'liberalization', differences of opinion have been expressed concerning just how far the Party can and should relax its grip. White has pointed out that there is a large area of contention between the notion that the Party cannot monopolize everything and the insistence that, as Deng Xiaoping put it, 'without Party leadership . . . there would be no force able to lead the four modernisations'.[81] The Party is caught in the contradiction of trying to keep intellectuals loyal to the basic tenets of Marxism—Leninism, thus requiring a fairly strict ideological orthodoxy while, at the same time, encouraging intellectuals to utilize their skills to promote the four modernizations, thus requiring a certain creativity.

One of the major criticisms of the 'Gang of Four' has been the charge that they promoted the mass organizations under their control as a direct challenge to Communist Party rule. As we have seen, it was not their, or Mao's, intention to replace the Party by other organizations but they did have a suspicion of the Party which opened the way to criticisms of their diluting the Party's leading role. History has shown that the Party does not tolerate the emergence of other bodies to challenge its rule. The present leadership has tried to restore the effective leadership of the Party while at the same time not negating the contributions that the masses can make to the modernization programme. This desire is reflected in the current view of the mass line. As Young points out, the current stress on the strengthening of Party leadership is seen to be entirely consistent with the mass line concept as the direction in which the masses are heading can only be the correct one if the Party is pointing the way.[82] The mass line becomes, in fact, another cog in the wheel for reaching the four modernizations, by helping to solve problems encountered on the road. This approach is reflected in the revival of organizations for the masses such as the Trade Unions, the Youth League and the Women's Federation which fell into disfavour during the Cultural Revolution. These organizations are now expected to provide the link between society and the Party.

The policy of relaxation, and its fluctuations, are seen most clearly with respect to policies concerning intellectuals. To provide their 'expert' advice this sector of society must be given certain freedoms and sureties to ensure their support. Despite recent retrenchments, intellectuals in many fields have enjoyed a freedom unparalleled since 1949. A number of 'forbidden zones' have been entered and it has been stated that 'without democracy, there can be no science' and that 'science and culture cannot develop without free discussion'.[83] Intellectual work and achievements are no longer downgraded and the vital role which intellectuals play in the modernization process has been stressed. Of the 340 model workers at the December 1979 National Model Workers' Conference, 160 were intellectuals.[84] Their status has been improved by the restoration of academic titles[85] and all intellectuals are to have their work and living conditions improved. Most importantly, intellectuals are now defined as a part of the working class — a long way from the 'stinking ninth category' as they were designated during the Cultural Revolution.[86] This means that in future when re-education for an intellectual is considered necessary, it will be dealt with in the same manner as other contradictions among the people. When Bai Hua was being criticized for his script 'Bitter Love', Chinese leaders were at pains to point out that the Cultural Revolution methods of criticism would not be used. In fact, at the same time as he was being criticized for 'Bitter Love', he received an award for another of his works.[87]

As has been noted, differences exist within the Party concerning the degree of freedom permissible. Leaders such as Deng Xiaoping and Hu Yaobang, while stressing the need for Party supremacy, seem to have supported greater freedom for intellectuals. Others in the Party have clearly sought to reassert tighter Party control. They, as in other periods, have been able to use the anti-Party sentiments and criticisms voiced in both the official and un-

official media to push through a crackdown on the extremes of freedom tolerated. During the period of greater freedom, views were expressed which desired greater freedom, and, in some cases, total freedom from Party control. Liu Binyan put forward a writer's defence of the right to criticize the Party when he wrote that 'when literature mirrors what is undesirable in life, the mirror itself is not to blame; instead, disagreeable things in real life should be spotted and wiped out. An ugly person cannot be turned into a beauty simply by smashing the mirror.'[88] Clearly, there are still those who would prefer to smash the mirror.

The changes in development strategy have also had a significant impact on the kind of person whom the Party wants to recruit from society. Although the Chinese Communist Party is one of the most exclusive Communist Parties in the world, recruitment of Party members has always been flexible. Since the fall of the 'Gang of Four' and more particularly since the 3rd Plenum, the emphasis of recruitment policy has been on cadres, intellectuals and those who possess technical skills. This has brought into the Party those with the high-level of technical skills to help with the programme of economic modernization. These groups of people are over-represented in recent recruitment when taken as a percentage of society as a whole. In 1979, Guizhou Province recruited 1916 intellectuals to be Party members.[89] Similarly, in other provinces emphasis has been on the recruitment of intellectuals and professionals. For example, in Shaanxi in 1981, 36.3% of new Party members were intellectuals and professionals while in the same time Henan recruited 4366 intellectuals.[90] From Beijing there is evidence to suggest that recruitment of intellectuals is increasing. In 1979, it was stated that 15% (2600) of the new recruits that year were intellectuals.[91] In 1982, it was stated that from 1979 to 1982, 20% of the new recruits were intellectuals. This same report mentions that most of the new recruits were outstanding factory, scientific, research and teaching workers or labour heroes.[92] The stress on recruiting professionals and technicians is reinforced by statistics from Shandong Province which show that of recent Party recruits, 20.9% were specialists and technicians.

However, problems have been encountered in recruitment. The relaxation of the Party's grip over the basic economic units could produce a reluctance of the part of the masses to join the Party.[93] For example, in the countryside, if the privileged access to goods etc. that Party membership gives is undermined and rivalled by other avenues for accumulating wealth, people may decide the gains of Party membership do not outweigh those that can be found elsewhere. Also, peasants and workers may feel that the stress on the model behaviour of Party members may prevent them from benefiting fully from current policies. Hu Yaobang in his report to the 12th Party Congress pointed out the 'grave situation' of the fewer Party members on the 'production front' and how this had 'weakened the direct link between the Party and the industrial workers'. When referring to the situation in the countryside Hu stated:

> in a number of rural areas . . . some Party members are interested only in their own productive activities and neglect the interests of the Party and the masses, and some Party branches have relinquished leadership among the masses.[94]

It seems probable that the stress from mid-1982 on the need to 'consolidate primary Party organizations' was inspired not only because of the problem of the 'poor quality' of Cultural Revolution recruits but also because of the weakening of the Party's grip over the economic sector.[95] Unless a satisfactory *modus vivendi* is found the Party could find itself. increasingly 'squeezed out' at the basic level by rival powerful groups.

7. CONCLUDING REMARKS

In this final section it is the intention to outline the differing views which exist concerning the Party in the Chinese political system.[96] I do not intend to look at views expressed by those writers in the Democracy Movement who proposed a multi-Party system primarily because there is no chance of such a view being realized in the foreseeable future.

Four main views can be discerned but they are not entirely distinct and it would perhaps be better to think of them as points along a continuum. Indeed, Deng Xiaoping appears to have given support to proponents of more than one view since his return, in the same way as the oscillating Mao did during the early years of the Cultural Revolution. The two ends of the continuum are dealt with first and then the two views which appear to occupy the centre and around which future policies will probably revolve.

First, there is the view of the Party which was dominant in the immediate post-Mao years. This view retains certain features from the Cultural Revolution years along with the ambiguities and was designed to complement

the optimistic proposals of the new 'Great Leap' strategy for economic development. Most of those associated with this type of view have been removed from power during the campaign against the 'Whateverists' and the campaign to eliminate 'Leftism'. Those who share these views and who have not been removed from power have had their power eclipsed. Essentially, this view proposed the continuance of the Party as a vehicle of mobilization to conduct mass campaigns, both economic and political, to achieve the ambitious targets set. While the Party was to be firmly in command, the masses were to exercise a monitoring function over abuses by Party members. Such a view was liable to allow suspicion of the Party to remain while failing to create organizations with legitimacy. It was too dependent on the more 'radical' aspects of Mao's legacy and the creation of a new personality cult around Hua to resist the policy shifts to the new economic programme. Defence of Mao's legacy and opposition to the current economic strategy and the 'open-door' policy has found powerful support in the army. Just before the 12th Party Congress convened, the *Liberation Army Daily* published an article which was critical of the current 'relaxation' in the ideological sphere and argued for the use of class viewpoint to explain things happening in social, material and spiritual life. The article accused 'certain leaders in China's theoretical, art and literary and press circles of taking the lead in supporting and propagating the erroneous viewpoints of bourgeois liberalizations'.[97] Following the Congress, an editorial was published in the *Liberation Army Daily* retracting the article claiming that it ran counter to the principles of the 12th Party Congress and propagated a 'Leftist' viewpoint while opposing 'bourgeois liberalization'.[98] It was also announced that the PLA's Political Commissar, Wei Guoqing, had been replaced by Yu Qiuli.[99]

The second view is that which has been denounced as reflecting 'bourgeois individualism'. In this speech to members of the Central Propaganda Department, in July 1981, Deng announced that liberalism as well as 'leftist' tendencies should be opposed.[100] Deng said that the core of this view was the rejection of the Party's leadership, a theme which was picked up by the *People's Daily* which described the trend as a 'wrong and dangerous tendency'.[101] The *Guangming Daily* stressed the importance of, and need to study, Mao's article 'Combat Liberalism' and reiterated that there should be no 'unprincipled peace' between proletarian and non-proletarian ideology.[102] This criticism has been most noticeable in the field of art and literature where the Party has sought to reassert stronger control. People such as Bai Hua and Ye Wenfu have been criticized and Hu Yaobang has called on Zhou Yang to compile a book dealing with the basic Marxist theories on art and literature for students and amateur writers.[103]

While it would be wrong to think that most of the people who have been criticized under the umbrella of 'bourgeois liberalism' reject the dominant position of the Party it is true that they seek a relationship with society different from that which the top Party leadership are willing to accept. They want to see a greater weakening of control by the Party over society, the opening up of other channels of communication for the masses and a system of supervision and defence of citizens' rights centred on a viable legal system. Thus, the resurrection of the legal system and a greater emphasis on constitutionalism are fundamental to this approach. The law is vital to protect the rights of citizens and to prevent arbitrary suppression should 'another "Gang of Four"' gain Party power. It is felt that if the Constitution had been properly upheld then the 'Gang of Four' would not have been able to proceed as they did. Also important to this view is the role of elections not just to prevent people such as the 'Gang of Four' coming to power but also to give citizens greater control over both Party and state machinery. Proponents of this view are suspicious of the Party's capability to act as society's control over the state and its coercive apparatus without greater supervision. The political participation of the masses is not to be restricted simply to channelling useful views into the Party but should help control access to positions of power. To this extent it does challenge the view that the Party has an exclusive claim to leadership over the masses. People's rights and interests, it is said, should also be protected by the Constitution supported by the legal system and not just by the Party.[104]

The two views which appear dominant at the moment could be termed the traditional and the pragmatic. The traditional view is that which seeks to operate the Party and its relationship to society predicated on orthodox Leninist lines. There can be no suggestion of a relaxation of Party control and supporters seek continually to institutionalize Party dominance. Such a view provides stability and assurances as well as status for Party cadres and ordinary members. However, at the same time, the view provides the institutional basis for the corruption and stifling of initiative which has been so heavily criticized in recent years. The reasons for this are the hierarchical structure of power and the lack of a genuine system of accountability. Measures adopted to cure problems within the Party are designed in such a way as to make sure that the Party's dominant position is in no way challenged. As a consequence, the proponents of this view focus criticism on the way in which cadres behave. The cure will come about by making cadres think correctly rather than by making the necessary structural changes which could help cure the problem at the source. Such an approach is, as Schram has referred to it, a 'dead end'.[105]

The term 'pragmatic' is used for the fourth view because those who take this approach are willing to introduce reforms which, while not in any way challenging Party supremacy, help meet the objective of the four modernizations. Proponents seek to introduce a flexibility into the Party which will prevent apathy and the stifling of innovation from ruining the modernization programme. The necessity for experts and intellectuals is fully recognized as is the need to give these people a greater degree of freedom as a prerequisite for their contribution to the new policies. These people must be given greater guarantees that they will not be punished tomorrow for what they say today. This leads not only to a greater tolerance of 'dissent' but also to a support for the protection of people's rights by the legal system upholding the Constitution. Genuine elections are seen as important not just for allowing mass participation in the decision-making process but also to ensure that those in leadership positions have the support of their constituencies. Finally, some structural reforms are supported to do away with corruption and inefficiency.

As recent history and the past history of the mid-1950s and early 1960s, has shown, this is a difficult position to maintain. Essentially, the view confronts the class dilemma of democratic centralism — how much democracy and how much centralism? This position comes under pressure from both sides. Some people push for greater democracy, while others use the 'excessive' criticisms put forward to demand a return to tighter Party control. It seems that some Party leaders were able to use the criticisms made by both official and unofficial media writers to force Deng to accept a tighter Party control over society. For the foreseeable future, the role of the Party will oscillate between these latter two views.

Finally, the question in the title must be addressed. It is hoped that this article has shown that although in part the changes in the

Party since the death of Mao have related to a change of workstyle, considerably more than this has taken place. The institutions now in operation and the views on the role of the Party represent a dramatic shift away from those of the early and mid-1970s. In major part these changes can only be understood in relation to the change in political direction and economic policy pursued in earnest since the 3rd Plenum. Whether the present institutions and codes of conduct can provide the necessary flexibility to promote the new development strategy and to contain arguments about future directions or whether they will disintegrate once major differences of opinion surface remains to be seen. Perhaps in this respect it is apt to quote from one of the present leadership's gurus:

> Ideological correctness must ultimately take precedence over any notions of organizational discipline.[106]

NOTES

1. *Red Flag* Editorial, 'Pull ourselves together in establishing a good party workstyle', *Red Flag*, No. 3 (1982).

2. *Ibid.*

3. See *Beijing Review*, No. 37 (1982), p. 15; and *Beijing Review*, No. 36 (1982), p. 5 respectively.

4. *The Manchester Guardian* (16 March 1982).

5. F. Schurmann, *Ideology and Organization in Communist China* (Berkeley: University of California Press, 1968), p. 107.

6. Mao, 'Talks at three meetings with Comrades Chang Ch'un-ch'iao and Yao Wen-yüan', in S. Schram (ed.), *Mao Tse-Tung Unrehearsed* (Harmondsworth: Penguin Books, 1974), p. 278. In the same talks, Mao denounces 'doing away with heads' as extreme anarchy.

7. See D. S. G. Goodman, 'The Provincial Revolutionary Committee in the People's Republic of China, 1967–79: an obituary' in *China Quarterly* (March 1981), No. 85, p. 70.

8. Schram notes that Mao used a Hunanese folk-saying 'straw sandals have no patterns; they shape themselves in the making' when illustrating his theory of permanent revolution. See S. Schram, 'The Cultural Revolution in historical perspective', in S. Schram (ed.), *Authority, Participation and Cultural Change in China* (Cambridge: Cambridge University Press, 1973), pp. 54–55.

9. See *The Tenth National Congress of the Communist Party of China (Documents)* (Beijing: Foreign Language Press, 1973); and *The Eleventh National Congress of the Communist Party of China* (Beijing: Foreign Languages Press, 1977).

10. *Documents of the First Session of the Fifth National People's Congress of the People's Republic of China* (Beijing: Foreign Languages Press, 1977).

11. S. Schram, 'The Party in Chinese Communist ideology', *China Quarterly*, No. 38 (1969), p. 11.

12. S. Andors, 'The political and organizational implications of China's new economic policies, 1976–1979', *Bulletin of Concerned Asian Scholars*, Vol. 12, No. 2 (1980), p. 46.

13. G. White, 'The new course in Chinese development strategy: context, problems and prospects', in J. Gray and G. White (eds.), *China's New Development Strategy* (London: Academic Press, 1982), p. 6.

14. *The Eleventh Congress of the Communist Party of China, op. cit.*, p. 124.

15. For the full text of the Constitution adopted by the 12th Party Congress see *Beijing Review*, No. 38 (1982), pp. 8–21. For a copy of an earlier draft see *Issues and Studies*, Vol. XVI, No. 9 (September 1980), pp. 81–109.

16. The General Programme or the Constitution adopted by the 10th Party Congress states that 'Comrades throughout the Party must have the revolutionary spirit of daring to go against the tide' while that adopted by the 11th dilutes this by stating that it only applies to tides which run counter to the three basic principles. See *The Tenth National Congress of the Communist Party of China, op. cit.*, p. 63 and *The Eleventh Congress of the Communist Party of China, op. cit.*, p. 125.

17. This suggestion was even included in the General Programme of the Constitution adopted by the 11th Party Congress. *The Eleventh Congress of the Communist Party of China, op. cit.*, p. 123.

18. For a detailed study of the breakdown and restoration of Party norms see F. Teiwes, *Politics and Purges in China* (White Plains, New York: M. E. Sharpe Inc., 1979).

19. 'Fundamental change in China's class situation', *Beijing Review*, No. 47 (1979), p. 1.

20. See, for example, Xue Muqiao, 'Economic work must grasp the laws of economic development', translated by T. Saich in B. Szajkowski (ed.), *Documents on Communist Affairs* (Houndsmill: Macmillan, 1981).

21. G. Young, 'Non-revolutionary vanguard: transformation of the Chinese Communist Party', in B. Brugger (ed.), *China Since the Gang of Four* (London: Croom Helm, 1980), p. 82.

22. Deng Xiaoping, Speech of 18 August 1980 in *Summary of World Broadcasts: the Far East (SWB:FE)* 6706 (1980).

23. Wang Renzhong, 'Unify thinking, conscientiously rectify workstyle', *Red Flag*, No. 5 (1982).

24. Chen Zihua, 'On China's electoral law', *Beijing Review*, No. 17 (1979), p. 18.

25. *Guangming Daily* (11 March 1979).

26. See the report of Li Xiannian's interview with the American journalist Harrison E. Salisbury in *The Times* (28 July 1980).

27. For the full text of the 'Resolution' see 'On questions of Party history — resolution on certain questions in the history of our Party since the founding of the People's Republic of China', *Beijing Review*, No. 27 (1981), pp. 10—39.

28. Deng Xiaoping, 'Report on the current situation and its tasks', *SWB:FE* 6363 (1980).

29. See Article 10 of the Constitution of the Communist Party of China adopted by the 12th Party Congress, *Beijing Review, op. cit.*, p. 13.

30. Article 4 of the Constitution of the Communist Party of China adopted by the 12th Party Congress, *ibid.*, p. 11.

31. Article 4 of the Constitution of the Communist Party of China adopted by the 12th Party Congress, *ibid.*, p. 11.

32. See, for example, *People's Daily* (11 January 1979).

33. These people have been referred to in the Chinese press as 'anarchists' and 'bourgeois liberals'. The 'Whateverists' are said to be those who adhere too closely to the two whatevers. The two whatevers are 'we resolutely support whatever policies are made by Chairman Mao; we resolutely follow whatever directives are made by Chairman Mao'. These were put forward in a 7 February 1977 joint editorial of the *People's Daily*, *Red Flag* and *Liberation Army Daily*.

34. For text see *SWB:FE* 6375 (1980). The 'Principles' were adopted by the 5th Plenum (February 1980).

35. *People's Daily* (1 February 1979).

36. Li Honglin, 'The leader and the people', *People's Daily* (19 September 1980).

37. For example the *People's Daily* announced that the Central Committee had drawn up 5 decisions to help cut down publicity for the individual. See *People's Daily* (4 September 1980).

38. This point is dealt with in more detail later.

39. Resolution on establishing the Secretariat of the Central Committee, *Beijing Review*, No. 10 (1980), p. 12.

40. Article 10 of the Constitution of the Communist Party of China adopted by the 12th Party Congress, *Beijing Review, op. cit.*, p. 13.

41. The translation in the Summary of World Broadcasts renders this sentence as 'The role of a convener is obviously different from that of a chairman'. See *SWB:FE* 7132 (1982).

42. Hu Qiaomu, 'Some questions concerning revision of Party Constitution', *Beijing Review*, No. 39 (1982), p. 17.

43. Article 16 of the Constitution of the Communist Party of China adopted by the 12th Party Congress, *Beijing Review, op. cit.*, p. 14.

44. Article 35 of the Constitution of the Communist Party of China adopted by the 12th Party Congress, *ibid.*, pp. 18—19.

45. Article 34 of the Constitution of the Communist Party of China adopted by the 12th Party Congress, *ibid.*, p. 18.

46. For a fuller account of the attempts to reform cadre policy see Hong-yung Lee, 'Deng Xiaoping's reform of the Chinese bureaucracy', *Journal of Northeast Asian Studies*, Vol. 1, No. 2 (June 1982).

47. *Red Flag*, No. 4 (1980).

48. *People's Daily* (28 October 1980).

49. See, for example, *Red Flag*, No. 2 (1981).

50. Commentator's Article, 'The glorious and sacred obligation of veteran cadres', *People's Daily* (3 March 1982).

51. *SWB:FE* 6969 (1982).

52. Article 37 of the Constitution of the Communist Party of China adopted by the 12th Party Congress, *Beijing Review, op. cit.*, p. 19.

53. See Article 32 of the Draft Constitution published in *Issues and Studies*. This stated that 'To ensure the accomplishment of the heavy tasks of modernization, the average age of members of the Party Central Committee should be from 55 to 65; the average age of members of the standing committee of provincial Party committees should be 50 to 60 . . .', *Issues and Studies*, Vol. XVI (September 1980), p. 103.

54. Hu Qiaomu, 'Some questions concerning revision of Party Constitution', *Beijing Review, op. cit.,* p. 29.

55. Articles 22 and 28 of the Constitution of the Communist Party of China adopted by the 12th Party Congress, *Beijing Review, op. cit.,* pp. 15–17.

56. *SWB:FE* 7129 (1982).

57. 'Resolution on establishing the Secretariat of the Central Committee', *Beijing Review, op cit.,* p. 12.

58. On 9 October 1979, the Central Party School reopened and, while priority was given to reopening those at the provincial level, it was made quite clear that if conditions permitted Party schools were to be set up at the county level.

59. The other two factors referred to as causes of the faulty workstyle are: (1) veteran cadres who have 'gone off the rails' and become corrupt, and (2) the institutional basis which gives cadres privileges which are said to be far above the average people's living standards. See *People's Daily* (15 August 1979).

60. Zhang Yun, 'Enhance Party spirit, strive for a fundamental turn in Party workstyle', *Red Flag,* No. 3. (1980).

61. 'Some questions concerning the building of the Party', *Beijing Review, op. cit.,* p. 19.

62. Commentator's Article, 'Carry out systematic theoretical education to raise cadres' political quality', *Red Flag,* No. 12 (1982).

63. Commentator's Article, 'Expel degenerate elements from the Party', *People's Daily* (11 August 1962).

64. Hu Yaobang, 'Create a new situation in all fields of socialist modernization', *Beijing Review,* No. 37 (1982), p. 38.

65. *SWB:FE* 7125 (1982).

66. L. Dittmer, *Liu Shao Ch'i and the Chinese Cultural Revolution* (Berkeley: University of California Press, 1974), pp. 185–186.

67. See, for example, *SWB:FE* 3400 (1971).

68. See *The Tenth National Congress of the Communist Party of China, op. cit.,* and *The Eleventh National Congress of the Communist Party of China, op. cit.*

69. *Red Flag,* No. 9 (1981).

70. F. Schurmann, *op. cit.,* p. 111.

71. G. White, 'The post-revolutionary Chinese State: dictatorship, democracy and the distribution of power', in V. Nee and E. Friedman (eds.) *State and Society in Contemporary China* (Ithaca: Cornell University Press).

72. Peng Zhen, Explanation of the Seven Draft Laws in *Main Documents of the Second Session of the Fifth National People's Congress* (Beijing: Foreign Languages Press, 1979), p. 219.

73. Hua Guofeng, Speech at the Third Session of the Fifth National People's Congress in *Main Documents of the Third Session of the Fifth National People's Congress of the People's Republic of China* (Beijing: Foreign Languages Press, 1980), p. 196.

74. The removal of Hua from the post of Premier can be interpreted solely in terms of the power struggle which sought his total removal from positions of power. However, it was also symbolically important to emphasize the need for a division between Party and state. When Hua was replaced as Party Chairman Hu Yaobang took the position, thus keeping the two 'top' posts in separate hands. The post of Chairperson was abolished altogether by the 12th Party Congress.

75. Article 30 of the new Draft Constitution for the State.

76. See Preamble to the new Draft State Constitution, *Beijing Review,* No. 19 (1982).

77. F. Schurmann, *op. cit.,* pp. 196–199.

78. State Planning Commission, Great Guiding Principle for Socialist Construction, *People's Daily* (12 September 1977).

79. The Four Fundamental Principles are adhere to socialism, the people's democratic dictatorship, Marxism–Leninism and Mao Zedong Thought and the leadership of the Chinese Communist Party.

80. See 'Some questions concerning the building of the Party', *Beijing Review* No. 28 (1982), p. 17. At the time of the Party's 61st Anniversary, meetings were held to commend advanced Party branches and groups and outstanding Party members. For example, the Fujian Provincial Party Committee commended 107 advanced Party branches, 71 advanced Party groups and 251 outstanding Party members.

81. See. G. White, 'The post-revolutionary Chinese State: dictatorship, democracy and the distribution of power', in V. Nee and E. Friedman (eds.), *op. cit.*

82. G. Young, 'Non-revolutionary vanguard: transformation of the Chinese Communist Party', *op. cit.,* p. 67.

83. 'Social sciences: a hundred schools of thought contend', *Beijing Review,* No. 14 (1979), p. 10.

84. *Beijing Review,* No. 13 (1980), p. 10.

85. See *People's Daily* (14 February 1980); and *SWB:FE* 6330 (1982).

86. During the early years of the Cultural Revolution intellectuals were designated the 'stinking ninth category' after landlords, rich peasants, counter-revolutionaries, bad elements, rightists, renegades, enemy agents and capitalist-roaders.

87. *People's Daily* (29 September 1981).

88. Liu Binyan, 'Literature as a mirror of life', *Beijing Review*, No. 52 (1979) p. 13.

89. *SWB:FE* 6362 (1980).

90. *SWB:FE* 7072 (1982).

91. *Beijing Review* No. 13 (1980).

92. *SWB:FE* 7072 (1982).

93. This idea was suggested to me by Dr. E. B. Vermeer of the Sinologisch Instituut, Leiden.

94. Hu Yaobang, 'Create a new situation in all fields of socialist modernization', *Beijing Review, op. cit.*, p. 36.

95. In June 1982 the Organization Department of the Central Committee held a forum on the question of the consolidation of primary Party organizations. This was followed by a detailed press coverage of how 'well' the process was proceeding. See, for example, *People's Daily* (27 June 1982) and *SWB:FE* 7066, 7072 and 7074.

96. The ideas in this last section have been influenced by those expressed in G. White, 'The post-revolutionary Chinese State . . .' *op. cit.* However, differences exist with White's analysis.

97. *Jiefang Jun Bao* and *Jiefang Ribao* (28 August 1982). In *SWB:FE* 7145 (1982).

98. *Jiefang Jun Bao* (27 September 1982) and *Jiefang Ribao* (28 September 1982). In *SWB:FE* 7149 (1982).

99. *SWB:FE* 7142.

100. *Beijing Review*, No. 36 (1981), p. 13.

101. *People's Daily* (29 September 1981).

102. *Guangming Daily* (18 September 1981).

103. *Red Flag*, No. 20 (1981).

104. See, for example, the article from *Zhongguo Qingnian* reprinted in *People's Daily* (13 November 1978).

105. S. Schram, 'To utopia and back: a cycle in the history of the Chinese Communist Party', *China Quarterly*, No. 87 (September 1981), p. 83.

106. Liu Shaoqi, 'Self-cultivation in organization and discipline' (July 1939), *Chinese Law and Government* (Spring 1972), p. 27.

Once Again, 'Making the Past Serve the Present': A Critique of the Chinese Communist Party's New Official History

BILL BRUGGER

Discipline of Politics, Flinders University,
South Australia

Summary. – The 1981 revised history of the Chinese revolution changes previous interpretations in fundamental respects. The 'people's democratic dictatorship' appropriate to the bourgeois-democratic revolution is taken to be synonymous with the 'dictatorship of the proletariat' which is appropriate to the process of socialist transition. As early as 1956 the Chinese had defined antagonisms as originating outside the socialist system, and in the anti-Right movement reverted to Stalin's notions which put such a view in an extreme form. Mao had denied the existence of 'economic laws of socialism' based on theoretical reasoning, but the post-1976 ideology of China has ignored Mao's warnings in this field. They have also passed over his contention that a change in formal ownership of the means of production might not mean a change in the commodity character of the means of production. One result is the rapid growth in China of *a-historical* positivist economics and a falling away of the important tradition of Marxian political economy, and non-socialist ideas like the 'law of planned and proportionate development' have consequently been able to experience a revival. The official history makes nonsensical comments on Mao and the Cultural Revolution and condemns the 'communist wind' of 1958, because its underdeveloped Marxism blinds it to the fact that socialism is a process whereby variations of the capitalist mode are negated and communist forms introduced.

In June 1981 the Chinese Communist Party rewrote its history to reflect the current line.[1] In this chapter I shall explore a number of issues raised in the 'Resolution on Questions of Party History' to indicate the confused state of Marxist thinking in China in recent years. To economize on space I shall deal only with the period since 1949.

NEW DEMOCRACY

Lenin broadened the Marxian term 'dictatorship of the proletariat' to include the peasants. His formula, 'the democratic dictatorship of workers and peasants' was further broadened by Mao to include 'national capitalists' and 'petty bourgeoisie' in a transitional stage known as 'new democracy'. The 'new democratic revolution', therefore, was (in Marxist terms) a species of bourgeois democratic revolution. The socialist revolution would begin at some later stage. But in the 1981 version of history we are told:

We have established and consolidated the people's democratic dictatorship led by the working class and based on the worker-peasant alliance, namely, the dictatorship of the proletariat.[2]

Thus the 'people's democratic dictatorship', appropriate to the bourgeois democratic revolution, is taken to be synonymous with the 'dictatorship of the proletariat' appropriate to the process of socialist transition. The present era, it seems, is both pre-socialist and socialist at the same time. Thus, it is possible arbitrarily to define policies as appropriate to whichever particular formula one likes. One may justify the payment of accrued interest to national capitalists according to the old formula of people's democratic dictatorship whilst suppressing dissidents in the name of the 'dictatorship of the proletariat'. Whilst I would welcome a theoretical argument showing the co-existence of socialist and non-socialist elements, such is avoided since it is probably too near the Trotskyist formula of telescoping stages. Indeed we are told most emphatically that a *socialist system* was established in 1956.

THE SOCIALIST SYSTEM

The achievement of a system defined as 'socialism' had been announced in the Soviet Union in 1936. It was because Stalin felt that a qualitatively new stage had been reached in Soviet society that he was able to justify his new constitution. I have described elsewhere Stalin's arguments on this issue, pointing out that Stalin invented a 'socialist form (mode) of production' which had basically been achieved.[3] Stalin's arguments assigned a very strong deterministic role to the forces of production; the new stage was ushered in once the same form of co-ordination was felt to have been achieved in the economy as a whole as existed in modern productive enterprises, i.e. when the planning system outside enterprises was a macrocosm of the economic accounting system within. Within the Marxist framework the construction of a socialist mode of production had to be arbitrary. Marx was clear about the major features of the capitalist mode of production and one might infer from his arguments what the communist mode of production might be like. They may be summarized as follows:

FORCES OF PRODUCTION

The capitalist mode of production co-ordinates human productive activity and the instruments of production in imperatively organized separate enterprises. *The communist mode of production* achieves co-ordination through voluntary co-operation among fluidly organized groups.

RELATIONS OF PRODUCTION

The capitalist mode of production requires ownership by separate capitals (enterprises or enterprises grouped as companies). Surplus labour takes the form of surplus value giving rise to a class division between those who appropriate surplus value and those from whom it is appropriated. There is thus a separation of labour from labour power (alienated labour), the latter being a commodity and exchangeable with other commodities. The technical division of labour at the workplace is determined jointly by the forces of production and the social division of labour. Finally, the relationship between production and distribution of the social product implies that society be integrated by the market or perhaps (and

this is a very contentious point) according to an asymmetrical principle of redistribution.[4]

The communist mode of production specifies common ownership. There is no class division and labour is unalienated. There being no social division of labour, the *technical* division of labour achieves a more co-operative form. Here one may only guess at the possible principles of distribution; the 'need' principle, however suggests integration according to some principle of reciprocity.

Using Marxist methods to construct a 'socialist mode of production' somewhere between the capitalist and the communist mode, one would have to specify some principle which might determine an intermediate point in all of the above dimensions. Failing that one merely has a Weberian ideal type:

> the synthesis of a great many diffuse, discrete, more or less present and occasionally absent concrete individual phenomena which are arranged according to . . . one sidedly emphasized viewpoints into a unified analytical construct.[5]

The ideal type gives merely a synchronic picture and the element of diachrony in Stalin's model is provided merely by asserting the deterministic role of the forces of production. Once they change all else follows:

> First the productive forces of society change and develop, and then, *depending* on these changes and *in conformity with them*, men's relations of production, their economic relations, change . . . however much the relations of production may lag behind the development of the productive forces, they must, sooner or later, come into correspondence with, and actually do come into correspondence with — the level of development of the productive forces, the character of the productive forces.[6]

This was the view which informed the Chinese Communist Party's Eighth National Congress in 1956 when an attempt was made to construct a Chinese equivalent of the Soviet model of 1936. There were, of course, a number of differences. As the 'Resolution on Party History' points out, such a view could accommodate Liu Shaoqi's demand that there should be a 'double track' system for labour (a system of temporary part-time employment coexisting with the full time labour force). It might accommodate also the demands of Deng Zihui and others for the introduction of a production responsibility system in agriculture. The differences here presumably reflected the more primitive development of the forces of production. Indeed the fact that the Chinese could pitch their socialist system at a lower level than the Soviet Union only points to the arbitrariness of constructing a socialist system in the first place.

The theoretical problems consequent upon constructing a model of socialism are immense. Stalin had announced in 1936 that the proletariat had ceased to exist and had become the 'working class' and the peasants had been transformed into '*kolkhoz* workers',[7] though this did not stop him invoking the 'dictatorship of the proletariat' later to justify the purges. The Chinese were not so silly but they likewise defined antagonism as originating outside the system. In Kuhnian terms, the 'revolution' was over and the task of planners and economists was to engage in 'normal social engineering' to fill out the 'socialist' paradigm.[8] Revolutions in the future would be peaceful and would be generated by anomalies within the existing paradigm ('internal contradictions') and would not stem from forces external to the paradigm (class struggle or antagonistic contradictions). Indeed Mao Zedong's speech 'On the Correct Handling of Contradictions Among the People' might be read as a Kuhnian text for 'puzzle solving'.[9] To be sure there was always the danger that internal contradictions (anomalies) incorrectly handled could become antagonistic and generate a paradigm change (though unlike Kuhn's picture this would be retrogressive.) But this was far from any analysis of class conflict generated from within the system.

The notion that antagonism could only be generated from outside the system led in the Soviet Union to the absurd justification of the purges in terms of foreign subversion and to charges that people like Marshal Tukhashevsky was a German agent. The Chinese official press in 1957 made the point that Stalin's error was to treat contradictions among the people as if they were antagonistic contradictions. Yet the official history tells us this was precisely what the Chinese Communist Party itself did during the Anti-rightist movement of 1957. What the official history cannot admit is that, since it was patently absurd to define all antagonistic struggles as originating outside the system and since that very formulation prevented the development of a theory of exactly how one determines the dividing line between internal and antagonistic contradictions, the scope for arbitrariness was very wide. The demarcation criteria offered by Mao rested, moreover, on the notion of a social system which was itself arbitrary.

OBJECTIVE ECONOMIC LAWS

According to the official history the mistakes made in economic planning up to 1958 were minor compared with those made during the Great Leap Forward (1958–60). During that Great Leap, Mao and many senior people in the Party were guilty of violating 'objective economic laws'. What are these objective economic laws?

Very clearly Marx had a notion of laws of motion which he felt were objective. These laws, however, were not the same as most natural laws. They were not universal nor even statistical; they were tendency statements. Mao was to point out in the early 1960s that Stalin, who lacked a thorough knowledge of dialectics, was confused on this score. In his criticism of the official Soviet textbook on political economy (based on Stalin's *Economic Problems of the U.S.S.R.*) he noted:

> Quite without foundation the book offers a series of laws, laws which are not discovered and verified through analysis of concrete historical development. Laws cannot be self-explanatory.[10]

Marx's method was not to posit a series of laws based on *a priori* reasoning about the operation of modes of production and transition between them but rather to strip away the appearances of the capitalist mode and uncover the change over time in the operation of certain tendencies (e.g. for the rate of profit to fall and for profits to be equalized), noting carefully the offsetting tendencies and the processes of dialectical interaction. Marx's focus was on *capitalism* and the laws (tendencies) he spoke about were peculiar to that mode of production. It is not at all clear how Marx might have envisaged the operation of laws peculiar to the communist mode in which exchange value had given place to use value. As for the intervening 'socialist mode of production', Marx had no such concept. Indeed, without a clear notion of what the socialist mode of production might be, all one may do is talk about the 'objective laws' of the capitalist system and show how they might operate differently when one or other of the relations of production have changed.

This is precisely what official Chinese spokespersons have done concerning the so-called 'law of value' (exchange between equivalent products of socially necessary labour time). The most authoritative statement on this score was made not by an economist but by the newly appointed head of the Chinese Academy of Social Sciences, Hu Qiaomu.[11]

As Clausen points out,[12] the fact that it was made by a historian is probably explained by major divisions amongst the ranks of political economists. The old orthodoxy, following Engels' *Anti-Dühring* and echoed in Stalin's *Economic Problems* . . . , was that the law of value continued to operate in socialist society and played an important role but would progressively be restricted as socialism developed. There were disagreements in China as to the pace and scope of this restriction, with people such as Zhang Chunqiao arguing for more rapid and widespread restriction and Xue Muqiao arguing for more liberal attitudes towards the law but, none the less, eventual restriction. Zhang Chunqiao's position stemmed from an implicit denial of Stalin's point that, once the nature of ownership changed, the means of production were no longer commodities. For Zhang (and I believe Mao) there was a dialectical relationship between ownership and the commodity system. A change in formal ownership did not imply a change in real ownership whereby the commodity system automatically changed. Both real ownership and the commodity system had to be changed by restricting the operation of the law of value and the class relations upon which it rested. Because, for Zhang Chunqiao the law of value was intimately bound up with the system of real ownership (the relations of production) the law of value was not an *economic* law, it was an objective law of *political economy* peculiar to the capitalist mode of production which was in the process of being negated.

The difference between economics and political economy here should be stressed. In the classical Marxist tradition, 'economics' was a reified discipline. It represented a partial abstraction from historically specific conditions of production, distribution and exchange, which (in that they included both forces and relations of production) were social and political as well as economic. As Clausen points out, both Zhang Chunqiao and Xue Muqiao remain within this classical Marxist tradition of political economy. The major person who stood out in opposition to that position and who was excoriated in the Cultural Revolution was Sun Yefang. In contrast to the definition of relations of production outlined earlier, Sun sought to redefine 'relations of production' as 'the conditions and forms of production exchange and distribution'. Ownership and, therefore, class relations did not appear in the definition. The way was open for an a-historical 'positive economics' and the

ground was cleared for consigning the study of political economy to the history books. In recent discussions with Chinese academics in various 'economic' institutions, I became aware that current thinking has done just that. For the moment Sun Yefang's view is dominant and, from it, stems the view that once formal ownership relations are considered to have changed, the law of value operates more effectively than under capitalism and should provide the basis for planning. The implications are profound!

Let us for a moment explore the operation of this 'objective economic law'. Assume for a moment that the transformation problem has been solved and one pursues a policy of making prices more equivalent to value, one would then have to make a crucial decision. Should one let value continue to be realized through the market; if so, one should not regulate wages and hope that the 'hidden hand' under 'socialism' operates more effectively than under capitalism. One has defined 'socialism' here purely as a system of state ownership and I fail to see how this might differ from capitalism once labour power is patently acknowledged as a commodity and how one might discuss that commodity relation outside some notion of class division. If one does regulate wages, then surely wages of industrial workers must be made to decline to the level of the peasants (or at least the more productive of them). What would be the consequences of this? Perhaps one would see a disincentive to pursue industrialization. But such a conclusion would depend upon another 'objective law' about the formation of consciousness unless one accepted the axiom of 'economic persons' which is supposed to be a historical product of capitalism. Indeed, if one wants to avoid an infinite regress, one has at some point to introduce historical discussion. Let us now suppose that we have overcome the problem of infinite regress and have reduced industrial wages to the level of the most productive peasants with no loss in incentive. Where does accumulation come from? Marxist Leninist orthodoxy, of a few years ago, argued that the only way to solve problems of primitive accumulation was to exploit the countryside (i.e. to violate the law of value). More recently some scholars have argued that the industrialization of the Soviet Union was in fact actually financed from the urban sector (involving a violation of the law of value there too). Do we now have an economic law which says that primitive accumulation requires a violation of the law of value? Clearly we do not; since funds may come from external sources. And any objective law which says that investment funds which do not come from external sources have to come from internal ones is pretty worthless; it boils down to saying that investment funds have to come from somewhere. What value is such a law?

Finally let us suppose that prices approximate to value and markets flourish. In conditions of scarcity this must lead to demand inflation. This is not an 'objective economic law' but a tautology. The Chinese answer to the problem is that such inflation might be countered by controlling the money supply. Indeed, Marxist monetarism has a long history and was employed in a most remarkable fashion in the Soviet Union during the days of the New Economic Policy. Though he has made himself available and has lectured in China, Milton Friedman is not necessary to give advice. To be quite honest, though, the idea of a state progressively restricting its activities in the interest of countering inflation is not what one usually associates with socialism. After all, restricting the money supply, which is more feasible in a relatively planned society than in a more capitalist one, will hit hardest those people whose income is more dependent upon state subsidies. It will exacerbate inequalities.

It is also claimed that once the ownership system changes, a further set of economic processes might come into operation grouped together under the rubric of the law of planned and proportionate development. At its simplest this cannot be said to even resemble a law and is merely a plea for better planning. At a more sophisticated level it is a restatement of the law of comparative advantage. Like so much else in first year economics textbooks, the law of comparative advantage depends upon a number of conditions. One of these is perfect information which never occurs and another is transportation facilities, the cost of which is lower than the extra value produced by specialization. China is glaringly deficient in both respects. But even if it were not, one has to acknowledge that the law begs a whole lot of questions about the psychological effects of regional self-reliance. If there is a trade off between the development of a socialist community spirit and economic growth, what are the units against which it might be assessed? Of course it might be argued that China is too poor to worry about the development of community feeling. Well, is it too poor for socialism? One may argue too that many cases cited in the past of communal spirit bred by self-reliance were fabricated and there is no empirical evidence showing the association

between self-reliance and socialist spirit. Such an observation would seem to fly in the face of common sense. Is it likely that the 'all round person' which people identify as 'socialist' is best fostered by those who only produce one product for sale in distant markets? Perhaps we need a few psychological laws here; but, being reified, will they be any more objective?

It is manifestly clear, moreover, that the law of comparative advantage will exacerbate inequalities between units and areas which are relatively well advantaged and those which have little or nothing. Again this is not what one usually associates with socialism, though to be sure, the old policy of self-reliance also did little to reduce such inequalities. As to whether the principle of comparative advantage or that of self reliance is the better able to produce equality is an empirical question which relates to a specific economy at a specific time. It cannot be solved by *a priori* reasoning nor by reference to totally different economic systems, differently endowed and developed in different times. A comparison with Taiwan, deliberately built up as a major agricultural component of the Greater East Asia Co-prosperity Sphere under the Japanese will tell us little about the prospects for mainland China. (Not that any Chinese official document would ever make this comparison common amongst Western economists.)

A final set of objective laws have been lumped together under the rubric of ensuring the identity of interests between the State, the enterprise and the individual. These surely can be no more than guidelines for planners. It seems obvious that one should not promote one of these interests at the expense of the other two and harmony between all three would secure economic growth. But what is harmony? Piecework, for example, might ensure harmony between individual income and enterprise planning but it might exacerbate disharmony between competing workers and their disaffection might hinder the harmony between them and certain institutions which constitute the state. Where is the objectivity?

All the above rests upon the notion that laws operate differently once ownership changes. One should bear in mind, however, that in the late 1950s, more people were employed in undertakings which were collectively owned than those defined as 'owned by the whole people'. Was it not premature to talk about the operation of such laws, if indeed they could be said to exist?

If we are not clear about what a socialist mode of production might be and what its laws are, how are we to assess the charge that 'objective economic laws' (or even objective laws of political economy) were violated in the Great Leap Forward? We can be sure some laws *were* violated but these (to my mind) were *scientific* laws and for these one may claim some universal objectivity. Crops were occasionally planted which would not grow (a violation of the laws of biology). The area sown in grain was reduced after miscalculations based on one atypical harvest (normal generalizations about meteorology were ignored). People were made to work too hard (physiological laws were disregarded). Machinery was employed too intensely (mechanics was ignored). Violation of objective laws there was but they were of natural science. A Marxist cannot know about what objective laws of political economy were violated until we have some detailed analysis of all the various modes of production which existed in China at that time and how they interrelated. The *idea* of a socialist system does not help and surely no Marxist would agree with the universal pretensions of 'positive economics'.

To my mind the various modes of production in China in 1956 were all some variations of the capitalist mode. Socialism should properly be used to describe the process whereby such modes were negated and communist forms introduced. The official history condemns the 'communist wind' which appeared in 1958. In so far as there were people who believed that pockets of communism might be established *in one country*, this criticism was undoubtedly apt. But features of the transitional system which did introduce communist elements (i.e. payment in part according to need) cannot be dismissed out of hand. The appropriateness of such experiments is an empirical question: such experiments are, after all, a way of testing how people's consciousness might be changing. Since the experiment only took place in a few areas and was ruled out of court by the Wuchang plenum, we are unable to assess the results.

The main types of capitalist mode which existed in China in the late 1950s were probably the state capitalist and the simple commodity modes. The official history takes the Larin version of Lenin's definition of the state capitalist mode: i.e. state control over the commanding heights of the economy and over financial institutions. One should not forget, however, the Zinoviev version which argued that capitalist relations continued to exist in that sector of the economy which was formally owned 'by the whole people'.[13] Zinoviev's argument was that the commodity nature of

labour power did not suddenly disappear once the formal ownership of the means of production was vested in the whole people. Labour power as a commodity only disappeared when the associated producers had control over the conditions of work, a point Zhang Chunqiao would have done well to explore. The Soviet model of 'one person management' (applied in the North East of China until about 1955 and formally abolished at the Eighth Party Congress) did not give them that. The abolition of 'one person management' was brought about because 'one person management' diluted the power of local Party committees and it was a while before collective Party leadership was tentatively integrated with worker participation in management. This was one of the positive achievements of the Great Leap Forward, as eloquently demonstrated by Steve Andors.[14] The balanced analyst has to assess this achievement against the undoubted costs of 'commandism' which current orthodoxy has done so much to highlight. Instead the official history merely praises Deng Xiaoping's efforts to promote worker representation through worker and staff congresses; a system which was apparently hindered by the Great Leap.

Let me summarize my position at this point. Rather than seeing the developments of the Great Leap in the context of a balanced socialist system we should assess the socialist potential and actuality of the Great Leap in terms of how the state capitalist mode was being negated, i.e. the extent to which labour power was becoming less of a commodity and in terms of a *telos* — workers becoming less alienated. It is possible, with the evidence now available to us, that our conclusions will be as negative as those of the present Party leadership: but let us not rule the question out of order by some appeal to a mythical 'socialist system' with its mythical 'objective economic laws'.

In my outline of the modes of production which existed in China in the late 1950s I have said nothing about 'feudalism'. This is because nothing like feudalism existed in China in the twentieth century in the sense that Marx understood it. Feudalism is a mode of production in which serfs are tied to land which is parcelled out in feoffs and cannot be alienated. Throughout the twentieth century land in China could be bought and sold and peasants were free (and often forced) to move in search of work once they lost their land. The dominant form of rural production in China which the Chinese Communist Party inherited was simple commodity production. Ground rent was capitalized and a significant volume of peasant production was for sale on the market. This is clearly a form of capitalism. What may be described as 'feudal' about the situation were simply the hierarchical, patriarchal and communal values which sustained the dominant ideology. No student of modern Japanese capitalism (one of the most vigorous in the world) would be at all surprised at the way feudal values may underpin a capitalist system more effectively than utilitarian individualism. We are here a very long way from the crude picture of cultural lag described by Stalin and quoted earlier.

The simple commodity form of capitalism in the Chinese countryside was not made any more 'socialist' by land reform. On the contrary, the subdivision of land encouraged the development of rural markets and it was not until co-operativization that we see the beginnings of change. Yet to define the higher stage co-ops (the Chinese equivalent of the *kolkhozes*) as 'fully socialist' is absurd. Distribution might be defined as socialist (in that payment was supposedly according to work done rather than initial investment) but production relations were probably more alienated than ever. One of the great tragedies of the communes was that units which were originally seen as 'do it yourself' organizations became quasi-military units solely pursuing the single minded goal of increasing output. For all that, the commune system *did* free a large number of women from being simply reproducers of and providers for male labour-power. It *did* help to promote rural industry and rural education, which *were* steps in the path of developing the all round person (*duomianshou*) demanded by the vision of 'socialist people'. One would have wished that the official history had been a little more balanced in its appraisal of those extremely exciting (if perhaps tragic) years.

MAO ZEDONG'S ERRORS

Mao's errors during the Great Leap, along with a great many leading cadres, stemmed from the fact that they had become 'smug about their successes, were impatient for quick results and overestimated the role of man's subjective will and efforts'. Such was probably the case. But Mao, it seems, was quite ready to correct those errors in the period which followed. Where he apparently became really incorrigible was in developing the theory of 'continuous revolution under the dictatorship of the proletariat'. Mao, it is said, deviated from Mao Zedong Thought which was defined as

the concrete application of Marxism Leninism to the Chinese conditions. The theoretical vacuity of such a statement is obvious. One may select any features of Mao's thought one likes, call it Mao Zedong Thought and declare that any other thought of Mao which one disagrees with is opposed to such Mao Zedong Thought. Marx faced with a similar situation called himself a 'non-Marxist'; Mao did not live long enough to chastise his apparent followers in such terms.

I have discussed elsewhere Mao's theory of 'continuous revolution' and the generative view of class. It originated in the repudiation of the line of the Eighth Party Congress which saw the main contradiction in society as being between the 'advanced socialist system and the backward productive forces' in favour of a view, emerging starkly in 1962, which saw that contradiction in terms of the continued struggle between proletariat (plus peasants) and bourgeoisie. Even more original was the idea that class struggle was not just a hangover from the past but that people and groups which exercised power and enjoyed high status might become the nuclei of a new exploiting class defined (in Marxist terms) in relation to the means of production. Thus these new class elements might be found in all organs of power; not the least in the leadership of the Communist Party itself. The 'vanguard' of the revolution, therefore, might be leading the revolution backward. To counter this, a mass movement of people outside the Party should be encouraged to criticize and repudiate erroneous leaders. Such a movement, which would originate in the cultural (superstructural) field, called into question the previous orthodoxy about the role of the productive forces. As well as leaving himself open to the charge of 'idealism', Mao offered an implicit challenge to the orthodox Leninist view of the Communist Party and, as I have outlined elsewhere, Mao was never game enough to explore the non-Leninist implications of his thinking. His new thinking was not only non-Leninist, it was more importantly non-Stalinist. Socialism, according to the new view, could not be defined as a state of affairs, a mode of production or a self-equilibrating system. Socialism was simply the process whereby capitalism was being negated. There must, therefore, be indicators as to how this process of negation was occurring. Mao was very confused in his identification of those indicators, merely praising such general developments as mass participation in decision making, showing an occasional enthusiasm for the Paris Commune and then a quick withdrawal when the non-Leninist implications became apparent. It was people later identified as the 'Gang of Four' who tried to add a little more theoretical weight to the argument by talking about policies which restricted 'bourgeois right'.

It is easy for the present leadership to attack Mao on orthodox Leninist and Stalinist grounds and attempt to save part of his reputation by pointing to times when he lost his nerve and retreated to the more orthodox formulae. This, together with an affirmation of Mao's role in the years of revolutionary war, have led the present Chinese leadership to consider Mao's errors those of a 'great proletarian revolutionary'. The orthodox rationale for the Party and orthodox Party norms have been restored; but have they? Mao's views on 'continuous revolution' might have challenged the role of the Party as an indisputedly 'correct' vanguard but the present justification of the role of the Party as a passive interpreter of 'objective economic laws' denies the party its rationale in terms of its knowledge of the way forward. From opposite ends of the spectrum Mao and the present leadership, between them, have destroyed the theoretical role for Party leadership. Is there any wonder that the Chinese Communist Party is totally demoralized?

THE CULTURAL REVOLUTION

It would be most misleading to conclude that Mao's generative view of class and his general views on 'continuous revolution' provided a clear theoretical guide for the Cultural Revolution. As Young has pointed out, the Cultural Revolution was informed by a hotch-potch of different theories of which that of the generative view of class was but one.[15] This view coexisted with Stalinist notions about cultural lag, the strange view that a bourgeois superstructure would thrive on a socialist base, crude conspiracy theories and a general set of complaints against the role of bureaucracy. The Cultural Revolution's incoherence stemmed from a variety of causes not the least of which was Mao's own theoretical incoherence. Not surprisingly the current official criticisms of the Cultural Revolution reveal a similar incoherence.

The official history points out that the Cultural Revolution was seen as an attack on 'revisionism'. This term is now considered to be meaningless outside the official pronouncements; though within them a discreet

silence is maintained due to the important role of revisionism (that of Bernstein and Kautsky) in the official Marxist-Leninist canon. In my view, the standard criticism of 'revisionism' — that it is an arbitrary label which may be used interchangeably with 'creative adaptation' depending on the position of the commentator — is somewhat too crude. It is theoretically possible over time to distinguish between policies at various stages of development which promote or hinder capitalism. But it is fair to say that the Chinese never did develop any theoretical sophistication on this score, in the absence of a coherent theory of transition and a coherent *telos*. A blanket statement in the official history that policies which were really Marxist were wrongly branded as 'revisionist' is meaningless without a coherent criterion of the latter. Neither Mao nor the present leadership provided such coherence but, as I have narrated elsewhere, Mao at least tried.[16]

Secondly, it is argued in the official history that the Cultural Revolution confused right with wrong. Again without some clear yardstick, one has no idea *what* this might mean. Mao is once again seen as deficient since in his famous speech 'On the Ten Major Relationships . . .' he did speak of such a contradiction.[17] The issue was as murky in 1956 as it was in 1966. Discussion of 'right' and 'wrong' can be undertaken, in a Marxist context, but only in the light of some socially determined theory of ethics; in China such has never been officially adopted. If all 'right' and 'wrong' may mean is an accurate or inaccurate picture of reality, the one may only decide the issue with reference to levels of analysis. It is said, for example, that the confusion of 'right' and 'wrong' led to the misidentification of Marxist leadership and enemies and the fabrication of a 'bourgeois headquarters' in the Communist Party. In the official history the issue is apparently to be decided at the empirical level; there was no smoke-filled room in which senior leaders plotted to restore capitalism. Who but the most bovine fundamentalist believed that there ever was? It is like saying that there is no ruling class in capitalist societies because one may not identify a smoke-filled room in which the barons of capital plot to keep the workers down. Most Marxists argue the case at a completely different level and bring into their analyses things like structural determination, hegemony and the like. Of course there was a lot of conspiracy theory in the Cultural Revolution but the revolution's more sophisticated defenders were surely talking about another level of analysis. But not the official history! There was no conspiracy to restore capitalism but there *was* a conspiracy to frame Liu Shaoqi as a 'renegade, traitor and scab'. Indeed I'm sure there was; but one cannot explain the case of Liu Shaoqi purely in those terms any more than one can explain the alleged absence of a 'bourgeois headquarters'.

Thirdly, the official history argues that the Cultural Revolution was not really a mass movement. This was apparently because the overwhelming majority of the population did not want to see Party organizations attacked. Thus the majority adopted a passive wait-and-see attitude until the movement was eventually rejected. The argument here resembles that of Young who maintains that the mass line was defined as a way of uniting Party policy with mass demands and when the Party organizations became paralysed, it could not operate.[18] But, Young also maintains, one can have mass activity without the mass line. And indeed there was a lot of mass activity. As for what majority public opinion may have been at the start of the Cultural Revolution, we may only guess. In that the bulk of the deep countryside was not affected by the activities of Red Guards and Red Rebels it is probably fair to say that the Cultural Revolution was always a minority movement. But I for one did witness a lot of mass activity, by workers and cadres as well as students, and did witness a lot of enthusiasm. That many of the early activists became disillusioned there is no doubt. But was this a result of extremist attacks on the Party, squabbling amongst factions or the result of the heavy hand of the Army in incidents like the 'February Adverse Current' of 1967 (which is now apparently not adverse at all). Even more serious, how much was the disillusionment due to the fact that Mao and other leaders lost their nerve and supported activities which actually suppressed mass spontaneity? Clearly the official history is correct in seeing disillusion and factionalism as providing a breeding ground for sheer opportunism. But has there ever been any political movement where that has not happened? Show me any political movement without opportunists!

Fourthly, the official history has decided that the Cultural Revolution was not a revolution at all; nor could it be. This is because 'under socialist conditions there is no economic or political basis for carrying out a great political revolution in which 'one class overthrows another''. The argument here hinges on the definitional problem dealt with earlier. It

is clearly true once one defines socialism as a system already realized in which the dominance of an exploiting class is abolished once and for all. It is not true if one adopts Mao's notion of 'continuous revolution': socialism is precisely the process in which one class overthrows another and the class which is being overthrown is represented in the very organizations which call themselves 'socialist'.

That the Cultural Revolution led to disaster is fairly clear. What is *not* clear is that it led to disaster for the reasons stated in the official history. What is most distressing is that *all* turmoil in 'socialist' societies now seems to be ruled out of order. Such a view is convenient for those in power. The prospect, however, is for the eventual attainment of either a more capitalist system or the same kind of dismal 'mature socialism' of the Soviet Union.

In explaining the origins and development of the Cultural Revolution, the official history makes much of the external environment in which it took place:

> Soviet leaders started a polemic between China and the Soviet Union, and turned the arguments between the two Parties on matters of principle into a conflict between the two nations, bringing enormous pressure to bear upon China politically, economically and militarily. So we were forced to wage a just struggle against the big-nation chauvinism of the Soviet Union. In these circumstances, a campaign to prevent and combat revisionism inside the country was launched, which spread the error of broadening the scope of class struggle within the Party, so that normal differences among comrades came to be regarded as manifestations of the revisionist line or of the struggle between the two lines. Thus it became difficult for the Party to resist certain 'Left' views put forward by Comrade Mao Zedong and others; and the development of these views led to the outbreak of the protracted 'cultural revolution'.[19]

To be sure, much of Mao's theory of continuous revolution drew upon his thinking about the Soviet Union and the matters of principle did become lost in the eventual struggle between the two nations. During the Cultural Revolution, however, people were well aware that one of its main objects was to prevent China becoming like the Soviet Union. That many Chinese might have had a rather distorted view of the Soviet Union should not detract from the worthwhile nature of that aim. Of course, today, the differences of principle have evaporated and all we have is a struggle between nations; a struggle without any apparent rationale in Marxist theory. In the early 1970s Zhou Enlai was to invoke classical views about the balance of power. Can one not do better than that?

How much was the Cultural Revolution Mao's fault? Chinese Communist Party theorists are here on thin ice. After Khruschchev's denunciation of Stalin in 1956, Mao and other commentators pointed out that the problems in Soviet society should be seen as structural and one could not explain them all away by focusing on the personality of Stalin. That this should later have led to a defence of Stalin is unfortunate but the point is well taken. Thus the 1981 official history goes to great pains to point out that Mao's errors in the Cultural Revolution should be seen in social and structural context. For all that, one cannot help getting the impression that the Chinese are, in fact, doing the same kind of thing they have criticized Khrushchev of doing in 1956. By focusing on Stalin, Khrushchev and the other leaders in the U.S.S.R. prevented an examination of their own role in maintaining the now criticized features of the Soviet structure. The same goes for the present Chinese leadership and it is not at all clear that some of the current heroes such as Zhou Enlai were consistent in their moderation of Mao's 'extremism'. We are presented with a picture of Mao, reminiscent of that suggested (by analogy) by Deng Tuo one of the first targets of the Cultural Revolution.[20] Mao became arrogant, divorced from the real world, subjective, arbitrary and obsessed with a sense of his own omnipotence. Of course the Central Committee was partly to blame for letting him act in this way and the main explanation of why it was said to do so is most interesting. Apparently the cult of the leader who holds absolute sway over his Party was due to the effect of 'feudalism'.

I have already said enough about feudalism to suggest that it could not provide a description of the Chinese economy in the twentieth century. If we take feudalism to mean simply the residue of the ideal which pervaded the traditional patriarchal bureaucracy then we have to concede that the criticism has a point. Yet, although abject obedience to authority was part of the Chinese bureaucratic tradition, the cult of the leader with a mass following was not. It was for this reason that Jiang Jieshi made such an unconvincing fascist in his brief flirtation with that doctrine.

The argument about feudalism (meaning the maintenance of patriarchal relations) is important theoretically because it may point to one weakness of the ideas about continuous revolution. If socialism is not a mode of pro-

duction or a system and is merely a process in which capitalism is being negated, how does one know that the direction is socialist (towards communism). As I have argued we do need some *telos* based on the notion of the unalienated producer. To my mind a major criticism of the Cultural Revolution was that this idea became lost in mindless faction fighting. It may have started out as the end justifying the means. After a while the end was forgotten. All one could do is fall back on fragments of Marxist hagiography. As Marx said in his *Eighteenth Brumaire*:

> Men make their own history, but they do not make it just as they please; they do not make it under circumstances chosen by themselves, but under circumstances directly encountered, given and transmitted from the past. The tradition of all the dead generations weighs like a nightmare on the brain of the living. And just when they seem engaged in revolutionising themselves and things, in creating something that has never yet existed, precisely in such periods of revolutionary crisis they anxiously conjure up the spirits of the past to their service and borrow from them names, battle cries and costumes in order to present the new scene of world history in this time-honoured disguise and this borrowed language.[21]

And here I am criticizing an earlier article of mine.[22] It is not sufficient to chart a process of negating capitalism. One should never lose sight of the human *telos* — to do that is to walk the road of Pol Pot. The Chinese however, now have abandoned the idea of *socialism as process* and have a peculiarly technological view of the *telos*. This is the road of Brezhnev and Andropov.

THE CULTURAL REVOLUTION: DID IT LAST TEN YEARS?

Until recently, it was generally maintained that the Cultural Revolution came to an end with the Ninth Congress of 1969 and that the attempts of the 'Gang of Four' after the Tenth Congress of 1973 represented an abortive attempt to revive it. Now the official view is that the Cultural Revolution lasted for fully ten years (from 1966 to the ousting of the 'Gang of Four' in 1976). This peculiar view has been advanced presumably to establish in the popular mind some continuity during the period when the 'Gang of Four' was influential, to establish a link between Lin Biao and the 'Gang of Four' and to avoid the strange conclusion that Mao suffered a major aberration in his thinking from 1966—69 which only recurred after 1973.

In fact, as the official history makes clear, the period after the fall of Lin Biao (or more particularly after the Second Plenum in 1970 when Mao began to turn against Lin) was characterized by the restoration of much that had existed before the Cultural Revolution under the aegis of Zhou Enlai. This was the period when the Party structure was restored, the Army was gradually sent back to its barracks, when the new initiatives in foreign policy favouring the West were undertaken and when major moves were made to import Western technology including numbers of complete plants. 1970–73 was a most unrevolutionary period.

Even now it is very difficult to establish the truth of the Lin Biao case. Despite the attempts to link Lin and the 'Gang', I see no reason to change my previous views that the case is best understood in terms of Mao emulating Stalin. Having demolished the right in the Party (Liu Shaoqi *et al.*), the new power accruing to the left was countered by a move against Lin Biao. As Lin's plans for a coup outlined in the '571 Engineering Outline'[23] suggest, Lin's attempted coup was a preemptive strike aimed to avoid this. As for the position of the 'Gang' at that stage, we cannot be sure, if indeed there was a 'Gang'. Judging from Jiang Qing's vitriolic comments on Lin Biao in her interviews with Roxane Witke, one finds it very difficult to believe that she shared Lin's position.[24] The fact that the 'Gang' was subsequently identified as 'left' is indicative more of a shift in what was defined as the political centre of gravity after 1973 than any identification of the 'Gang' with Lin Biao. To complicate the issue, it is quite clear from the catalogue of complaints of the various military officers who surrounded Lin Biao in 1971 that no coherent line (left or right) may be established amongst Lin's followers. Huang Yongsheng, for example, who from the post-1978 perspective had behaved quite correctly in ruthlessly and brutally suppressing Guangzhou's Red Guards during the February current (no longer 'adverse') was identified as a prominent member of the group.

Whatever the truth about Lin, his demise did see the negation of many Cultural Revolution initiatives. The anti-Confucius Campaign of 1974, the Campaign to Study the Theory of the Dictatorship of the Proletariat in 1975, the campaign to criticize 'the Water Margin' of the same year and the Campaign to Beat Back the Right Deviationist Wind to reverse Previously Correct Verdicts (anti-Deng Xiaoping) of 1976 were all attempts to reverse the trend. Clearly those identified as the 'Gang' were out to discredit Zhou Enlai, Deng Xiaoping and many cadres they had been responsible for rehabilitating; but there was more to it than that. The official history does not mention the nature of the political movements of those years. True, a lot of nonsense was said about Confucius and the First Emperor of Qin in 1974 but the anti-Confucius movement did promote an evaluation of the role of women more profound than anything that had happened in the Cultural Revolution. It promoted also a 'revolution in education' which sought to broaden the base of education in a process of 'open door schooling' which was not a fundamentalist denigration of standards. The Campaign to Study the Theory of the Dictatorship of the Proletariat in 1975 did stimulate some writing in political economy which was far from the mindless fundamentalism with which the 'Gang' was subsequently accused.[25]

CONCLUSION

The Official History makes much of the conspiracies and political thuggery of the 'Gang of Four' and, as I have recounted elsewhere, a lot of the charges, though exaggerated, probably rest upon an accurate description of their inept political style.[26] Doubtless too their theoretical position revealed major weaknesses. Just how does one operationalize their notion of the 'dictatorship of the proletariat'? Certainly not as was exhibited in 1976 by the use of the public security apparatus. For all that, the 'leftist' thinking in political economy of 1974–76 deserves to be taken very seriously indeed. As I have suggested, 'the law of value' is not an 'objective economic law' yet it cannot be denied that the 'Gang's suggestion that in a transitional society it might be used as an ideological mask to legitimize inequalities, and the congealing of those inequalities into class relations deserves to be explored. After all of the criticism of positive economics circulating in the West, Chinese thinkers may not be allowed to get away with the absurd notion that once a socialist system (albeit underdeveloped) is declared to be in existence, capitalist 'laws' automatically change for the better.

Similarly arguments about 'bourgeois right' deserve to be taken very seriously. Clearly the use of the yardstick 'payment according to work' discriminates in favour of those who are most productive, and those whose income is higher are in a better position to maximize the chances for their families. What the 'Gang' failed successfully to do was to integrate their arguments about distribution into a general argument about the relations of production as a whole. But there is another aspect of bourgeois right about which little has been said. This is the *legal argument* that bourgeois right gives equal rights to people made unequal by their location *vis-à-vis* the means of production. No student of affirmative action or positive discrimination in the West may fail to notice how this aspect of liberal ideology preserves inequalities and helps to reproduce class relations. In a society pursuing socialism, there needs to be some active intervention in this process and such intervention must of necessity violate the legal principle of equality of treatment. Marxist theory usually discusses such positive discrimination in terms of the interests of the working class — according to a *telos*. It is a point which those in China charged with establishing the rule of law have forgotten. It is by means of such positive discrimination that Marxists believe the socialist revolution might be completed and it is idle to believe that the process will always be peaceful. Indeed one wonders what is meant by the statement in the Official History that the Chinese revolution has 'entered the period of peaceful development'. As I have suggested this is just a way of preempting occurrences such as those in Poland where people claiming to be Marxists could denounce Solidarity as 'counter revolutionary' purely on the grounds that unionists disturbed public order. While classes still exist, it is a strange kind of Marxism which condemns 'widespread turbulent class struggle'. To be sure the Official History recognizes that under certain conditions class struggle could in future still be acute. But what are those conditions? Are they all generated externally or simply the products of ageing remnants of the past?

One does not know how long it will be before the Chinese Communist Party produces another Official History. When I first went to China in the early 1960s, I soon became aware that the 'turning point' was reached in the Great Leap Forward and history was reinterpreted in the light of its rationale. In the Cultural Revolution I found that history began first in 1962 and then 1966 and all which occurred before was constantly rewritten. This was the position I found on returning to China in 1976. Now, Chinese history is rewritten from the perspective of developments since the Third Plenum in 1978 so that even the pseudo 'Great Leap' of that year can be associated with the 'Left' thinking of previous years. It is with a vengeance that the past is made to serve the present. But history does not repeat itself, neither (in Marx's words) as tragedy nor farce. Even the Eighth Party Congress, so magnificently rehabilitated, has had its basic line changed. No longer is the principal contradiction seen as lying between the advanced socialist system and the backward productive forces. The main contradiction, read back to 1956, is seen as lying between the 'growing material and cultural needs of the people and the backwardness of social production'. So China is just like anywhere else in the third world. To say no more than that is to ignore the exciting things that were said and the exciting things that were done in analysing and formulating a new view of modernization with a consideration of how needs were generated. A statement about relative deprivation should lead to a critique of political economy. That, after all, is what Marx did with statements about alienation.

NOTES

1. CCP, 6th Plenum of 11th CC; 'Resolution on Certain Questions in the History of Our Party Since the Founding of the People's Republic of China', 27 June 1981, *Beijing Review*, **27**, 6 July 1981, pp. 10–39.

2. *Ibid.*, p. 13.

3. B. Brugger, 'Soviet and Chinese Views on Revolution and Socialism — Some Thoughts on the Problem of Diachrony and Synchrony', *Journal of Contemporary Asia*, Vol. 11, No. 3, 1981, pp. 311–332.

4. The idea of 'market', 'reciprocal' and 'redistributive' integration is taken from K. Polanyi, *The Great Transformation: The Political and Economic Origins of Our Time* (1944), Boston, Beacon Books, 1957.

5. M. Weber in *The Methodology of the Social Sciences*, New York, The Free Press, 1949, p. 90.

6. J. V. Stalin, 'Dialectical and Historical Materialism', September 1938, in J. Stalin, *Problems of Leninism*, Moscow, Foreign Languages Publishing House, 1947.

7. J. V. Stalin, 'On the Draft Constitution of the U.S.S.R.', 25 November 1936, in Stalin *Problems of Leninism, op. cit.*, pp. 540–588.

8. See T. Kuhn, *The Structure of Scientific Revolutions*, University of Chicago Press, 1970.

9. Mao Zedong, *Selected Works*, Beijing Foreign Languages Press, 1977, pp. 384–421.

10. Mao Zedong, *A Critique of Soviet Economics*, New York, Monthly Review Press, 1977, p. 108.

11. Hu Qiaomu, speech to State Council, 7 July 1978, 'Observe Economic Laws, Speed up the Four Modernisations', *Beijing Review*, **45**, 10 November 1978, pp. 7–12; **46**, pp. 15–23; **47**, pp. 13–21.

12. S. Clausen, 'Chinese Economic Debates After Mao and the Crisis of Official Marxism' in S. Feuchtwang and A. Hussain, *The Chinese Economic Reforms*, London, Croom Helm, 1983, pp. 53–73.
The argument about Xue Muqiao and Sun Yefang is brought out in this article.

13. See R. Fischer, *Stalin and German Communism*, Cambridge Mass., Harvard University Press, 1948, pp. 471–495 on the background to the CPSU 14th Congress. Zinoviev's views are in his 'Excerpt from Minority Report to 14th Party Congress' December 1925 in R. V. Daniels, *A Documentary History of Communism*, New York, Random House, 1960, pp. 274–277.

14. See S. Andors, *China's Industrial Revolution*, New York, Pantheon Books, 1977.

15. G. Young, unpublished paper to appear in his forthcoming book on 'continuous revolution'.

16. See my introduction to B. Brugger, *China: The Impact of the Cultural Revolution*, London, Croom Helm, 1978.

17. Mao Zedong, 'On the Ten Major Relationships', 25 April 1956, *Selected Works*, Vol. V, pp. 301–302.

18. G. Young, 'On the Mass Line', *Modern China*, Vol. VI, No. 2, 1980, pp. 225–246.

19. 'Resolution . . .', *loc. cit.*, p. 25.

20. Deng Tuo, *Yanshan Yehua*, Beijing Chubanshe, 1963.

21. K. Marx, 'The Eighteenth Brumaire of Louis Bonaparte' in K. Marx and F. Engels, *Selected Works*, Moscow, Progress Publishers, 1969, p. 398.

22. B. Brugger, 'Soviet and Chinese Views . . .', *loc. cit.*

23. Partial text in CCP.CC *Zhongfa* (1972) **4**, 13 January 1972, *Issues and Studies*, Vol. VIII, No. 8, May 1972, pp. 79–83.

24. R. Witke, *Comrade Chiang Ch'ing*, Boston, Little Brown, 1977.

25. See e.g. the famous textbook *Shehuizhuyi Zhengzhi Jingji xue* (draft 2nd printing) Shanghai, Renmin Chubanshe, June 1975.

26. See B. Brugger, *China: Radicalism to Revisionism*, London, Croom Helm, 1981, pp. 170–200.

Chinese Marxism Since 1978*

COLIN MACKERRAS†

School of Modern Asian Studies, Griffith University, Queensland

Summary. – The comprehensive re-evaluation of Maoism at the official level in China extends to historiography, political ideology and the Arts. The most significant change has been the demotion of the role of class struggle; no longer the 'key link' from the time of the Third Plenum, it has come to rank fairly low in the minds of Chinese Marxists. As a result, in considering the motive forces of history much weight can be transferred to the role of the productive forces or elsewhere. The significance of mass movements declines. It is no longer necessary or even desirable to restrict 'bourgeois right' as a principle of income distribution and an encouragement to high productivity. Humanitarianism becomes an important component of Marxism rather than something to be treated with suspicion.

Above all, 'continuing the revolution' becomes not the transformation of social relations between classes in the intermediate time-horizon, but a question of modernization and expanding diffusion of modern technology.

In his later years, however, far from making a correct analysis of many problems, he (Comrade Mao Zedong) confused right and wrong and the people with the enemy during the 'cultural revolution'. While making serious mistakes, he repeatedly urged the whole Party to study the works of Marx, Engels and Lenin conscientiously and imagined that his theory and practice were Marxist and that they were essential for the consolidation of the dictatorship of the proletariat. Herein lies his tragedy.[1]

This statement is part of the resolution of the Sixth Plenary Session of the Eleventh Central Committee of the Chinese Communist Party (CCP) adopted on 27 June 1981 and hence official policy. It tells us in so many words that Mao was wrong in considering himself a Marxist in his later years and that the Cultural Revolution which he led had nothing in common with Marxism. This article aims to explore developments in Chinese Marxists' thinking since 1978, and especially the Third Plenum of the Eleventh Central Committee in December, against the background of the ideas of Mao Zedong in his last years and of his followers at that time. While it does not presume to cast a judgement, as does the statement, on whether 'true' Marxism has been espoused or rejected, it will conclude that the principal determinant in the transformation of Chinese Marxism has been politics, and that adherence to the slogan 'seeking truth from facts' (*shishi qiushi*) has been much less important.

The sources for this article are in Chinese and English and mainly published in China itself. Perhaps the most important of all is the *People's Daily* (*Renmin ribao*), which is the newspaper of the Central Committee of the CCP as well as China's main official daily. In contrast to the West, it is standard practice in China for philosophical discussion to be carried on in the main and most widely read dailies, including the national ones. There is of course also a wide range of periodical literature, some of which focuses extensively, or exclusively, on philosophy, including Marxism; and the number of journals has grown greatly in recent years.

Fortunately, digests of the periodicals' and newspapers' content also exist. The most important of them is the monthly *New China Digest* (*Xinhua wenzhai*) published by the People's Press in Beijing. Since its inception in January 1979 it has gathered together the main articles in various fields of study, one of them being philosophy. The English-language *Beijing Review*, entitled *Peking Review* before January 1979, also includes digests of the Chinese press. It frequently carries summaries of academic debates on various topics and this is of obvious and great value to the researcher. It is only in

* Reprinted from *Journal of Contemporary Asia*. Vol. 12, No. 4, 1982.
† Professor and Chairman of the School of Modern Asian Studies, Griffith University, Queensland, Australia.

recent years that the practice has been adopted, so the range of available published material is considerably more extensive now than it was during the decade from the beginning of the Cultural Revolution, 1966, and the fall of the 'gang of four', 1976.

Yet it needs to be emphasized that the present article is based more or less entirely on published documents which reflect or are themselves official policy. The unpublished dissident view, even the debates which perhaps occur in private intellectual circles or the classroom about Marxism, lie outside the scope of this paper.

THE MOTIVE FORCES OF HISTORY

Karl Marx himself introduced his famous summation of what he elsewhere called 'the materialist conception of history' by describing that doctrine as 'a guiding thread for my studies'.[2] So it is reasonable to start a discussion of Chinese Marxism with historical materialism (*lishi weiwuzhuyi*), as most people, following Engels and others, usually call it.

All Chinese Marxists of all periods claim to uphold historical materialism. However, this did not solve the debate over whether the motive forces of history lay in class struggle or the productive forces. The view supported by Mao's followers was that class struggle was decisive, it would produce revolution which would liberate the productive forces. The slogan was 'grasp revolution, promote production'. It was necessary to continue the revolution in the superstructure, even after the revolutionary classes had taken over ownership of the means of production, so for a time the productive forces might not correspond with the relations of production. The adherents of this concept had strongly attacked Liu Shaoqi for his 'theory of the productive forces'. According to them, this 'describes social development as a natural outcome of the development of productive forces only', so that the productive forces and relations of production would need to harmonize. 'There is no need at all for the proletariat to make revolution, it argues, because capitalism will "peacefully evolve" into socialism as long as the productive forces develop'.[3]

Mao's supporters were not opposing the role of the productive forces or rapid economic growth, but they did give primacy to class struggle which they believed would result in a flowering of the productive forces. Marx and Engels had begun the first major section of

The Communist Manifesto with the ringing statement that 'the history of all hitherto existing society is the history of class struggles'.[4] The whole idea of the Cultural Revolution was based on class struggle, which, as long as Mao was alive, remained the key link on which everything else depended.

However, class struggle was in effect demoted in favour of economic progress as the 'key link' in Chinese politics at the Eleventh Central Committee's Third Plenum of December 1978. Its communique stated that 'the large-scale turbulent class struggles of a mass character have in the main come to an end' and decreed that the Party and people should shift the emphasis of their attention to socialist modernization. It also observed that the implementation of the four modernizations 'requires great growth in the productive forces' and that 'those aspects of the relations of production and the superstructure not in harmony with the growth of the productive forces' would need to undergo major changes.[5] In conflict with the notion of the Cultural Revolution's supporters, this appeared to make class struggle an obstacle of the productive forces, not their liberator.

So it is not surprising to find far greater stress on the forces of production and their connections with the relations of production as the fundamental motive force of history. Marx himself stated that 'at a certain stage of their development, the material productive forces of society come into conflict with the existing relations of production' and 'then begins an epoch of social revolution'.[6] This particular passage appears to support the new emphasis; it seems to imply that the productive forces and relations of production will again harmonize *after* the period of revolution.

Class struggle under socialism does not disappear in this view, but it does cease to be primary. One senior Chinese Marxist holds that 'the advance of human society is, in the last analysis, determined by the development of productive forces', a view which underpins the decisions of the Third Plenum. As for class struggle, he contends that its status as the primary motive force for historical development 'refers mainly to the turbulent transformation from the old society, the old social system to a new society, a new social system'.[7] This is a neat solution, since class struggle becomes something which was vital in past eras, but is no longer really relevant in the present.

Another argument used to reinforce the de-emphasis on class struggle is the one which holds that the material needs and economic interests of human beings are the fundamental motive force of history. Again justification is found in the works of Marx and Engels who wrote that 'the first premise of all human existence and, therefore, of all history' is that 'men must be in a position to live in order to be able to "make history",' and life 'involves before everything else eating and drinking, housing, clothing and various other things'.[8]

Two Chinese Marxists apply this dictum to China's history and note that the real reason why the CCP made revolution was to improve the livelihood of the masses. Referring to still more recent times they use Marx and Engels to discredit the consequences for the unfolding of Chinese socialism posed by the Cultural Revolution:

> One of its results was that, despite their industrious labour . . . , the material and cultural life of the labourers underwent no corresponding improvement. Their reasonable needs did not reach minimum satisfaction. The productive forces made no advances, and even went backwards. In contrast to this, since the Third Plenum of the Party's Eleventh Central Committee, the Party Centre has corrected left errors in economic work, and clarified that the aims of socialist production are to the utmost extent to satisfy the constantly expanding material and cultural life needs of the whole of society.[9]

So the failure of the gang of four can be explained by an appeal to the theory of productive forces which is held to constitute the essence of Marxism. Class struggle becomes, in this view, 'merely a means for a class to realise its material or economic interests'. It is 'only a direct motive force of history, not the basic motive force'.[10]

A particularly sophisticated line of ideology in recent times sees a combination of various motive forces in history, but the emphasis is less on a hierarchy than on categorization by type. A forceful exponent is Pang Zhuoheng who wrote a learned article aimed at enquiring how Marxist theory could assist economic development in the 'new period' after Mao. Pang appeals to such terms as 'the ultimate motive (driving) forces of history',[11] 'the immediate driving power of history' and 'great lever', which derive from Marx and Engels.[12] He concludes:

> In a word, the economic movement is the ultimate force in historical movement. The class struggle between the newly emerging and decadent classes is the main 'immediate driving power' or 'great lever' driven by the 'ultimate motive forces'. At the same time, there are many other immediate driving powers or levers imbedded in different classes and facets of life. Consequently, all these forces, governed by the general law of the economic movement, are merged into a common resultant of forces which produces all the events which unfold before our eyes and make up history.[13]

Chinese Marxists, then, have come up with various interpretations of what constitutes the ultimate motive force or forces in history, and there are others which I have not considered here. But all can be interpreted as attempting justification for the general direction of Chinese politics since the Third Plenum. They tend to downgrade the class struggle and they directly or indirectly attack the Cultural Revolution. They also justify the transfer of full Party and governmental emphasis to socialist modernization.

HISTORY WRITING – THE PERSONALITY CULT

Up to this point I have considered only those problems of a theory of history which have asked the question 'what?'. But Marx wrote also in a famous passage that 'men make their own history', suggesting that 'who?' is a legitimate question. Marx went on to argue that people make history under circumstances transmitted from the past.[14] Both this statement and the whole concept of productive forces, class struggle and so on in the determination of history suggest that people must be seen as groups, not individuals.

No Chinese Marxist of the pre-1976 period would have formally denied that it is the masses, not individuals or leaders, who make history. Mao himself was too insistent on the vital role of the masses in history for that.[15] But the constant and almost exclusive credit for the revolution which was given to Mao Zedong during the Cultural Revolution left the impression that his followers regarded him as a moulder of history in and by himself and not simply as the embodiment of the will of the proletariat. Merle Goldman argues that by 1974 the power of the will, especially Mao's, to shape history had been downplayed by comparison with the preceding years.[16] Nevertheless, from a theoretical point of view, the leaders of the Cultural Revolution made a big mistake in allowing the cult of Mao Zedong to reach the proportions familiar in the late 1960s and early 1970s. This has allowed the Marxists of the post-Mao years a golden chance to attack Maoism, an opportunity which they have not neglected.

On the academic plane, Pang Zhuoheng, among others, presents cogent reasons for arguing that it is 'the people' from whom the motive forces of history derive.[17] On a more popular level, writers in *People's Daily* have taken up the same cudgel. One (unnamed) commentator, in particular, acknowledges that in Marxist theory great characters play a big role in history. However, he attacks any exaggeration of the role of the individual, which would amount to the error of historical idealism. He points out that China's own Communist Party fell into such errors as following only one person and calling this following the Party's leadership or implementing the Party line.[18]

Other writers have appealed directly to the authority of Marx and Engels to justify their opposition to the cult of the individual. One author reminds his readers that when the first volume of *Capital* was published in 1867 'the bourgeois press tried silently to smother it', but 'the proletariat saw it as a strong ideological weapon for its own emancipation', so that many friends sent Marx congratulations. One correspondent had passed on a view he had heard from a Berlin economics professor that 'its appearance was the greatest event of the century etc., etc'. Marx reacted strongly against such adulation.[19]

The developments just described in Chinese Marxism are obviously inspired by the political needs of de-Maoification. Bill Brugger has drawn attention to the conflict between the 'whatever' (*fanshi*) and the 'practice' (*shijian*) factions over the evaluation of Mao Zedong during the meetings leading up to the Third Plenum.[20] The 'whateverists' held that 'we firmly uphold whatever policy decisions Chairman Mao made, and we unswervingly adhere to whatever instructions Chairman Mao gave'.[21] The slogans of the other group were 'practice is the only standard for evaluating truth' and 'seek truth from facts'.[22] The victory of the 'practice' faction led on to the progressive discrediting of Mao's last years and the Cultural Revolution, and ultimately to formal attacks on Hua Guofeng as a 'whateverist' at the Sixth Plenum in late June 1981.

While it is arguable that the major ideological documents of the Cultural Revolution placed far too much emphasis on Mao's role in the modern Chinese revolution, its followers appear to have generally applied a materialist view in their study of the centuries before the twentieth.[23] Mao Zedong, above all, gave a very high evaluation to the roles of peasant rebellions as progressive forces in Chinese history and true examples of class struggle. He even claimed that they 'constituted the real motive force of historical development in Chinese feudal society'.[24] The new post-Mao historiography takes a broader view which gives less importance to the peasant rebellions, and assesses them much less positively. The basic reason is that 'in the old society, the peasants were scattered small-scale producers, they were not representatives of advanced modes of production'.[25] However, this topic has been well covered elsewhere,[26] and needs no detailed recapitulation here.

Attitudes towards the role of peasant rebellions or 'motive forces' involve general theories of history. But Chinese Marxists have also been concerned to find a balance between studying the specifics of what actually happened and devising an appropriate framework to accommodate the details. In other words, Marxism helps to evaluate policy and strategy for the Party to follow in relation to historical and economic studies not only through its theory of history but also its methodology.

The prerequisite for a proper Marxist study of history, according to contemporary Chinese historians, is that 'everything proceeds from historical reality'; the guiding principle is the familiar slogan 'seeking truth from facts'. However, this does not mean that theory is unnecessary. Indeed, it is for their lack of theory that present historians criticize those of the Cultural Revolution most severely. 'It was especially the negative influence of the "ten years of calamity" on historical work that caused some history workers' theoretical interests to weaken, so that they became more and more preoccupied with research into trivial problems'.[27]

Under the title 'historical research must use Marxism as its guide', the historian Dai Yi of People's University in Beijing warns in an article against forcing facts into an inappropriate framework, an unMarxist approach. He points to three slogans, all of which have played a useful role since liberation, but only one of which really suits the present. One is 'guide history with theory' (*yilun daishi*), necessary in the context of the traditional Chinese approach in which a mass of unprocessed data might make very little sense. The second is 'theory emerges from history' (*lun cong shi chu*), the converse of the first, suggesting that no concepts lacking a firm basis in historical fact have any value. The slogan which Dai Yi favours, however, is 'integrate history and theory' (*shilun jiehe*), itself an amalgamation of the earlier two epigrams giving due weight both to historical detail and to theory.

This balanced approach he sees as the correct application of Marxism.

This slogan expresses a methodology which places equal emphasis on theory and on 'the importance of historical materials for research work'. The historian must understand the ramifications of historical materialism in order to apply it correctly, without distortion. He must also 'collect and master rich materials, sort them out, carry out textual research, discard the dross and select the essence, reject the false and preserve the true',[28] and so on, in other words the good historian must really master the sources. The slogan is a kind of balance very typical of China since the Third Plenum. Extremes are reminiscent of the Cultural Revolution when, it is argued, neglect and distortions of theory, as well as inadequate attention to sources and fact, were rife.

CONTINUING THE REVOLUTION

One of the most fundamental doctrines and justifications of the Cultural Revolution was the need for continuing the revolution (*jixu geming*). This propounded the view that the revolution was anything but complete with the accession of the CCP to power. It was necessary to continue struggle against class enemies and the bourgeoisie within society more or less indefinitely. Certainly there was no expectation that class struggle would die out in the foreseeable future. The Cultural Revolution was part of this continuing revolutionary process, designed to prevent a complete takeover by the bourgeoisie.

The Party itself, the vanguard of the proletariat, was not without bourgeois representatives, hence the need to dismiss so many leading members. Liu Shaoqi and Deng Xiaoping were the two most famous and senior examples. Right down to the end of his life Mao never changed his mind about the presence of the bourgeoisie in the Party. During the anti-Deng campaign of 1976 he is quoted as declaring: 'You are making the socialist revolution, and yet don't know where the bourgeoisie is. It is right in the Communist Party — those in power taking the capitalist road'.[29]

But there was more. Mao came to think that a new bourgeoisie was actually engendered after the victory of the Communist Party. His ardent follower Zhang Chunqiao, one of the 'gang of four', wrote of his anxiety because 'our economic base is still not firm'. More serious still was the situation in 'the various spheres of the superstructure' in some of which the bourgeoisie was still actually in control so that old ideas and forces of habit continued to obstruct the growth of socialism, even after the Cultural Revolution itself. 'Following the development of urban and rural capitalist factors, new bourgeois elements are engendered (*chansheng*) group by group',[30] small-scale production being a major culprit in this process. Hence the Cultural Revolution must continue and recur. The numerous campaigns of the 1970s were justified as part of the ongoing attempt to forestall the restoration of the bourgeoisie and hence preserve the gains of the Cultural Revolution.[31]

In the early days after the fall of the 'gang of four' the theory of continuing the revolution and the prevention of bourgeois restoration remained intact. In his political report to the Eleventh National Congress of the CCP given on 12 August 1977, Hua Guofeng even described the 'theory of continuing the revolution under the dictatorship of the proletariat' as 'the most important achievement of Marxism in our time'.[32] He also accepted, as Zhang had done, that there may be need for revolution in the realm of the superstructure so that it 'will correspond better with the socialist economic base'.[33] Above all he retained the notion of newly engendered bourgeois elements and of their presence within the Party. However, he attacked the 'gang of four' and others for wildly exaggerating the scope of the problem. They had carried out their worst distortion by 'equating veteran cadres with "democrats" and "democrats" with "capitalist-roaders"', whereas Mao had 'explicitly pointed out that there were only a handful among the cadres in our Party'.[34] A few representatives could not be described as a bourgeois class within the Party.

By the beginning of 1978 the distinction drawn between the situations in the economic base and the superstructure had come under attack. 'It is inconceivable' wrote one Marxist ideologue, 'that shortly after building its own economic base, our socialist superstructure should . . . be in disharmony with its base'.[35] The other main arms of the theory of continuing the revolution were unchanged.

It was the attack on the Cultural Revolution that led to the negation of the 'capitalist restoration' concept. This was well under way among intellectuals by the autumn of 1978, as I found during a visit to China at that time, and was made possible officially by the Third Plenum. Statements opposing anything remotely in defence of the Cultural Revolution have since become more and more strident, reaching a climax in its official decisive rejection at the Sixth Plenum of late June 1981.

Naturally, the Central Committee majority at that meeting also formally discarded the theory which underpinned the Cultural Revolution. It attacked the thesis that many bourgeois elements had found their way into the Party, government, army, and cultural circles and asserted that there 'were no grounds at all' for defining the Cultural Revolution as a struggle against the capitalist road.[36] It denied that small-scale production would continue to engender the bourgeoisie after the basic completion of socialist information.[37] Above all, it declared that 'class struggle no longer constitutes the principal contradiction after the exploiters have been eliminated as classes',[38] a happy state in which China found itself both at the time of the Cultural Revolution and of the Plenum. The idea that political revolutions in which one class overthrows another would recur in the future was also rejected.[39]

The Central Committee denounced the theory of 'continuing the revolution under the dictatorship of the proletariat' as Mao and his followers had understood it at the time of the Cultural Revolution. However, the members of the Central Committee upheld the theory as such. They reinterpreted it, however, to signify that revolutionary goals would be reached through a lengthy and orderly process without 'fierce class confrontation and conflict'. The aims of China's revolution were now set out to include the expansion of the productive forces, presumably both a byproduct and result of a successful modernization programme, but also the elimination of 'all class differences and all major social distinctions and inequalities'.[40]

So the long-range objectives of continuing the revolution remain basically unchanged, but the methods by which the followers of Mao and Deng expect to reach them are fundamentally different. A contemporary follower of the ideas of Mao in his last years would most certainly argue that current policies are exacerbating social distinctions and inequalities, not tending to eliminate them, but neither the Plenum nor Mao, nor indeed Marx, predicted when the society without major inequality would arrive.

A precursor to the concept of 'continuing the revolution', which is similar but not identical to it, is that of uninterrupted revolution (*buduan geming*). According to Stuart Schram, it dates, as a Maoist theory, from the period just before the Great Leap Forward and is characterized by two main strands. 'It refers to the ceaseless changes and upheavals' which always occur in a rapidly changing society 'riven with contradictions'. It is also a demand to the leadership constantly to rouse the people's enthusiasm by setting new and higher tasks.[41] The first of these fits well with the Cultural Revolution, but would be anathema to the Sixth Plenum. John Bryan Starr argues that the link between the earlier 'uninterrupted revolution' and the later 'continuing the revolution' is 'the idea of intentional destabilization of the society as a means for realising revolutionary goals'.[42] So both these Maoist concepts are alike in being totally at variance with the theory proposed at the Sixth Plenum. Only one arm of Mao's thought on this subject has been praised and emphasized since the Third Plenum: that which calls for the technological revolution.[43]

Mao and his followers may well have worked out a more carefully formulated theory of uninterrupted revolution or 'continuing the revolution' than achieved by his Marxist predecessors. It was a theory based upon the actual conditions he saw around him. Nevertheless, there are references to uninterrupted revolution in the works of Marx himself, and they have drawn comment from Marxists in China today.

The most famous passage occurs in *The Class Struggles in France 1848 to 1850*, written in 1850, and is worth quoting:

> While this *utopian, doctrinaire Socialism*, which subordinates the total movement to one of its moments, which puts in place of common, social production the brainwork of individual pedants and, above all, in fantasy does away with the revolutionary struggle of the classes and its requirements by small conjurers' tricks or great sentimentality; . . . wants to achieve its ideal athwart the realities of present society; . . . the *proletariat* rallies more and more round *revolutionary Socialism*, round *Communism* . . . This Socialism is the *declaration of the permanence of the revolution*, the *class dictatorship* of the proletariat as the necessary transit point to the *abolition of class distinctions generally*, to the abolition of all relations of production on which they rest, to the abolition of all the social relations that correspond to these relations of production, to the revolutionising of all the ideas that result from these social relations.[44]

The Chinese use the term *buduan geming* for 'the permanence of the revolution', so this phrase and 'uninterrupted revolution' both translate into Chinese through the same characters.

The passage quoted above makes no reference to whether the bourgeoisie continues either to operate or be engendered within the vanguard party after its victory, since Marx never saw a consolidated socialist state. But he scoffs at the type of socialism which aspires to avoid class struggle, although he does not make it clear how important he expected class struggle to be *after* the establishment of the dictatorship of the proletariat. Moreover, the phrase 'declaration of the permanence of the revolution' has a ring about it which accords nicely with either of Mao's two concepts.

Contemporary Chinese Marxists have not skirted the apparent problems in reconciling Marx with current viewpoints. Several explanations have emerged. One is that it was not surprising for Marx to take this view because of the events of the years 1848 to 1850 in France. Later on, with hindsight, Marx developed a more sober view of those years, so it is unreasonable for ultra-leftists to appeal to that passage for support of their own ideas.

> In short, the basic points making up Marx's and Engels' idea of 'uninterrupted revolution' in the period of the 1848 revolution, were one by one abandoned and negated by them following historical development. This abandonment and negation were inevitable and wise, and an important symbol of the progress of their revolutionary thought and theory towards maturity. To regard 'the theory of uninterrupted revolution' as Marx's scientific thesis is a frightening misunderstanding in the history of the development of Marxist doctrine.[45]

The author is here trying to make a serious indictment not only of the Marx of 1850, but also of Mao, whether of the late 1950s or the Cultural Revolution.

Another view, put forward by Xin Zhongqin and Xue Hanwei, agrees that the idea of uninterrupted revolution characterized only one phase of Marx's career. It argues that the object of the passage quoted from *The Class Struggles* was 'not specially to expound and prove uninterrupted revolution, but to explain the essential differences between revolutionary socialism and empty socialism'.[46] This is true, but hardly comes to grips with why Marx listed the declaration of the permanent revolution as the first hallmark of genuine proletarian socialism.

Another line of argument has been to ask what precisely Marx meant by the 'genuine socialism' which declares the permanent revolution. True, he has listed four of its characteristics, but not stated at which stage of social development it falls. Xin Zhongqin and Xue Hanwei claim that he was talking about the period *before* the victory of the socialist revolution.[47] Applied to China this would mean that uninterrupted revolution became

irrelevant with the establishment of the People's Republic of China. One scholar has challenged this view directly, arguing that Marx's phraseology shows that 'the uninterrupted revolution does not stop with the time when the proletarian dictatorship is established, but permeates the whole period of the proletarian dictatorship'. Marx, he believes, was referring to the period 'right down to when all classes are thoroughly eliminated in the economic, political, ideological and social spheres'.[48] Applied to China, this includes not only the democratic revolution but also the socialist period, up to and beyond the present. The writer does not define the concept of uninterrupted revolution, but presumably would understand by it a vision much closer to the Sixth Plenum's than to Mao's either of the late 1950s or the Cultural Revolution.

Still, it must be admitted that his theory could be consistent with the Cultural Revolution. It is the only one of those suggested which is anything but a rather obvious academic ideological preparation for and defence of the Sixth Plenum's line. Once again it looks as though Chinese scholars are looking to Marx for support of current policy and interpreting his work in accordance with political needs.

SOCIAL INEQUALITIES — BOURGEOIS RIGHT

The Sixth Plenum removed from the theory of uninterrupted revolution one of the principal features which Mao had included in it during the Cultural Revolution. This was that continuous campaigns would be necessary to maintain the purity of the revolution and prevent backsliding. One key concept of the last years of Mao's leadership revolved around the theme of 'bourgeois right', a term which Karl Marx used and developed in his *Critique of the Gotha Programme*, written in 1875. The movement to limit bourgeois right took place principally in 1975,[49] and raised a number of issues which continued to arouse great interest in the years after the fall of the 'gang of four'. As in so many other areas, *formal* adherence to Marxism has remained while the political line on the specific issues has changed fundamentally. Mao is charged with having misunderstood Marx's exposition on bourgeois right, while Zhang Chunqiao and the 'gang of four' are accused of having wilfully distorted it.[50]

In the section of the *Critique of the Gotha Programme* over which debate has raged most fiercely, Marx discusses the distribution of the product of labour in what he calls the first phase of communist society. This is equivalent to what the Chinese know as socialist society, before the arrival of 'communist' society or, as Marx named it, 'a higher phase of communist society'.

Deductions are made from the product of labour to cover administration costs, social welfare, such as schools and health services, and funds for those unable to work. After that, the individual producer receives back exactly what he has given, although in a different form because he gives in labour but receives a certificate which entitles him to draw on the social stock of means of consumption. So the harder a producer labours, the more he will receive from society.

Inequalities inevitably emerge because some workers are stronger than others, physically or mentally, and can work harder or longer. Some are married with children, others not. To achieve perfect equality would require inbuilt inequalities aimed against the strong. Marx does not advocate these counterbalances to prevent the harder worker receiving more in the first phase of communist society. The inherent inequalities he terms bourgeois right. They are inevitable when a society 'has just emerged after prolonged birth pangs from capitalist society'. Marx then writes:

> In a higher phase of communist society, after the enslaving subordination of the individual to the division of labour, and therewith also the antithesis between mental and physical labour, has vanished; after labour has become not only a means of life but life's prime want; after the productive forces have also increased with the all-round development of the individual, and all the springs of co-operative wealth flow more abundantly – only then can the narrow horizon of bourgeois right be crossed in its entirety and society inscribe on its banners: From each according to his ability, to each according to his needs![51]

Marx thus clearly recognized and accepted that there would be inequalities in socialist society. He did not condemn them, but he did see them as a phenomenon which should and would disappear eventually.

So what policy should a Marxist adopt towards contemporary Chinese society? In 1975 Zhang Chunqiao and Yao Wenyuan, the latter also a member of the 'gang of four' were quite clear that inequalities would grow unless the Party attempted to restrict bourgeois right. This was indeed one of the factors which they believed would engender a new bourgeoisie. The only way to prevent the exacerbation of

the inequalities was to strengthen the dictatorship of the proletariat.[32]

Of all the campaigns of Mao's last years that on bourgeois right was notable for the frequency and extent of reference to the works of Marx, Engels and Lenin.[53] On the other hand Mao was naturally also quoted. 'Our country at present practises a commodity system', he is reported to have said, 'and the wage system is unequal too, there being the eight-grade wage system, etc. These can only be restricted under the dictatorship of the proletariat'.[54] Mao thus followed Marx in accepting the inequalities for the time being, but cautioned against allowing them to increase. Probably the 'gang of four' pushed, with Mao's support, for greater efforts to close the social gaps. The signs are that they were alarmed at the direction China was moving after the Fourth National People's Congress in January 1975. They feared, with good cause, that growth in social and regional inequality would mean not only the end of their political power but the demise of the revolution as they understood it. As one of their ideologues put it, 'Whether such inequalities should be gradually restricted and ultimately eliminated under the dictatorship of the proletariat or strengthened and extended at will is an important mark of distinction between Marxism and revisionism'.[55]

In other words the central issue was the trend, the direction in which the Chinese society was going on this issue. All accepted that inequalities could lawfully exist. What mattered was whether they grew or shrank. Restricting bourgeois right meant pressing for the latter tendency. Certain forms of material incentive, such as 'raising wages, bonuses and payments for manuscripts',[56] were denounced as leading to the former.

It was not long after the fall of the 'gang of four' that all these ideas came under attack. As early as the Eleventh Party Congress in August 1977, when the general theory of the Cultural Revolution was still intact, Hua Guofeng had already denounced the 'gang of four' for 'waving the revolutionary banner of "restricting bourgeois right" ' in order to describe the 'differences in distribution' between the leading Party, army and government cadres on the one hand and the masses on the other as tantamount to class exploitation.[57]

As from 1 October 1977 nearly half the workers of China were given a wage rise for the first time since the Cultural Revolution. In later months the trend towards material incentives accelerated and bonuses, overtime, piecework etc. were reintroduced. A theory to justify the changes gathered momentum in 1978. The Constitution adopted by the First Session of the Fifth National People's Congress on 5 March 1978 stipulated that 'the state applies the socialist principles: "He who does not work, neither shall he eat" and "from each according to his ability, to each according to his work".'[58] Meanwhile a press campaign emphasized the correctness of these principles according to Marxist criteria.

The document to which most appeal was made was again the *Critique of the Gotha Programme*. Rather than arguing, as Yao and Zhang had done, that bourgeois right, if unrestricted, would widen, the new ideologues stressed that it was not only acceptable but could exist *only* in a socialist society where no exploitation existed. 'The prerequisite for the enforcement of the principle "to each according to his work" is the public ownership of the means of production'. It follows from this reasoning that bourgeois right is desirable at the present stage of development. It cannot possibly engender capitalism or a new bourgeoisie. Eventually the communist principle enunciated by Marx, 'from each according to his ability, to each according to his needs', will be implemented, but not for many generations.[59]

Another arm of the new argument was to defend the whole idea of 'material interests' through an appeal to the works of Marx, Engels, Lenin and Mao. I already noted that economic material interests were seen by some Chinese Marxists as the main motive force of history, but the aim in combating the 'gang of four's' attitude towards bourgeois right was to show that the classical Marxists advocated material interests as desirable. If workers do not receive material benefits, their labour enthusiasm will suffer.[60]

Another element was added to the discussion when Hua Guofeng declared at the Second Session of the Fifth National People's Congress on 18 June 1979 that the exploiting classes had ceased to exist in China. He said:

> Owing to the adoption of correct and reasonable measures, supported by the vast majority of the people, the feudal and capitalist systems of exploitation have already been abolished, the system of small-scale production has been transformed, and the socialist system has been through rigorous tests and established its own firm rule. The landlords and rich peasant classes have been eliminated as classes. Under the historical conditions of our country, the capitalists are a part of the People's Republic of China. Our government adopted a correct policy towards them of buying them out

and has successfully transformed capitalist industry and commerce. The capitalists no longer exist as a class.[61]

So all the claims of the 'gang of four' that small-scale production would help engender a new bourgeoisie were said to be groundless because of its elimination through popular means. Unlike the 'gang of four', Hua was confident that the socialist system was firmly established. Since there are no Chinese exploiting classes, the argument for struggle against them loses force. There is no reason to strive for equality if the forces preventing it have mainly vanished.

This appears to me to be a prescription for the reemergence of greater inequality, and such measures as the reintroduction of key schools and bonuses, as well as the return to a measure of private farming, all suggest that this is precisely what is happening.[62]

Chinese ideologues now argue that Marx's description of the distribution of the product of labour is essentially what prevails in China, and Marx's defence of bourgeois right justifies the analogous situation. But what of the question of trend? One official response is that 'the differences will gradually be narrowed with the development of the productive forces and labourers' skills, as well as with the general enhancement of their scientific and cultural levels'.[63] The 'Manifesto of the Chinese Socialist Democrats', an unofficial body which opposes what it sees as the authoritarian bureaucratism of the Chinese Communist Party but basically supports its aims, states: 'We think that socialism has not eliminated, but is eliminating and will eliminate, all classes'.[64] No evidence is given for either the official or unofficial prediction. It is arguable that measures such as the increase of sideline production raise the living standards of the peasantry and hence relieve social inequalities. However, developments in other countries would appear to suggest that the elimination of classes is not likely to be the end result of current Chinese policy.

What the Chinese have done is to give up systematically seeking social equality by redistribution of class and regional income. They have devised a theory based on Marx to justify present inequalities and to convince the masses that equality must come eventually, but so far off that nobody need worry about the problem for the present.

THE PARIS COMMUNE, THE MASSES AND PEASANTRY

Marx had raised the problem of social equality not only in his *Critique of the Gotha Programme*, but also, a few years earlier, in *The Civil War in France*. This document is the text of a speech Marx gave to the General Council of the International Workingmen's Association in London on 30 May 1871; it is an obituary on the famous Paris Commune the final defeat of which had occurred only two days earlier.

In his address Marx praised the Commune highly and, in particular, listed several features of its administration which he believed should be copied. Some of them follow. (1) The municipal councillors were chosen by universal suffrage and subject to recall at short term; (ii) control of the Commune was in the hands of workers or their representatives; (iii) all officials of the administration, which was at once executive and legislative, were subject to recall at all times; and (iv) all public service was carried out at workmen's wages.[65]

Marx later showed himself well aware of the shortcomings of the Paris Commune. In a private letter dated 22 February 1881, he even wrote that 'the majority of the Commune was in no way socialistic, and could not be'.[66] On the other hand, Engels concluded his Introduction to *The Civil War in France*, written on the twentieth anniversary of the Commune and dated 18 March 1891, with a resounding reference to it as an excellent example of the dictatorship of the proletariat.[67]

In the early stages of the Cultural Revolution, the Paris Commune was regarded as a model of administration. The ninth of the Sixteen Points of 8 August 1966, the guidelines for the conduct of the Cultural Revolution, even called for 'a system of general elections, like that of the Paris Commune, for electing members to the cultural revolutionary groups and committees'[68] and stated that they must be subject to recall. In January 1967 the Shanghai Commune was set up based specifically on the model of the Paris Commune.[69] It is true that, like its predecessor, the Shanghai Commune did not last long, but two overall points made Mao and his followers of the Cultural Revolution retain the Paris venture as an appropriate model. One was that it 'sought to destroy the existing state structure and to rebuild a new one'.[70] The other was mass participation in the dictatorship of the proletariat which would replace the old order.

In the mid-1970s the adherents of Mao's radicalism used the examples of Marx's statement on the Paris Commune to justify their campaigns on preserving the revolution and restricting bourgeois right, discussed in the previous sections. In particular, they pointed to the equality of wages between public servants and workers.[71] On a more general plane, they cited Engels' contention that the Paris Commune had adopted means to prevent the 'transformation of the state and organs of the state from servants of society into masters of society – an inevitable transformation in all previous states'[72] and support for their own attempts to forestall the very real threat of a capitalist restoration in China.[73]

In the 'new period' since the fall of the people who proposed such views there have appeared two related basic strands in a 'new look' approach to the Paris Commune: its application to cadre policy, and the role of the masses.

On 29 February 1980 the Fifth Plenum of the Eleventh Central Committee adopted a communique which declared that the members had discussed the draft of the revised CCP Constitution. Among a number of new provisions on the Party's cadre system was one putting 'an end to the practice of being a life-long cadre'.[74] Naturally there has been opposition to the suggestion from those who see their own interests threatened by it, but the Party remains committed to preventing people who are too old from occupying important positions, and thus to creating opportunities for the recruitment of younger talented people into leading bodies.[75]

Part of the ideological justification for this policy comes from the Paris Commune. One writer summarizes the history of revolutionary attitudes towards administrators. He notes with approval that the officials of the Commune had been subject to recall and received the same wages as workers; as well as Engels' dictum, which he wrongly ascribes to Marx himself, that these policies prevented the 'servants of society' from turning into the 'masters of society'. After quoting Lenin to the same effect he concludes: 'from this we can see that to abolish the life-long tenure system which actually exists in cadre posts is in total accordance with what Marxism-Leninism teaches on the cadre problem'.[76] The writer cites no evidence that the Paris Commune developed a policy on lifelong tenure. Moreover, he does not use its example to suggest that Chinese cadres should receive the same wages as workers or be subject to recall. Nevertheless, he is surely right to stress that cadres 'must make up their minds, no matter under what circumstances, to serve the people to the end'; and to suggest that Marx and Engels saw and supported such an attitude in the Paris Commune.

'Serving the people' was also a Maoist slogan and implied the mass line. Despite its departure from so many of Mao's ideas favoured during the Cultural Revolution, the Sixth Plenum came out with a strong and unequivocal restatement of the mass line. 'Isolation from the people', it declared, 'will render all the Party's struggles and ideals devoid of content as well as impossible success'. The Party must rely on the masses and serve them wholeheartedly.[77]

But this does not mean that all mass movements are desirable. The historian Li Yuanming has taken the opportunity of the 110th anniversary of the Paris Commune to consider the attitudes of Marx and Engels towards it and other mass movements. Although he retains a generally positive evaluation of the Commune as a mass movement, he is also at pains to point out that Marx was not wholly supportive of its aims and behaviour and was quite prepared to 'undertake a calm analysis' of it, in other words criticize its failings. Marx and Engels were very discriminating in their attitude towards mass movements in general, and, with documentation and detailed footnotes, Li Yuanming cites specific cases which they strongly opposed.[78]

The lesson for the present is as follows:

Mass movements of differing natures exist in the same way under conditions of socialism. Therefore we should likewise make specific analyses of them. We should fully support those which in general push forward the development of the history of society and the productive forces. But we should also make a clear-headed analysis of certain defects and abuses which the movements manifest, and point them out warmly so that the mass movements can develop healthily along a correct road. As to those mass movements which impede the development of the history of society and the productive forces and even play a retrogressive role, no matter whether they are spontaneous, or launched from above or below, we should not only 'shake our finger' at them, but also . . . take up a clear stand against them. This alone is the Marxist attitude.[79]

Although Li does not say so in so many words, the most obvious example of his last category is the Cultural Revolution, so the weight of Marx and Engels is being indirectly enlisted against it.

Where does all this leave the role of the masses? It is still affirmed as positive both as a historical force and as a current one. But in history it is hemmed around with reservations which cannot but detract from it. Despite the positive statement of the Sixth Plenum, the power of the masses is explicitly more subjected to directors, executives, technicians and experts now than was at least in theory the case in Mao's late years. In fact, the mass line may survive, but with quite clearly reduced emphasis and priority.

In China, the largest part of the masses is the peasantry. The high evaluation which Mao gave to their role in society and the revolution has been well documented.[80] In his last years his view was symbolized in the praise lavished upon the Dazhai Brigade in Shanxi Province.

After the Third Plenum a study group was sent to Dazhai to investigate it. As a result, in mid-1980 the model was discredited and the provincial Party committee even accused of corruption in promoting it. An 'official' opinion emerged as to the lessons to be learned from the Dazhai fiasco. One of them, that 'the scope of class struggle must not be arbitrarily enlarged', repeats a point that has come forward several times already in this article. Another bears on the whole question of the status of the peasantry in society: although their political consciousness has risen greatly since liberation, 'the peasants have a long tradition as small producers and this must not be overlooked'. It is wrong not to heed their material rewards and compensations, or to take away their private plots. A serious way of violating their interests is arbitrarily to switch 'the system of ownership without regard to the degree of development of the forces of production'.[81]

All this is to downgrade the peasantry as a revolutionary force. It also attacks the commune system, because it implies that the forces of production in rural China were not ready for the change in the system of ownership when the communes were set up.

The reference to 'small producers' is particularly interesting. In his *The Eighteenth Brumaire of Louis Bonaparte* Marx criticized the small-holding peasants in French society as conservative and unable to represent themselves, although he acknowledges the existence of the 'revolutionary' peasant in the same passage.[82] It was largely on the grounds that Marx had viewed the peasants as conservative small-scale producers that historians, as discussed earlier, came to ascribe them a less positive and important role in history.[83] Marx's attitude appears to be the justification also for the new assessment of the peasantry as a class.

The differing function of the idea of small-scale production in works by the Maoist radicals of the mid-1970s and those since 1978 is worth noting. Zhang Chunqiao and Yao Wenyuan followed Lenin in seeing petty-commodity production as the source which engenders capitalism and the bourgeoisie. The dictatorship of the proletariat must act against it to preserve the revolution,[84] which otherwise small-scale production may destroy. The new official theoreticians have changed the thrust completely. While agreeing that small-scale production is a force for conservatism they single out the peasants as particularly susceptible to its influence. This becomes a reason for allowing a partial return to private production in the countryside. In other words one concept is used by one group to implement the very policies which the other, appealing to the same notion, wished to prevent.

HUMANITARIANISM

The change in interpretation of the implications of small-scale production is part of the general retreat from the Cultural Revolution. Another very important aspect is the discussions on the relationship between humanitarianism (rendaozhuyi) and Marxism. These began just after the Third Plenum took the lid off official criticism of the Cultural Revolution as such, as distinct from just the role of the 'gang of four' in it.

These are basically two approaches to the subject of humanitarianism: one is that humanitarianism is a fundamentally different stream of thought from Marxism, and the other is that it is a component part of Marxist philosophy.

We begin with the first of these viewpoints. One writer summarizes its arguments as follows:

Humanitarianism takes the nature of man as the highest criterion in observing history, but Marxism recognises the contradictions between the productive forces and production relations as the fundamental motive force of social development. Under definite historical circumstances Marxists may make use of humanitarian slogans, but this does not at all imply that Marxism can contain humanitarianism. This kind of viewpoint also considers that Marx's early works were influenced by Feuerbach's humanism (renbenzhuyi), and retained traces of humanitarianism, but that the mature Marx was no longer a humanist. The formation of the Marxist world view begins precisely from criticising Feuerbach's humanist thought. Marx did not negate human nature or humanity, but he clearly did tie human nature and humanity tightly with human social relations; neither did he negate human 'natural essence', but he clearly did consider that reliance on 'natural essence' was inadequate to explain the difference

between man and the world of living organisms, it can only explain that man is a special 'genus' in the world of organisms. Humanitarianism is an idealist view of history, and cannot be confused with Marxism.[85]

This view notes also the humanitarianism derived from the European Renaissance and arose at almost exactly the same time as capitalism. In the light of all these arguments it can be characterized as a bourgeois system of thought.

The reference in the quotation to 'Marx's early works' is interesting. In fact, most of the discussion has centred around certain of Marx's writings which antedate the *Communist Manifesto* (1848). They include the *Economic and Philosophical Manuscripts*, written in 1844, where Marx developed his ideas on 'alienation' most fully; the 'Introduction' to his *Contribution to the Critique of Hegel's Philosophy of Law*, published the same year; and the very short *Theses on Feuerbach*, written in 1845 to develop some of the ideas of the materialist German philosopher Ludwig Feuerbach (1804–72).

But the most important point about the quoted passage is that it is redolent of the sort of view on humanitarianism which prevailed during the Cultural Revolution, even though it uses somewhat different terminology. The major reason why the adherents of the Cultural Revolution opposed humanitarianism as anti-Marxist was because they perceived it as ignoring, and hence attacking, the key link of class struggle. Since the idea of the incompatibility between Marxism and humanitarianism appears to hold links to the Cultural Revolution, it is not surprising to find this view as very much that of the minority since 1978. In the selection of articles in the April 1981 issue of the *New China Digest* it finds not a single supporter.

It is the demotion of class struggle from its position as 'key link' that allows for the dominant attitude, namely that Marxism, far from being opposed to it, is essentially and tightly linked to philosophical humanitarianism.

This line begins by looking at humanitarianism as a broad phenomenon. The term refers not to the specific humanism so closely associated with the European Renaissance but to the general idea that one should regard human beings according to the dignity of their species and treat them in a way appropriate to their value.

The dominant view emphasizes that Marx gave humankind an extremely central place in his philosophy. An important article by Xue Dezhen in *People's Daily*, entitled 'The Status of "Man" in Marxist Philosophy',[86] demonstrated how high and valuable it was by reference to such passages as that in Marx's 'Introduction' to his *Contribution to the Critique of Hegel's Philosophy of Law* where he applauds the 'theory which proclaims man to be the highest being for man'.[87] ' "Man" is the starting point of Marxist philosophy', states Xue, 'and also its objective'. Other authors,[88] leading to a similar conclusion, cite the almost identical wording elsewhere in the same work that '*man is the highest being for man*' and Marx's consequent call '*to overthrow all relations in which man is a debased, enslaved, forsaken, despicable being*' (italics in original).[89]

Marx was at pains to point out the difference between the idealist notion of the abstract man, as espoused by philosophers like Hegel,[90] and his own of the material, real man who lives within a society and belongs to a class. Chinese Marxists have generally followed him in denying the existence of 'the ordinary man' (*yibande ren*) or of a 'human nature' existing beyond classes.[91]

An alternative view is, however, possible. One scholar, Li Lianke, has explicitly challenged both assertions in the last sentence. He has picked up Marx's statement in his *Theses on Feuerbach* that the human essence 'is the ensemble of the social relations'[92] and supplemented it with a thorough study of Marx's other works of the same period to suggest that 'human nature (or the essence of man) is the social nature of man, it is the generality of humankind, it is the activity of humankind in pursuing freedom'.[93] Such a conclusion brings Marxism closer to a contemporary Western bourgeois view, though Li certainly claims to make his observations from a Marxist and materialist viewpoint. He is on firm ground in seeing Marx as emphasizing human emancipation. But it must be noted that for Li 'communist freedom' is not merely a collective matter but is 'the only real freedom of the individual',[94] whereas Marx, including the young Marx, emphasized the universal role of working classes: 'The *emancipation of the German* is the *emancipation of the human being*. The *head* of this emancipation is *philosophy*, its *heart* is the *proletariat*' (italics in original).[95]

One feature of Marx's approach to humanitarianism was his theory of alienation which, put in its simplest terms argues that man becomes alienated from nature, himself and others if estranged from the product of his labour, if, as in capitalist society, his labour is merely sold to someone else and so brings him no satisfaction.

The theory received very little attention in China during the Cultural Revolution and succeeding years.[96] It was not until August 1980 that public discussion began with an important and full-page article in *People's Daily* by a Marxist writing under the pen-name Ru Xin. The author recapitulates Marx's ideas on the dehumanization of labour in capitalist countries and refutes any suggestion that humanitarianism might be revisionist. He warns that to ignore this aspect of Marxism could bring about a new form of alienation. 'Have there not been lessons of this kind in the history of the international communist movement?', he asks.[97]

This is a fairly clear reference to the Cultural Revolution. It came at a time when the press was beginning to print statements from individuals on the traumas which the Cultural Revolution had inflicted, especially on the young people who had supposedly benefited most from the campaign.[98] Alienation provided the Marxist ideological justification for a full-scale attack on the human effects of the Cultural Revolution. The language that official commentators increasingly came to use was strong. During the 'ten years of turmoil, the phenomenon of human alienation was not only not overcome, but underwent malignant development', said Xue Dezhen. 'The leader of the people', he went on in an obvious reference to Mao, 'was alienated into a god, and frenzied modern superstitions appeared'. Perhaps worst of all was that 'the power of the people was alienated into a force which suppressed the people'.[99] So in the revived 'Marxist theory' Mao became not only an alienated but an alienating influence.

Because of the effects of the Cultural Revolution alienation is perceived to function still in China today. Society stands at the socialist stage, in other words Marx's lower communist phase, which it has entered 'directly from the semi-colonial, semi-feudal society', that is, 'without passing through the capitalist stage of development'. So the influences of feudalism and capitalism survive. This means that 'in the economy, the alienation of the labourer and the product of his labour still exist'.[100] The authors do not relate the concept of alienation to Hua Guofeng's declaration of June 1979 that the bourgeoisie and landlords no longer survive as classes, but it is honest of them to admit in effect that alienation persists in China without exploiting classes.

What happens to the status of class struggle in the Chinese Marxist theory of alienation? It may no longer be the 'key link', but continues to occupy an important place. 'In the past we constantly made class struggle the objective', wrote Xue Dezhen, putting forward the official line, whereas the correct attitude is to regard class struggle as 'a means of overcoming human alienation'.[101] In other words Xue is accusing Mao in the Cultural Revolution of making class struggle an end in itself, not merely the means of progression towards communist society where alienation will have become extinct.

One final point on alienation is that the Chinese contemporary Marxists have had to confront the question, at what stage of Marx's career did he really stress the concept? The answer is unequivocal. It is found in the writings both of the young and mature Marx.[102] Thus it cannot be passed off as an aberration of his early thought, before he really came to terms with the reality of class struggle.

This verdict naturally strengthens the importance of alienation and its concomitant humanitarianism. The rediscovery of these notions in Marx is undoubtedly one of the most significant developments in Chinese Marxism since 1978. Like other ideas discussed in this paper it is used to buttress current political attacks on the late Mao and the Cultural Revolution. In particular Ru Xin was quite specific that 'the key link on whether or not Marxist humanitarianism can be acknowledged lies in the emancipation of the mind (jiefang sixiang)'.[103] He thus refers to a movement which was part and parcel of the process of deMaoification.

CONCLUSION

The slogan 'to emancipate the mind' was one of a group to be adopted officially by the Third Plenum; others included 'practice is the only standard for evaluating truth' and 'seek truth from facts'. All resulted from the victory of the 'practice' faction over the 'whateverists' and set the style for ideological debate in the following period. Like the other two dictums, 'emancipating the mind' was designed clearly to fit in with and support the supremacy of Deng Xiaoping. It was not really a call for Marxists, or anybody else, to think what they liked. This is obvious from the government's moves to end the 'democracy movement' at about the same time. Rather, 'emancipating the mind' meant to clear it of ideological patterns hitherto taken for granted; or as Zhao Yang, Vice-President of the Chinese Academy of the Social Sciences, put it in a speech: 'to break down all the taboos placed by Lin Biao and the 'gang of four', and to get rid of the pernicious

influence they had spread over the years'.[104] In the place of this 'trash of the Cultural Revolution' presumably goes an ideology appropriate to the modernization programme of Deng Ziaoping and his followers of the practice faction.

This is not to say that there has been no broadening in the Chinese approach to Marxism since the Third Plenum. In fact, within the confines of an official attitude which opposes the Cultural Revolution, there have been major attempts to rethink Marxism. To judge from what they write, Chinese Marxists show greater familiarity with the works of Marx and Engels than was ever the case during the decade 1966 to 1976. Far more scholars have been writing theoretical articles in a much wider range of journals and newspapers. Their publications not only quote far more from Marx and Engels but from many more of the works of the two fathers of communism. Whole new areas of thought, such as Marx's humanitarianism, have come up for discussion. There are still limitations: contemporary Chinese Marxists rarely cite the works of their European contemporaries and appear uninterested in such thinkers as Louis Althusser; but then neither did the Chinese Marxists of the 1966 to 1976 decade take heed of their European counterparts.[105] The one who is now quoted drastically less than earlier is Mao Zedong.

Hand in hand with this 'limited broadening' has gone greater emphasis on formal attempts to encourage research into Marxism. For example from 28 May to 6 June 1979 a national planning conference was held in Lüda, Liaoning Province, on the theme 'Marxism Today'. It suggested new areas of research and encouraged scholars to 'proceed from reality to find scientific answers to a series of new issues confronting our country and the world as a whole'.[106] Again, in mid-1981 a symposium specifically devoted to research on Volume II of Capital took place in Fuzhou, capital of Fujian Province, with over 100 people attending. It had a particular political/economic purpose, and 'emphasised discussing Marx's theory on reproduction and their significance as guides to our country's socialist construction'.[107] Still, academic conferences on such topics were notable by their absence in the Cultural Revolution, and their convention shows greater activity in research on Marxism in China today.

One feature of the Cultural Revolution decade under particular attack is its dogmatism. The new Marxists see themselves as more balanced and open. Dai Yi's verdict, noted in an earlier section, on how to use Marxism as a guide to historical research shows favour given to the median or moderate option, as against extremes. The discussions on approaches to the motive forces of history, the continuing revolution and humanitarianism indicate that a range of views on particular topics is not only possible but encouraged, provided it does not overstep the mark of support for the Cultural Revolution.

This openness even extends to recognition of the contribution of opposing systems of thought, except that of the Cultural Revolution. One writer in *People's Daily* stated: 'we do not advocate idealism, but we do advocate giving idealism a scientific evaluation'. Having examined German classical and other philosophies, he concluded through 'concrete analysis' that 'to affirm that under certain conditions idealism . . . played a progressive role is not at all to sing the praises of idealism, but is required by respect for reality'.[108] Of course it is quite arguable that without Hegel there would have been no Marx. Nevertheless, there is a certain irony in a Chinese Marxist's being able to find something positive to say about the antithesis of materialism, but not about the Cultural Revolution.

The political negation of the Cultural Revolution is part and parcel of the ideological criticism of Mao in his last years. The CCP still adheres formally to Mao's thought as the Sixth Plenum made clear. But it insisted on making 'a distinction between Mao Zedong Thought — a scientific theory formed and tested over a long period of time — and the mistakes Comrade Mao Zedong made in his later years'.[109] This separates the Mao Zedong of the Cultural Revolution and later from Mao Zedong Thought. What has happened in fact is that Chinese Marxists have renounced virtually all that Mao advocated in his late years. The discussions on the continuing revolution, on the writing of history, and bourgeois right bear out this assertion. The major exception is Mao's doctrine on the mass line, but the reservations expressed on mass movements in history and on the Paris Commune suggest that, even here, contemporary understanding differs somewhat from Mao's. Such is the extent of the negation of his last years that Chinese ideological circles no longer regard the Cultural Revolutionary Mao as a genuine Marxist and appeal to Marx and Engels themselves to discredit the personality cult which he once unwisely allowed to develop around him.

The most important single idea which has changed with the demotion of the late Mao is in the evaluation of class struggle. No longer the 'key link' from the time of the Third Plenum, it has come to rank fairly low in the minds of Chinese Marxists. The Sixth Plenum decreed it no longer the principal contradiction and went on:

> Because of domestic factors and international influence, class struggle will still exist within certain limits for a long time, and under certain conditions may perhaps grow acute. We should oppose both the view which enlarges class struggle and that which reckons it has died out. . . . It is necessary to recognise that there are many diverse surviving social contradictions within our country's society which do not belong to the scope of class struggle, and we must adopt methods other than class struggle to resolve them correctly, otherwise we shall endanger the stability and unity of society.[110]

Although the Central Committee foresees the possibility that class struggle may grow acute in the future, the whole tenor of this statement is to downgrade its significance. Certainly there are wide implications in this decision for contemporary Chinese Marxism. In virtually all ideological areas discussed in this paper, the current line has been influenced by the demotion of class struggle. In considering the motive forces of history much weight can be transferred to the role of the productive forces or elsewhere. The significance of mass rebellions or mass movements in China declines, whether it be of the peasants in China or of the workers in the Paris Commune. It is no longer necessary or even desirable to restrict bourgeois right. 'Continuing the revolution' becomes a question of modernization and expanding technology. Humanitarianism becomes an important component of Marxism, not one to arouse suspicion and distrust.

The re-evaluation of the status of class struggle accords well with the renewed emphasis on stability which followed immediately upon the fall of the 'gang of four'. In fact, the ideological change succeeded and resulted from the political, not the other way round. The same conclusion follows in virtually all other areas of Marxist thought. The political line demanded more freedom to apply material incentives, so the ideological justification came to back it up; arguments were found in Marx himself why it was good and useful to cater for the people's 'material interests'. Economic pressures required promoting directors and experts, so the new ideologues found reasons, again from Marx himself, why social inequalities need not be prevented from growing, at least for the time being. The same line of thought could be recapitulated from any section of this paper.

Topics not treated here point in the same direction. For example, the Fifth Plenum of February 1980 adopted the 'Guiding Principles for Inner-Party Political Life' which advocated such slogans as 'uphold collective leadership, oppose the making of arbitrary decisions by individuals' and 'speak the truth and match words with deeds'.[111] Later *People's Daily* called on the people to 'learn from the thought of Marx and Engels on party style'. It showed that 'seeking truth from facts was part of the style of Marx and Engels' that they 'opposed the worship of the individual' and 'advocated the style of criticism and self-criticism'.[112] The ideas embodied in the slogans are all good ones

but one cannot help wondering if the Chinese have not read some of their own current catchcries into the mouths of the fathers of communism for political purposes.

In any event, the Chinese still claim to be Marxists. Indeed they argue they are more so than ever, because leading authority in Marxist ideology has been transferred from Mao Zedong to Marx, where surely it rightfully belongs. Few would wish to take issue with that. But it is ironical to find Marxism used to justify two such different political ideologies as that of the Cultural Revolution on the one hand and, on the other, that of the period since the Third Plenum of December 1978.

NOTES

1. 'On Questions of Party History — Resolution on Certain Questions in the History of Our Party since the Founding of the People's Republic of China', *Beijing Review* Vol. XXIV, No. 27, 6 July 1981, p. 23. See the original Chinese in 'Guanyu jianguo yilai dang de ruogan lishi wenti di jueyi', *Hongqi* (*Red Flag*), No. 13, 1 July 1981, p. 14.

2. 'Preface' dated January 1859, to *A Contribution to the Critique of Political Economy*, in *Karl Marx and Frederick Engels Selected Works*, 3 vols, Moscow, 1969—70, I, 503.

3. See Writing Group of the State Planning Commission, 'Continuing the Revolution or Restoring Capitalism? — Criticising the "Theory of Productive Forces" of Liu Shao-chi (Shaoqi) and Other Political Swindlers', *Peking Review* Vol. XIX, No. 37, 10 September 1971, pp. 6—11.

4. Marx and Engels, 'The Communist Manifesto', in *Marx-Engels Selected Works* Vol. 1, Moscow 1962, p. 43.

5. *Beijing Review*, Vol. XXIV, No. 27, 6 July 1981.

6. 'Preface' to *A Contribution to the Critique of Political Economy, Selected Works*, I, 504—5.

7. Liu Danian, 'Class Struggle is the Motive Force in Private Ownership Society', *Beijing Review* Vol. XXIII, No. 35, 1 September 1980, pp. 14—15.

8. *The German Ideology*, in Karl Marx and Frederick Engels, *Collected Works, Volume 5*, London, 1976, pp. 41—2. Among others, P. A. Baran and E. J. Hobsbawm have pointed out that historical materialism does not see history as determined only by economic interests of people, but is 'a powerful effort to explore the manifold, and historically changing connections between the development of the forces and relations of production and the evolution of the consciousness, emotions, and ideologies of men'. See 'The Stages of

Economic Growth', *Kyklos* Vol. XIV, No. 2, 1961, p. 241.

9. Yin Jizuo and Yao Bomao, 'Guanyu shengchan li fazhan dongli wenti de tansuo' ('Explorations on the Problem of the Motive Force in the Development of the Productive Forces'), *Xinhua wenzhai* No. 9, 25 September 1981, p. 14, reprinted from *Guangming ribao* (*Guangming Daily*), 11 June 1981.

10. Yan Zhongkui, 'Material or Economic Interests of Mankind', *Beijing Review* Vol. XXIII, No. 35, 1 September 1980, p. 17.

11. See *Ludwig Feuerbach and the End of Classical German Philosophy, Selected Works*, III, 367. Pang talks of 'motive' forces, the translation in the Selected Works is 'driving' forces.

12. Marx and Engels, *Selected Letters*, Peking, 1977, p. 69.

13. Pang Zhuoheng, 'The Marxist Theory of the Motive Force in History and its Significance Today', *Social Sciences in China, A Quarterly Journal*, Vol. I, No. 4, December 1980, p. 149.

14. *The Eighteenth Brumaire of Louis Bonaparte, Selected Works*, I, 398.

15. For instance, Mao says in 'On Coalition Government' that 'The people, and the people alone, are the motive force of world history', *Selected Works of Mao Tse-tung, Volume III*, Peking, 1965, p. 257.

16. *China's Intellectuals, Advise and Dissent*, Cambridge, Mass., 1981, p. 178.

17. 'The Marxist Theory of the Motive Force of History', p. 169.

18. *Renmin ribao*, 4 July 1980, p. 2. See also an abridged translation of the article under the title

'On the Role of the Individual in History' in *Beijing Review* Vol. XXIII, No. 32, 11 August 1980, pp. 17–21. See 'Correct Approach to Marxism', *Beijing Review* Vol. XXII, No. 47, 23 November 1979, pp. 9–13.

19. *Renmin ribao*, 4 September 1980, p. 5.

20. *China: Radicalism to Revisionism 1962–1979*, London, 1981, pp. 218–19.

21. 'On Questions of Party History', p. 26.

22. On the 'practice is the only standard' campaign see Brantly Womack, 'Politics and Epistemology in China Since Mao', .*The China Quarterly* No. 80, December 1979, pp. 768–92.

23. See the study of Wang Gungwu in 'Juxtaposing Past and Present in China Today', *The China Quarterly* No. 61, March 1975, pp. 1–24. Wang states (p. 22) that, since the early 1960s, at least some historians 'show a much greater awareness of how Marxist analysis should re-order the facts and trends of Chinese history'. He describes Marxist analysis as 'pervasive'.

24. 'The Chinese Revolution and the Chinese Communist Party', *Selected Works of Mao Tse-tung, Volume II*, Peking, 1965, p. 308. The passage is included in *Quotations from Chairman Mao Tsetung*, Peking, 1972, p. 9, and consequently applies to the period of the Cultural Revolution as much as to its original date of authorship (1939). See also James P. Harrison, *The Communist and Chinese Peasant Rebellions: A Study in the Rewriting of Chinese History*, New York, 1969.

25. Chen Mingkang and Zheng Zemin, 'Nongim zai jindai Zhongguo geming shishang de zuoyong' ('The Role of the Peasantry in Recent Chinese Revolutionary History'), *Xinhua wenzhai* No. 10, 25 October 1981, pp. 52–3, reprinted from *Guangming ribao*, 27 July 1981.

26. Kwang-Ching Liu, 'World View and Peasant Rebellion: Reflections on Post-Mao Historiography', *Journal of Asian Studies* Vol. XL, No. 2, February 1981, pp. 295–326.

27. *Renmin ribao*, 25 August 1981, p. 5.

28. *Renmin ribao*, 2 April 1981, p. 5, reprinted 'Lishi yanjiu yao yi Makesizhuyi zuo zhidao', *Xinhua wenzhai* No. 5, 25 May 1981, pp. 61–3.

29. See Fang Gang 'Zouzi pai jiushi dangnei de zichanjieji' ('Capitalist-Roaders Are the Bourgeoisie inside the Party'), *Hongqi* No. 6, 23 May 1976, p. 15. I have followed the official translation in *Peking Review* Vol. XIX, No. 25, 18 June 1976, p. 7.

30. 'Lun dui zichanjieji de quanmian zhuanzheng' ('On Exercising All-Round Dictatorship over the Bourgeoisie'), *Hongqi* No. 4, 1 April 1975, p. 8. For a discussion of the theory of the engendering of the bourgeoisie under socialism see Bill Brugger, 'Introduction: The Historical Perspective', in Bill Brugger, ed., *China The Impact of the Cultural Revolution*, London, 1978, pp. 25ff. Brugger believes that Mao was developing the theory already in the early 1960s.

31. Raymond Lotta has collected numerous documents on this theme in *And Mao Makes 5. Mao Tse-tung's Last Great Battle*, Chicago, 1978, especially pp. 53–397.

32. *Peking Review* Vol. XX, No. 35, 26 August 1977, p. 31.

33. *Ibid.*

34. *Ibid.*, pp. 32, 33.

35. Wu Chiang, 'The Tasks of Continuing the Revolution Under the Dictatorship of the Proletariat', *Peking Review* Vol. XXI, No. 3, 20 January 1978, p. 7.

36. 'On Questions of Party History', pp. 20, 21.

37. *Ibid.*, p. 25. See also Xue Mou, 'Will Small Production Lead to Capitalism?', *Beijing Review* Vol. XXV, No. 3, 18 January 1982, pp. 14–16.

38. 'On Questions of Party History', p. 37

39. ' "Continuing the Revolution" ', *Beijing Review* Vol. XXIV, No. 34, 24 August 1981, p. 3.

40. *Beijing Review* Vol. XXIV, No. 27, 6 July 1981, p. 39.

41. 'The Marxist', in Dick Wilson, ed., *Mao Tse-tung in the Scales of History*, Cambridge, 1977, p. 56. See also Schram, 'Mao Tse-tung and the Theory of the Permanent Revolution, 1958–69', *The China Quarterly* No. 46, April/June 1971, pp. 221–44. The term *buduan geming* continued to be used positively during the Cultural Revolution (see pp. 243–4).

42. *Continuing the Revolution, The Political Thought of Mao*, Princeton, 1979, p. 303.

43. See Mao's article, dated January 1958, p. 11. The article is actually the twenty-first of Mao's 'Sixty Points on Working Methods'. See Jerome Ch'en, ed., *Mao Papers, Anthology and Bibliography*, London, 1970, pp. 62–4.

44. *Selected Works*, I, 281–2. Italics in original.

45. Kuang Cuijian, 'Makesi he "buduan geming lun" – yidian zhiyi ('Marx and "the Theory of Uninterrupted Revolution" – a Query'), *Shangr shizhuan zuebao (Bulletin of the Sangrao Norr Technical College)* No. 1, 1981, reprinted, slig' revised, in *Xinhua wenzhai* No. 8, 25 August 1 p. 27.

46. 'Zai tan Makesi de buduan geming lun' ('More on Marx's Theory of Uninterrupted Revolution'), *Wen shi zhe (Literature, History, Philosophy)* No. 3, 1981, reprinted in *Xinhua wenzhai* No. 8, 25 August 1981, p. 34.

47. *Renmin ribao*, 19 June 1980, p. 5.

48. Xu Jingze, 'Ye tan "shehuizhuyi jiushi xuanbu buduan geming" – yu Xin Xhongqin, Xue Hanwei er tongzhi shangque' ('More on "Socialism is the Declaration of the Uninterrupted Revolution" – Consultations with Comrades Xin Shongqin and Xue Hanwe'), *Wen shi zhe* No. 1, 1981, reprinted in *Xinhua wenzhai* No. 8, 25 August 1981, p. 32.

49. On this campaign see also Merle Goldman, *China's Intellectuals*, pp. 191–201.

50. For example, see Shi Zhongquan, 'What is Meant by "Bourgeois Right"?', *Beijing Review* Vol. XXIV, No. 52, 28 December 1981, pp. 11, 20.

51. *Selected Works*, III, 19.

52. The two key articles are Zhang Chunqiao, 'Lun dui zichanjieji de quanmian zhuanzheng', pp. 3–12, already cited in No. 30 above and Yao Wenyuan, 'Lun Lin Biao fandang jituan de shehui jichu' ('On the Social Basis of the Lin Biao Anti-Party Clique'), *Hongqi* No. 3, 1 March 1975, pp. 20–9. The official translations, contained in pamphlets and elsewhere, are given in Lotta, *And Mao Makes 5*, pp. 196–208 (Yao's) and pp. 209–20 (Zhang's).

53. See thirty-three passages on the dictatorship of the proletariat reproduced in *Hongqi* No. 3, 1 March 1975, pp. 6–19 translated *Peking Review* Vol. XVIII, No. 9, 28 February 1975, pp. 6–12.

54. *Hongqi* No. 3, 1 March 1975, p. 1, translated *Peking Review* Vol XVIII, No. 9, 28 February 1975, p. 5.

55. Chuang Lan, 'Capitalist-Roaders are Representatives of the Capitalist Relations of Production', *Xuexi yu pipan (Study and Criticism)* No. 6, 1976, as translated in Lotta, *And Mao Makes 5*, p. 370. A measured and scholarly view which would support the fears of Mao and the 'gang of four' is that of Martin King Whyte. In his article 'Inequality and Stratification in China', *The China Quarterly* No. 64, December 1975, pp. 684–711, he argues that 'fairly marked inequalities still exist' (p. 710), even though 'recent policies may have checked and limited the emergence of a rigid system of stratification' (p. 711).

56. *Ibid.*, p. 371.

57. 'Political Report to the 11th National Congress of the Communist Party of China', *Peking Review* Vol. XX, No. 35, 26 August 1977, pp. 35–6.

58. *Peking Review* Vol. XXI, No. 11, 17 March 1978, p. 7.

59. Li Hung-lin, 'To Each According to His Work: Socialist Principle in Distribution', *Peking Review* Vol. XXI, No. 7, 17 February 1978, p. 7.

60. See *Renmin ribao*, 12 September 1978, p. 3, and abridged translation in 'How Marxists Look at Material Interests', *Peking Review* Vol. XXI, No. 41, 13 October 1978, pp. 5–10.

61. *Renmin ribao*, 26 June 1979, p. 1. See also 'Report on the Work of the Government', *Beijing Review* Vol. XXII, No. 27, 6 July 1979, p. 9, where an alternative translation is given.

62. For confirmation of this assertion in the agricultural sphere as early as the end of 1979, see Greg O'Leary and Andrew Watson, 'Current Trends in China's Agricultural Strategy: A Survey of Communes in Hebei and Shandong', *The Australian Journal of Chinese Affairs* No. 4, 1980, pp. 119–65.

63. Shi Zhongquan, 'What is Meant by Bourgeois Right?' p. 11.

64. See the Manifesto, 'dedicated to the National Unofficial Publications Convention', reprinted, in English, in the mainly Chinese-language Hong Kong journal *Shiyue pinglun (October Review)* Vol. 8, No. 9, 30 September 1981, p. 49.

65. *Selected Works*, II, 220–1.

66. Marx to Ferdinand Domela Nieuwenhuis, founder of the Dutch Social Democratic Party, in Saul K. Pądover, *The Letters of Karl Marx, Selected and Translated with Explanatory Notes and an Introduction*, Englewood Cliffs, New Jersey, 1979, p. 334.

67. 'Introduction by Frederick Engels', *The Civil War in France, Selected Works*, II, 189.

68. 'Decision of the Central Committee of the Chinese Communist Party Concerning the Great Proletarian Cultural Revolution', *Peking Review* Vol. IX, No. 33, 12 August 1966, p. 10.

69. See John Bryan Starr, 'Revolution in Retrospect: The Paris Commune Through Chinese Eyes', *The China Quarterly* No. 49, January/March 1972, pp. 118–19.

70. *Ibid.*, p. 124.

71. Chuang Lan, 'Capitalist-Roaders are Representatives', in Lotta, ed., p. 371.

72. 'Introduction by Frederick Engels', *The Civil War in France, Selected Works*, II, 188.

73. Fang Gang, 'Zouzi pai jiushi dangnei de zichanjieii', pp. 16–17.

74. *Beijing Review* Vol. XXIII, No. 10, 10 March 1980, p. 8.

75. 'Quarterly Chronicle and Documentation (October–December 1980)', *The China Quarterly* No. 85, March 1981, pp. 186–7.

76. Wu Liping, 'Ganbu zhidu shang yixiang zhongda de gaige' ('A Major Reform in the Cadre System'), *Hongqi* No. 11, 1 June 1980, pp. 6–7.

77. 'On Questions of Party History', *Beijing Review* Vol. XXIV, No. 27, p. 34.

78. 'Zhengque renshi Bali gongshe de lishi jingyan' ('Correctly Understanding the Historical Experience of the Paris Commune'), *Hongqi* No. 6, 17 March 1981, p. 24.

79. *Ibid.*, p. 25. For an alternative translation see 'On the Historical Experience of the Paris Commune', *Beijing Review* Vol. XXIV, No. 15, 13 April 1981, p. 19.

80. See, for instance, Stuart Schram, *The Political Thought of Mao Tse-tung*, Praeger, New York, 1963, pp. 236–64.

81. Zhou Jinhua, 'Appraising the Dazhai Brigade', *Beijing Review* Vol. XXIV, No. 16, 20 April 1981, p. 28.

82. *Selected Works*, II, 479.

83. Kwang-Ching Liu, 'World View and Peasant Rebellion', p. 300.

84. For instance, see Yao Wenyuan, 'Lun Lin Biao fandang jituan', p. 21, and Zhang Chunqiao, 'Lun dui zichanjieji de quanmian zhuan-zheng', p. 4.

85. Cui Wenyu in *Renmin ribao*, 19 October 1981, p. 5. See a summary of Cui's article in 'Discussion on Humanism', *Ta Kung Pao* No. 799, 29 October 1981, p. 10. Similar ideas are expressed in the summary of the debate by Li Wen, in 'Marxism and Humanitarianism', *Beijing Review* Vol. XXIV, No. 50, 14 December 1981, pp. 21–3.

86. Xue Dezhen "Ren' zai Makesizhuyi zhexue zhong de diwei', *Xinhua wenzhai* No. 4, 25 April 1981, pp. 21–2, reprinted from *Renmin ribao*, 25 December 1980, p. 5.

87. Karl Marx and Frederick Engels, *Collected Works, Volume 3,* London, 1975, p. 187.

88. Zhang Kuiliang, Bi Zhiguo and Wang Yalin, 'Lun shehuizhuyi shehui ren de jiazhi wenti' ('On the Problem of the Value of Man in Socialist Society'), *Xuexi yu tansuo* (*Studies and Explorations*) No. 1, 1981, reprinted in *Xinhua wenzhai* No. 4, 25 April 1981, p. 24.

89. *Collected Works, Volume 3*, p. 182.

90. For example, see his attack on Hegel on this point in *The Holy Family*, in Karl Marx and Frederick Engels, *Collected Works, Volume 4,* London, 1975, p. 192.

91. See Cui Wenyu, in *Renmin ribao*, 19 October 1981, p. 5. In his 'Talks at the Yenan (Yan'an) Forum on Literature and Art', Mao had written that in class society 'there is only human nature of a class character; there is no human nature above classes'. See *Selected Works of Mao Tse-tung, Volume III*, p. 90.

92. *Selected Works*, I, 14.

93. 'Lun ren de benzhi "shi yiqie shehui quanxi de zonghe" ' ('on the Human Essence's "Being the Ensemble of the Social Relations" '), *Xueshu yuekan* (*Academic Monthly*) No. 1, 1981, reprinted in *Xinhua wenzhai* No. 4, 25 April 1981, p. 28.

94. *Ibid.*, p. 31.

95. 'Introduction' to *Contribution to the Critique of Hegel's Philosophy of Law*, in *Collected Works, Volume 3*, p. 187.

96. See Donald J. Munro, 'The Chinese View of "Alienation" ', *The China Quarterly* No. 59, July/September 1974, pp. 580–2.

97. *Renmin ribao*, 15 August 1980, p. 5.

98. See also 'Eastern Diary', *Eastern Horizon* Vol. XIX, No. 9, September 1980, p. 3.

99. *Renmin ribao*, 25 December 1980, p. 5.

100. Zhang Kuiliang, Bi Zhiguo and Wang Yalin, "Lun shehuizhuyi shehui ren de jiazhi wenti", p. 26.

101. *Renmin ribao*, 25 December 1980, p. 5.

102. See Ruan Ming, 'Ren de yihua dao ren de jiefang' ('Human Alienation to Human Liberation'), *Xin shiqi* (*New Period*) No. 1. 1981, reprinted in *Xinhua wenzhai* No. 4, 25 April 1981, p. 17. In his book on *Marx's Theory of Alienation*, London, 1978 ed., p. 227, István Mészáros writes: 'It should be clear by now that *none* of the meanings of alienation as used by Marx in the (*Economic and Philosophical*) *Manuscripts of 1844* dropped out from his later writings'.

103. *Renmin ribao*, 15 August 1980, p. 5.

104. 'The Third Movement to Emancipate the Mind', *Beijing Review* Vol. XXII, No. 21, 25 May 1979, p. 11.

105. Other than to Marx, Engels, Lenin or Stalin, the number of references I have found to European Marxists in articles on Marxism in journals like *People's Daily* or *New China Digest* is astonishingly small. The Chinese have recently become aware of other European Marxists. For instance, see Xu Chongwen, *Baowei weiwu bianzheng fa* (*Defend Materialist Dialectics*), People's Press, Beijing, 1980. However, the discussion of Althusser on pp. 67–71 is a little superficial.

106. 'Research on "Marxism Today" ', *Beijing Review* Vol. XXII, No. 31, 3 August 1979, p. 5.

107. *Renmin ribao*, 6 July 1981, p. 5.

108. Wang Shuren, in *Renmin ribao*, 18 August 1980, p. 5.

109. 'On Questions of Party History', p. 35.

110. 'Guanyu jianguo yilai dang de ruogan lishi wenti de jueyi', p. 25. See an alternative, the official, translation in 'On Questions of Party History', p. 37.

111. See *Beijing Review* Vol. XXIII, No. 14, 7 April 1980, pp. 11–20.

112. *Renmin ribao*, 8 June 1981, p. 5.

Bureaucratic Privilege as an Issue in Chinese Politics

RICHARD KRAUS*
University of Oregon

Summary. – Since December 1978, social policy in China has followed a more openly elitist direction than in any period since 1949. The conservative drift in many policies is unmistakable, but in one respect there is concern – Party opposition to the rapid growth of bureaucratic privilege and abuse of political position. Mao had struck harshly at non-Party intellectuals, urban entrepreneurs, scientists and politically inactive youth. These groups are part of the social base for the new top leadership. A set of demobilizing reforms and purges aimed to rout the radical leaders have been ordered by the Deng faction to intimidate their followers, as well as to discredit the mass-campaign style of work in order to replace it with orthodox Party-state structures. Some resistance has followed, but the increasing privatization of the economy created an absolutely larger petty-bourgeoisie which formed a new social layer supporting Deng. Generous back-pay and compensation for those weeded out by the Cultural Revolution gave a material basis for new inequalities. Upper-class communists were once again able to organize privileged, elitist education for their progeny. Finally, economic policy, including the new tolerance of patriotic Hong Kong capitalists, gave a new lease of life to entrepreneurs, some with foreign ties. A coalition of Party bureaucrats, civil servants, academics and businessmen has little time for socialist egalitarianism and Mao's radicalism.

1. INTRODUCTION

After the death of Mao Zedong, and especially after the 3rd Plenum of the Communist Party Central Committee in December 1978, social policy in China followed a more openly elitist direction than in any period since 1949. Not surprisingly, this policy shift was accompanied by a marked diminution in official attention to class struggle, a phrase which was centrally placed in Party rhetoric until 1957, and again from 1962 until 1978.

But while policies became less egalitarian in most obvious respects, there emerged a lively concern for one category of elitism, the abuse of high political position to obtain distinctive privileges available only to bureaucrats. This development seems curious, in that it appears to be at odds with the general conservative drift of other policies. This paper will examine the issue of bureaucratic privilege in terms of tension over the distribution of the limited material benefits to be found in Chinese society. In brief, the argument is that the successes of the post-1978 administration in pacifying the class conflicts which Maoist politicians formerly encouraged gave rise to new conflicts. The new tensions were most sharply posed between two elite groups that have flourished in the post-Mao period: a conservative set of bureaucrats led by Deng Xiaoping and Hu Yaobang, and a more loosely associated grouping of non-Party intellectuals, scientists, urban entrepreneurs and politically disenchanted youth. These two groups shared a hostility to the Maoist radicalism that struck harshly at them both. However, with the defusing of radical class struggle, their own differences become more apparent. The issue of bureaucratic privilege has provided an opportunity in which their rival quests for advantage clashed.

2. BUREAUCRATS AND BOURGEOISIE AS A SINGLE CLASS ENEMY

For a decade and a half, China's Communist Party operated with a doctrine that was always loud, if not clear; socialist society, no less than its predecessors, is divided along class lines, and these classes are engaged in ceaseless

* The author wishes to acknowledge helpful comments from several participants in the 1982 Oxford Conference on 'China in Transition', as well as the suggestions of Andrew Nathan.

battle for power and privilege. This fascination with class was unusual for a ruling Party, and its impetus can be traced directly to Mao Zedong and a shifting band of his closest political allies. Mao's insistence at the Party's 10th plenum in 1962 that it should 'never forget class struggle' can be understood on two levels, both as a rather simple political slogan and as an indication of a deeper theoretical concern for the failure of revolution and socialist transformation to extirpate the roots of inequality.[1]

Mao needed a good slogan in 1962. His political weakness since the failure of the Great Leap had permitted more conservative leaders to pursue what he deemed to be excessively elitist policies in the arts, health care, education, agriculture, military affairs, and commerce.[2] The class struggle slogan was intended to steel the nerves of his beleaguered supporters and to unnerve his adversaries. The forceful, if transient radical victory in the Cultural Revolution did permit considerable social experimentation with policies designed to strengthen worker and peasant interests. It also showed that class struggle could mask a confusing hubbub of rhetoric in which sometimes viciously narrow interests could be passed off as the public good.

Political sloganeering was accompanied by a more abstract effort to understand the forces in Chinese socialist society that gave rise to class conflict. Longstanding hostility toward the bourgeoisie encouraged a sensitivity to its capacity to wield influence indirectly, using ideology and culture as sources of power even after its private property had been socialized. Party traditions of thought reform were reaffirmed, as ways were sought to protect workers, peasants and cadres from succumbing to the lingering ideology of class enemies formally overthrown.

Late in the Cultural Revolution Maoists became dissatisfied with a simple cultural explanation for why state officials often behaved as selfishly as capitalists. The new explanation was that officials took the capitalist road not merely because they were ideologically weak, but also because of their material interests that were deeply embedded within the political machinery created by the Party itself. The structure of state-engendered inequalities encouraged cadres to treat their posts as commodities, to be used for their personal advantage. Although Maoists sought to reassure cadres that 90% or more of their number were politically reliable, the thrust of the 1975–76 campaign to restrict 'bourgeois rights' was clearly

menacing to state bureaucrats as a whole, as it identified their interests in contradiction to those of ordinary working people.[3]

The radicals were not especially concerned to draw sharp distinctions between an old elitism associated with the former bourgeoisie and a new elitism arising from the Party and state bureaucracies. Both worked against the underprivileged coalition of workers, poor peasants, frustrated junior officials and other disadvantaged persons that the leftist band of renegade bureaucrats sought to mobilize. Indeed, the representation of bureaucrats as a species of bourgeoisie provided a common target which might encourage the diverse components of the radical alliance to overlook their own, more profound internal contradictions.

3. THE DEMOBILIZATION OF THE CULTURAL REVOLUTIONARY COALITION

Maoist politicians were skilled at harnessing the revolution's traditions of mass mobilization, sometimes in order better to build constituencies for radical social experimentation, often for purposes of strengthening personal political advantage. The Maoist drive to equalize frequently has been overstated. Maoist politicians in power were never levellers, but were carefully tolerant of class differences both between and within working class and peasantry. Nonetheless, the politics of mass mobilization provided a pressure for extending greater benefits to relatively underprivileged groups by bestowing legitimacy on their demands. But after the 1978 3rd Plenum there was a conscious withdrawal of central political support for the mass mobilizing tradition, along with a consequent weakening of worker and peasant voices in politics.

One set of demobilizing reforms was direct. Most obvious was the purge of radical leaders, a process which ranged far beyond the show trial staged for Jiang Qing and her associates. Exemplary units, such as the Seventh Ministry of Machine Building, were selected as national models for their success in purging leftist officials.[4] Other radicals were publicly humiliated in mass rallies, such as Nie Yuanzi, who spearheaded the Cultural Revolution at Beijing University, and Li Suwen, a Shenyang vegetable hawker who became vice-chairman of the National People's Congress.[5] Even more emphatically, former Red Guards were executed in 1979 for crimes committed in 1967–68.[6]

The most difficult purge was of the memory of the great mobilizer himself, the dead Mao.[7] Initiated cautiously, with careful distinctions between the 'good' Mao of the 1950s and the 'bad' Mao of the Cultural Revolution, the extent of successful iconoclasm could be seen in a comment in a 1982 *Red Flag* article: 'Many of the works by Mao Zedong are still well worth our reading'.[8] This was a striking tone in a land not long ago given to the collective waving of little red books of the Chairman's wisdom.

Less direct than the removal of leftist figures was a broader discrediting of the whole campaign style, which sought to introduce changes by encouraging popular participation, rather than bureaucratic administration of new programmes. Indeed, among the last mass mobilizations were those staged against the mass mobilizers. In a political world where power flows along regular official channels, those groups furthest removed from those bureaucratic channels may expect to receive the least attention from the state.

There also were concrete policy decisions which served to weaken lower-class voices in politics. The widespread decollectivization of the rural economy not only tended to divide peasants among themselves by diminishing their collective stake in the production system, but also threatened some of the proudest radical programmes in the countryside. Barefoot doctors, for instance, often found it unpalatable to tend to health care when their friends and neighbours were all working so hard at individualistic ways of increasing their incomes.[9] In addition, the government postponed its commitment for universal middle school education in the countryside, a choice which should in the long term make it more difficult for peasants to understand the political world they inhabit, as well as deter the emergence of articulate representatives of their interests.[10]

In place of mass mobilization, the administration offered a mass trivialization of politics. However arid and formalistic many past study sessions of Marxist classics may have been, they at least denoted an encouragement by the Party to ordinary citizens to think about state affairs. Instead of seeking political engagement, post-1978 propaganda emphasized such themes as the importance of good manners. The regime's decision to lower the rate of savings reflects an encouragement of consumerism, a development no doubt welcomed by many Chinese, but clearly a force that pushed people away from the stormy collective arena of politics and into a retreat toward individual concerns.

Some index to the speed with which many of these steps toward political disengagement may have taken hold is found in visitors' reports that 'comrade', that venerable appellation of shared struggle, had often become reserved for ironic use.[11]

There are some indications that demobilizing policies were not accepted without resistance. For instance, steps to decollectivize agricultural production were sometimes delayed.[12] But there is little evidence to suggest any effectively organized resistance. Indeed, in the absence of mass mobilizing leadership, China seems to follow the pattern described for Eastern Europe by Frank Parkin: 'the long run tendency seems to have been for the proletariat to relinquish many of the advantages which accrued to it in the early period of socialist rule'.[13]

4. THE COUNTERMOBILIZATION OF OLD AND NEW ELITES

Leftists engaged in class warfare often turn to class slogans for arousing the enthusiasm of their supporters. Conservative politicians, however, seem more comfortable waging class warfare while pretending that they are not. Perhaps this is because they are so often closer to established centres of power, and can rely more readily upon such catchwords as discipline, efficiency and reward of individual accomplishment. In any event, the lack of explicit class slogans did not prevent the Deng Xiaoping administration from waging a class struggle no less fierce than that of the Gang of Four.

As a complement to the demobilization of worker and peasant politics, there was a steady number of reform measures intended to arouse the spirits of groups formerly attacked by the radicals. Both the old elite left over from China's days of private property and the newer bureaucratic top echelon were well served by measures designed to elicit their support.

'Bourgeoisie' is a very loaded word, but I turn to it in the absence of any obvious alternative shorthand characterization for the mixed agglomeration of former property-owners, urban shopkeepers, technical intelligentsia, alienated youth and non-Party intellectuals who have so often been linked together as supporters of market-oriented reforms in the economy and procedural democracy in the polity. This group has some of the flavour of a bourgeoisie, although in socialist China there are some other tastes mixed in as well, including the important factor of shared persecution in the past.

For these groups the new regime made dramatic gestures. The official supplantation of class-based mass line politics with the refurbished united front was proclaimed by the rehabilitation of the old 'democratic' parties, which recruited new members and received unanticipated public attention. The increasing privatization of the economy led, by 1981, to 700,000 people working in individual enterprises, many of whom presumably were so engaged prior to the Cultural Revolution, and others of whom were no doubt offspring of traditionally merchant families.[14] The people labelled as bourgeois rightists in 1957 had their labels removed; in addition, the Party retroactively determined that 81% of those classified as capitalists in the 1950s were erroneously identified, but were actually 'working people'. Even the remaining 19% became 'working people', so that there were no persons who had to bear the taint of capitalist class designation.[15] There is some irony in the disappearance of officially designated capitalists at the same time as the state restored property to its former private owners. In addition to such concrete measures of state favour, the old bourgeoisie and its family members were also accorded dramatically increased access to Westernized (and often depoliticized) forms of art and entertainment.

A parallel set of measures was extended to members of the socialist bureaucracy who suffered during the years of radical rule. Rehabilitated cadres received new posts, and were free to spend generous back-pay settlements on housing or consumer goods. The new administrative style emphasized the bureaucratic discipline and respect for authority that the radicals so resisted.[16] Equally gratifying to the old bureaucrats must have been the stress on 'normal' promotion procedures, in which seniority was honoured instead of the radicals' eager sponsorship of young and inexperienced officials with good class backgrounds.[17] In addition, there were explicit defences of the children of high officials, a group which the leftists allegedly victimized.[18]

There were also reforms which appealed simultaneously to both of the upper-class groups about whom the Maoists so worried. Thus the newly restored entrance examinations for university admissions tended to give advantages to children of both elites, to the disadvantage of worker and peasant applicants, as was the case prior to the Cultural Revolution. Other reforms in intellectual life, such as new provisions for protection of patent rights, were designed to appeal to a technical intelligentsia

drawn from among children of both elites. Finally, both officials and private citizens were enjoined to partake of China's new spirit of material acquisition. Indeed, the Party was to take the lead: 'If we ourselves do not have the ability to get rid of poverty and become rich, how can we help others to get rich? . . . If we ourselves are getting rich, this shows that we are capable and have taken the right path'.[19]

5. ECONOMIC DEVELOPMENT AND THE QUESTION OF PRIVILEGE

By focusing upon the redistribution of opportunities and benefits in China, I have not considered broader changes in economic policy. Part of the context for these class changes was a shift in economic development strategy. The former Maoist policy of suppressing immediate consumer demand in favour of greater public investment for future industrial growth was replaced by a kind of Chinese Keynesianism, in which economic growth was to be stimulated by consumer demand. This change demanded abandoning the former radical asceticism in favour of developing markets for consumer goods, a change no doubt especially welcome in those parts of society where disposable income is available.

In this climate of opportunity-seeking, and with the old Maoist checks against luxury relaxed, it is not surprising that problems arose as some officials overstepped the bounds of propriety. The concern for privilege has a long history in the People's Republic, having figured in political discussions of the 1950s and 1960s, but it became a special focus of concern in the period before and after the 3rd Plenum, as class changes and new economic policies were being felt. Privilege, or 'tequan' (which is often redundantly translated as 'special privilege') typically identifies inappropriate claims to privilege by officials. The concept is ultimately a moral notion, subject to enormous variation in relative judgment of cadre rectitude. The common element is use of official position to obtain benefits that are not widely available or to which a person is not strictly entitled.

Classic abuses of power which have been castigated as bureaucratic privilege include the construction of private housing with workers and material officially assigned to build state warehouses, vacationing in Shandong while officially on a study mission to Dazhai, enjoyment of free meals at restaurants eager to curry favour with leaders of their bureaucratic hierarchy, securing scarce tickets to performances not available at the box office, old-fashioned extortion of subordinates through gifts, and using personal connections to gain access to jobs or education for one's relatives. The list could be extended, but this should suffice to convey the idea that this is the stuff of jealousy and of outraged senses of fairness. The charge of bureaucratic privilege is as likely to be raised by someone only marginally less well situated as it is by the truly impoverished. The former may feel indignant, knowing that they might do better, while the latter may well regard such privileges as natural and wonder what all the commotion is about.

Bureaucratic privilege is a very dangerous issue for the Party, as it evokes public discussions of corrupt behaviour and threatens to undermine public confidence. To some extent the concern with privilege as an issue in a time of elite aggrandizement may have reflected a small bit of posthumous revenge by Mao upon his unfilial successors. Certainly all those years of ascetic class struggle made Chinese sensitive to gross violations of at least superficial egalitarianism. Ultimately, however, privilege became a national issue neither because of Mao's heritage nor because China's officials had become especially greedy. It became an issue because it figured in the conflict between the bourgeois and bureaucratic segments of the rehabilitated Chinese elite. Fighting not just over how to divide the booty of the political wars against the radicals, but over what kind of society China should become, the question of privilege became a weapon which was used with far greater finesse by conservative bureaucrats than by non-Party reformers.

6. DISCREDITING THE MAOIST APPROACH TO BUREAUCRATIC PRIVILEGE

There have been three fundamentally different analyses of the problem of bureaucratic privilege, and three distinct political solutions to it. One comes from the non-Party bourgeois elite (and would-be elites), and calls for restricting Party power as a solution. Another comes from the bureaucrats themselves, and sees the answer in greater self-discipline. The third approach, however, is Maoist, and is sufficiently menacing to both branches of the post-Mao elite that they could agree on the need to suppress it.

The radical analysis of privilege is, of course, that it is a class issue. In the last years of Maoist rule, the campaign to restrict bourgeois rights was a drive against bureaucratic privilege by another name, calling attention as it did to the use of official posts by cadres as commodities by which they might personally profit. The left advocated a series of practical measures to handle the problem, all of which centred around the necessity of supervising bureaucrats by the masses. Examples are to be found in the poor and lower-middle peasant associations which the radicals sponsored in the 1960s, or in downward transfer of cadres to work in production through a variety of programmes, including the 7 May schools. In addition, leftists sought to open up cadre ranks to members of underprivileged groups, thereby creating a more class-loyal officialdom.

None of these measures were popular with the post-Maoist regime in China. Neither bureaucratic nor bourgeois veterans from the once-defeated side of the Cultural Revolution wanted the question of privilege to lead to a reopening of class analysis and official 'class conflict'. Efforts to discredit the radical programme took two forms. One was the memory that radical solutions did not solve the problem when the leftists were in power. Cadre privilege was a public issue in the controversies of the early 1970s over back-door admission to universities.[20] In addition, there was a secret life of privilege enjoyed by many of the radical leaders themselves, who did not spare their own comforts as they directed the masses in class struggle. The trial of Jiang Qing provided an opportunity to publicize this formerly discreet feature of 'life at the top' of the Chinese left.

A second thrust against any possible public re-emergence of Maoist ways of analysing privilege was to draw a sharp distinction between bureaucratic privilege (a legitimate subject for concern) and a privileged 'bureaucratic class' (a forbidden line of inquiry). The latter was held to be an 'unscientific' term; a bureaucratic stratum is always a part of the ruling class of an epoch, and thus for China today, bureaucrats must be a part of the workers and peasants who form the official ruling classes.[21]

There was some elaborate, if unpersuasive footwork to justify this position. Deng Liqun, the head of the Party Propaganda Department, attempted in 1981, when he was a prominent adviser to Deng Xiaoping from the Academy of Social Sciences, to present evidence that there was no empirical basis for making a class analysis of bureaucrats. According to Deng, the wages of China's top 80,000 cadres, both civil and military, constituted less than 0.2% of the total national wage bill. When the incomes of 800m peasants are also considered, the share of high officials drops to 0.1%. 'Comrades, please make a comparison, how can one say that our country has any privileged stratum?'[22] One has enough confidence in the sophistication of a figure such as Deng Liqun to realize that this rhetorical flourish must be disingenuous. First, he certainly knows his Marx well enough to recognize that class issues refer to questions of ownership and control of assets, not shares in distribution. Second, he must also realize that his wage total excludes important extra-wage benefits that high officials enjoy, such as use of automobiles, access to entertainment, travel, servants, etc. Depending upon one's point of view, these matters are necessary perquisites of office, or they are the heart of bureaucratic privilege. But they are an expense to the state, and thus should be counted. If Deng Liqun may not have persuaded all of his readers with his argument, he no doubt did convince them of the more important message: to analyse the special privilege issue in class terms is off-limits.

7. A 'BOURGEOIS' APPROACH TO BUREAUCRATIC PRIVILEGE

But Deng Liqun was not only trying to send a message to unrepentent Maoists. He was also addressing the loose association of non-Party critics referred to here by the shorthand of 'bourgeoisie', which analysed the special privilege issue as one of concentrated power demanding the creation of countervailing extra-bureaucratic power centres.

This market-oriented approach rested on an analysis of China as a society still feudal in many respects, in sharp contrast to leftist inclination to emphasize lingering capitalist influences. Bureaucratic privileges were a feature of the Imperial past, and radical political movements such as the Cultural Revolution only intensified the personalistic politics that feed such privileges.[23] Power corrupts, and the way to restrict its corruption is to encourage alternative sources of power to the Party. This requires democratic institutions, due process, and legal reforms to lessen the Party monopoly of power.

The best-known expressions of this analysis of privilege were found in the 'underground' press associated with Beijing's democracy wall in 1979. In this period the problem of special privileges (*tequan*) was linked to the problem of human rights (*renquan*). The two concepts

are at odds in Chinese, a tension which is lost in translation.

Many are the echoes in this period heard from the earlier era from which one of its slogans was borrowed — the 1956–7 Hundred Flowers. The earlier period was also a time of class change (in the wake of socialist transformation), there was a democracy wall (at Beijing University), there was renewed activism within the so-called 'democratic' political parties (which tripled then in membership),[24] and there was also a direct attack upon high Party officials as a privileged group.[25] Even some of the critics were the same, as the charge against cadre privilege was made in 1957 by journalist Liu Binyan, who was labelled a rightist for his remarks. Undaunted after his rehabilitation, in 1979 he wielded a fearsome pen against bureaucratic privilege as an investigative reporter for *People's Daily*.

Literary continuities were also evident in the heavy reliance upon the arts as a base from which the bourgeois writers could attack Party privilege. Wang Meng's celebrated 1956 story, 'The Young Man Who had Just Arrived at the Organization Department', had its analogue in such works as the popular satirical play, 'What If It Were True?' and the poem, 'General, You Cannot Act This Way'.

Many of the lines of criticism from the two periods bore the same tone of resentment toward greedy officials who threaten the limited privileges available to a non-bureaucratic elite. Cadre children received unfair advantages that they had not earned, and non-Party intellectuals were not promoted quickly enough — left in the cold, according to Zhang Bojun, Vice-Chairman of the Democratic League, in 1957.[26]

In addition, the political dynamics of the two periods of bourgeois criticism were similar. In 1957 Mao and other leaders sought to enlist bourgeois critics (presumably rendered harmless after socialist transformation) to spur on changes within a hidebound Party. So in 1978–79 did Deng Xiaoping and his associates find it expedient to use the democratic movement's critique of privilege as an external lever to complete what they could not accomplish from within the Party alone — the overthrow of remaining top leaders still maintaining allegiance to Mao and his ways, if not to the Gang of Four.

For Deng, the issue was not privilege in general, but the particular privileges enjoyed by the Party's surviving leftist leadership. Thus public criticism was directed against vulnerable leftists, as a way of eroding Hua Guofeng's political support. In discussing officials who abused their authority to build fine houses, the most common example was that of the unrepentent radical Wang Dongxing, Mao's former bodyguard. A fine case of bureaucratic ineptitude was offered by the sinking of the Bohai No. 2 oil rig, arrogantly administered, it turned out, by personnel from the 'petroleum faction', a group of leftover Cultural Revolutionaries with roots in the Maoist model, Da Qing. Similarly, Chen Yonggui was attacked for falsifying production figures for the Maoist agricultural model, Dazhai, as well as for personal extravagance and concupiscence. The most notorious case of cadre protection of errant children involved the Xiong brothers of Hangzhou, multiple rapists — whose father happened to be an army officer with leftist affiliations. I do not mean to suggest that these and other cases were fabricated, and it may in fact be true (if unlikely) that leftist politicians are somehow more susceptible to corrupt behaviour than are conservatives. The point is that the conservatives within the Party were able to use the situation very skilfully — the bones they threw to the non-Party 'bourgeois' critics of privilege had been sticking uncomfortably in their throats for too long, anyway.

The outcomes of the two periods of bourgeois critique of privilege were similar as well, in that the harshest critics were silenced after a relatively brief time. The 1957 Hundred Flowers ended messily, amidst considerable political confusion and with a wide-ranging purge that left countless careers in shambles. The termination of the later movement was more controlled. Big character posters were outlawed, democracy wall was shut down, and show trials were staged for a handful of activists, such as Wei Jingsheng and Fu Yuehua. Bourgeois criticism continued, although limited generally to the field of culture and the arts. But the message was clear: the problem of bureaucratic abuse was not to be criticized from a bourgeois point of view, with demands for fundamental and liberal political change.[27]

8. THE BUREAUCRATS' SELF-CRITIQUE

The conservative leadership was successful in controlling the discussion of privilege so that the concern was typically over the shortcomings of individual officials, rather than the collective behaviour of the corps of high-level cadres. Still, having encouraged public attention to the problem of bureaucratic abuse, conservatives had to have an explanation of their own for the

bad apples in their barrel. The Party's legitimacy in a time of rapid social change was not likely to be strengthened by an image of indifference to selfish plundering of scarce resources.

The self-analysis which emerged focused upon weaknesses internal to the bureaucracy, rather than external corruption by capitalist or feudal influences in an insufficiently transformed society. The weakness is above all one of will, an inability to withstand temptation which can be rectified only by returning to some of the Party's traditional methods of self-policing. Rather than looking to forces outside the Party, whether lower-class supervisors or bourgeois counterweight, the bureaucratic self-critique emphasized an organization managing its own affairs. The posthumous rehabilitation of Liu Shaoqi in 1980 added a sometimes nostalgic tone to this return to first principles.

The Confucian strand in Liu's conservative approach to Party affairs stressed the cultivation of Communist virtue, here summoned up as a solution to the problem of privilege. A very traditional moral reproach at the abandonment of the responsibilities of leadership was apparent in passages such as this:

> The masses have seen all this with their own eyes and have felt anger in their hearts. They have said: Since you have acted this way, how can the people trust our party? You have already modernized your personal living standards even before the modernization of the country.[28]

Party members should avoid arrogance, conceit and bureaucratic airs, improving their 'party spirit' and their 'work style' in ways long familiar to Chinese organizations.

Liu Shaoqi's legacy also includes a strongly legalist side, stressing organizational discipline to complement personal self-cultivation. Through the development of rational regulations, the Party can undermine the basis for unwarranted claims to privilege. This tough side was stressed by the 1980 National People's Congress, which held that bureaucratic abuse should be solved 'first of all' by thorough eradication of the irrationalities within the state administration, the cadres system and other administrative networks'.[29] A Central Discipline Inspection Commission was re-established in the manner of a traditional censorate, and new regulations sought to restrict special privilege by limiting such matters as the numbers of limousines available to bureaucratic offices. More visible reorganizations of the State Council to reduce the number of ministries were also presented as evidence of a serious assault on the problems of bureaucratic abuse, but it is unclear that this went far beyond the renaming of offices. It did, however, provide yet another opportunity by which conservative bureaucrats could dislodge well-entrenched comrades still hankering after old-fashioned Maoist ways.

Similarly, the Discipline Inspection Commission had functions beyond mere self-policing, including reassuring the population that matters were under control. In the wake of the scandal over the father who protected the Xiong brothers from prosecution for their misdeeds, the Commission investigated children of high officials. Its conclusion gave little support to critics who saw them as a blatant manifestation of bureaucratic privilege, as 98% were held to have good or average behavior. But the remaining few were bad indeed: 'their nature is even worse than that of ordinary bad youths in society, and their influence is also worse'.[30]

Another internal reform which received much attention was the effort to develop a retirement system for older cadres, who were frequently the ones with the greatest number of privileges. This of course made them uneager to retire, despite recurring encouragement to do so.[31] It should be noted that the terms offered old cadres were generous — after 1978 it was possible for those who joined the revolution prior to Japan's surrender to retire at 90% of full pay, while those who joined prior to 7 July 1937 could receive full pay.[32] But retirement takes cadres away from personal connections and extra-income perquisites. There may be good administrative and political arguments for retiring more older cadres, but this reform was unlikely to change the *system* of privilege, but only to circulate the people who enjoy its benefits.[33]

The bureaucratic self-critique was thus a strongly self-protective approach to special privilege. While it strongly resisted efforts to pose the issue in terms which made cadres look like a class, it used class offensively, as a weapon against bourgeois critics. The suppression of the 1979 human rights movement was followed by a campaign against 'bourgeois liberalism', aimed at critical writers and artists. A theme of that campaign was the harmful influence of bourgeois ideology imported from outside China through cultural commodities. This line of analysis was subsequently extended, with new discussion of class struggle. Class struggle was tied to 'economic crimes' in the following manner.[34] Exploiting classes exist *outside* China, especially in Hong Kong and other places from which contacts can be made with Chinese citizens, leading them into temptation. The

thrust of this discussion was to warn the non-Party critics to be on their best behaviour — the Party may have decided that there are no longer any exploiting classes within China, but if it ever changed its mind, it would certainly look for them among former bourgeois, and advocates of political liberalism, not within the ranks of state officials. By this stroke, the onus for bureaucratic privilege was placed on the Party's bourgeois critics and their foreign ties, not on Communist officials who were 'victimized' by capitalist corruption.

9. CONFLICT VERSUS COLLABORATION IN THE POLITICS OF BUREAUCRATIC PRIVILEGE

While the language of class conflict in China was altered sharply after Mao's death, the kinds of competition over scarce resources and benefits that one should expect in a poor, industrializing society remained quite lively. Class conflict was not pacified, even though its discussion assumed new forms, such as the debate over the significance of privilege.

The Maoists uncharacteristically combined two into one when they comingled bureaucrats and bourgeoisie as a common class enemy. With the removal of radical political pressure, it became apparent that there were divergent interests within the group formerly treated as an undifferentiated elite. In the bureaucratic privilege discussion, we can identify three intellectually coherent approaches to the appearance of distinctively advantaged groups in socialist society. The left saw special privilege as a threat to the revolution, arising from the embourgeoisement of socialist institutions. They sought to resolve the problem by organizing workers and peasants to supervise their officials. The bourgeois version of special privilege regarded cadre abuse of power to be a threat to the material and intellectual interests of non-bureaucratic elites. Its source is a lumbering feudal influence that persists despite decades of revolutionary change, and will only be rendered impotent if countervailing powers can be institutionalized and society made modern. The bureaucrats themselves identified cadre privilege as an embarrassment which must not be allowed to undercut their authority. But their China is neither too capitalist nor too feudal, rather cadres themselves have been insufficiently diligent, especially during organizationally lax periods of radical rule. The solution is better cadres, better organized from within. In addition, as long as the issue arose, bureaucrats were skilful at manipulating it to purge their own ranks of officials with either Maoist or bourgeois inclinations.

The bureaucratic treatment of privilege was not simply to use an opportunity to weaken rivals through conflict. Conservative officials also sought to protect their own privileges by extending similar ones to other groups in society. The strategy seems to have been to build a united front of the advantaged, thereby eroding potential bases of opposition.

One aspect of this drive was to bureaucratize increasing numbers of intellectuals, thereby defusing criticism by creating a commonality of interest. There were changes in Party composition, as the Cultural Revolutionary stress on recruiting candidates of worker and peasant origin was replaced by a search for intellectuals.[35] Intellectual work was bureaucratized by the addition of new hierarchies of formal titles, with the claim that this increased efficiency, although it can also be argued that this entangled potential critics more thoroughly in the bureaucratic web.[36]

Special attention was given to the 5.7 million middle-aged intellectuals, against whom considerable prejudice was still felt by leftists within the bureaucracy. Underpaid and undervalued, this group would be coopted rather cheaply, according to one analysis.[37] After all, there were so few of them — for Shanghai, less than 3% of the population, while only 1 and 10% of this small total was made up of high and middle level intellectuals; few resources would have to be expended to give them all better-paying jobs. Still another cheap way of buying off potential adversaries of the bureaucrats was to follow the example of Nanchang, where in 1980 houses illegally built by miscreant officials were turned over to high-level technical personnel and 'famous personages'.[38]

Nor can one ignore efforts to extend special privileges to segments of other classes, as well. Urban workers were favoured by policies that permitted them to bestow their scarce factory jobs to their children.[39] Such a policy was likely to enhance long-term divisions among the urban working population. Similarly, the introduction of the responsibility system into agriculture probably divided peasants into those who were situated to prosper with greater reliance upon market mechanisms and those who could not. In both cases, the development of internal contradictory interests should diminish the capacity of the group to approach the political system with a common voice. If this assured protection against the emergence of a coalition of disgruntled intelligentsia and unhappy workers and peasants, such policies then contributed to an environment in which the privileges of high officials could pass more easily without external challenge.

NOTES

1. Some of this section is based upon my *Class Conflict in Chinese Socialism* (New York: Columbia University Press, 1981), pp. 63–164.

2. See Byung-joon Ahn, *Chinese Politics and the Cultural Revolution* (Seattle: University of Washington Press, 1976).

3. For example, see Li Hsin, 'Leading cadres must consciously restrict bourgeois rights', *Red Flag* (1 July 1976), in *Survey of People's Republic of China Magazines*, Vol. 881 (26 July 1976), pp. 18–22.

4. See the *People's Daily* report in *Foreign Broadcast Information Service* (*FBIS*) (3 March 1978), pp. E1–5.

5. For criticism of Nie, see *Beijing Ribao* (19 January 1979), in *JRPS*, 073201 (11 April 1979), pp. 14–16. Rallies against Li Suwen and Yao Lienwei, a factory worker who also became a vice-chairman of the NPC, are reported in *South China Morning Post* (19 December 1978), in *FBIS* (19 December 1978), p. E2.

6. Hong Kong AFP (1 February 1979), in *FBIS* (2 February 1979), p. E1.

7. Ye Jianying, *Speech at the Meeting in Celebration of the 30th Anniversary of the Founding of the People's Republic of China* (Beijing: Foreign Languages Press, 1979).

8. Article by Guan Jian, in *FBIS* (3 June 1981), p. K8.

9. *Renmin Ribao* (25 March 1981).

10. AFP report in *South China Morning Post* (10 December 1979). See also Suzanne Pepper, 'Chinese education after Mao: two steps forward, two steps back and begin again?', *The China Quarterly*, Vol. 81 (March 1981), pp. 1–65.

11. As early as 2 December 1978, *Renmin Ribao* found it useful to print an article to 'Encourage the common practice of addressing each other as Comrade', a sure sign of the term's disuse. *FBIS* (5 December 1978), p. E7.

12. Xian radio (6 January 1981), in *FBIS* (8 January 1981), p. T1.

13. Frank Parkin, 'Class stratification in socialist societies', *British Journal of Sociology*, Vol. XX, No. 4 (December 1969), p. 364.

14. Shanghai, *Shijie Jingji Dabao*, Vol. 37. (15 June 1981), in *FBIS* (24 June 1981), pp. K17–18.

15. Beijing radio (10 June 1981), in *FBIS* (17 June 1981), pp. K1–2.

16. Among many accounts, see *Renmin Ribao* (19 July 1977).

17. *Renmin Ribao* (6 December 1977), in *FBIS* (14 December 1977), pp. E11–14; and Beijing *NCNA* (11 April 1978), in *FBIS* (12 April 1978), pp. E11–12.

18. *Renmin Ribao* (3 November 1978).

19. Taiyuan *Shanxi Ribao* editorial (6 July 1982), in *FBIS* (23 July 1982), pp. R4–5.

20. For instance, *Renmin Ribao* (29 January 1974), in *FBIS* (14 February 1974), pp. B2–3.

21. Lin Yoye and Shen Che, 'Commenting on the so-called opposition to the class of bureaucrats', *Red Flag*, Vol. 5 (1 March 1981), in *FBIS* (31 March 1981), pp. L1–8.

22. Deng Liqun, 'Communism is an eternal and lofty undertaking', Beijing, *Gongren Ribao* (27 March 1981).

23. For example, see Yuan Shi, 'The ideology of special privilege is the root of exploiting class ideology', *Xinhua Yuehao* (August 1979), pp. 26–29; as well as the account of an academic forum to criticize feudal dictatorship in *Renmin Ribao* (25 December 1979).

24. David Arkush, *Fei Xiaotong and Sociology in Revolutionary China* (Cambridge: Harvard University Press, 1981), p. 240.

25. See Roderick MacFarquhar (ed.), *The Hundred Flowers* (London: Sevens & Sons, 1960), pp. 73–75.

26. 'Forum of democratic parties and groups in the rectification movement', *NCNA* (8 May 1957), in *Survey of the China Mainland Press*, Vol. 1543 (4 June 1957), pp. 18–21.

27. See Harbin, *Heilong Ribao*, 'Commenting on a viewpoint of the main contradictions in socialism', in *FBIS* (17 June 1981), pp. K12–20, for a critique of bourgeois democracy as a solution to China's bureaucratic ills.

28. *Renmin Ribao* (15 May 1979), in *FBIS* (17 May 1979), p. L6.

29. Shi Zhongquan, 'The "Cultural Revolution" and the struggle against bureaucracy', *Beijing Review*, Vol. 24, No. 49 (7 December 1981), pp. 19–20.

30. Hong Kong, *Ta Kung Pao* (23 March 1981), in *FBIS* (25 March 1981), p. H2.

31. *Renmin Ribao* (11 November 1979).

32. *Beijing Review*, Vol. 24, No. 43 (26 October 1981), p. 22.

33. See the remarks in Li Fu, 'I am an element of the specially privileged stratum', *Zhengming*, Vol. 57 (July 1982), pp. 30–33.

34. See *Tianjin Ribao* (13 July 1982), in *FBIS* (23 July 1982), pp. R5–8; Nanjing, *Xinhau Ribao* (19 January 1981), in *FBIS* (10 February 1981), pp. O1–3; Beijing, *China Daily* (13 August 1982), in *FBIS* (13 August 1982), pp. K1–2; *Beijing Review*, Vol. 25, No. 33 (16 August 1982), pp. 17–19.

35. Guiyang radio (27 July 1981), in *FBIS* (24 July 1981), p. Q2; *Renmin Ribao* (19 July 1982), in *FBIS* (23 July 1982), pp. K5–6.

36. Beijing Xinhau (14 January 1981), in *FBIS* (14 January 1981), p. L2; Beijing Xinhau (29 July 1982), in *FBIS* (3 August 1982), pp. K12–13.

37. *Guangming Ribao* (15 July 1982), in *FBIS* (27 July 1982), pp. K12–16; see also *Shaanxi Ribao* editorial (21 July 1982), in *FBIS* (11 August 1982), pp. T2–3.

38. Beijing, *Gongren Ribao* (18 March 1980).

39. See Thomas B. Gold, 'Back to the city: the return of Shanghai's educated youth', *The China Quarterly*, Vol. 84 (December 1980), pp. 763–766; and Susan Shirk, 'Recent Chinese labour policies and the transformation of industrial organization in China', *The China Quarterly*, Vol. 88 (December 1981), pp. 575–593.

Post-Mao China's Development Model in Global Perspective*

SAMUEL S. KIM

Institute for World Order, New York

Summary. – This essay is a preliminary normative analysis of the meaning and implications of post-Mao China's entry into the capitalist world-economy. In assessing the nature and extent of shift in the Chinese model of development in global perspective, there is need to focus more on international than on domestic aspects. Specifically, this essay is concerned with the following issues. What are the contending models of the global political economy that can be used as a theoretical frame of reference for macro-inquiry into model shift into the post-Mao era? What were the central characteristic features of the Chinese model during the Maoist era, and to what extent, and in what manner, have they been retained, revised, or repudiated in the post-Mao era? What are the explanatory variables for shifts in the political economy of post-Mao China? By way of conclusion, some normative and policy implications of the shifts and changes initiated by the post-Mao leadership are suggested.

To industrialize our country, the primary issue before us is to learn from the Soviet Union. . . . We must set going a tidal wave of learning from the Soviet Union on a nationwide scale, in order to build up our country . . . 'follow the path of the Russians'. (*Renmin ribao*, 1953)[1]

If we do not rely mainly on our own efforts but, as Teng Hsiao-ping [Deng Xiaoping] advocated rely solely on importing foreign techniques, copying foreign designs and technological processes and patterning our equipment on foreign models, we will forever trail behind foreigners and our country's development of technology and even its entire national economy will fall under the control of foreign monopoly capital. (*Peking Review*, 1976)[2]

We are standing at another turning point in Chinese history. . . . China has now adopted a policy of opening our doors to the world, in a spirit of international cooperation. (Deng Xiaoping, 1980)[3]

The emerging reentry of China into the capitalist world economy raises new issues in the study of the development process. For years, Sinologists and comparative development economists have been preoccupied with China's development experience, testing various theories of political economy or debating that experience's relevance for the developing countries.[4] For the *dependencia* and world-system theorists, China has been the exception (an anti-Centre model, as it were) that supported their thesis about global political economy of core capi-

talism.[5] Johan Galtung argued, for example, that the Centre countries were 'not only on the decline in terms of power, but also as *models* — which, of course, is one aspect of their total power decline' and then suggested that 'if any country is a model, it would rather be China.'[6]

This paper examines continuity and change (a diachronic analysis) in the development model of post-Mao China, with greater emphasis on international variables. The term 'model' — *moxing* in Chinese — is used in the paper in its *normative* sense as a behavioural standard to be followed or emulated. This is also the sense in which the Chinese generally use the term. Such 'model' approach is useful in this diachronic analysis because the normative components are so salient in the ongoing dialectics of the Chinese development process.

In pursuit of this line of normative inquiry, the paper focuses upon the following questions. What contending models of the global political

* This is a revised version of a paper originally presented at the 'Post-Mao China's Interaction with the World Economy' Panel of the 23rd Annual Convention of the International Studies Association, Cincinnati, Ohio, 24–27 March 1982 and Columbia University's Contemporary China Seminar on 8 April 1982. The author is grateful to Gavin Boyd and William Feeney for their critical comments on an earlier draft of this paper.

economy can be used for macro-inquiry into the political economy of post-Mao China? What were the central features of the Chinese model during the Maoist era, and to what extent have they been retained, revised, or repudiated in the post-Mao era? What variables explain the changes and shifts? By way of conclusion, some normative and policy implications of the development process of post-Mao China are suggested.

CONTENDING MODELS OF THE GLOBAL POLITICAL ECONOMY

The decade of the 1970s, suddenly sensitized by global economic crises, has generated various contending models of the world economy.[7] These can be grouped under three separate rubrics: system-maintaining; system-reforming; and system-transforming. Despite differences in assumptions, methodology, and prescriptions, they share several similarities. First, they are expressions of concern about the state of the world economy. Second, most of them are *global* political economy models since they bear directly or indirectly on the mechanisms for negotiated and unilateral allocations of global goods and resources. Third, they are imbued with futurism, projecting preferred goals and targets based on different value assumptions. And finally, their prescriptive strategies express different images of the underpinning structure of global society.[8]

System-Maintaining Models. Central to system-maintaining global models is the assumption that the existing economic order can — and should — be preserved and that the present world economic system only needs to be managed in a more orderly and efficient manner, relying on the vehicles of international division of labour and comparative advantage. The main operational concern is to prevent a breakdown of existing patterns of order and stability in a period of rapid change and disruption. The system-maintainers have neither the normative rationale nor the cognitive urgency that international stability requires structural reform. The economic well-being of the developing countries is to be secured only through their full integration into the capitalist world market — the internationalization of the 'trickle-down theory.'[9] In the parlance of *dependencia* theory, these models are variants of the Centre model.

What may be called the 'Trilateral model,' espoused by the Trilateral Commission, especially in its early phase (1973–1976), is a good example of the system-maintaining approach to world economic order. In an age of hegemonic decline, world order rhetoric (co-operation, partnership, solidarity, etc.) is invoked as 'a master strategy' to restore *la belle époque* of the immediate postwar era and shore up the crisis-ridden capitalist world-economy. Inter-capitalist rivalries and disputes have to be avoided to form a united trilateral front and thus 'make the world safe for interdependence.'[10] An implicit linkage between geopolitical and geoeconomic factors in the model has become more salient in recent years. An attempt to sustain the viability of the model has been joined by four Western 'think tanks' in an unprecedented collaborative report, *Western Security*, proposing a series of strategies to meet 'enhanced Soviet military threats' and 'an increasingly unstable and volatile Third World upon which it [the West] will depend more and more for its economic survival.'[11]

System-Reforming Models. Drawing normative energy from the reform tradition of Hobson, Keynes, and Mitrany, system-reforming models seek a more efficient and equitable management of the global economy through incremental institutional reforms. The underlying assumption is that the maladies afflicting the world economy should be cured through functional and institutional reform measures. At no point do the system-reformers seek to *transform* the statist paradigm in their quest for a more efficent, equitable, and lasting international order.

Most vocal supporters of system-reform confine their proposals to the advancement of inter-state social and political justice and inter-state economic well-being. They believe that greater international efficiency can be combined with greater international equity, greater international protection of national autonomy (the principle of permanent inalienable resource sovereignty of each nation) with greater international cooperation (the common-heritage-of-mankind principle concerning the global commons), greater international justice with greater international law and order. In short, the system-reforming models affirm the functionalist belief that both North and South — and East and West — can indeed come together for the joint management of 'complex interdependence.'

The prime move for system-reform emanates from the Group of 77, articulating demands for the New International Economic Order (NIEO) through the United Nations Conference on Trade and Development (UNCTAD) and the UN General Assembly. To the extent that OPEC became a vanguard as well as a political and financial supporter of the NIEO in the mid-1970s, system-reforming models (or we may simply call this the NIEO model) enjoyed serious leverage. Indeed, the formation of the Trilateral Commission can be interpreted as an effort to forge a countervailing response.

RIO: Reshaping the International Order (a report prepared under Jan Tinbergen for the Club of Rome) and the Brandt Commission report present system-reforming models.[12] Stirred by the crisis of global inequalities and the failure of the present system to make an adequate response, both reports sought to achieve 'an equitable international social and economic order' and suggested short and long-term reforms on a wide range of global developmental issues. Both reports advance measures for strengthening the United Nations system and restructuring international financial and monetary institutions.

System-Transforming Models. The reconceptualization of the development *problematique* to reject the assumption of automatic transmission of the benefits of economic growth to all regions and peoples is central to system-transforming models. A model is system-transforming if it challenges the legitimacy and viability of the present global dominance/dependence system and presents alternative visions and structure.

System-transformation is a preferred norm, not a working reality, in global politics. Marxism has long represented the most powerful anti-systemic force in the development of the world capitalist system, but its potency is considerably weakened by rampant statism, bureaucratization, unaccountability, and the inability to reconcile all kinds of contradictions within and between socialist states, let alone inter-socialist fratricidal warfare. There are simply too many contradictions in the world today that cannot be explained by class conflict alone. Clearly, there are crises of faith in Marxism in China, Poland, and even the Soviet Union. That there is also a crisis in Marxian theory among its exponents outside the communist world is acknowledged by no lesser a Marxist than Paul M. Sweezy.[13]

Dependencia theory explores the incorporation of the periphery into the capitalist world economy through a global division of labour, and the implications of 'underdevelopment' of periphery capitalism.[14] The *dependencia* model rejects the statist paradigm, conceptualizing the global political economy in terms of the dominant and dependent roles,

positions, and relationships. The penetration of peripheral economies by centre actors occurs in a variety of economic, political, and cultural modes. The resulting internal structural distortions contribute to the maintenance of centre capitalism. This model seems to call for national self-reliance as the only way of first delinking from the capitalist world economy and then reassociating these detached parts with a socialist world economy.

The neo-Marxist 'world system' approach, exemplified in Immanuel Wallerstein's historical investigation of the emergence of world capitalism, presents another system-transforming model. A variant on *dependencia* theory, it conceptualizes the global political economy as essentially based upon an international division of labour in which an exchange of unequal values takes place between core, peripheral, and semi-peripheral areas. This model anticipates the eventual demise and replacement of the world capitalist system by 'a socialist world-government' through continual class struggle.[15] A global socialist transformation will evolve out of the dynamics of national revolution at the periphery and semi-periphery. This process of transformation is expected to strengthen socialist values and structures. Wallerstein has not yet specified a transition path, but his vision seems to depend on the process of disintegration of the world capitalist system brought about by accelerating contradictions, on the one hand, and the coalition of anti-systemic forces — or what he calls 'real worldwide intermovement links' — on the other.[16]

The non-Machiavellian and non-Marxist system-transforming models are represented by *What Now*, the 1975 Dag Hammarskjold Report on Development and International Cooperation, prepared for the Seventh Special Session of the UN General Assembly, and the WOMP (World Order Models Project), a cross-cultural, transnational research enterprise committed to world peace, economic well-being, social justice, and ecological balance. 'The existing "order" is coming apart and rightly so,' the Dag Hammarskjold report observes, 'since it has failed to meet the needs of the vast majority of peoples and reserved its benefits for a privileged minority.' The key to the process of struggle and transformation is 'another development,' which calls for the satisfaction of human needs, the strengthening of Third World capacity for self-reliant development, the reorientation of science and technology, and the transformation of existing social, economic and political structures in the world today.[17]

Based on the assumption that the transformation of global actors, values and institutions is necessary and possible, the WOMP is engaged in (1) a diagnostic/prognostic task of describing present world order conditions and trends, (2) a modelling task of designing preferred futures, and (3) a prescriptive task of mapping a transition process, including concrete steps and an overall strategy.[18] Both models give much weight to political and cultural factors as well as to alternative attitudes and values in pressing for a concerted mobilization to achieve basic structural changes at domestic and global levels.

THE CHINESE DEVELOPMENT MODEL

Given the weight of Sinocentric tradition, modern Chinese nationalism, Marxist ideology, Maoist perennial quest for normative order, and long exclusion from the world economy, the Chinese development model is *sui generis*, defying easy identification with any of the contending global models. Then there is the harsh reality of providing basic human needs of nearly one-fourth of humanity (now officially confirmed by the 1982 census) with only 7% of the world's cultivated land in an age of resource scarcity. The imperative of 'mobilization politics' is embedded in this adverse geodemographic reality.

Social and political mobilization of people for the development process calls for three major functions: the descriptive function (policy popularization); the normative function (policy legitimation); and the prescriptive function (policy implementation). The Chinese mobilization politics has often invoked model heroes (Zhang Side, Lei Feng, Yugong, Norman Bethune, Lu Xun, and more recently Luo Jianfu and Jiang Zhuying) to galvanize people to greater diligence, self-sacrifice, obedience, and patriotism.

Another notable feature of the Chinese development process is a constant resort to the Marxist-Maoist dialectics to find the correct line of thought and action. The dialectical imperative for a continuing process of experimentation with various strategies and the perennial quest for normative social order largely account for the volatile and unpredictable zigzag pattern of radical upsurge and revisionist retreat in the course of the Chinese development process.

The People's Republic of China during the first decade of its 'encircled' and 'embargoed' existence followed the Soviet Union in foreign policy (the lean-to-one-side alliance policy) and developmental politics, as shown in the opening epigraph of this paper. The decision to go it alone in China's development was made in 1958, according to Mao's secret speech in 1962.[19] With the withdrawal of Soviet technical experts, managers, and industrial blueprints from China in mid-1960, which inflicted maximum damage on the Chinese economy at a time of maximum vulnerability,[20] there was simply no alternative to the self-reliance model of development.

The self-reliance model was a logical outcome of Mao's objections to the political economy of Soviet socialism expressed as early as 1956 ('Ten Major Relationships') and later elaborated in his trenchant critique of Stalin's political economy textbook, *Economic Problems of Socialism in the Soviet Union.* For Mao, the most troublesome feature of the Soviet (Stalin) model was the lack of dialectics and balanced development, i.e. excessive stress on the economic base, heavy industry, cadres and technology and are too little emphasis on the ideological superstructure, light industry and agriculture, the peasant, and creative human energy.[21]

Since the Sino-Soviet split, the dominant component of the Chinese model has been independent and self-reliant national development. Despite the shifts in the specific formulation and actual implementation of self-reliance, responding to changing correlations of political forces at home and abroad and their resulting opportunities and constraints, general commitment to the principle persisted.

The self-reliance model did not imply autarky. It was a general and flexible guide for maximal self-realization. The Chinese term *zili gengsheng* literally means 'regeneration through one's own strength', connoting a means, not an end. In terms of the global political economy, it followed the logic of the *dependencia* model by stressing (1) the *maximization* of internal autocentric development; (2) the *minimization* of external dependency; and (3) the *transformation* of the capitalist world-economy.

What is unique about the Chinese self-reliance model was its normative assumptions: that development is both desirable and feasible only by mobilizing the creative energies of the people to serve the people; that distribution should not be separated from growth of the economic pie; that equity is as important — and sometimes more important and desirable — as efficiency; and that an egalitarian social order cannot be maintained without continuing struggle to keep the superstructure pure and proletarian. In short, this model conceptualized development as a continuous value-shaping and value-realizing process.

In popularizing self-reliance, Mao used three national models. First, there was the Yugong model to energize the masses with the spirit of strategic optimism. Using the ancient Chinese fable in which God is finally moved by the dogged determination of the Foolish Old Man (Yugong) to remove the mountains, Mao tried to imbue the masses with a breakthrough (the Great Leap Forward) mentality. Based on the assumption that a poor and underdeveloped political economy can hardly afford to offer the material rewards of meritocracy without undermining distributive justice, Mao also popularized two models for agricultural and industrial development — the Dazhai model (or 'In Agriculture Learn from Dazhai') and the Daqing model (or 'In Industry Learn from Daqing') — as mobilizing techniques with which to conquer extremely adverse material conditions. All three national models were designed to spur China's development by the infusion of a spirit of national independence, the triumph of human willpower, and the mobilization of human resources.

The Sixth Special Session of the General Assembly on Raw Materials and Development, which ended by calling for the establishment of a New International Economic Order, provided the first opportunity for China to relate its development model to the global political economy. The three founding resolutions — the NIEO Declaration, the NIEO Programme of Action, and the Charter of Economic Rights and Duties of States — were taken up to project China's model to the global level. The authoritative *Renmin ribao* [People's Daily] began to report international development issues in terms of the NIEO (*Xinde guoji jingji zhixu*) model. The NIEO model thus became the strongest symbolic and normative link between China and the Third World in their mutual engagement in global developmental politics.[22]

In NIEO politics, Maoist China projected the self-reliance model as the best means that Third World countries could adopt in order to keep the initiative in their own hands, preserve their resource sovereignty, prevent the structural penetration of their economies by imperialist predators, and liberate themselves from the vicious process of the exchange of unequal values in international economic relations. During the debate at the Sixth Special Session of the General Assembly, Huang Hua singled out 'interdependence' and the 'international division of labour' as being particularly susceptible to a co-option strategy by the superpowers. Using a vivid Chinese metaphor, he argued that interdependence in the contemporary world economic system could easily turn into an asymmetrical interdependence 'between a horseman and his mount.'[23]

The dominance of associative linkage strategies in the NIEO has been made clear by Gamani Corea who, as Secretary-General of UNCTAD, played an instrumental role in the formulation of the NIEO model: 'I am of the opinion that the underlying desire, indeed demand, of all is that the countries of the Third World be *incorporated* into the system of world-wide trade. They want to belong to it and to participate in the decisions and events that influence its development.'[24] Although the NIEO did not fully conform to Maoist China's image of individual and collective self-reliance — or the *dependencia*'s ideal of a real solution to the development of underdevelopment — China became a strong symbolic supporter of the NIEO aligning itself with the Group of 77 as a counterbalance to the superpowers.

By casting its lot with the radical faction of the Third World in the struggle to break up the global dominance/dependence system and by advocating not the conventional mode of politics as power-seeking and power-wielding but a new style of politics as value-realizing and structure-transforming, Maoist China tried to fill a leadership deficiency in 'world-order politics,' though its own analysis of world contradictions was much more radical than that of the progressive national bourgeoisie of the Third World which produced the NIEO.

Although the self-reliance model was elastic, it nonetheless had established certain policy parameters and precedents during the Maoist period. First, foreign trade was used as a balancing factor in the development process, largely to eliminate certain sectoral weaknesses, for example by importing specific capital goods that were becoming a bottleneck on production growth or key military items. Second, China managed to avoid foreign debts by balancing imports and exports and by rejecting new foreign borrowing. The debt owed to the Soviet Union was fully paid by 1964. However, the repeated assertion that China is a socialist country without internal or external debt was made possible through the use of 'supplier credits,' a device whereby China's suppliers arranged financing with their own commercial banks with interest payments simply added to the price of the goods sold to the Chinese. Third, Maoist China managed to portray itself as the most powerful national symbol of self-reliance in global developmental politics, a poor and developing socialist country that admirably met basic human needs at home and extended both bilateral and multilateral aid abroad at the same time, but one that as a matter of principle absolutely declined foreign aid in any form. And finally Maoist China not only was absent from international monetary and financial institutions but repeatedly criticized them as strongholds of resistance to the NIEO.[25]

CHANGES AND SHIFTS IN THE POST-MAO DEVELOPMENT

Phases of Conceptual Shift. The political economy of post-Mao China has been marked by several phases of policy-making and model-seeking. All the twists and turns in this ongoing search of the development path that is politically viable and economically sustainable reflect the dynamics of political struggles in the successor regime, in particular, the gradual ascendancy of Deng Xiaoping and his attempts to balance contending political factions for a broadest possible 'united front' in the modernization drive. For our analytical convenience, the post-Mao era can be divided into four phases.

During the first phase (September 1976 through the end of 1977), the post-Mao leadership seems to have recognized the necessity of Maoist continuity to assure a degree of stability and legitimacy. This was indeed a period of behind-the-scenes soul-searching and preparation. The purge of the 'Gang of Four' or even Deng's return to power in mid-1977 did not produce any discernible erosion of the self-reliance model. The Chinese press in 1977 was filled with articles extolling Mao's three-world theory and in the most elaborate and comprehensive foreign policy posture statement issued in recent years, the editorial department of *Renmin ribao* devoted its entire issue (six pages) of November 1, 1977, to an essay, entitled 'Chairman Mao's Theory of the Differentiation of the Three Worlds Is a Major Contribution to Marxism-Leninism.' Thus, Mao's three-world theory, a geopolitical variant of the system-transforming *dependencia* model, was canonized − or so it seemed at the time − as the primary strategic principle to guide Chinese global policy in the post-Mao era.

During the second phase (from February 1978 when the modernization drive was offi-cially launched to the end of 1979), the post-Mao leadership had shifted discernibly. Under Hua there was in practice, if not in theory, a move from the self-reliance model to the more interdependent model, or at least self-reliance was drastically reinterpreted and revised to seek a better interface with the Trilateral model. When Deng replaced Hua as the leading political force at the Third Plenum in December 1978 this process accelerated. In 1978, Chinese activity in the capitalist world economy suddenly exploded, with overall trade increasing by 40% (from $15 billion in 1977 to $21 billion in 1978). Tensions, contradictions, and discrepancies between the functional requirements of the modernization drive and the normative requirements of self-reliance were resolved by establishing an ends-means complementarity between the long-term objective of national self-reliance and the short-term imperative of utilizing foreign capital, technology, and market.[26]

During the third phase (from February 1980 when Deng made a public declaration of the 'open-door' policy as 'another turning point in Chinese history,' as shown in the last of three epigraphs cited at the beginning of this paper, to mid-1981) the post-Mao leadership continued to discard additional features of the self-reliance model. The most notable feature of this period was a drastic reformulation (and relegitimation) of China's future in terms of such hitherto proscribed concepts as the open-door, international interdependence, division of labour and specialization. By late 1981, the open-door policy was elevated to one of the 'Ten Principles for Future Economic Construction' in Premier Zhao Ziyang's Report on the Work of the Government, delivered at the Fourth Session of the Fifth National People's Congress.[27]

The fourth period since mid-1981 seems to have marked another, certainly not the last, phase in the ongoing quest for the proper development path. Although there is no evidence that this new phase has had major practical impact on the open-door policy, the conceptual pendulum seems to have shifted from the right to the centre as the normative components of Chinese mobilization politics have regained their salience in the Chinese development process. This shift has expressed itself in a rectification campaign against the 'liberalization trends' and renewed search for a more 'legitimate' open-door/self-reliance nexus in domestic politics.

This latest period has also witnessed a number of symbolic moves in Chinese foreign policy. At the level of policy pronouncement, Mao's three-world theory has reappeared, though in a reactive form. Inquiries from concerned Third World heads of state during their state visits in 1981—1982 evoked a somewhat apologetic response: 'China *still* holds Chairman Mao's theory of the three worlds in its foreign policy.'[28] Such a reassertion has been matched by more active identification with the Third World — notice the repeated vetoes against the re-election of Kurt Waldheim as Secretary-General of the United Nations in late 1981 and Premier Zhao Ziyang's 11-nation African tour in early 1983 — on the one hand and by the revival of the 'hegemonist' tag to both superpowers and an equidistance posture between Washington and Moscow, on the other. It is still premature to say definitely whether this posture shift in 1981—1982 is a diplomatic bargaining ploy designed to enhance the value of 'the China card' as a *de facto* geopolitical and economic partner of the West and/or a necessary concession to the left in domestic intraelite conflict.

Shifts at Home. The most discernible feature of the reinterpretation of self-reliance has been a decisive shift from the model's political and ideological dimensions to its empirical and economic components. The opening salvo was launched in the form of an article entitled 'Practice Is the Sole Criterion for Testing Truth,' published in *Guangming ribao* (Guangming Daily) on 11 May 1978. This provided the new epistemological rationale for demythologizing late (post-1957) Maoism. In October 1979, Ye Jianying defined a 'pragmatism/modernization' nexus as follows: 'The work of every district, every department, and every unit, right down to every single individual, as well as the credit due to it, will be judged by its direct and indirect contribution to modernization.' Debunked in the process was the Maoist belief that 'man could effect at will a so-called change or transformation of the superstructure and the relations of production.'[29]

The extent to which self-reliance was subjected to a progressive normative erosion can be seen in the current status of the three national models alluded to earlier. In August 1980, a Chinese commentator demythologized the Yugong model by deriding the foolish old man for his 'imbecility' and declaring the happy ending of the fable as an example of superstition.[30] Yet by early 1982 the Yugong model seems to have made a spiritual resurrection of sorts, as the Central Committee of the Chinese Communist Party (CCP) now calls on cadres to emulate the dogged *spirit*, if not

the specific *action*, of the foolish old man. An analogy between the Yugong spirit and Yanan spirit is made as if to admit the limits of material incentives in removing the mountains standing in the way of the modernization drive.[31]

From 1964 onward Dazhai was an integral part of the Maoist development model. Like Yugong, Dazhai too was popularized as a transformation model designed to break the fatalistic tradition of Chinese peasants, to demonstrate the irrelevance of cost-effectiveness, and to distribute the benefits fairly among its various households. The process of debunking the Dazhai model in the post-Mao era got off rather slowly at first, then quickly gained momentum. By September 1979, it was killed for all practical purposes. In February 1981 the Party rendered its final judgment for its official burial — that it had become a model in implementing the erroneous leftist principle of absolute egalitarianism.[32]

The reaffirmation of the Daqing model in a revised form in late 1981 suggests the kind of 'balancing' process in the fourth phase shift earlier alluded to. In December 1981 the CCP Central Committee distributed the 'Report on the Question of Learning from Daqing in Industry' and an accompanying circular for the Party's authoritative interpretation of the Daqing model. Due to the pernicious influence of the 'left' over a long period in the past, the circular argues, the Daqing model was linked to the two-line class struggle. As a result, it is now argued, numerous problems cropped up in 'publicity and popularization.' Yet Daqing was reaffirmed, not repudiated, because its 'key experiences' are still of practical significance. This reaffirmation is based on the newly-gained recognition of resolving the contradictions between normative and material incentives and redness and expertise:

While eliminating the influence of 'left' ideas, it was totally necessary to repudiate the erroneous viewpoint that 'consciousness can achieve everything.' However, we should by no means reject the dynamic role of revolutionary consciousness in transforming the objective world on this account. While transforming the objective world, man's varying metal [sic] outlooks might produce different results under largely identical material conditions. At present, as the national economy is being readjusted, some leading cadres must resolutely and quickly change such mental outlooks as passiveness, fear of difficulties, blaming everybody and everything but themselves and tending to believe that nothing whatsoever can be done . . . it is most urgent, under the new ～n and for the new tasks, to build a com ideologically advanced, vocationally proficient and highly disciplined workers and staff members who work hard and cooperate.[33]

Still, it cannot be said that the Daqing model has been reaffirmed as *the* national model for industrial development. In 1981 and 1982, Shanghai was also advocated as a model that 'has assimilated the advanced techniques and methods of management of foreign countries' and is therefore 'a most practical way in tapping the potential and raising the economic results of China's industries at present.'[34] As a follow-up, Chinese scholars proposed in mid-1982 an establishment of 'urban economic circuits' with large cities as props in order to bring into fully play their leading role in the national economy.[35]

China and the NIEO. China's symbolic support of the NIEO has continued, though in a revised and muted tone. This change has taken place in a variety of forms and manifestations. First, Maoist China's unique representational style of expounding its principled stand on developmental issues in support of the general interests of the global underdogs (the Third World) rather than in its own has been replaced by a more 'realistic' redefinition of NIEO politics in terms more compatible with perceived national interests.[36]

Second, the two *bêtes noires* — global interdependence and the division of labour and specialization — are no longer feared or attacked. A qualitative content analysis of the articles published in *Hongqi* [Red Flag] and the *Beijing Review* between January 1977 and December 1981 shows the extent to which self-reliance has been reconceptualized in all of its crucial dimensions: (1) the superiority of the division of labour and specialization in production over that of all-around, balanced, and self-reliant development; (2) the deepening and inevitable trend of international interdependence in world economic development; and (3) the downgrading of China's role in the transformation of the capitalist world-economy.[37]

And lastly, China's supportive commentaries on and references to the NIEO have been declining. The coverage of 'North-South' issues in *Peking Review* showed a significant drop from 34 articles (totalling more than 99 pages) in 1974 to 10 articles (totalling 19 pages) in 1977.[38] The number of articles bearing the NIEO title in the *Renmin ribao* also dropped from 21 in 1977 to 7 in 1978.[39]

The 11th Special Session of the General Assembly in 1980 brought to light two significant shifts in the Chinese perception of the

NIEO model. First, there is now more explicit articulation of, and more active campaigning for, the linkage approach coordinating assorted global geopolitical and economic struggles. Second, Chinese perception of the NIEO has shifted from the *dependencia* model to the Trilateral model of 'interdependence.' Post-Mao China has not abandoned its support of the Third World's NIEO struggle. Instead, it has moved from a position of system-transformation to one of system-maintenance in the Third World's ideological spectrum.

The Cancun Summit Conference attended by 22 nations in October 1981 has received extensive coverage as the 'North-South Dialogue' (*Nanbei duihua*) in the Chinese press.[40] This suggests some shift from the right to the centre in Chinese global policy in 1981–1982. China followed a double track at Cancun, designed to minimize losses in the Third World and maximize gains with the United States. The central theme of Chinese public pronouncements was that there are both contradictions *and* interdependence between the North and the South and that 'a new kind of international relationship is beneficial to both the developing and the developed countries, and is conducive to world peace and stability.'[41] According to the current Chinese image, the world economy has gradually changed from the East-West contradiction of the early postwar period to the mutually dependent and mutually conflictive structure among the four major groups of countries: the capitalist imperialist countries, socialist imperialist countries, socialist countries, and developing countries.[42]

Premier Zhao Ziyang's militant public attack on the 'unjust and unequitable economic system' at Cancun[43] was part of the renewed attempts to paper over the steady peripheralization of the Third World in the global political economy of post-Mao China and to renew a closer identification with the Third World in the public (symbolic) domain of global development politics. Nonetheless, the centrepiece of Zhao's summit diplomacy at Cancun was more political than economic — to dissuade President Reagan from arms sales to Taiwan.

Cancun may well prove to be the denouement of the NIEO. The central issue that stalemated the 11th Special Session of the General Assembly remains unresolved, namely, the irreconcilable conflict over the forum in which global negotiations should take place and the mechanisms for implementing any eventual agreements. The Third World took an integrated and centralized approach focusing upon the General Assembly to link simultaneously policy measures in several sectors, while the North, in particular the United State, Great Britain, and West Germany, insisted on a fragmented and decentralized approach through the specialized agencies such as the Bank Group (where they still dominate) and continued compartmentalization of the dialogue along sectoral lines.

Viewed against this background, Cancun was a triumph of the Northern strategy of 'divide and delay.' In fact, the Declaration of the 1980 Venice Summit had already ruptured the assumption of the postwar economic liberalism by advancing a new 'divide and rule' formula — that the burden of helping developing countries must be equally shared by the trio of the OPEC, OECD, and industrialized Communist countries. That the Conference took place outside the UN framework also ran counter to the NIEO spirit of 'participatory democracy' on global developmental issues.

Moreover, the Conference was characterized by numerous anomalies. The Soviet Union was invited but declined. The exclusion of Cuba's Fidel Castro was the precondition for Ronald Reagan's participation. The superaffluent ambience of the Conference in a Third World country also symbolized a problematic linkage to the basic needs of the world's poor. And there was the anti-NIEO but self-serving declaration of Brazilian foreign minister Ramiro Elysio Sarairva Guerreiro: 'The countries of the South have the greatest interest in preserving the stability of the Bretton Woods institutions [the World Bank and the IMF].'[44]

International Trade. What used to be regarded in China's view as an 'exchange of unequal values' has now become 'international trade practices and norms.' It is now repeatedly argued that the 'left' deviationist thinking of the past under the influence of the 'Gang of Four' failed to 'proceed from reality' by adopting a closed-door policy. Exports have been elevated to the status of being 'the foundation of China's foreign trade.'[45] An 'objective reality ' — this term recurs in the current Chinese vocabulary and presumably refers to the global political economy dominated by capitalist powers — obliges all countries to engage in commodity exchange. In view of the current global reality, we are told, no country can manage without developing trade with foreign countries, and it is absolutely impossible for any economically backward country to realize modernization with a closed-door policy.[46]

In order to promote export trade, the post-Mao leadership has initiated a number of novel measures. There is an attempt to improve China's terms of trade (the ratio of export prices to import prices) by changing the structure of the export trade from raw materials to finished goods. Such restructuring, which follows the export-oriented development strategy of the newly industrializing countries (NICs), is justified by the need to earn more foreign exchange. By the late 1980s, China's economic experts now estimate that machinery exports will acount for one-half of China's total export of manufactured goods.

The post-Mao leadership has established four 'special economic zones' (SEZs) in the cities of Shenzhen, Zhuhai and Shantou of Guangdong Province and the city of Xiamen of Fujian Province. These are modelled after the 'free trade zones' (FTZ) in many Third World countries, an artificial socioeconomic environment characterized by an exceptionally favourable infrastructure, special tax exemptions, low wages, export subsidies, and the prohibition of strikes. China's rationale for setting up special economic zones is 'to make better use of foreign funds, import technology, increase exports, increase employment and increase foreign exchange earnings in order to more successfully assimilate useful foreign experience on management and administration, to prosper the special economic zones and to accelerate the progress of the four modernizations.'[47] 'Foreign businessmen making investments or running factories in these zones will be allowed to get a reasonable amount of profit,' it is now conceded, 'which is indeed a kind of exploitation.' But that kind of exploitation involved 'is nothing to be afraid of.'[48]

As if to emulate the NIC growth model, the post-Mao leadership has also joined the race to outbid Taiwan, South Korea, and the Philippines in the exportation of cheap labour to the Middle East. The China Construction Engineering Corporation, which was originally set up in 1957 to undertake government foreign aid projects abroad (including the Tan-Zam Railway) and major construction projects at home, was transformed in 1979 for this new task. By May 1980, the Corporation 'with some 80,000 architects and workers with experience in different climates and working conditions' had already signed 40 contracts worth almost $100 million.'[49] In 1981, China sent more than 17,000 workers abroad. Having too many people is China's great problem, it is argued, but the abundance of the labour force is also China's greatest superiority; hence, it is imperative to promote the business of 'international labour cooperation' (*quoji laowu hezuo*) to capitalize on such strength.[50]

International Monetary and Financial Issues.
The year 1978 witnessed perhaps the most
dramatic departure from the self-reliance model
when the post-Mao leadership plunged into the
international race for bilateral and multilateral
aid from capitalist countries, transnational
corporations, international commercial banks,
and even international organizations. The shift
from an aid-giving to an aid-seeking state was
made in mid-1978. In July 1978, China cut off
all assistance to its heretofore largest recipients,
Albania and Vietnam, in a manner reminiscent
of Soviet 'hegemonic' behaviour *vis-à-vis*
China itself in mid-1960. It was also reported
officially in the fall that 'China was cutting its
foreign aid program drastically and that the
present level of aid giving was about one-tenth
that of 1970.'[51]

In a carefully reasoned study of China's
Third World Policy, Harry Harding argues that
the year 1978 witnessed a decisive shift. 'As
part of this shift in emphasis,' he argues, 'China
(1) showed less interest in the "new international economic order" and a growing preoccupation with the political and military
threat posed by the Soviet Union to the security
of the developing world; (2) reduced its foreign
economic assistance program, while maintaining
relatively constant levels of military aid to
developing countries; and (3) virtually ended
its attempts to portray itself as a model for
economic development and social change in
the Third World.'[52]

In the latter half of 1978 China crossed the
Rubicon by seeking UNDP technical aid. This
request from a poor and developing member
state was received as a complete surprise, and
with mixed reactions. With this single act,
China shifted from the posture of overstating
its strengths and virtues as a donor to one of
understating its economic and scientific strength
to elicit assistance from international organizations.

In spite of some opposition, the Governing
Council of UNDP approved a $15 million pack-
age for China.[53] By the end of 1981, UN
development agencies were supporting some
200 projects in China, ranging from installation
of computers and training of technicans for
tallying China's 1982 census to improvements
in livestock breeding and fisheries.[54] In the
short span of three years, China transformed its
status as the only developing country declining
any multilateral aid to the one with the largest
number of UN aid projects.

Both symbolically and substantively, China's
entry into the International Monetary Fund

(IMF) on 17 April 1980 and the World Bank
(and its affiliates, the International Development Association and the International Finance
Corporation) on 15 May 1980 marked another
turning point. Only a few years ago it was
unthinkable that China might accept the
stringent membership requirements and con-
ditionality for loans — such as permitting a
complete monitoring of the Chinese economy
by the Fund-Bank staff, agreeing to set a
renminbi exchange rate that would not damage
competitive currencies, consulting annually
with the World Bank on the state of China's
economy to meet the usual conditions for
credit borrowings, and furnishing statistics for
official foreign exchange reserves, gold production, price indices, and foreign debts.

Apparently, the lure of the IMF's large pool
of lending capital, the World Bank's project
financing, and IDA's interest-free credit for
poor developing countries was such that China
was willing to bend its rigid principle of 'permanent and inalienable resource sovereignty.'
A high-level Chinese Communist Party conference in late December 1980 is reported to
have made a decision to set an arbitrary limit
on interest rates for foreign borrowings at
8.5%, which explains its parsimonious use of
the ample credits extended by the trilateral
countries (some $26.2 billion by February
1980), and its active pursuit of concessionary
low-interest loans from multilateral development agencies like the Bank Group.

Instead of maintaining a low profile and
retreating into its accustomed, unobtrusive,
apprentice-like posture on the sidelines as in
the Maoist period,[55] China immediately started
lobbying to increase its quotas which determine
borrowing rights and voting power in both
institutions. At the time of its entry, for
example, China's quota in the IMF was 550
SDRs (Special Drawing Rights), the equivalent
of about $693 million. In September, China
succeeded in having its quota raised from SDR
550 million to SDR 1,200 million, and in
December 1980 the China quota was increased
to SDR 1,800 million, as part of a general quota
increase for all IMF members. As a result,
China now has the eighth largest quota, equal
to 3.02% of the total and 2.89% of the voting
power in the IMF. Likewise, China managed
to have its subscription increased from the
original 7,500 shares to 12,000 shares of the
capital stock of the World Bank in September
1980, moving up to the sixth place in the
hierarchy of the Bank, below Japan and above
India. China now has 12,250 votes, or 3.55% of
the total, in the World Bank.

During the first year of its participation in the IMF, China drew assistance in the amount of nearly $1.5 billion. The World Bank's first loan to China was approved in June 1981 for $200 million — $100 million from the Bank and $100 million from the IDA — for a University Development Project that is the 'first phase of China's higher education development for the 1980s.' The World Bank is now considering two other loans for China totalling nearly $300 million — one for improving irrigation and drainage facilities in Anhui, Hebei, Jiangsu, Henan, and Shandong Provinces and the other for expanding container facilities in Shanghai, Huangpu, and Tianjin.[56]

The shift from aid-giving to aid-seeking placed China in the unaccustomed rivalry with the Third World in the politics of resource allocation. A dispute occurred in the General Assembly in 1979 when China for the first time submitted 'complete national income statistics' to the Committee on Contributions. According to the submitted statistics, China's per capita income amounted to only $152 (ranking 125th among the 152 member states), which would have reduced China's assessment rate from the existing 5.5% to 0.95%. This was perceived by many Third World countries as a self-serving deflated figure. Embarrassed by this controversy, China agreed to assume, for the three-year period 1980—1982, a major portion of the assessment increase that would have devolved on the developing countries from the change in China's assessment rate. As a result, China's assessment was fixed at 1.62%, not 0.9%, for the financial years 1980—1982. In the latest assessment for the financial years 1983—1985 adopted by the General Assembly on 17 December 1982, however, China's assessment was fixed at 0.88%.[57]

In the summer of 1980, there were strenuous complaints that China had understated its per capita GNP at $230 to secure more concessional loans from the IDA. Like the General Assembly, the World Bank accepted the Chinese data even though its own estimates placed China's 1978 per capita GNP at $460. In explaining the concept of 'average per capita GNP' to its readership, *Beijing ribao* noted that 'China's per capita GNP was $155 in 1975, $152 in 1976, $171 in 1977, $208 in 1978 and around $240 last year.'[58]

In contrast, the *Financial Times* (1979), based on the figures given to its delegation at the Foreign Trade Ministry of the PRC, placed China's 1978 per capita GNP at $650, while US CIA's estimate was $442.[59] Economist Dwight Perkins estimates that China's per

capita GNP in 1979 was in the range of $400—500, while economist Irving Kravis, by converting each commodity one by one, arrived at the conclusion that China's real per capita GDP for 1975 was about 12.3% of the U.S.'s.[60]

The most comprehensive analysis/projection of the Chinese political economy, or for that matter of any country's political economy, was carried out by the World Bank with Chinese blessing — the Chinese provided data and statistics that the World Bank's 28 roving economists wanted — and completed in mid-1981 with a Chinese stamp of approval. The central message of the World Bank report is a familiar chorus sung by mainstream American China specialists and the CIA for many years, but which has risen to a crescendo only after the passing of Mao — that the most rapid way for China's economic development lies in extensive reliance on foreign (read capitalist) aid, loans, technology, and participation.[61]

Both as a benefactor and a 'detached' analysis, the World Bank postulated two economic growth scenarios to the Chinese for the 1980s. *The high growth scenario*, with GNP increasing 5% annually in 1980—85 and 6% in 1985—90, is based on the assumption of optimal performance in highly successful energy savings, light industrial manufactures and exports, and a high level of borrowing. *The moderate growth scenario*, with 4% GNP growth in 1980—85 and 5% growth in 1985—90, projected a fall-back position with fewer dangers but leaving China that much farther behind its modernization goals. In the final analysis under the moderate growth scenario China's total debt in 1990 would amount to about $41 billion (or $20 billion in 1980 prices), whereas under the high growth scenario its debt level in 1990 would rise to $79 billion (or $40 billion in 1980 prices).[62]

China's current strategy on international monetary and financial issues is to seek the cheapest possible loans from foreign governments and international organizations while at the same time accepting loans from foreign commercial banks if their conditions are 'fair and reasonable.' The priorities for the use of foreign funds are the development of energy sources, the construction of railways, ports, and telecommunications, and the expansion of those medium and small-sized projects which require a small investment but are capable of earning more foreign exchange.

According to Minister of Finance Wang Bingqian, foreign loans totalled 4.3 billion yuan (or 126.9% of the budgeted figure) for 1980. Wang further reports that 'revenues from foreign loans' for 1981 are projected to be 8 billion yuan (or 7.6 percent of total revenues for 1981) and the total of outstanding foreign loans borrowed as part of state revenue will be an estimated 4 billion U.S. dollars by the end of 1983.[63] In short, foreign loans are now regarded as part of governmental *revenues* in China's budgetary process. It is not possible to predict the full extent of foreign borrowing to fuel the modernization drive, but the Chinese government disclosed to visiting members of the Trilateral Commission in May 1981 that it had decided to limit its external debt to 15% of foreign exchange earnings.[64]

Global Commodity Problems. The steady and long-term deterioration in the terms of trade for the exchange of commodities for industrial goods has been, and continues to be, of crucial importance to Third World countries. The terms of trade of commodities in relation to manufactures deteriorated by almost one-third between the mid-1950s and the early 1970s. At least 25 developing countries are dependent on only one primary commodity for more than half their export earnings, and another 13 nations on just two primary commodities. It is not surprising, then, that improvement of the terms of trade for the commodity-exporting developing countries has been one of the central demands of the NIEO.

There are several problems in improving and stabilizing international commodity markets: asymmetrical interdependence between producers and consumers; worldwide inflation and volatile exchange rates; wide fluctuations in prices; elasticities in demand; the largely uncontrolled intermediary role of transnational corporations; and relative low prices (and the derivative problem of mounting external debts). In addition, there is an asymmetry of interests between producers and consumers to cooperate on the joint management of global commodity problems. Consumer countries lose interest in negotiations when prices fall, just as producer countries become apathetic when prices rise.

The UNCTAD proposal for an 'Integrated Programme for Commodities' (IPC) has served as a focal point for the debate on global commodity issues. How does China fit into this evolving debate on global commodity issues? Although China is a commodity-exporting country, its interests coincide more with commodity importers than with commodity exporters. Of the ten core commodities making up the IPC, for example, China's imports averaged $1.06 billion annually and its exports only $143.2 million annually during 1974–1975.[65] China's major exports, crude oil and

tungsten, are excluded from the IPC. As noted earlier, there is an attempt to restructure China's export trade by importing more raw materials and converting them into manufactures. China's unique role in the group politics of UNCTAD and the negotiations to establish a NIEO commodity regime needs to be examined against this background.

In spite of its continuing self-definition as a developing socialist country belonging to the Third World, China has refused to join the Group of 77, the Third World economic caucus representing 123 developing countries and PLO (as of late 1982) in global development politics. This has posed a serious problem for the group politics of UNCTAD, the dominant platform for Third World attempts to restructure international commodity markets. China is the only member state of UNCTAD that has insisted on — and succeeded in — playing an independent role as a 'group of one.' China's anomalous role and status in NIEO politics was most clearly highlighted in the controversy surrounding the voting structure of the Common Fund, the most divisive issue of the Third Session of the United Nations Negotiating Conference on a Common Fund under the Integrated Programme for Commodities, held in Geneva from March 12–19, 1979. If successful, this will be the first commodity regime born out of NIEO politics. Hence, the institutionalization of China's role in the Common Fund may set a precedent for the construction or transformation of other international economic regimes.

China participated in all the preparatory meetings for the negotiation of a Common Fund as well as in the United Nations Negotiating Conference on a Common Fund under the Integrated Programme for Commodities. Such active participation reflected a convergence of Chinese economic and normative interests in the establishment of a global commodity regime. From the beginning of NIEO politics, the Chinese have conceptualized the integrated program for commodities as the centrepiece of the Third World's struggle to restructure the existing economic order. The Chinese have continued to give public support to the Third World's struggle to establish a NIEO commodity regime in the post-Mao era, but as one observer remarked, 'where it really matters, when negotiating, they're in there as business people, bargaining hard and defending their interests.'[66]

In spite of the four-year negotiations and controversies over its size, organization, management and operational procedures, the Common Fund as finally agreed upon was substantially scaled down from the original $6 billion that the UNCTAD secretariat estimated was needed to finance the buffer stocks of the ten 'core' commodities. The Agreement now stipulates that there will be two accounts: the first account will receive an initial endowment of $400 million in cash and callable capital in order to serve as a bank to help individual commodity organizations purchase buffer stocks, and the second account will receive contributions of $350 million to function as an aid organization for commodity research, development, and diversification (local processing and marketing in the Third World).

The Common Fund, as currently envisaged, may be characterized as a 'pooling scheme' sought by the industrialized countries. As such, it is a breakthrough of sorts for the North and a defeat for the South. Even the compromise voting structure — which established parity between like-minded States by granting the Group of 77 47% and China 3% (thus 50% for the South) and Group B (the North minus the Soviet bloc) 42% and Group D (the Soviet Union and Eastern Europe) 8% (thus 50% for the North) — may well prove to be a recipe for stalemating the decision-making process within the new regime.[67]

The fact that the Group of 77 would consent to such a diluted and downsized commodity regime indicates the central dilemma of the Southern trade unionism: how to translate the grandiose objective of system reform into an effective and credible tactic in a specific issue area. There is a 'desperation mentality' that a small concession is better than none when the commodity boat is sinking. For the non-oil developing countries, the year 1982 witnessed the fifth consecutive year of deterioration in the terms of trade, leaving them with a composite terms of trade some 12—13% lower than that in 1972.[68] Between 1980 and 1982, world commodity prices, excluding oil, have dropped by 35% to the lowest real levels in three decades. To buy a seven-ton truck in 1981, for example, Tanzania had to grow and export three times as much coffee (or cashew nuts), four times as much cotton, or ten times as much tobacco, as it took to buy the same vehicle five years earlier. A 41% decline in sugar price, 22% decline in coffee price, and 17% decline in cocoa price all occurred in spite of support operations of the International Sugar Agreement (since May 1981), the International Coffee Agreement (since October 1980), and the Cocoa Buffer Stock (since September 1981).[69]

Be that as it may, the future of the Common Fund is uncertain. Apparently, both producer and consumer countries have had second thoughts about the Common Fund, reassessing its advantages and disadvantages. The Agreement was supposed to enter into force on 31 March 1982 if, by that date, at least 90 States whose total subscriptions of shares comprise not less than two thirds of the directly contributed capital of the Fund have ratified. On 16 December 1981, the General Assembly, finding that only 14 States had ratified the Agreement, passed a resolution prodding member states that have not yet done so to ratify the Agreement for its entry into force by the specified date. China ratified the Agreement on 2 September 1981. As of 31 March 1982, however, only 12 more states ratified the Agreement, thus falling far short of the Article 57 requirement. On 3 June 1982, UNCTAD decided to extend the ratification deadline to 30 September 1983.[70] Many developing countries now insist that what has finally emerged is too diluted a version of the original scheme initially proposed at UNCTAD-IV, while the United States under the Reagan Administration is proselytizing 'the magic of the market place' and private foreign investment as the salvation for Third World development.

MOTIVES FOR CHANGE

How can all the twists and turns in post-Mao Chinese political economy be explained? Whatever may be the long-term intentions and consequences, the short-term policy of the post-Mao leadership seems powerfully motivated by an intense catching-up drive. The dogged determination to redirect the developmental course of China's political economy in its New Long March to the promised land of modernity has become a new religion. But this is no longer, if it ever was, the promised land of communism where the state as an instrument of exploitation of man by man would wither away. It is the promised land where China would emerge as a powerful multinational state. Such statism is one primary motivating force behind China's 'great leap outward.'

Having redefined security and status in terms of material power via the modernization drive, one Maoist principle after another was subject to revision or repudiation. The principal contradiction [*zhuyao maodun*] is no longer the contradiction between the proletariat and the bourgeoisie, we are told, but the contradiction between people's needs and backward economy and culture.[71]

The ascendancy of arch-realist Deng Xiaoping in the post-Mao leadership has brought about a shift from the value-oriented self-reliant model to the interest-oriented 'realist' model in the Chinese conceptualization of the global political economy. During the Maoist era, there was a recurring propensity to make a virtue out of weakness by defining 'national power' as a sum total of both material and normative power, as shown in an editorial of the *Renmin ribao* (25 November 1957): 'Though, for the time being, the output of some products is smaller on our side than in the imperialist countries, yet since we are on the side of socialism, the socialist system plus a certain level of material strength gives us superiority in the entire balance of power.'

Such a conception of national power has been abandoned as the post-Mao Chinese leadership increasingly defines status in terms of material power. That China's exports amounted to only 0.9% of the global total in 1979 — as compared to 10.9% for the U.S., 10.5% for West Germany, 6.3% for Japan, 6% for France, and 5.6% for Great Britain — is bewailed as being incongruous with 'a country as big as ours.'[72] The post-Mao leadership takes no issue with the conventional experts' assessment that 'China's industrial and technical level lags about 20 years behind the developed capitalist countries and its agricultural production level is about 40—50 years behind.'[73] Thus, there is a huge discrepancy between China's proper place in the world as the oldest civilization and the most populous state and its low ranking in material and scientific status that calls for rectification. Even the structure of China's exports is derided as 'still quite backward,' because its machinery products account for only 0.1% of the world's trading volume.

But how can China rectify its status inconsistency in the 'robber's world'? The shift to the Trilateral model is a 'realistic' strategy to survive in the robber's world dominated by core capitalist powers — 'if you can't beat them, join them!' Deng came close to making that suggestion when he said: 'To accelerate China's modernization we must not only make use of other countries' experience. We must also avail ourselves of foreign funding. In past years international conditions worked against us. Later, when the international climate was favourable, we did not take advantage of it. It is now time to use our opportunities.'[74]

Dengist 'realism' entails acceptance — and adjustment to — the opportunities and constraints imposed by the trilateral managers of the capitalist world-economy. China's cultural, economic, political, and strategic ties with Japan, Western Europe, and the United States apparently represent the answer to the key foreign policy question: how to *maximise* external inputs — foreign capital, investment, joint ventures, technology, management techniques, concessional aid, and preferential trade treatment — and to *minimize* defence costs by forming a broad united (trilateral) front against the Soviet Union. One close observer of Chinese politics has argued that 'the contemporary Chinese contradiction is just another ordinary consequence of the inevitable national egoism-global ethics contradiction which affects all nations' and 'to end one's perceived victimization, one becomes complicitious with robbers.'[75]

China's breaking away from self-reliance is not a socialist anomaly. Cuba has recently passed a law allowing transnational corporations to engage in joint ventures with state-run enterprises. Algeria is trimming its socialist goals. Guinea's Marxist regime is also adopting many elements of capitalist economy. The familiar 'development virus' has also spread and affected the socialist countries of Eastern Europe: excessive borrowing in the latter half of the 1970s and early 1980s to finance imports of Western machinery and technology on which to build modern industries that would in turn pay for themselves through exports to the West. At the end of 1981, the COMECON countries owed more than $80 billion to the Western governments and banks. Viewed in this light, China's 'great leap westward' seems to be part of the global trend. In the short run, such trend seems to support the contention of the world-system theorists that 'these so-called socialist states are in fact socialist movements in power in states that are still part of a single capitalist world-economy.'[76]

What about China's transformative role for a new world economic order? Despite the slippage in China's commitment to the NIEO, it may be easier to explain that China has merely accepted the limitations of the NIEO and acted accordingly. In recent years, OPEC, far from being a system-transforming vanguard for the NIEO, has become a problematic partner as its member states, especially Saudi Arabia, have been coopted to join system-maintainers by detaching oil pricing policy from wider NIEO issues as well as by reducing (from 2.59% of GNP in 1975 to 1.35% of GNP in 1980) their official development aid.[77] In spite of a flurry of global developmental activities in the 1970s, no other effective commodity cartels have been organized. The post-Mao Chinese 'realism' means accepting — and adjusting to — these basic systemic constraints rather than trying to transform them.

In the meantime, the economic conditions of the Third World, especially the thirty-one least developed Third World countries, have rapidly deteriorated by such key measures as growth rate, indebtedness, and trade.[78] The post-Mao realism is not exclusively home made; it is being influenced by the changing reality of the global political economy, and that reality at the present time is that the NIEO model is in disarray. The quest for a more just international economic order, in all of its forms bearing on access to capital, markets, resources, and technology as well as in the restructuring exercise, has been derailed.

It can also be argued that post-Mao China has become part of the NIEO problem. The changing realignment of China's Third World 'friends' and 'foes' along the Moscow-Washington bipolarity may be China's way of enhancing its geopolitical and economic value to the United States — punishing the Soviet Union — but such a strategic minuet with the Nemesis of the NIEO can only erode China's own credibility and influence in the Third World.[79] Even in the domain of global developmental politics, Peking has considerably complicated — and weakened — NIEO politics by linking the issues of world peace and world development. The NIEO is weak enough to carry on its own burden without any excessive luggage.

NORMATIVE AND POLICY IMPLICATIONS

Given the traumatic experience of dependency under Western semi-colonialism and Soviet semi-imperialism, no Chinese leadership can do without the legitimizing principles of national independence and self-reliance. The years 1981 and 1982 witnessed a renewed debate on the proper strategy of balancing and integrating the empirical and normative approaches in the New Long March to modernity. It has become evident to the post-Mao leadership that the new politics of modernization cannot live by bread alone. Hence, the Chinese quest for a new development model is not finished; it represents an ongoing process of experimentation with a variety of models and approaches. In this fluid and unsettled situation, new and unexpected turns and twists are bound to crop up with every passing year. The latest twist in the dialectics of the Chinese development process is a call for a new form of class

struggle, to be distinguished from the past mistake of taking class struggle as the key link. Instead, the new class struggle is needed to build 'socialist spiritual civilization' and to energize the development of material civilization. In this way, there would be a guarantee to prevent the imperialists *and* hegemonists from 'making every attempt to infiltrate, disrupt and subvert our country politically, economically, ideologically and culturally.'[80]

Despite the renewed attempts to strike a dialectical balance between extreme and no class struggle, it can still be argued that all the normative and policy changes initiated by the post-Mao leadership in the last five years (1978—1982) taken as a whole constitute an across-the-board assault on the traditional Chinese (Maoist) model of development. In his report to the 12th National Congress of the CCP, held in September 1982, Hu Yaobang stressed the open-door/self-reliance complementarity. On this premise, the open-door is characterized as 'firm strategic principle' and 'irreversible policy' to 'speed the entry of Chinese products into the world market and vigorously expand foreign trade.'[81]

The political economy of post-Mao China has undergone a remarkable reorientation from Mao's value-oriented self-reliance model to Deng's open-door model, through shifts from superstructure to base (or from politics in command to economics in command), from regional self-reliance to regional specialization through the SEZs and other schemes, from social egalitarianism and normative incentives to the economic division of labour and specialization and material incentives, from symbolic diplomacy to 'realist' diplomacy, from mass participation in decision-making to a more explicit hierarchy of authority and responsibility, from aid-giving to aid-seeking, from model-projecting to model-seeking, from fear of dependency to fear of isolationism and backwardness, and from autocentric social development to export-oriented growth.

The normative structures and substance of the Maoist model have been treated as being either irrelevant to or hindering the modernization drive. The current slogan, 'to take practice as the sole criterion for testing truth,' is a euphemism designed to downgrade the Maoist model. A wall poster on the now defunct Democracy Wall seemed to summarize the situation well: 'What kind of modernization does China hope to realize? The Soviet type, the American type, the Japanese type, the Yugoslavian type . . . on these issues the masses know nothing!'

In spite of the recent pronouncement that 'China's modernization will be accomplished while adhering to socialism,'[82] the defining characteristics of the political economy of post-Mao China are still in a state of dialectical struggle. Nonetheless, the general contours and parameters of post-Mao China's political economy have been drawn. In pursuit of foreign capital, investment, technology, and entrepreneurship, China has adopted an open-door policy on an evolving and experimental basis. China now unabashedly uses this discredited term in describing its current policy toward foreign (read trilateral) countries and transnational corporations. Technology, which used to be conceptualized as an instrument of imperialist predatory penetration, is now claimed to have no class character.

Despite the continuing rhetorical support of the NIEO, Chinese behaviour since late 1978 has shifted from the *dependencia* model to the interdependence model, and closer to the system-maintaining models in the domains of global geopolitics and developmental politics. Chinese behaviour in the global system has shifted from the 'revisionist' posture of seeking *new* rules, *new* values, and *new* norms[83] to the 'realist' posture of accepting (and taking advantage of) existing rules, structures, and processes of the international economic regimes.

The notion that China can capture its share of the world market through a dynamic export-oriented growth strategy seems unrealistic in the light of the deepening structural problems plaguing the world market: (1) wide price fluctuations of commodities; (2) rising protectionism in the North; (3) chronic stagflation in industrial countries, which reduces the demands for developing countries' exports and simultaneously increases the prices of their imports; and (4) oil price volatility (and China's own energy constraints).[84] Although China had a lower degree of dependency on foreign trade than today and was just entering the world market as an exporter of crude oil, the 1973–74 world economic crisis adversely affected China's political economy.[85] Moreover, post-Mao 'realism' seems to be anchored in the sanguine assumptions about robust economic prospects of core capitalist countries and China's ability to maximize the opportunities and minimize the constraints of the capitalist global political economy.

What about the internal normative implications of the 'realist' model? Can the leadership manage to maximize the payoffs of capitalist loans, joint ventures, special economic zones, and technology transfer and minimize the penalties or what it calls 'Western pollutants'? *Embourgeoisement* has already begun to affect the modernization drive, although its social and political implications are far from clear. The open-door policy brought in not only foreign capital and technology but also luxury contraband, pornography, and other cultural 'bads' that corrupt China's ideological superstructure. The extent of smuggling through the SEZs is estimated to run about $500 million worth annually.

Even in purely economic terms, the miscarriage of the Baoshan Steel Mill, begun in 1978 as a showpiece of the modernization drive, serves as a reminder of China's capacity to absorb and assimilate foreign capital and technology. This incident also reminds of the disjuncture between policy enunciation and policy implementation in the Chinese development process. The tradition of *guanxi* — that quintessential reward system made up of interpersonal connections cemented by shared interests, obligations, and vulnerabilities — still persists in Chinese politics. A recent study of the Chinese economic policy-making process based largely on field research concluded: 'To a considerable extent, power remained vested in individuals rather than institutions. One sensed that changes in the top leadership could easily produce changes in structure and policy at the top.'[86]

We are left with a number of imponderables. Can the New Long March move far enough and fast enough to satiate the revolution of rising consumerism for the Chinese *and* the revolution of rising expectations for the trilateral corporate managers? Can it succeed at all without a legitimizing Chinese model? Can it help to mitigate the centre-periphery, urban-rural, and expert-red contradictions? Can the current normative crisis[87] be resolved without resuscitating the two-line class struggle again? In the final analysis, the legitimation of the post-Mao successor regime is dependent on the resolution of these questions and a fair and equitable distribution of the material benefits of the modernization drive. Given the demonstrated volatility and unpredictability of the Chinese body politic, as evidenced in the repeated failures of all previous attempts to Sinicize Western models in the course of modern Chinese history, and also given the deepening crises and contradictions in the world economic system, there is no reason to be sanguine about the stability of the open-door policy.

NOTES

1. *Renmin ribao* (People's Daily) [hereafter cited as *RMRB*], editorial, 14 February 1953, cited in A. Doak Barnett, *China's Economy in Global Perspective* (Washington, D.C.: The Brookings Institution, 1981), p. 583.

2. *Peking Review*, No. 35 (27 August 1976): 8.

3. Deng Xiaoping, 'Why China Has Opened Its Door,' in Foreign Broadcast Information Service: Daily Report — People's Republic of China [hereafter cited as FBIS-PRC or FBIS-China], 12 February 1980, pp. L1—L2.

4. For discussion on the transferability of the Chinese model, see Robert F. Dernberger, ed., *China's Development Experience in Comparative Perspective* (Cambridge, Mass.: Harvard University Press, 1980); Alexander Eckstein, *China's Economic Revolution* (New York: Cambridge University Press, 1977); John G. Gurley, *China's Economy and the Maoist Strategy* (New York: Monthly Review Press, 1976); and Dwight H. Perkins, ed., *China's Modern Economy in Historical Perspective* (Stanford, Calif.: Stanford University Press, 1975).

5. See John Galtung, 'Conflict on a Global Scale: Social Imperialism and Sub-Imperialism — Continuities in the Structural Theory of Imperialism,' *World Development* 4 (March 1974), pp. 153—65; 'Implementing Self-Reliance,' *Transnational Perspectives* 3 (1976), pp. 18—24; Richard C. Kraus, 'Withdrawing from the World-System; Self-Reliance and Class Structure in China,' in Walter L. Goldfrank, ed., *The World-System of Capitalism: Past and Present* (Beverly Hills, Calif.: Sage Publications, 1979), pp. 237—59; Immanuel Wallerstein, *The Capitalist World-Economy* (New York: Cambridge University Press, 1979); and Edwin A. Winckler, 'China's World-System: Social Theory and Political Practice in the 1970s,' in Goldfrank, *The World-System of Capitalism*, pp. 53—69.

6. Galtung, 'Conflict on a Global Scale,' p. 162; emphasis in original.

7. See Sam Cole, *Global Models and the International Economic Order* (New York: Pergamon Press for UNITAR, 1977); Antony J. Dolman, *Resources, Regimes, World Order* (New York: Pergamon Press, 1981).

8. For further elaboration and analysis along these lines, see Samuel S. Kim, *The Quest for a Just World Order* (Boulder, Colorado: Westview Press, 1983), chap. 5.

9. The logic of this argument is elaborated in the OECD 'interfutures' global model. See OECD, *Facing the Futures: Mastering the Probable and Managing the Unpredictable* (Paris: OECD, 1979).

10. Bruce Cumings, 'The Political Economy of Chinese Foreign Policy.' *Modern China* 4 (October 1979), pp. 450—452.

11. Karl Kaiser, Winston Lord, Thierry de Montbrial, and David Watt, *Western Security: What Has Changed? What Should be Done?* A Report Prepared by the Directors of Forschungsinstitut der Deutschen Gesellschaft für Auswartige Politik (Bonn), Council on Foreign Relations (New York), Institut Français des Relations Internationales (Paris), and Royal Institute of International Affairs (London) (New York: Council on Foreign Relations, 1981), p. 11.

12. See Jan Tinbergen (Coordinator), *RIO: Reshaping the International Order*, A Report to the Club of Rome (New York: E. P. Dutton & Co., 1976) and *North-South: A Program for Survival*, The Report of the Independent Commission on International Development Issues under the Chairmanship of Willy Brandt (Cambridge, Mass.: The MIT Press, 1980).

13. Paul M. Sweezy, 'A Crisis in Marxian Theory,' *Monthly Review*, 31 (June 1979).

14. See James A. Caporaso, ed., *Dependence and Dependency in the Global System*, Special Issue of *International Organization* 32 (Winter 1978); Fernando Henrique Cardoso and Enzo Faletto, *Dependency and Development in Latin America*, trans. Majory M. Urquidi (Berkeley, Calif.: University of California Press, 1979); and Andre Gunder Frank, *Reflections on the World Economic Crisis* (New York: Monthly Review Press, 1981).

15. Wallerstein, *The Capitalist World-Economy*, pp. 35—36.

16. Immanuel Wallerstein, 'Friends and Foes,' *Foreign Policy*, No. 40 (Fall 1980), pp. 119—131. See also Christopher K. Chase-Dunn, 'Socialist States in the Capitalist World-Economy,' *Social Problems*, 27 (June 1980), pp. 505—525.

17. *What Now*, The 1975 Dag Hammarskjold Report on Development and International Cooperation (Uppsala, Sweden: The Dag Hammarskjold Foundation, 1975), pp. 12—21.

18. For elaboration, see Richard A. Falk and Samuel S. Kim, *An Approach to World Order Studies and the World System*, WOMP Working Paper No. 22 (New York: Institute for World Order, 1982), pp. 17—23.

19. Mao made this point in his speech of 30 January 1962, at an Enlarged Central Work Conference, See *Mao Zedong sixiang wansui* [Long Live Mao Zedong's Thought] (n.p., August 1969), p. 416.

20. For a detailed elaboration of this point, see *Peking Review* (5 May 1964), p. 14.

21. See *Mao Zedong sixiang wansui* [Long Live Mao Zedong's Thought] (n.p., 1969), pp. 156—166; *Mao*

Zedong sixiang wansui (1969), p. 204; 'On the Ten Major Relationships,' in *Selected Works of Mao Tsetung*, Vol. V (Peking: Foreign Languages Press, 1977), pp. 284–307.

22. For elaboration, see Samuel S. Kim, *China, the United Nations, and World Order* (Princeton, N.J.: Princeton University Press, 1979), pp. 242–333.

23. GAOR, 6th Special Sess., *Ad Hoc* Committee, 10th meeting (18 April 1974), para. 15.

24. Cited in Dorman, *Resources, Regimes, World Order*, p. 86; emphasis added.

25. Kim, *China, the United Nations, and World Order*, pp. 315–328.

26. See *RMRB*, editorial, 1 January 1979, p. 1.

27. See Zhao Ziyang, 'The Present Economic Situation and the Principles for Future Economic Construction,' *Beijing Review* [hereafter cited as *BR*], No. 51 (21 December 1981): 6–36.

28. Mu Youlin, 'Opposing Hegemonism,' *BR*, No. 32 (9 August 1982); 3; emphasis added. See also Shen Yi, 'China Belongs For Ever to the Third World,' *ibid*, No. 39 (28 September 1981): 23–25.

29. Ye Jianying, 'Comrade Ye Jianying's Speech – At the Meeting in Celebration of the 30th Anniversary of the Founding of the People's Republic of China,' *BR*, No. 40 (5 October 1979): 7–32; quote at p. 17.

30. Liu Maoying, 'A New Explanation of the Story of Yugong Who Removed the Mountains,' *Wenhui bao* (Shanghai), 15 April 1980.

31. See FBIS-China, 28 December 1981, pp. K3–K5; *BR*, No. 2 (11 January 1982), pp. 5–6.

32. *RMRB*, 12 February 1981, p. 1. For a detailed analysis, see Tang Tsou, Marc Blecher, and Mitch Meisner, 'National Agricultural Policy: The Dazhai Model and Local Change in the Post-Mao Era,' in *The Transition to Socialism in China*, edited by Mark Selden and Victor Lippit (Armonk, New York: M. E. Sharpe, Inc., 1982), pp. 266–299.

33. FBIS-China, 28 December 1981, p. K4.

34. See *BR*, No. 28 (13 July 1981); No. 1 (4 January 1982).

35. FBIS-China, 9 August 1982, pp. K5–K6.

36. See Samuel S. Kim, 'Whither Post-Mao Chinese Global Policy?' *International Organization*, 35 (Summer 1981): 447–455.

37. For elaboration, see Friedrich Wu, 'Socialist Self-Reliant Development Within the Capitalist World-Economy: The Chinese View in the Post-Mao Era,' (A paper presented at the 23rd annual convention of the International Studies Association, Cincinnati, Ohio, 24–27 March 1982).

38. Barnett, *China's Economy in Global Perspective*, p. 659.

39. This is based on my own count for 1977–1978.

40. In October 1981, for example, the *Renmin ribao* carried no less than 66 articles under the rubric 'North-South Summit Conference' (*Nanbei shounao huiyi*). In November 1981, however, not a single article appeared in the *Renmin ribao* under the NIEO or North-South dialogue. See *Renmin ribao suoyin* (People's Daily Index) (October 1981) and (November 1981).

41. *BR*, No. 32 (10 August 1981): 3.

42. See Qian Junrui, 'The Outlook of the World Economy and the Chinese Economy in the 1980s,' *Shijie Jingji* (World Economy), No. 7 (10 July 1982): 1–5.

43. For Premier Zhao Ziyang's statement and speeches delivered at the Cancun Meeting on 22–23 October 1981, see *China and the World* (1) (Beijing: Beijing Review Foreign Affairs Series, 1982), pp. 5–15.

44. Cited in *Far Eastern Economic Review* (Hong Kong) (6 November 1981): 110.

45. FBIS-China, 22 October 1981, p. K3.

46. See *RMRB*, editorial, 17 January 1981, p. 1; Li Dai, 'Independence and Our Country's Foreign Relations,' *Shijie Zhishi* (World Knowledge), No. 19 (1 October 1981): 2–4.

47. FBIS-China, 6 July, 1981, p. W3; *BR*, No. 50 (14 December 1981): 14–17.

48. *BR*, No. 12 (23 March 1981), p. 3.

49. FBIS-PRC, 23 August 1979, p. D2; 4 June 1980, p. A3.

50. Editorial Department, 'On the Questions Concerning Our Country's Foreign Economic Relations,' *Hongqi* (Red Flag), No. 8 (16 April 1982): 2–10; quote in the text at p. 7.

51. John F. Copper, *China's Foreign Aid in 1979*, Occasional Paper/Reprints Series in Contemporary Asian Studies, No. 8, p. 1. See also U.S. Central Intelligence Agency, National Foreign Assessment Center, *Handbook of Economic Statistics* (Washington, D.C.: August 1979).

52. Harry Harding, 'China and the Third World: From Revolution to Containment,' in Richard H. Solomon, ed., *The China Factor: Sino-American Relations and the Global Scene* (Englewood Cliffs, N.J.: Prentice-Hall, Inc., 1981), p. 270.

53. For further analysis, see Kim, *China, the United Nations, and World Order*, pp. 315–328; 'Whither Post-Mao Chinese Global Policy?' pp. 449–451.

54. *BR*, No. 24 (14 June 1982): 3; FBIS-China, 8 April 1982, p. A1.

55. For elaboration of this argument, see Kim, *China, the United Nations, and World Order*, chap. 7.

56. For details, see the following: K. Berney and D. Jones, 'China's Activities in the IMF and World Bank,' *China Business Review*, 8 (March–April 1981): 47–48; *The Economist* (London) (7 March 1981), pp. 70–71; *The New York Times*, 3 March 1981, p. D1; 15 June 1981, p. D17; *Finance and Development* (September 1981): 2–3.

57. With the reduction of an assessment rate from 5.5% to 1.62% and its continuous refusal to pay its assessed and thus legally binding contributions to the expenses incurred by UN peace-keeping operations (the new defunct UNEF-II and the continuing UNDOF and UNIFIL), China was moving perilously close to losing its voting rights under Article 19 of the UN Charter. Against this background, China through its close ally, Pakistan, came out with an ingenious, if not ingenuous, device with the following conditions at the 36th Session of the General Assembly in 1981: (1) China's outstanding past withholding arrears from peace-keeping operations (which amounted to $55 million for the period 25 October 1971–31 December 1981) be transferred to a special account; (2) Article 19 should not be invoked for the past arrears; and (3) China shall assume its share of assessed expenses for UN peace-keeping operations as of 1 January 1982 based on the reduced assessment rate. On 10 December 1981 the General Assembly passed by a recorded vote of 115:13:0 this Pakistani draft resolution embodying all three Chinese conditions as Resolution 36/116 with the title, 'Financial Emergency of the United Nations.' See UN Docs. A/C.5/36/28 (29 October 1981); A/36/701 (20 November 1981); A/C.5/36/SR.56 (7 December 1981). For the latest decision to fix China's assessment at 0.88% for the financial years 1983–1985, see General Assembly Resolution 37/125 of 17 December 1982.

58. FBIS-PRC, 17 November 1980, p. L24.

59. See U.S. Central Intelligence Agency, National Foreign Assessment Center, *China: A Statistical Compendium* (Washington, D.C.: July 1979).

60. Dwight Perkins, 'The International Consequences of China's Economic Development,' in Solomon, *The China Factor*, p. 118 and Irving B. Kravis, 'An Approximation of the Relative Real per Capita GDP of the People's Republic of China.' *Journal of Comparative Economics* 5 (March 1981): 60–78. When extrapolated from Kravis' method, China's 1978 per capita GNP comes to $1,198 (or 12.5% of $9,590 for the 1978 U.S. per capita GNP).

61. Cumings, 'The Political Economy of Chinese Foreign Policy,' pp. 420–421.

62. See *The Economist* (7 March 1981), pp. 70–71; *Far Eastern Economic Review* (14 August 1981); and Nicholas Ludlow, 'World Bank Report,' *China Business Review* 8 (July–August 1981): 6–8.

63. Wang Bingqian, 'Report on the Final State Accounts for 1980 and Implementation of the Financial Estimates for 1981,' *BR*, No. 2 (11 January 1982): 14–23; Wang Bingqian, 'Report on the Implementation of the State Budget for 1982 and the Draft State Budget for 1983,' *BR*, No. 3 (17 January 1983): 16–17.

64. FBIS-China, 27 May 1981, p. A1.

65. Barnett, *China's Economy in Global Perspective*, p. 240.

66. Bhushan Bahree, 'China Stepping Up Its Role at World Commodity Talks,' *Asian Wall Street Journal*, 17 October 1978.

67. See *Agreement Establishing the Common Fund for Commodities*, UN Doc. TD/IPC/CONF/24 (29 July 1980).

68. *World Economic Outlook* (Washington, D.C.: International Monetary Fund, June 1981), p. 52; *World Economic Outlook* (Washington, D.C.: International Monetary Fund, April 1982), p. 150.

69. *World Economic Outlook* (1982), pp. 137–138, 210.

70. This account is based on the author's field interviews at UN Headquarters, New York City, 9 June 1982.

71. See Jie Wen, 'Class Struggle and the Principal Contradiction in Socialist Society,' *Hongqi*, No. 20 (16 October 1981): 26–31, 6.

72. FBIS-China, 15 September 1981, pp. K15–K16.

73. Ren Tao and Zhang Jingsheng, 'Why a Change in Emphasis?' *BR*, No. 1 (3 January 1983): 16.

74. Deng, 'Why China Has Opened Its Door,' p. L3.

75. Edward Friedman, 'On Maoist Conceptualization of the Capitalist World System,' *China Quarterly*, No. 80 (December 1979): 836–837.

76. Wallerstein, *The Capitalist World-Economy*, p. 280.

77. *World Development Report 1981* (New York: Oxford University Press Published for the World Bank, 1981), p. 165.

78. For a most recent and comprehensive description and analysis of the Third World's economic problems, see UNCTAD, *Trade and Development Report 1982*, Report by the Secretariat of the United Nations Conference on Trade and Development (New York: United Nations, 1982, Sales No. E.82.II.D.12).

79. For further elaboration of this point, see Samuel

S. Kim, 'The Sino-American Collaboration and Cold War II,' *Journal of Peace Research*, 19, No. 1 (1982): 11–20.

80. Zhou Yan, 'On China's Current Class Struggle,' *BR*, No. 33 (16 August 1982): 18.

81. Hu Yaobang, 'Create a New Situation in All Fields of Socialist Modernization – Report to the 12th National Congress of The Communist Party of China, 1 September 1982,' *BR*, No. 37 (13 September 1982), pp. 11–40. See also *RMRB*, 20 September 1982, p. 5.

82. Ren and Zheng, 'Why a Change in Emphasis?' p. 18.

83. For a detailed analysis, see Samuel S. Kim, 'The People's Republic of China and the Charter-Based International Legal Order,' *American Journal of International Law* 62, No. 2 (April 1978): 317–349.

84. See *World Development Report 1982* (New York: Oxford University Press Published for the World Bank, 1982).

85. See Eckstein, *China's Economic Revolution*, pp. 253–277.

86. Michel Oksenberg, 'Economic Policy-Making in China: Summer 1981,' *China Quarterly*, No. 90 (June 1982): 192.

87. See Li Honglin, 'What Does the "Crisis of Faith" Explain?', *RMRB*, 11 November 1980, p. 5.